CONSTANTINOPLE

BY
GEORGE YOUNG

BARNES
&NOBLE
BOOKS
NEW YORK

This edition published by Barnes & Noble, Inc.,

1992 Barnes & Noble Books

ISBN 1-56619-084-3

Printed and bound in the United States of America

M 9 8 7 6 5 4 3 2 1

CONSTANTINOPLE

CONTENTS

CONSTANTINOPLE

INTRODUCTION

Two ways there are to Swindon :
One is by Timbuctoo ;
And one by Jerry Hammond's 'bus,
Which way you will pursue.
("Marlborough School Song.")

TWO ways there are to Constantinople. One lies along the Golden Road to Samarkand through the Kingdoms of Romance to Der-el-Saadet, the City of Felicity. And if you are for taking that magic way you have no need of a Slave of the Lamp like me. You have only to get the right spells from some Wizard of the Books, like Mr. Cox of the London Library. Then, sitting on that magic carpet, your own hearthrug, you will be transported in the twinkling of an eye or the turning of a page to the Gorgeous East.

For such a journey you might take for heavy baggage, such as the respectable Englishman loves, some of those leather-bound quarto volumes of old Eastern travels that you can find in any public or private library. You should also have intro-ductions to distinguished diplomats, such as no self-respecting Englishman would travel without. For example, to Busbequius, Lady Mary Wortley Montagu, "Odysseus," and "Eothen." If you are travelling light, so to say with a pilgrim basket, you may be satisfied with Pierre Loti, Adalet Hanum, and Mr. Davey; while as travelling companions I would recommend Baron de Tott, the original of Baron Münchausen, and his Turkish confrère the Khodja Nasreddin Effendi. But you will find no lack of good company on that road.

This book is, however, intended for those who wish to see the real Constantinople, not that tantalizing mirage that floats over the eastern horizon of our workaday world. And, lest you be disappointed with Constantinople as it is, I shall have to try and make you see the city as it was, to rebuild for you royal palaces from a few scattered ruins and to restore to life again from the dust the Golden Lads and Chimney-sweepers of other days. This will mean a good deal of digging in historic dust-bins. But I shall not give each column of print a plinth of learned footnotes—partly because I am afraid of the fate of one of my predecessors who quoted as his authority "that learned historian Anonymos."

But, first of all, I have to get you out to Constantinople. The 'bus route that comes nearest to the Magic Carpet is of course a journey by aeroplane. Travel by air, especially if you don't land when you get there, will least disturb your ideas of the Gorgeous East. And then there is the other extreme—to go on foot. This is even less usual; but there is much to be said for it. For the great compensating principle of travel is that those who pay most see least. The perfect traveller is the tramp. And the way to get to the bottom of that strange hotchpotch of races, religions, and raw humanity that bubbles and boils between Vienna and Constantinople is to go through them on foot. But it is a long and an arduous special course, and I do not recommend it unless you have already taken your degree as a Master of Arts in the universities of Bohemia or Alsatia.

Putting on one side both the cloudlands of the air and the peaks of high adventure, there remain the train and the steamer. You can get to Belgrade by many routes, and from there you can either go straight by train, or make a diversion to the right by Salonika and thence by steamer, or to the left by Constanza and so by steamer again.

Most of us will probably go all the way by train; so let us take that first—not forgetting that there are many ways of travelling by train. You can take the Orient Express which, for twenty pounds about, and in four days or so, will take you from Paris to Constantinople in a fairly watertight compartment of western comfort. But those who pay most see least, and in the Orient Express you will see the Balkans from behind the plate glass and plush curtains that protect the dignity of diplo-mats and demi-reps. For half the fare and more than double the fun you can travel with second-class sleepers to Belgrade; whence the "Conventional," again with second-class sleepers and dining-car, will take you on to Constantinople in about the same time and almost the same comfort. It will, moreover, turn you out at each frontier to study life and language in the Balkans in Ollendorfian controversies with Customs officials. You might even travel third class all the way and almost as quickly. And,

on the wooden benches of a Balkan box car, you can, at considerable cost of comfort, get better entertainment than you would
in the express. But you must have an eye for local colour and
a nose for information—and for nothing else.

The last time I made this journey I was in company with a
party of Spanish Jews who were paying their way as they went.
At each frontier the member of the party who was an expert in
that country took charge and opened business with the joint
stock in trade. On every occasion, before the train left, the
party had paid its way to the next frontier. But living on
the country like this is beyond most of us. We shall have to
be content with not letting it live too excessively on us.

Once past Vienna, even the polished veneer of the Orient
Express will not conceal from you that you are travelling over a
thin crust of civilization, precariously covering seething subterranean fires. Even the railway lines are not always a reliable
bridge across the barbarism of the Balkans. It is still just as
well to avoid a compartment in the rear of the trains; which, after
the war, developed a lizard-like trick of quietly dropping their
tails if they found them in the way going up a hill. Patriots
with Mills bombs and Mausers may still come round collecting
for some local entertainment. You may find yourself stuck in
the snow on the Dragoman Pass with the heating turned off and
the dining-car eaten out; or held up by some wash-out on the
Maritsa, or by some oversight in your visa. But all these incidents are part of the game, and make for good-fellowship with
your fellow-travellers. What may seem at first merely an
annoying delay often becomes an experience that one would
not have missed, and there is generally some one to save the
situation. I remember once being held up at a Balkan bridge
with a young King's Messenger, who was inspirited by his fellow-
passengers into putting a literal construction on his orders to
proceed to Constantinople without delay by the quickest route.
So he chartered a special train to Dédé-agatch and a special
steamer on to Constantinople. It was a charming picnic he gave
us all, and what the authorities said when they saw the bill is
not suitable for publication.

Once through the hill country and picturesque costumes of
Serbia you get among the dull plains and duffel-clad peasants of
Bulgaria, where it becomes clear that you have reached a civilization of " Arms and the Man." After another night, and crossing
the Turkish frontier into Thrace, you find that you have reached
a sort of No-man's-land between the " fronts " of Asia and

Europe—a limbo between the Western and Eastern Worlds. The train has gone slower and slower as it got farther East, and now, for hour after hour, it jolts heavily across the bare uplands and deserted farmlands of Thrace. This is a country that any of us might have seen populated and prosperous but that is to-day peopled only by ghosts. Ghosts of great armies that have fought good fights in our own day and that have marched already into oblivion. Ghosts of long caravans of exiles, driven from their own land by the follies of men whose names even were unknown to them. Looking at the rough track that winds alongside the railway I can see again the little " Army of Liberation " hurrying eastward from Macedonia under Shefket Pasha to free Constantinople from Abdul the Damned and found an Ottoman Empire of Liberty, Equality, and Fraternity. Or the great Ottoman hosts of the Balkan wars slowly rolling westward to defend the Islamic Empire against disruption into nations of warring Christians. Or the interminable bullock trains of the victorious Bulgars crawling eastward to supply the Christian armies at Tchataldja in their crusade to recover the first capital of Christianity. Or the Turkish cavalry under wiry little Rafet Pasha cantering westward to wrest from the Ghiaour, Adrianople, the first European capital of the Caliphate. Then comes the Great War, and Thrace can be seen of no English eye except from some adventurous aeroplane hovering like a hawk high in the air and watching the white " Balkan luxuszug " creeping along below with its load of German generals and high explosives for the Dardanelles.

The last time I came through there was another transformation scene in progress. The Angora Turks, with the support of the French, were pushing out the Greeks and their patrons the British. At every station were flying Turkish and French flags, and the kolpaks of the Turkish Nationalists were fraternizing with the fezzes of the Ottoman Imperialists. British pickets were keeping the peace along the Maritsa between the lines of the defeated Greeks and the advanced bands of the Angora national army which had no business to be there at all. I remember a curious little scene in the dining-car of the " Conventional " during a long halt at the Maritsa Bridge. Behind a table sat a portly French Consul-General arbitrating between a Greek major and a mysterious officer whose French cap and waterproof thinly disguised a Turk of the Angora army. The Greek officer was demanding the surrender of a young Thracian Greek whom the Turks proposed to shoot as a spy. The wrangle was interrupted by a sergeant of the old Ottoman army who came in to report that the Greek had escaped and hidden on the train. The Angora intruders began to search the train, upon which it began to back over into the Greek lines. The Turks dropped off and the train then went ahead again towards Constantinople, which was still in British occupation. And all the time the British officers in charge of the station strolled up and down the platform in Olympian oblivion to what was passing. Our British aloofness is no doubt a help in governing Eastern subject races; but only so long as they remain subject.

The ancients showed that they had grasped the principles of political geography when they put the birthplace of Mars in Thrace. This land bridge between East and West used to support a large mixed population of Greek townsmen, Turkish farmers and Bulgar peasants. But it has been swept again and again by the tide of war. In the Balkan wars the Bulgar occupation scared out a good many of the Turks and Greeks. Then the Turkish reoccupation scoured out the Bulgars. Then came the Greeks after the Great War, swept out the Turks and substituted Greeks. And now again reoccupation by the Angora Turks has cleared out the Greeks, who are to be replaced some day by Turks from Greece. This last is the " exchange of populations " policy sanctioned by the Treaty of Lausanne and the League of Nations. No doubt it makes no difference to a diplomat or his productivity whether he works in London or Lausanne. But a Turkish tobacco planter from Macedonia cannot, as a matter of fact, do much with a Bulgar market garden or a Greek orchard in Thrace. Peasants are like plants. These transplanted households perish before they can take root in their new home.

No one can travel through Thrace without wondering how people who mean well come to do so much harm, and whether the suffering they cause can ever be atoned.

> Quo tanto crimine tellus
> Laesisti superos—ut te tot mortibus unam
> Tot sceleris premerent. Eheu, Quod sufficit aevum
> Immemor ut belli donet tibi damna vetustas.

So wrote Lucan in his crabbed Latin. How, he asks, can Thrace so have offended the Powers that they have so often overwhelmed it with death and devilry—and how long will it take those Powers to pay off the reparation they owe to Thrace? Long as is the journey across Thrace or the time since Lucan asked the question, you will not have found the answer before you get to

Constantinople. For what the future of Thrace will be, whether it will go on being a wasted border between East and West, or whether it will become a bridge between them as the European province of an Asiatic nation—nobody yet knows.

As the railway gets nearer the Lines of Tchataldja, the outermost fortifications of Constantinople, it begins to loop itself round the barren downs in apparently meaningless meanderings. These writhings represent the wanglings of the promoter, Baron Hirsch, to increase his kilometric guarantee, and of Baron von der Goltz, the fortifier of Constantinople, to bring the line nicely under fire of his batteries. But we, weary with a long, dull journey, watching the train chase its own tail interminably round these dreary uplands, will curse impartially both the Austrian Jew and the Prussian Junker.

Coming down to the Marmara coast we run past San Stefano and get a glimpse of the great walls. The line breaks through them, between the Seven Towers Castle and the sea. On a neighbouring tower is a tablet recording that it was built by " ROMANUS, THE MIGHTY DESPOT OF THE ROMANS THE MOST MIGHTY." But whether the most mighty Romanus was Romanus I, who had a beautiful daughter, Helena, whom he married to Constantine Porphyrogenitus, whose throne he subsequently usurped until he was forcibly made a monk ; or Romanus II, the son of Constantine Porphyrogenitus who married a beautiful wife, Theophano, a barmaid, poisoned his father at her instigation and died of dissipation ; or Romanus III, an old gentleman who came to the throne at sixty and was poisoned by his wife Zoe, who was in love with an epileptic footman whom she made Emperor ; or Romanus IV, a reformer, whose army consequently abandoned him in battle and who was thrown prostrate before Alp Arslan so that a Turkish Sultan might place his foot on the neck of an Emperor of the East—which of these was " the most mighty Romanus " nobody knows and nobody cares. But I have put in this paragraph to show you the sort of people you are going to meet.

Breaking our way in, thus, through a hole in the wall the City turns its back on us with the contempt it has always shown to a barbarian invader. We drive our destructive way along the Marmara sea front, across ancient harbours that the line has filled up and ancient palaces that it has pulled down, first inside, then outside the seawalls. Passing close under the shell of the Bucoleon Palace, the line rounds Seraglio Point to the Sirkedji Terminus. There, as other invaders of the city have found, the real fight begins. And we are soon engaged in a hand-to-hand battle with porters, interpreters, cab-drivers and other banditti. Leaving you to deal with them as best you can and make your way to your Pera hotel, I shall go back to look after the travellers by steamer.

Coming to Constantinople by train you crawl into the town as other invaders have done, through a drain. Coming by steamer through the Black Sea and the Bosphorus you reach it by the back door. And this variant has great advantages. You reduce the long dull railway journey; and the last stage by sea is altogether attractive, in summer. I would not, if I were you, risk the night on the Black Sea in winter unless you are an old salt.

We will suppose you, then, getting up after a restful night on a fine summer morning. The smart white Roumanian mail-boat is racing towards a low line of hills to the south that marks the coast of the Chersonese. Coming from the Black Sea you will be able to grasp one of the reasons that has always made Constantinople a golden apple of discord. Somewhere in that coast-line is the mouth of the water-way between the outer oceans and this inland sea, whose coasts are rich in the two main necessaries of modern civilization—grain and oil. Before the war you would have seen the invisible channel marked by the spiring smoke trails of a long line of steamers coming up with coal and wares, or going out with wheat and oil. But since Denikin, Wrangel and the Poles ravaged the wheat provinces of White Russia, since the French and British fleets swept off and sold all the Russian shipping of the Black Sea, and since the boycott of Russia, this trade, so essential to all the peoples of Europe, has been crippled and is only now being restored. First opened by the Argonauts, this channel has been ever since one of the main arteries of civilization, and the main source of the wealth of Constantinople. The city was a distributing centre and warehouse both for the maritime trade north and south through the waterway, and for the land trade east and west across the isthmus.

But enough of economics; for we are already entering the land of legends. The Bosphorus opens before us, and the mail-boat runs boldly in through the once-dreaded strait—

> Where the narrowing Simplegades whiten
> The straits of Propontis with spray.

Under the tall cliffs and the bare hill-sides of the eastern shore you can still see an isolated rock pinnacle rising from the sea with a white object on the summit,—the marble pedestal of a statue to an Emperor, put up there for a sailing mark. There is no trace left of the other of the two " Cyanean Rocks " that legend tells used to come clashing together to the destruction of adventurous navigators. No one has yet suggested a working explanation of this tradition. Geologists find traces of volcanic action in the surviving rock ; archæologists find traces of fortifications. But none of their explanations carry conviction. Here is a new theory for your consideration. To the west of the Strait is a bay of evil repute to shipping, called the False Bosphorus. So dangerous has it proved even in modern times that a special international life-saving and light service was established there at Phaneraki in the last century, and a light of some sort has been maintained on it throughout history. An ancient navigator before the days of lights, who believed that he had safely entered the Bosphorus but found himself embayed on this lee shore and wrecked on its rocks, might well, if he survived, explain to his owners, and possibly believe himself, that the jaws of the Strait had closed on him. Taller stories than that have been sworn to in Admiralty cases.

Phaneraki is where King Phineus entertained the Argonauts and, in return, was freed by them from the raiding Harpies— winged man-vultures who used to sweep down and clear off all eatables. This too we can fit into the real story of Constantinople. The wealthy Propontis has always been exposed to raids from the less civilized tribes of the Black Sea coasts. This legend probably records the earlier raids of these pirates in their sailing canoes and their winged hats just as later chronicles describe them, until the Byzantine navy and fortifications ended their ravages.

Running into the Strait the steamer wheels left and draws in to Anatoli Kavak for pratique. The two castles of Roumeli Kavak on the European shore and this Anatoli Kavak are the gates of the Bosphorus. On a calm day you can still see under the water the foundations of a mole that ran out to meet another from Roumeli Kavak, the channel between the two being closed by a chain. With all due respect to the accuracy of Byzantine historians and the ability of Greek engineers, this seems to-day impossible in view of the depth and width of the Strait. Erosion cannot account for the widening in view of the hardness of the rock. So here is a new explanation. The Strait geologically is a rift, the two continents having broken apart at the junction. Looking at the map you can see that if the two shores were brought together again, the European bank would fit neatly into the Asiatic, allowing for some widenings of the bays by the scoop of the current. The latest theory of our earth's surface is that the continents float in a viscous lava, and that America has even shifted in historic times some little distance westward. Here may be historic evidence that Europe has got a move on too.

Anatoli Kavak, with its fine old Crusaders' Castle above, its green plane trees and little brown wooden Turkish houses leaning over the water below, and the Giants' Mountain behind, is a pretty coloured frontispiece for your new picture-book of the East. And when you hear that Haroun al Raschid besieged it and Godfrey de Bouillon took it, you will realize that you are already on the frontier of the realm of the Arabian nights and of the Romaunt of the Rose. But the yellow flag at the masthead will by now have been hauled down and your steamer will be under way again before you have had more than a glimpse. You may be glad that on the mail-boat you run no risk of the experience I had on last putting in to Kavak. It was on a Bolshevik steamer, and when, after a long delay, we started again, I saw, to my horror, that the yellow flag was still flying. This meant that, after two days and nights of a Black Sea winter gale on a bench in a crowded saloon, I was carried past the hotels of Constantinople down to a desolate quarantine station in the Gulf of Ismid there to be purged of any revolutionary infection.

Below Kavak the scenery changes from the grim bare cliffs at the mouth of the Strait to the green banks of a broad swift stream lined with stone quays and villages of wooden houses. Behind are walled gardens and meadows with giant planes, and a background of low hills crowned with umbrella pines. Here and there are marble palaces and pleasure-houses. In the shallow bays stand wooden structures on piles, the "daglians" of the fishermen. Everywhere are nets and fishing-boats. Shoals of small fish shimmer past and on warm summer nights you can hear the booming splash of the great sunfish as he leaps from the water. Of the many fish, great and small, perhaps the best-eating is the loufer, a sort of grey mullet. The oysters too are notable and also notorious. Do not eat them uncooked. There is good sport to be got along the quays scooping at fish in the clear water with a sort of landing-nct on a long pole.

Your steamer passes shipping of all lands and ages, from the motor yacht that is swiftly squandering the fortune of an Asiatic prince to the old steam tramp that is slowly building up the fortunes of a future British peer—from the centre-board cat-boat that corrects the digestion of a South American diplomat to the mediæval galleon bringing charcoal to cook his dinner. The rowing kaik with the gay liveries of its crew, its slender swiftness and its bundled-up beauties of the hareem is gone. But you can still see the degenerate descendant of the ancient galley in the mahona, a wooden barge rowed by men who at each stroke step up on to a bar and throw themselves back against the heavy sweeps, giving the time by a monotonous chant. As they toil painfully along, there shoots past them a flock of the Lesser Shearwater, skimming the surface of the water. Naturalists may be able to explain why these graceful little birds spend their lives flying at top speed up and down the Bosphorus, never apparently stopping anywhere or stooping at anything. We may however be satisfied with the local legend which holds they are the souls of the dead galley slaves who now enjoy eternally an ecstasy of motion where they had so often passed before in labour and pain.

I shall not deal here with the places you pass on the run down the Bosphorus. For the mail-boat races past them on the swift current and we shall return to visit many of them in the last chapter. Just below Kavak on the European side is Therapia, the diplomatic summer resort. The Argonauts put in here on their return with the Golden Fleece and with the witch Medea : the former the symbol of the Angora goat that has always been a gold mine to Turkey—the latter the symbol of those Eastern arts that have always been the bane of Greece. The place was originally called Pharmakia because Medea here left behind her travelling medicine chest. But a mediæval patriarch, who had invested in local real estate, rechristened it " Therapia "—the Place of Healing. Facing, as it does, the cool northerly breeze that blows every summer day with business-like regularity from ten to five, it quite justifies its new name.

The most striking scenery in the Straits is at the Narrows, where the Bosphorus makes a right-handed turn round the bluff on which stands the fine Turkish castle of Roumeli Hissar. The current here at times is almost a rapid and navigation is complicated by the crook in the channel and the cross-currents of wind. You can sometimes stand on the point and see vessels running past you down the channel before the northerly breeze from the Black Sea, while others breast the current to meet them before the southerly draught from the Marmara. Moreover, though the surface stream, here known as the Shaitan Akindi or Devil Current, runs south at a rate of knots, there is said to be a northerly under-current which, if you lower a bucket deep enough, will tow a boat up the Strait. I have never seen it done and do not believe it. But there are quite enough queer natural phenomena about here to account for this point having been held to be the home of particularly dangerous devils and put under the special supervision of Poseidon, who had a temple on the summit. In modern times Poseidon's duties were taken over by an International Board; but since the Treaty of Lausanne the devils have had it pretty well their own way.

Even steamers are sometimes led astray in the Bosphorus by the fogs and currents. I remember seeing a wooden house overhanging the water at Anatoli Hissar, with its whole front sliced off by an errant tramp. Another night, on a balcony at Therapia in a sea fog, I had the sensation of something silent and unseen near by. I dashed into the room, seized my tin bath, and, coming out on the balcony, thumped it vigorously. Immediately the mist was rent by a clanging of engine bells, churning of engines, and clamour of voices while the towering bow of a drifting steamer loomed large over the house and then faded as she backed away.

If you want to enjoy the sensation of swimming from one continent to another do not try it, as I did, from Roumeli Hissar to Kandilli. You will get on swimmingly, so to say, until almost within reach of Kandilli quay, when the devil current will catch you and carry you away back again to Europe. It can be done the other way across; as it was by a tribe of Danube horsemen serving under an early Byzantine Emperor in Asia Minor. Getting homesick one day they rode straight away for the Danube, until the Bosphorus barred their way. Shouting "Who goes home?" their leader spurred his horse headlong in, and the tribe, following, all got over safely.

Just above the Narrows was the original crossing. The name Bosphorus, or ox-ferry, marks what the Strait meant to the early pastoral peoples of these regions who had to move their cattle backwards and forwards across it from winter to summer pastures. And this old grazing road is still followed annually by great flocks of sheep. The opportunity this gave the Lords of the Straits for tolling and taxing was not likely to be missed. And the ordeal established the popular name for ever. The legend of Europa crossing on the back of a divine bull was no doubt a religious sugaring of the pill, much as the figure of Britannia ruling the waves on a penny consoles us for the large number of them we must contribute to the naval estimates.

The Turks, with their contemptuous candour, sum this up in their name for the Straits, " Boghaz Kessen " or the Cut-throat. The ancient Greeks more politely expressed the same idea by calling them the Gates. Only the Crusaders missed the point, with their " Arm of St. George." But then the Latin Empire never made anything of Constantinople.

Below Roumeli Hissar, a short run past the Bosphorus palaces and round another point, and then the sky-line of Stamboul, with its domes and minarets, slowly lengthens itself before us, as the steamer turns toward the Golden Horn and draws alongside its Galata quay. And you will be able to land armed with a vision of the beauty of Stamboul that will enable you to face the dingy disillusionments of Galata.

As we arrive from the Black Sea, we may perhaps see some enormous Atlantic liner on tour, sliding slowly up from the Marmara, dwarfing our Roumanian mail-boat to a steam-launch and making Stamboul itself look like one of those toy cities built by ingenious children out of the parlour ornaments. And the route followed by the liner from Athens of classic memories, through the Greek islands of the Ægean, the Homeric Dardanelles and the classic Marmara, is the high road to the Golden City. Along this road you approach her, as an Empress of the East should be approached, by the front gate and step by step through each successive court until you come to where she sits enthroned.

The great water-gate of the Dardanelles and the towering heights of Gallipoli put even a Transatlantic liner in its place. Looking up to the western heights of Gallipoli, conquered for a few brief moments by our brothers in arms from the other side of the world, and looking out on the east over the low-lying Troad, where are the foundations of the seven Troys, all destroyed by sieges, we can realize what the command of this water-gate and land-bridge has always meant to the world. Until lately it looked as though the future of Gallipoli was to be an Eastern Gibraltar. And whether that would have been any advantage to us is now likely to remain an open question.

I shall not deal here with the two great campaigns that have immortalized the Dardanelles. Some of us have learnt all about the one at school and others have learnt all about the other in the stern school of war. The story of these campaigns is an epic for poets only ; and you can take Pope and Masefield with you.

But as we steam past the batteries on Cape Helles under which the *River Clyde* was run ashore and the beaches of the Scamander where the Greek ships were fired by the Trojans, we may wonder at the little improvement in the Powers that rule the affairs of men. Men still exterminate each other for the same policies, at the same places and under the same little tin gods; only the names are changed. For on the east you can see the snowy peaks of the Bithynian Olympos and Mount Ida where squabbling gods and goddesses squandered the lives of the heroes fighting for Troy. And away in the west we can imagine the gods of our day in equally remote altitudes of Whitehall and the Wilhelmstrasse while heroes, beside whom Achilles would look like a manikin, gathered here from all the Seven Seas to fight for Constantinople.

Steaming through the Hellespont we are all the time among the relics of long-forgotten fights. The piles of great stone cannon balls we see in the Turkish batteries were for those mediæval cannon, whose reputation alone defended the Strait for centuries. They were never really tested until in the Napoleonic wars Admiral Duckworth braved them without damage and brought his fleet of wooden three-deckers safely up to Constantinople; though coming back, the fleet suffered heavy damage. In the last war the big guns were on the other side, and on the shore you may still see the wrecks of a Turkish transport and cruiser sunk by the heavy guns of the *Queen Elizabeth* shooting from the Gulf of Saros, by balloon observation, right across the Gallipoli range.

The Hellespont is not so beautiful as the Bosphorus; but it has played an even larger part in the world's history. From Alexandria Troas, near by on the Asiatic side, St. Paul started to carry the cross to Rome and martyrdom. Hither from the west came the Christian Emperor Barbarossa to carry the Cross to Jerusalem, and to meet an equally obscure death. Hither too from the east came the Saracens and Turks to carry the Crescent as far as the walls of Vienna. And, last of all, the ebb and flow of the Great War, in which both Cross and Crescent, both Orthodox Church and Ottoman Caliphate, have been swept away by the new religion of Nationalism.

You will probably get your first sight of Constantinople as you come on deck in the early morning. Away to your right, the sun will have risen over the hills of Asia, lighting up the white villages along the Thracian coast on your left. Far away ahead, along the northern horizon, beyond a mother-of-pearl sea, will be a silver-grey outline of domes and minarets. As it grows higher and longer you will see the whole city before you, from the Castle of the Seven Towers that marks the end of the Great Walls on the west, along the Seven Hills and Seven Mosques like the arches of a long bridge, down to the black pins of the cypresses on Seraglio Point. As the steamer gets nearer and the sun rises higher, the pearly greys begin to take colour and the outline gains depth. The long battlemented line of the sea walls appears and the Seraskierate Tower marks the valley of the Grand Bazaar. As the steamer draws in round Seraglio Point the great Ahmediyeh Mosque bulks large above the heavy buttresses and flat dome of Saint Sophia.

By then we shall have passed, on the right, Prinkipo Islands, the prison of many Byzantine Emperors and, not long ago, of a British general. Like some of the Emperors, General Townsend from his prison played a considerable part in the politics of his jailers. From this waterway between Prinkipo and Stamboul, many a Turkish Pasha under the late Abdul Hamid of impious memory, has taken his last look at this world before being thrust under water over the side of the Yildiz Palace launch. Many a more fortunate Pasha has fled in his kaik or launch across this water to the British colony; to sail later, hidden in the hold of a British yacht or a British steamer. To these islands also was exiled my friend the Kaptan Pasha when the Turks started to clean up Constantinople. For years I had watched him rule his province in the Grande Rue de Pera with dignity. In battle with neighbouring tribes his great yellow dingo head raged supreme. But any bona-fide traveller who arrived at his frontiers with lowered tail, and who observed the proper formalities by there lying on his back until allowed to get up, was courteously escorted through his territory. Every dog has his day, and the day of the Kaptan Pasha had passed like that of his Turkish prototypes, the Derebeys and Bairakdars. His race were the first victims of the deportation policy. The Turks were kind to their street-dogs, just as they were to Armenians, Greeks and other sons of dogs. But the time came when they believed they had to clean their community from all that was contaminating it. So the dogs were deported in barges to die of thirst and starvation on the rocky islets of the Marmara. The Armenians were driven along the barren tracts of Anatolia until they died as miserably. And now the market-gardens of the Greeks along the Gulf of Ismid and the Greek villages along the coast of Thrace are inhabited only by a few starving Turkish deportees from Macedonia. It was a Near-Eastern diplomatist, Edward Bulwer Lytton, who wrote that " the pen is mightier than the sword " ; but he did not realize what a sinister significance his successors at Lausanne might give to his aphorism.

Let us hope that your steamer will not be too big to go along-side, or that you will be met by some one capable of dealing with the harbour boatmen. They are the worthy progeny of the corsairs and the progenitors of a Communist Trade Union. On my last arrival the only way I could reduce the rate from two pounds to the proper two shillings was by getting into a boat and sitting there for about two hours, smilingly repeating at intervals, " Bir lira " (one florin), while the storm of expostulation and vituperation raged around.

Patience is the one suitable weapon in Turkey, and it always wins. But another time, crossing from Galata to Stamboul to catch the " Conventional " which then left at dawn, I found the bridge open for shipping and had to take a boat. Arrived off Sirkedji, the boatmen refused to land me unless I gave them four times their bargain. The alternative of losing my reser-vation or of being robbed was too much for my temper. " What is this ? " I said : " you dress as Moslems but you deal like Chris-tians." Without a word they rowed me to the quay and pushed off again without deigning to take my fare. In all dealings with Asiatics injury is no excuse for insult.

Clear of the boatmen, the next business of all travellers is to find a hotel. Do not be too adventurous. Rule out at once any idea of collecting local colour at a Turkish Khan in Stamboul or at a Greek Xenodokheion in Galata. Such experiences are only for the expert. On the other hand, the Pera Palace or Therapia Summer Palace may have to be renounced as too expensive. The next class, of which there is a good choice in the Grande Rue de Pera, will do for a start. Moreover too much regard for economy may prove expensive. At a recent visit I put up at a small hotel in the Grande Rue, which was clean and comfortable. But the first night I lost money. The next night I took more precautions and lost more moncy. The third night I surrounded myself with trip-strings tied to water-jugs over tin pails and similar man-traps, only to wake up in the small hours, to see the thief disappearing through the door, and to fall into all my own useless booby-traps. No doubt through some spy-hole he had watched my preparations for him with much appreciation.

You should also give up all ideas of Oriental establishments *à la* Pierre Loti. And if you must seek social adventures in the Levantine half-world of Russian "countesses" and Greek "clergyman's daughters" do not do so under the guidance of the disreputable touts who hang about the hotels. Pera cannot bait its man-traps so well as Paris, and their bite is far more dangerous. The back streets of Galata after dark are quite unsafe.

If you are staying more than a few days and have local friends you can easily find a pleasant lodging with some family. If you can get admitted as a visitor to the Constantinople Club you can get there reliable information as to the usual diversions of foreign colonies, such as catching fish, shooting birds and beasts, collecting antiques and hunting concessions. And if you want culinary adventures you can get plenty of variety in the restaurants. I put the Russians first, of which there is a good example almost opposite the entrance to the British Embassy Chapel. Then you should try the Turkish, where you can make even more exciting experiments. The best are in the Grande Rue, where is also an Armenian restaurant of longstanding reputation. Before long you should find out how to live cheaply and comfortably.

But most of us who arrive in Constantinople are just travellers, tired with the long journey. So I will suppose you resting at some window, looking out on the most wonderful view in the world, the long outline of Stamboul across the Golden Horn, or at the scarcely less beautiful outlook on the villages and wooded hills across the Bosphorus. For you have before you some strenuous sight-seeing that will call for all your energies.

Sight-seeing in a city with so long a past and so large an area as this must be arranged with an eye both to chronology and convenience. If you see what is to be seen just as it comes, you will end with your head all in a dither with dates and befogged with strange names. You will muddle up the Constantine who founded the city and the Constantine who fell with it—Mohammed the Conqueror who founded the old Empire, and Mahmoud the Reformer, who founded the new—Mustapha Bairakdar, who fought for reform in 1808 and failed, and Mustapha Kemal, who has done the same with better success to-day. We must get landmarks like these leading characters well fixed in our minds in their proper order if we are not to get lost in a history ranging over 2,000 years. On the other hand, we must also arrange the sights with some regard for their situation, or we shall spend all our time bumping or tramping backwards and forwards over some of the worst-paved streets in Europe.

The story of Constantinople falls conveniently into five chapters. The first two cover the period when Constantinople was the capital of the Christian Empire. The first of these two chapters I have distinguished as the period of the Roman Empire, representing, as it does, the period from the building of New Rome by Constantine for a capital of the World Empire, down to the time when it became the metropolis of an Empire of the East. During this chapter the Latin law and language was predominant over the Greek, and I have considered it as ending with Heraclius. The second chapter is that of the Byzantine Empire, during which the dominant Greek slowly declined until his Empire was interrupted by the Latin conquest, and, after a short revival, ended finally with the Turkish Conquest. The period of the Turkish Empire I have also divided into two chapters, calling the first the Osmanli Empire, to distinguish the mediæval and feudal regime of Mohammed the Conqueror. The next chapter I call the Ottoman Empire, as representing the modern reconstruction by Mahmoud the Reformer. Finally comes a chapter dealing with the latest and most striking change of all—one that has passed almost unnoticed under our own eyes. When a bitter war as to whether Constantinople should again become a Christian capital, or should remain the seat of the Caliphate, ended by the city being reduced to the commercial port of a Turkish National State.

For each of these chapters I have arranged an excursion to the principal monuments of the period, so that in five days you can cover a range of some twenty centuries and a radius of as many miles.

The monuments will be taken in chronological order, and will be used as a memoria technica to mark the stages in the long story of the city. The first day we shall be in Stamboul, the second out at the Wall, the third in Stamboul again, the fourth in Pera-Galata, and the fifth up the Bosphorus. If you want to reduce the programme to one day, you could do the first excursion in the morning, read the second during lunch, do the third in the afternoon, and read the other two chapters in bed.

I will leave you then for the present, at your magic casement. Let us hope that it will be a summer night, with the moon turning the Golden Horn to a silver moat between you and Stamboul, that faery land forlorn. If you have only eyes for such obvious beauty as this, then be content with your vision of the City of Felicity and take the morning train home again. The vision will, in itself, be worth the journey.

But, if you are true travellers and have the eye of fancy that can make dry bones and dead dust live again, then we will start together on that long journey to which Constantinople is only the ruined gateway.

> Master of the Caravan:
> Open the gate, O Watchman of the night.
> Watchman:
> Ho, travellers, I open. For what land
> Leave you the dim-moon city of Delight?
> Merchants:
> We take the Golden Road to Samarkand.

CHAPTER I

THE ROMAN EMPIRE

How many miles to Babylon ?
Three score miles and ten.
Can I get there by candlelight ?
Yes—and back again.

(Nursery Rhyme.)

THE Old Serai on Seraglio Point in Stamboul is the site of the earliest settlement. It is also the centre of the city. And it is in itself one of the sights best worth seeing. So you should make it your first excursion.

You can get to Seraglio Point from Pera all the way by tram, or you can go down to Galata by tram or " tunnel " (a funicular railway) and then walk across the bridge and up the hill.

The bridge from Galata to Stamboul, that is, from Europe to Asia, gives you a fine view of the city and of the shipping in the Golden Horn. Below it are moored the ocean-going steamers, above it little thickets of masts mark the coasting and fishing fleets of all manner of rigs and races. Further up again is a curious collection of more or less derelict warships. The bridge was at one time a sight in itself. For, until a generation or so ago, every race, every religion and every occupation had its distinguishing dress, some of them most fantastic. The wide windows and balconies of the old cafés at either end of the bridge remind us that it was then one of the shows of the city to sit and look at the bridge. But these highly coloured and characteristic costumes were killed by the general impoverishment of the latter part of the last century. The crowd took to wearing the cast-off clothes of Europe, and the official uniform became the black Stambouli, a curate's coat, with the red fez made in Austria. The fez continued to give a note of colour until it was in its turn replaced by the kolpak, or woolly bonnet, of the Angora Nationalists. The fez was the symbol of the Ottoman Empire, the kolpak that of the Turkish nation. The change symbolized the replacing of a regime of Levantine clerks by the rule of Turkish

Highlanders. The fez made you bald and the kolpak does not help in keeping a cool head. The size and shagginess of your kolpak is proportionate to the wildness and wooliness of your nationalism. When the allied armies left Constantinople, and the Angora Nationalists marched in, the Ottoman Imperialists expected to be massacred, and for several days the Bosphorus ran red, with fezzes. But to-day they have again reappeared and each fez may be looked upon as a danger-signal for Angora.

A sort of conical kolpak means a dervish, a more or less unorthodox Islamic monk. The round cap of the army officer is the French cap with visor removed, as a verse in the Koran has always been understood as prohibiting a Moslem from shading his face. But the visor is, I hear, now to be restored. A fez, with a turban wound round it, means an orthodox Islamic mullah ; and, if the turban is green, he has been to Mecca. But, with a few such exceptions, the crowd is uninteresting, and there is little to distract one from the beauty of the view of Stamboul, with the Valideh mosque facing the bridge in the foreground.

We enter Stamboul, in which very name the long war between Turks and Greeks for the city is waged. The Turks maintain that Istambol is their way of pronouncing Constantinople, just as they cut Thessalonika down to Selanik. The Greeks say that Stamboul is a corruption of 'ς τὴν πόλιν (to the city), just as we speak of going " to town." However this may be, there is no doubt about two essential facts—that the Turks are now, for the first time, getting rid of the Greeks for good and all, and that the Greeks were there several thousand years before the Turks.

Byzantium and the Museum

On our left, as we go up the hill in the tram or following the tram lines, is the still recognizable eminence of the first Greek acropolis, now enclosed by the old Seraglio walls. This was the citadel of the first colonists from Megara, whose fortifications have been built first into a Byzantine then into a Turkish wall, as was shown by excavations for the railway in 1871. This first city, saved by Xenophon in the retreat of the Ten Thousand, was destroyed by Darius the Persian during his invasion that ended with Marathon and Salamis. Byzantium was then rebuilt by Pausanias within a new line of wall running from the Golden Horn, where the bridge now is, through the valley of the Grand Bazaar to the Marmara ; a wall built in the best Greek style of squared blocks with metal clamps, of which traces survive. This

Pausanias was the Spartan statesman who tried to sell Greece to Xerxes. Evidently, even as early as this, the Persian depravity of Byzantium was too much for the Spartan tradition. Pausanias was only the first of a long succession of public men who have been corrupted by this Circe of cities. It was these Pausanian walls that for two years kept out Philip of Macedon, until the town was relieved by sea from Athens as a result of the eloquent appeals of Demosthenes. Many of us may regret that a similar situation was not as successfully solved in our own day by the eloquence of Mr. Lloyd George. The story goes that Philip's men had scaled the wall by surprise, when they were revealed by the sudden rising of the moon, and that thenceforward the crescent has been the emblem of the town. But the city of Pausanias need trouble us little, for it was wiped out by Septimius Severus in a dynastic squabble in 176 B.C.

We will go straight into the Old Seraglio Garden, through the Demir Kapou (Iron Gate), and on to the Column of Theodosius, or Claudius Gothicus, and take a look round. It is the duty of a travel book of this sort to mark a fine " Aussichtspunkt " with a purple patch, just as a guide-book marks it with a star. So please consider this view as patched and starred. The beauty of Constantinople colouring cannot be conveyed in print. The pleasure in such beauty must be all your own ; we writers can only give interest to what you might otherwise overlook.

You would not in any case overlook the Column of Theodosius ; for in its setting of trees, it is in itself a beautiful thing. But when it was crowned with the golden statue of the Emperor, it must have been a worthy ornament of the famous garden of the Great Palace. The victory that its inscription commemorates has been forgotten like so many other elaborately commemorated victories. It may be that of Claudius Gothicus at Nissa in A.D. 269. During the Roman Empire the column became an object of popular interest by accommodating for twenty years a pillar hermit.

Leaving the column, and coming back along the north wall of the Old Serai, we come to the Museum, our next destination. We are going there now to see the sarcophagi, which perhaps does not sound like a sight worthy of being given a first place among so many. But the classic beauty that you may there see is something quite out of the common, and it should be enjoyed with a clean palate, uncloyed by the picturesque.

The sarcophagi are of two sorts. Those of the Byzantine Emperors are only historically interesting. You will find them in the rooms to the right of the entrance. They have been recently collected from all over the city, and there is little or no doubt that these massive porphyry or verde antique coffins are those which held the remains of Constantine and the early emperors in their shrines at the Church of the Holy Apostles; though it is impossible to assign them to their respective tenants. These tombs were broken open by the Crusaders when they captured the city in order to rifle the bodies. They were later repaired by the Greeks, as you still may see. But, after the Ottoman Conquest, they were scattered all over the city and used for various purposes, sometimes as public fountains. The lids of two of them were known to be buried under the roots of a great plane in the Old Serai, and were dug up by Turkish archæologists in 1920. As these great masses of stone were practically indestructible they have now been rescued from their various menial duties and restored to the respect if no longer to the veneration of men. But their tenants who thought that in them they had secured an eternal and imperial repose cannot be rescued from such useful occupation as they may have found, so that still:

> Imperial Caesar dead and turned to clay
> May stop a hole to keep the wind away.

The other series of sarcophagi are works of classic art not historically connected with the city, but that would alone justify a visit to Constantinople had it nothing else to offer. The best of them were found in one seven-chambered tomb at Sidon by Dr. Eddy, an American, and together they give you excellent examples of the various schools of Greek classic art. For example, in the rooms to the right you will find the sarcophagus of the " Satrap " assigned to the Ionian School of about 450 B.C. The reliefs on one side show an Oriental prince with tiara and sceptre between two women, presiding at a chariot race. On the other side he appears in a hunting scene, and at the end he is on his bier with the two women mourning. Another is in the Lycian style with Amazons lion-hunting and a boar-hunt. The riders remind us of the Parthenon frieze. To the left of the Museum entry is another, that of " The Mourners," which is of the Attic school, with traces of the original colouring still very visible. The preservation of this, as indeed of all of them, is otherwise perfect. But the finest of all is the so-called " Alexander " sarcophagus. The date is about 300 B.C. and Alexander is the central figure; though the evidence is all against his having been buried in it. The reliefs on one side and end show a cavalry combat between Macedonians and Persians, perhaps the battle of Issus. Alexander, attended by a General, possibly Parmenio, is overthrowing a Persian. On the other side Alexander is rescuing a Persian Satrap, who has got into difficulties lion-hunting.

After these examples of Greek classic art in its perfection you may find of interest the good collection of more primitive work. I myself, at my last visit, coming straight from Communist Russia, was interested to find, on primitive reliefs from Asia Minor, the symbols of the Virgin and Child and of the Good Shepherd that I had just seen used in Communist child-welfare posters for the Ukraine villagers. Thus do religions come and go while their human symbols remain. Among other interesting things in the Museum are—a piece of a white marble column of the fifth century, with the earliest known representation of the baptism of Christ in the Jordan, the earliest known relic of the temple of Herod at Jerusalem—a tablet with a Greek inscription forbidding strangers to pass the balustrade round the Hieron on pain of death, and a Phœnician inscription from the Pool of Siloam, dating probably from Hezekiah. There are also gold ornaments from Troy, and part of one of the serpents' heads from the Delphic Column.

Leaving the Museum and turning left-handed up into the main court of the Old Serai we can as we go make our first excursion into history. The history of Constantinople proper begins with Constantine the Great, whose reign (A.D. 306 to 337) began at York and who rebuilt Byzantium as the first Christian capital of the Roman Empire, calling it New Rome. This may suggest to us the curious resemblances between the position and politics of New Rome and New York. One that we can note here is that both are in 40° 42′ 40″ N. Lat., Seraglio Point being 5,622 miles due east of Battery Point. As the story goes on, you will find even more significant likenesses between the growth of the two cities.

CONSTANTINE AND THE CHURCH

With the personal and political conditions that brought Constantine out of the ruck of some half-dozen rival emperors, and set him to building a new capital, we need not bother. But owing to the rush of population to the new capital of the world, the Emperor soon had on his hands a housing problem which he disposed of with an efficiency we may envy. The forests of Belgrad, which still exist to the north of the town, supplied unlimited timber, and the island of Proconnesos no less unlimited marble. And, as the building unions of the day were unable to provide a sufficient number of architects and artificers, the Emperor diluted them with apprentices from his own technical schools. The work was done at surprising speed; and, judging from contemporary complaints of jerry-building, the capital was run up very much on the lines of a modern Empire Exhibition. If Rome wasn't built in a day, New Rome very nearly was. Themistius, a contemporary chronicler, reports that the city had to be practically rebuilt by Constantine's successor Constantius.

One advantage that Constantine had was that he could lay the whole empire under contribution for ornaments, tombs, trophies, and statues of gods and heroes. These with a north-country thoroughness he "conveyed" in cargo loads from Rome, Athens, Alexandria, and all the cities of Europe and Asia. So that the chronicler Cedrenus, describing the opening ceremonies, declared with an acid irony " that nothing was now wanting save the souls of the illustrious dead." Was this want possibly the reason why it comes that of the Great Palace built by Constantine, enlarged by his successors and enriched with the wealth of the ancient world, of its marble staircases, of its hanging gardens, and of its port on the Marmara, nothing remains. These " cloud-capped towers and gorgeous palaces " all " like an insubstantial pageant faded have left not a wrack behind." Gone are the university, the two theatres, the eight public and one hundred and fifty-three private baths, the fifty-two porticoes, the four law courts, the fourteen palaces, and the four thousand three hundred and eighty-eight family mansions, all built by Constantine for the establishment of the first Christian capital.

One building alone remains—one of the smaller of the fourteen churches, St. Irene that we are now passing in the outer court of the Old Serai. This most interesting church, thanks to its protected position, escaped conversion into a mosque, was used as an armoury and since 1839 has become a museum of arms. This, though apparently a satisfaction to the orthodox, is very unfortunate. For the interior is so disguised and disfigured by the collections of arms and costumes that there is nothing of the church to be seen. It is much to be hoped that the Angora Government will make the restoration of this most interesting historic monument one of their next reforms. The collections, which are well worth larger quarters, we shall visit later, and until they are moved you had better take the inside on trust from me.

In moving the capital to New Rome Constantine was only

following a shift in the gravity centre of World Empire that had already caused Diocletian to move to the east of the Adriatic. But the main reason for making a fresh start was the religious revolution that Constantine had decided to carry out by making Christianity the State religion. He realized that autocracy could no longer clothe itself in divine right by borrowing the attributes of the debased Greek gods or the monstrous and mystical Egyptian deities. He saw that the new Christian religion offered an opportunity of rebuilding autocracy on a better foundation of legal principles and personal loyalty. This new divine right required a new capital where its adherents would not be offended at every turn by monuments to their persecutors, and where its opponents would not be further alienated by the destruction of pagan works of art. In Constantinople the Phidian Apollo could safely be converted into a Christian Emperor and a pagan basilica could be transformed into a church. For, as Constantinople shows us, Christian ecclesiastical architecture developed out of the Roman basilica, the Court of Justice, not out of the Greek Temple, the Shrine of Beauty. The Byzantine church is, in its structural origin, the Western basilica with an Eastern dome superimposed. It is a true architectural expression of the alliance of Western and Eastern ideas and institutions that went to make the early Church.

Byzantine architecture, born of the union of Greek and Persian art, is the only creation that a thousand years of Byzantine civilization gave the world. Even so, Byzantium only provided the conditions of peace and prosperity in which old forms could be combined in new formulæ. There were domes in Europe and Asia before that of St. Sophia. Columns had been bridged by arches instead of architraves in the palace of Diocletian and walls faced with coloured marbles in the pavilions of the East. Even such a device as the pendentive—the vaulting filling the triangular space where arches meet at an angle—was not new. But it was left to the Byzantine church to combine all these in an artistic expression of spiritual emotion as lively and as lovely as any Greek temple or Gothic cathedral.

The Roman basilica was an oblong nave ending in an apse with aisles on either side divided from the nave by colonnades of pillars bearing a flat roof. In Constantinople we can see how this simple model of the earliest Christian church develops through transitions in which the dome and arch become more and more dominant, until we have the square edifice with a central and four subsidiary domes characteristic of the complete Byzantine style. The growth and decline of this style was only slightly affected by the Moslem conquest and it reaches its highest expression in the great mosques of Constantinople.

In St. Irene we have its beginnings. The building was obviously at first a simple basilica, with nave, aisle, apse, narthex (porch), and atrium (cloister). Whether built by Constantine or only beautified by him is uncertain, but it is certainly the only building left that has any association with him. It was before the altar of St. Irene that the aged Catholic bishop Alexander lay all day long, praying that the saints would deliver him from the sacrilege of obeying Constantine's order to receive into communion the arch-heretic Arius. In the words of Gibbon : " On the same day that had been fixed for the triumph of Arius he expired— and the strange and horrid circumstance might excite a suspicion that the orthodox Saints had contributed more efficaciously than by their prayers to deliver the Church from the most formidable of her enemies." Constantine seems to have had the same idea, for the Catholic bishops Athanasius of Alexandria and Paul of Constantinople were soon afterwards banished. When Constantine on his death-bed underwent his long-deferred baptism it was from an Arian bishop, and thereafter that sect were for some time in authority.

The churches of Constantinople in those days were fortified citadels round which the fanatics of the homousion and the homoiousion dogmas settled their controversy in the only way it ever could be settled. St. Irene was half-ruined in the course of the riots and had to be rebuilt by Justinian, who added the dome (A.D. 533). It had again to be restored in A.D. 740, when the second dome was added and the narthex included in the church. The atrium with its pointed arches is probably Moslem. The rows of marble seats round the apse with a passage underneath are an interesting transitional feature from the basilican to the Byzantine style. The carved columns and capitals are of the first transition. Over the chancel arch is a half-effaced inscription calling on the Hope of the Earth to enter his Temple. The mosaics are just discernible under the colour-wash, from which they will no doubt be soon relieved by an unsectarian administration. The great black cross of tesseræ on the vaulting will then again become an impressive feature, and when the church is restored it will give us a fine emotional expression of the austere asperities of the age of Athanasius. For the architecture and associations of St. Irene belong to the atmosphere of the damnatory clauses.

With the thunder of that tremendous denunciation in our ears and the din of dogmatic disputants fading away again into the forgotten past we leave the Old Serai for the present and cross the Hippodrome, passing St. Sophia on our left. And we may marvel at the perversity of man, who after dedicating one church to the Peace of God (eirene) should have used it for faction fights on the nature of God, and who having created such a monument of human extravagance and inhuman extortion as is St. Sophia should have then dedicated it to the Divine Wisdom.

THE COLUMNS AND THEODOSIUS

Making our way across the Hippodrome to the trim public garden under the Achmediyeh Mosque, we shall find the Delphic Column sandwiched between an Egyptian obelisk and the fountain presented by Kaiser Wilhelm. This serpent column from Delphi, the most ancient and archæologically interesting of the monuments of Constantinople, can now be seen to the full extent of what remains of it, thanks to the excavations of it by British officers during the Crimean War. It has stood here for sixteen centuries and was looted by Constantine from Delphi, where it had stood for eight. When at Delphi it bore the golden tripod, dedicate to Apollo, and its inscription still records in archaic Greek characters the City States which took part in the victory of Platea. You can still read there the names of the Tenians whose trireme brought the news of the Persian Armada, just as that careful historian Herodotus tells us. " For this service the Tenians were enrolled among the victors on the tripod at Delphi." The Dutchman Gyllius, who saw the column in the sixteenth century, describes it as " encircled with the cable coils of three serpents. Their heads arranged in a triangle project from high up on the shaft of the column." These heads are now missing. They were first knocked off in A.D. 835 by fanatical monks in a nocturnal devil-hunt round this shrine of pagan magic. They must then have been replaced; for Mohammed the Conqueror, riding in on the capture of the city, struck off the lower jaw of one serpent as an act of defiance against the much-dreaded magic of the Greeks. We have in fact here a relic of early serpent worship which retains something of its mystic prestige to the present day.

The column of the Colossus in the Hippodrome is an ancient monument of which practically nothing is known, except that it was once covered with bronze plates, and was probably the column from which the Latin Crusaders threw the Greek insurgent Alexius the Beetlebrowed. Perhaps even our Duke of York's column may some day in some such way justify its existence.

The column that corresponds to our Nelson monument, as being the centre of the life of the city, is the Column of Constantine that stands a little farther along the tram-line where was the centre of Constantine's Forum. It bore a colossal statue of Apollo by Phidias, transmogrified into Constantine with a sceptre in one hand and an orb in the other ; while the golden sunrays of Apollo were converted into a sort of halo and further sanctified with nails from the true Cross. The art critics of the day all unite in ardent admiration of this product of hybrid piety. The other name of the column, the Porphyry Column, is explained by its eight drums of porphyry, once encircled by bronze laurel wreaths. The Turkish name, Tchemberli Tash (hooped stone), is accounted for by the iron rings that now hold it together, and that have been recently renewed by the Angora government. It is also called the Burnt Column, from the marks of many fires left upon it. In an arched chamber under the marble stylobate were enshrined relics that were as priceless to the ancients as they would be to antiquaries to-day. Such were the adze with which Noah built the ark, the alabaster box of Mary Magdalene, and the Palladium of Troy. The stylobate was encased in masonry early in the eighteenth century, and the relics are supposed still to be inside. Some years ago two adventurous archæologists hired a house near by and tried to reach them by tunnelling, but were discovered.

Returning towards the Hippodrome again from Constantine's Column we can imagine ourselves passing through the reaction that followed the fanaticism of his day and led to the pagan revival under Julian the Apostate. Even an ecclesiastic like Gregory of Nissa had had to admit that one could have too much theology. Thus he complains that " the very workmen and slaves have become profound theologians, and preach in the streets. If you ask anyone for change he tells you how the Son differs from the Father—if you ask the price of a loaf you are told how the Son is inferior to the Father—and if you ask for a bath you hear how the Son is as nothing to the Father."

With the bakers and bathmen turned theologians fashion turned to paganism again. Julian had been born and bred in Constantinople and was educated in the university. He seems to have been the only Emperor who had a real affection for the city. " I love her as my mother," he writes in one of his letters, and he left his fine library to his alma mater when he died. He reconstructed the government and tried to reform the Court, where the cooks, footmen, and hairdressers were already counted in thousands. " I sent for a valet not a viceroy," he complained when a gorgeous official bowed himself up to his bedside. But the Court and the Church were too many for him. The one pestered his life with intrigues, and the other poisoned his memory with calumnies. The only monument left of his able administration, and that a significant one, is the port he built on the Marmara shore just below the Hippodrome. Under him New Rome surpassed in population and prosperity Rome itself, and the mere sight of it was enough to scare away an invading army of Goths. To this period of rapid growth belong another utilitarian monument, the great aqueduct of Valens (A.D. 366), which is a conspicuous object striding across the valley between the third and fourth hills.

This period of quiet growth ended in the brilliance of the reign of Theodosius the Great (A.D. 378–395). Theodosius went in for a general rebuilding that made him almost as much belauded as Constantine himself. Moreover, like Constantine, he was a good churchman and so got a good press ; while it is interesting for us to note that both these emperors first made their mark in Britain. The Picts and Scots, represented by Jerome as cannibal savages of great ferocity, were raiding the Roman settlements of Britain. Theodosius landed a punitive expedition at Sandwich, marched on London, drove out the raiders, and pacified the country.

The successors of those savages will now have arrived back at the public gardens in the Hippodrome where, beside the Serpent Column, they will find a most noteworthy monument of Theodosius. The top of it is an Egyptian obelisk, brought by him from Heliopolis, which is only interesting as suggesting that the Byzantine decorators of the Hippodrome had much the same taste as the British decorators of the Embankment. But the bas-reliefs round the pedestal are a most entertaining historic document. They show us what we should have seen, had we visited a State performance at the Hippodrome, attended by the Court. On the north side, above a representation of the transport and erection of the obelisk, we have a picture of Theodosius inspecting the games. The Labarum, the mystic symbol of the unity of the Empire, is above him, and on either side Honorius and Arcadius his two sons, between whom the Roman Empire was, at his death, finally divided. On the west, over a Greek inscription in which the municipal engineer Proclus records his achievement, is a picture

of the Empress and other spectators.   On the south side is a
chariot race rounding the cone, or turning-point.   In big shows
there were as many as twenty-four heats, each of seven laps, and
the number of laps run was shown by balls hoisted on the cone.
As there were no rules against fouling, and the upsetting of rivals
was part of the game, and the competitors represented rival
political factions, the races often ended in a free fight.   But
Greek culture never allowed the introduction into Constantinople
of the Roman gladiatorial combats.   Above the race, we have a
picture of the Imperial family in the royal box presiding over a
ballet and orchestra.   On the east, above an inscription in Latin,
is the Emperor surrounded by his courtiers, about to present a
wreath.   Looking at the lifelike portraits, the detailed costumes
and the characteristic incidents, we can imagine again the whole
gorgeous scene out of the bare dust and scattered ruins of the
At-Meidan.

The Circus and the Court

At the north end of the Hippodrome was the Milion, a gilded
column, canopied by a triumphal arch on four piers which bore a
great cross, with Constantine and his mother as supporters.   The
Milion, like London stone, was the centre of the Empire, and from
it all the milestones along the Imperial roads were numbered.
The south end was built up in a great curved structure, the Sphendone, that stood out over the port of Julian, like the stern of an
enormous vessel.   If we go a few steps down over the southern
edge of the Hippodrome plateau, we can see the lower tiers of
the Sphendone, which is represented as still fairly intact in the
mediæval picture of the town reproduced at p.126. The Hippodrome
was encircled, except at the north end, by tiers of marble benches,
with a covered promenade running round the top.   At the
northern end, between two towers, was the Manganon, or " shooting off " place—a row of offices, stables and dressing-rooms,
above which was the kathisma, or royal box.   The terrace round
the kathisma was reserved for the Court, and another one below
for the guard.   Behind were dining-rooms and dressing-rooms,
whence a winding staircase, the scene of more than one royal
assassination, communicated with St. Stephen's Chapel, the
colonnades of Daphne and the Great Palace.

As the association of St. Stephen's Chapel suggests to us, the
attendance of the Emperor at the Circus had something the same
political importance as that of an English king in Parliament.
The Constantinopolitans, having no regular democratic repre-

sentation, gave expression to public opinion in uproar, which easily passed into uprising. It was in the Circus that citizens clamoured to the Emperor for the redress of their grievances, or that the opposition tried issues with the faction in power. The remedy was often no less rough-and-ready. Thus, the Emperor's attention having been called to an act of oppression committed by the prefect of the city through a humorous allusion to it in a comedy, he at once had the offending officer thrown in full uniform from the terrace into the arena and beheaded.

In these early days games were fairly frequent ; and, as the cost of each is estimated to have been about fifty thousand pounds in our money, the wealth of the city can be appreciated. Later, they were held only on Founder's Day, May 11, and Christmas Day. The last race took place about the year 1200, and the ruins of the Hippodrome were used to build a palace by Ibrahim, the Greek vizier of Suleiman the Magnificent.

The games opened with a religious ceremony, followed by a Court reception. Thereafter, the whole assembly sang anti-phonally a hymn of praise. On the Founder's Day celebration on May 11 this hymn was an ancient Spring Song, of which two lines have been preserved. The Green faction on the east would open with : " All hail the spring, the lovely spring." The Blues on the west would respond with : " That joy and health and wealth doth bring." Which charming ceremony, compared with the brutality of the Coliseum, makes us regret that the Roman mind so much dominated that of the Greek in our Western civilization.

Of the many works of art that adorned the Hippodrome, only one still survives. The bronze horses of Lysippus that crowned the Imperial box were carried away to Venice by the Crusaders and to-day adorn St. Mark's. Many of the remainder we should, no doubt, have considered rather interesting than beautiful ; as, for example, the brazen statue of one Victor and his donkey Victoria, auspiciously met by Augustus on the day before his victory over Mark Antony at Actium. But the Hippodrome itself, with its tiers of marble benches and colonnades, 400 yards long and 150 yards wide, with the terraced Manganon at one end and the great curved Sphendone at the other, must have been an imposing sight.

Theodosius should, however, rather be associated with the Codes and with the Church than with the Circus. The Codes of Theodosius are outside our range, and they were anyhow soon superseded by those of Justinian. But they remain a precious record of the life of the age and of the restoration of the Greek mind as the lawgiver of the civilized world. The claim of Constantinople to be the capital of Christian culture and the connecting link between the ancient and modern civilizations rests on these Codes.

As for the Church, it was Theodosius the Great who presided over the death of Paganism and the birth of Orthodoxy. The general destruction, by his orders, of the shrines of the earlier religions provided more pagan works of art for conversion to church decoration, while the substitution of relic worship for the older idolatry made the city quite an emporium of relics. Thus, the great Church of the Holy Apostles had the honour of receiving the bodies of St. Andrew, St. Luke, and St. Timothy; who were followed a few years later by the prophet Samuel. But this magnificent Mausoleum of apocryphal saints and imperial sinners cannot be included in our programme, for there is not one stone of it left. A dead Turk having been found in the porch soon after the Ottoman Conquest, the church was abandoned by the Patriarch in a panic. It was then pulled down and the materials used for building the mosque of Mohammed the Conqueror. The six great Byzantine columns of red porphyry, and the twelve of verde antique built into the mosque, with the sarcophagi we have seen in the Museum, are all that remains to-day of the Church of the Holy Apostles.

Theodosius was the first Emperor to be baptized in Orthodoxy on his accession. The ceremony over, he issued his famous edict, which became the charter of the Orthodox Church:

It is our pleasure that the nations governed by our clemency and moderation should steadfastly adhere to the doctrine taught by St. Peter, as professed by the Pontiff Damasus, and Peter, Bishop of Alexandria. According to the discipline of the Apostles and the doctrine of the Gospel, we believe in the sole deity of the Father, Son, and Holy Ghost under an equal majesty and a pious Trinity. We authorize the followers of this doctrine to assume the title of Catholic Christians, and we affirm that all others are extravagant madmen, hereby branded with the infamous name of heretics. Besides the condemnation of divine justice they must expect to suffer the severe penalties which our authority, guided by heavenly wisdom, shall think proper to inflict upon them.

This edict was confirmed by a synod of 150 bishops, was carried out by a sort of Grand Inquisitor, and was further reinforced by the appointment of Gregory of Nazianzen as Bishop of Constantinople with authority second only to the Bishop of Rome. The authority thus acquired by St. Gregory began a long duel between the Crown and the Church. The duel became acute under the next Emperor, Arcadius, whose Empress, Eudosia, came into collision with John Chrysostom. Chrysostom was a great preacher and a prophet of the people who alienated the Church by his discipline and the Court by his diatribes. To these latter we owe much of our knowledge of the shady side of Byzantine life, while his intolerance for much that we consider innocent makes us inclined to sympathize with the indignation of Eudosia when, in preaching at the formal inauguration of her silver statue, he compared her to Herodias and himself to John the Baptist. The pedestal of this statue can still be seen within an iron railing close to St. Irene ; and it is perhaps not surprising that Chrysostom died a martyr to the hardships of exile. His tomb was desecrated by the Crusaders in 1204, and his head is preserved in the cathedral at Pisa. The liturgy of the Orthodox Church is attributed to him.

We might now leave the Hippodrome and descend the hill toward the Marmara sea wall. The next Emperor to Arcadius, Theodosius II, was the builder of the walls. The city had by now reached its full growth, filling the present girdle of the sea and land walls ; though it was not to reach its full grandeur until Justinian. The walls were building from 413, under Anthemius, Regent of Theodosius. In 447 an earthquake threw most of them down, just when that tidal wave of barbarism, Attila and the Huns, was sweeping down on the city. It was one of the great crises in the history of civilization, and the city rose to the emergency. The chronicler Marcellinus Comes tells us the walls were rebuilt in two months, and

> Theodosiae iussis gemino nec mense peracto
> Constantinus ovans haec moenia firma locavit.

The citizens not only rebuilt the single wall of Anthemius, but added a second wall with 192 towers and a moat, which tremendous task was carried out by an interesting combination of socialism and the sporting spirit. The money was raised by a capital levy. The two great factions of the Greens and Blues, corresponding to our Radicals and Tories, started building in competition with one another from different ends, and proved their equal enthusiasm and efficiency by meeting almost exactly in the middle. The triple wall that they built, which we shall visit in a later chapter, was formidable enough to scare away even Attila, who expressed his willingness to make terms. But the magnificent embassies sent by Theodosius, of which the sufferings in the barbarian camp are feelingly described by Priscus, only excited the cupidity of Attila ; while the secret diplomacy of the eunuch Chrysaphius, aiming at Attila's assassination, only evoked his contempt. We read how the Hun ambassadors, Orestes and Eslav, boldly came before Theodosius with the *pièce de conviction*, a purse of gold, hanging round the neck of Orestes, who unkindly asked Chrysaphius, as he stood behind the throne, whether he recognized it. Receiving no reply, Eslav thus addressed the Emperor of the East : " Theodosius has forfeited his paternal honour and by paying tribute has degraded himself to the position of a slave. He should therefore respect those above him in station, instead of conspiring against them like a wicked slave." Thus was the centre of civilization saved by its democracy and shamed by its diplomacy. And it was left for the successor of Theodosius, Marcian, to score off Attila in his turn, by replying to a demand for more tribute : " Our gold is for our friends, our steel for our enemies."

Theodosius II has been called the first Greek Emperor, and in his reign Greek inscriptions begin to predominate. But this Byzantine Greek intellect and inspiration is very different from that of ancient Greece. When it now reappears from under the Roman supremacy that had overlaid it, it resumes its normal development. It is no doubt without the Roman virtue, but it is also without the Roman vulgarity. And there is already something senile about it. It collects old masters, gets heated over party politics, and hates all that is new. Its only art is architecture, its only science the amassing of wealth and the mechanism of law.

The two main contributions to our modern civilization that we owe to this Byzantine Greek are court ceremonial and official procedure. Gold lace and red tape are Byzantine. The red ink with which the Secretary of State minutes despatches is a pale copy of the purple ink in which the Byzantine Emperor signed his death warrants. Our gold rods and silver sticks were first carried by courtiers in the palace that we are now about to visit.

Along the sea wall to the eastward we can find overhanging the Marmara the ruin of a palace of the early Empire, the Palace of Hormizdas, or Bucoleon. Hormizdas was a Persian prince who, under Constantius the second Emperor, here lived a life of elegant and epigrammatic exile. He it was who observed that the one disadvantage of New Rome was that " one died there like anywhere else." His villa was enlarged into a palace called the Bucoleon, from the statue of a lion killing a bull which stood on the quay outside till after the Turkish Conquest. The palace is only a shell, but thanks to the new government it is now clean enough to visit.

To the east of the Bucoleon was the precinct of the Great Palace, which, as the Emperors achieved a Chinese seclusion, was walled off from the Hippodrome and became a forbidden city. This " God-guarded city " was a regular labyrinth of palaces, porticoes and pavilions, of courts, cloisters, and corridors. On its sea-front was a great marble stairway down to the port where floated the imperial galleys and pleasure boats. Near by were towers with organ pipes that wailed and moaned unceasingly in the wind. The gardens were in the south-east corner, where also was the Pharos or lighthouse from which messages were flashed by light signals from one station to another throughout the Empire. It still survives, a shapeless mass of masonry. Near the shore on a line with the Bucoleon Palace was a square building with conical roof lined with purple marble, the Porphyry Palace reserved for imperial confinements ; whence the phrase, " born in the purple." Near by was the Hall of Nineteen Couches where State banquets were served, and where behind the Emperor's chair stood the Bed of Tears on which some day he would lie in state. Overlooking the Hippodrome was a white marble pavilion called Daphne which was an auditorium and half-way house between the riotous publicities of the Hippodrome and the secret recesses of the God-guarded city. In Daphne were played many of the dramas of Byzantine history.

Here in Daphne you might have found a scene of some agitation in A.D. 491, the date we have now reached. The political situation was delicate. The Emperor Zeno had just been formally entombed while in an epileptic fit and the sentry reported that he was clamouring to be let out. The city having got news of this was pouring into the Hippodrome shouting " give the Romans back their Emperor." On the advice of the Chief Eunuch the Empress Ariadne went into the kathisma and pacified the populace by promising that an Emperor should be immediately appointed. An elderly courtier Anastasius was chosen, and the obsequies of Zeno were solemnly performed at his tomb, while he, as later investigation showed, was eating his boots inside. The next day was the coronation of Anastasius in the Hippodrome, which went off very well. Some years later we find Anastasius, who had made an excellent ruler, being hurried from Daphne to the kathisma in abject terror at a riot he had raised by publishing a revised (monophysite) version of the

Trisagion hymn. He only made his peace after he had sung the authorized version to the Hippodrome.

Close to where we now are is a locality of special interest to Anglo-Saxons. Vlanga Street, to the west of the Church of St. Serge near Koum Kapou, marks the quarters of the Varangian Guard that for centuries protected the Emperor and preserved order. Tacitus mentions the Saxon tribes " Angli et Varini." And when the Angles went west, settled on the land and became a nation, the Warings seem to have gone east and become an Imperial ruling class over Slavs and Greeks. As rulers of Russia they appeared before Constantinople in the tenth century, when their leader Olaf, *pour épater le bourgeois*, hung his shield on the cross over St. Sophia. Their next appearance was as an Imperial Guard, whose good looks and firm loyalty made them one of the most useful and ornamental of the imperial institutions. Their special church was the Panaya Varanyistica (Our Lady of the Warings) west of St. Sophia, later replaced by the Church of St. Augustus of Canterbury, which survived as a mosque until 1868. The Waring tombs from this church recorded by Paspates might perhaps yet be traced by an energetic archæologist.

After the Norman Conquest the Varangian Guard was recruited from English malcontents. Ordericus Vitalis tells us of these English : " Not a few fled into exile either just to escape from the Norman ruler or to get rich so as to renew the fight at home. Some of the younger and stronger went far afield and entered the service of the Emperor of Constantinople, a prudent prince against whom Robert Guiscard Duke of Apulia was then arming. These exiled English were put in line against Robert's Normans, whom the Greeks could not face in a mêlée. As the Norman peril grew Alexius put his Great Palace and all his treasure in charge of these English." We shall later meet them again re-fighting the Battle of Hastings in Macedonia. After the Turkish Conquest the colony emigrated to the Crimea, but it is said that a fair-haired type still exists in this quarter.

The quaintly named little church of St. Serge and St. Bacchus near the Koum Kapou (Sand Gate) is our next historical land-mark. It is called by the Turks Kutchuk Aya Sophia (Little St. Sophia), which reminds us that it was built by Justinian just before he built the cathedral. It has since served as a model for the Greek Church in London, and you can study it at no greater cost than a trip to Bayswater. In this church, the square-domed Byzantine type definitely replaces the oblong flat-roofed basilica. The church has been compared to an octagonal reliquary in a square box ; the awkward angles of the square under the domed vault are avoided by columned exedras, and the round dome with sixteen flutings rests on an octagon of piers. The narthex remains, but the aisles only survive in a vestigial form on one side. The vine leaves of the capitals are, no doubt, an allusion to the rather ambiguous antecedents of one of the patron saints. Bacchus was too good a fellow to excommunicate altogether, though he generally appears in church as the " drunken St. George." Here we find, for the first time and in its simplest form, the impost capital. This was a daring device for dealing with the difficulty of adapting a capital designed to carry a flat architrave, to the different work of carrying the base of an arch.

Justinian dedicated this church to the soldier saints martyred under Maximianus. It was long used for services according to the Roman Catholic rite, and Gregory the Great (590–614), while Papal Envoy, officiated there. An inscription commemorates Justinian's clemency, and refers to the Empress Theodora as " divinely crowned." And as we reclimb the hill again to St. Sophia we may beguile the way with the strange romance of this royal pair.

THEODORA AND JUSTINIAN

Justinian was a new type of Emperor. The son of a Bulgar soldier of fortune, he had the sober virtues of that sturdy people. He was also well endowed with that civic conscience which generally was so conspicuously lacking in Byzantine Emperors. Theodora, on the other hand, was like Aphrodite a Greek of Cyprus. Her father was a keeper in the Constantinople Zoo. From an early age the audacity with which she defied the proprieties of a community already thoroughly corrupt, won her the position of Queen of the Half-world. From this she rose by a higher audacity to be Empress of the Eastern Hemisphere. The character of her public performances is best left veiled in the verbosity of Gibbon or in the obscurity of Byzantine chroniclers. For the theatre, from which women and children were excluded, was by now quite unbridled in its licence. The accounts we have of it in the anecdotes of Procopius and in the epistles of Chrysostom show that the Greek drama had degenerated into a ribald review. The law prohibited absolute nakedness on the stage ; but the Byzantine censor was satisfied with the most transparent concessions, and if you want an idea of what the Byzantine stage was like I must refer you to Act. Apost. Hom. XLIII. 3 of St. Chrysostom. As for Theodora, we may estimate her popularity from the fact that, under the Theodosian Code, XV, § 7, anyone running away with an actress was punished with the same fine that he had to pay if he withdrew a favourite from a race. But Theodora was no mere light-hearted votary of Vanity Fair. She was equally shameless, whether making herself a career as a sinner or as a saint. It was a sacrifice to respectability that, for once, shocks the cynical old pedant Gibbon out of his pomposity into what rings like real indignation.

Once and once only (he writes) she became a mother. The infant was saved and educated in Arabia by his father, who imparted to him on his deathbed that he was the son of an Empress. Filled with high hopes, the unsuspecting youth hastened to Constantinople and was admitted to the presence of his mother. As he was never more seen after, Theodora deserves the foul imputation of extinguishing with his life a secret so offensive to her imperial virtue.

There have been attempts to whitewash Theodora, but the hard brilliance of her character gleams through them like Byzantine mosaics, whitewashed over to save offence to the faithful. The marble pallor, jewelled eyes and chiselled features of her portrait in mosaic, now at Ravenna, still dazzle us through the rigid conventions of Byzantine art. And there can be no doubt that her repentance and retirement into private life was a trap set for Justinian, who used to find her day after day sitting demurely at her spinning wheel in a modest attic. Justinian was then principal adviser and heir-presumptive to his uncle, the worthy Justin ; and he risked his whole career when he determined to marry her. Having overborne the opposition of his own mother, and of Justin's Empress, he passed an act legalizing marriage with a prostitute, until then prohibited by Roman law. This was, indeed, the first legislative enactment of the great jurist and author of the Edicts. On becoming Emperor he was not satisfied with the usual position of royal consort for his wife, but associated her with himself in the Imperial dignity. Theodora responded by becoming most rigidly respectable, though insatiably rapacious. She undoubtedly saved Justinian his crown when the lawlessness of the Circus factions nearly destroyed the city in the Nika riots. And as by now we are again crossing the Hippodrome we can conveniently deal with this turning-point in the political fortunes of Constantinople. For these faction fights had far more political meaning than is recognized by most historians.

The Circus factions that we last saw rebuilding the walls against Attila had, by now, become themselves a danger to the city. Of the four colours that distinguished the competing chariots, red, white, blue and green, the two last had become the badges of powerful political parties, at bitter feud with one another throughout both Empires. In Constantinople a dense and disorderly population made the collisions of these parties quite catastrophic. In a previous reign the Greens, by concealing stones and daggers in the fruit and flowers of a festival, succeeded in massacring three thousand Blues. Men do not kill each other by thousands without cause, or at least without a cause. And these outbreaks of the Greens were really the rising of a Radical faction, ordinarily repressed by a reactionary faction. The Greens claimed to be the representatives of the landed interests, especially of the provincial peasantry ; while the Blues claimed to represent the maritime interests of the middle class. The Greens, moreover, had the support of all dissenters and of the discontented ; while the Blues were associated with Imperial orthodoxy and the ruling class. We have, in fact, the ordinary two-party division between Progressives and Conservatives ; and, by the reign of Justinian, no one who had not the support of one of these factions could hope for success in any candidature or in any law court. The two factions competed for the control of the wards (demes) into which the municipal government of the city was divided, much as Republicans and Democrats, or Moderates and Progressives, compete in New York or in London. But these wards were both civil and military administrations—the " demarch " being the civil, the " democrat " the military authority. The prefect, on the other hand, was an Imperial official; though the autocracy had little to do with the organization through which the city governed and guarded itself until the faction fights forced it to interfere. But Blue and Green politics had also penetrated the Imperial court, where military officers and court officials greedily canvassed for lucrative appointments as democrats or demarchs.

Justinian and Theodora themselves were notoriously Blue—the Emperor because he believed in sound conservative principles, the Empress because her father owed his place at the Zoo to the Blues, and she herself had once been hissed off the stage by the Greens. So the Blues, out of compliment to Justinian, dressed themselves up as Bulgar barbarians and, in this disguise, proceeded, like the Mohawks of eighteenth-century London, to make life unbearable for peaceable citizens. In vain did Justinian threaten and thunder. Gibbon tells us that—

the ministers of Justice who had the courage to punish such crimes became the victims of their indiscreet zeal ; a Prefect of Constantinople fled for refuge to the Holy Sepulchre; a Count of the East was ignominiously whipped, and the Governor of Silicia was hanged by order of Theodora on the tomb of two assassins he had executed for murder.

At last matters came to a head in the Hippodrome on the festival of the Ides of January (552). This place of public assembly had so adapted itself to the two-party system that it had already become the prototype of our legislative chamber. On either side of the kathisma, or Imperial box, sat the two factions—the Blue, or Government party, on the Emperor's right; the Green, or Opposition, on his left. Each had their separate entry on either side of the Manganon. The Emperor's awards could be challenged by either party as being against the rules and as a pretext for airing public grievances. On this occasion, when the Greens had questioned his verdict for the twenty-second time running, the Emperor lost his temper and, through the official crier, engaged in a wrangle with the Opposition. The dialogue, in the colloquial Greek of the day, has been preserved for us verbatim by Theophanes. " Shut up, you Jews, you Samaritans, you Manichees," thundered the Emperor through his " loud speaker." " Get out, you murderer, you ass, you cheating tyrant," clamoured the Greens. Whereupon the good Conservative true Blues hunted those aliens and anarchists, the Greens, out of the Hippodrome.

At this crisis, seven assassins, arrested impartially from both factions, were being taken by the imperial prefect through the city to execution on the heights of Pera. The two factions thereupon stopped breaking one another's heads, and shouting their watchword " Nika " (Victory), joined forces to rescue the prisoners, burn down the prefect's palace, and break open the prison. The Imperial Guard tried to restore order. But the Heruli Guards, savage barbarians all, not understanding the object of a religious procession that was intervening in the interests of peace, by overturning the priests and their holy relics poured oil on the flames. The tumult rapidly grew into a trial of strength between the municipal militia and the Imperial Guard ; in other words, between democracy and autocracy. It raged for days until the greater part of the city was burnt down, including the original wooden St. Sophia, most of the Great Palace, the world-famous Baths of Zeuxippus, and many churches.

Justinian appeared more than once in the Hippodrome, but had each time to fly for his life. He finally conceded all the demands of the Greens, including the surrender to them of their candidate for the throne, Hypatius, nephew of the unorthodox Emperor Anastasius. The Greens then carried the reluctant Hypatius to the forum of Constantine, and there crowned him with an improvised coronet. Justinian had already embarked his treasure on a galley in the port of the palace, and was preparing to follow it, when, at a last Council, Theodora refused to fly without a fight. With the help of Belisarius, the greatest general of the age, a body of Blues was rallied and, with three thousand veteran guards, was rushed through the gates on to the Hippodrome against the triumphant and unwary Greens. Above thirty thousand perished. The Emperor would have spared poor Hypatius, but Theodora saw to his execution. The Green party was crippled for a generation, and the Hippodrome was closed for several years. And though this Progressive party revived again later, it could never again make head against the autocracy. There was thenceforward no democratic check upon extortion and corruption—thanks to Theodora the " divinely crowned."

The rule of the " green " Anastasius had been one of peace, retrenchment, and reform. It had reduced the income tax, popularly known as the " Gold of Affliction," and had accumulated great reserves of capital. The commerce of the Empire had grown until it was draining into the city the wealth of the world from China to Caledonia and from the snows of Scythia to the sands of the Sahara. But the imperial expenditure of Justinian had soon exhausted these reserves and had to find new resources. For the first time heavy customs duties were collected at both straits. Prices rose and trade declined. Industry in the provinces profited; and as the import of silk from China died off, the manufacture of it in Anatolia developed and survived there until the expulsion of the Greeks last year. But this was small comfort to the population of Constantinople that found itself starving. And most of the devices of modern taxation can be found in the budgets of Justinian's much-hated minister, John of Cappadocia. Says Gibbon—" the edifices of Justinian were cemented with the blood and treasure of his people."

St. Sophia and Justinian

We are now going to see the principal of those edifices and of the sights of Constantinople, the Church of St. Sophia. It was the fourth church on the site. The basilica of Constantine was rebuilt by Constantius with a "trick" dome which fell, on the accession of Julian the Apostate. The third church, built by Theodosius, was burnt in the Nika riots. The architect of this fourth church was Anthemius of Tralles, a mathematician. He invented a primitive steam-engine and a searchlight, with which he used to play practical jokes on his neighbours. Under Anthemius ten thousand workmen finished the building in about six years, by which time it had cost, according to the estimate of Professor Paparrigopoulos, about ten million sterling in our values. Such extravagance strained even the resources of Constantinople in the Golden Age. The chronicler Zonaras laments that the schools had to be shut as the teachers were starving, and that washing had become impossible as all the lead pipes had been melted down for the gutters.

Justinian on his solemn entry, looking up at the great mosaic of Solomon in his glory, exclaimed with emotion—" Glory be to God who has found me worthy to finish so great a work and to excel thee, O Solomon!" What the city thought is not recorded, but possibly its feelings are expressed in a little-known legend. On the morning of the opening ceremony it was found that the inscription on the corner-stone—" This Church was given to God by Justinian the Emperor "—had been changed to " This Church was given to God by Euphrasia the Widow." The inscription was recut and the scandal hushed up. But the next morning the importunate widow was back again, and the affair was the talk of the town. Justinian sent out his guards to find Euphrasia and they presently returned with a terrified young woman. She denied having had anything to do with the cathedral, but confessed to having often given water to the oxen that drew the stone up the steep hill from the quay, past her lodging. Justinian rose to the occasion, and ordered her name to be left on the stone. All the same you won't find it there to-day, and no doubt the Blues thought it a mighty clever trick of the Greens. We may think it a miracle or the true voice of the city, as we please.

The impression made by the building on the public imagination of the day is shown by the web of legend woven into the story of the church. For example, the story of a man in white who appeared to a boy minding the workmen's tools during the dinner hour and who asked why they were so long away. The boy said he would go and hurry them up, and the apparition promised to mind the tools until he came back. The boy reported the matter, and was at once sent to a distant province by the ingenious Emperor, who thus trapped an angel into acting as permanent churchwarden.

The outside of the church is, to us, disappointing. The architect sought an effect of sheer mass and height by an experiment on an unprecedented scale in a novel style. He impressed his own day and many succeeding centuries. Procopius says:

> It presents a most glorious spectacle, extraordinary to those who behold it and indescribable to those who are told of it. It rises to the heavens and overrides the surrounding buildings as a ship the waves. The dome is as it were suspended from heaven by golden chains.

But Michelangelo outbid it in bulk, and to many modern eyes familiar with larger structures and a more finished architecture the first impression is heaviness without either grace or grandeur. The buttresses that have had to be piled round the dome to support it spoil the beauty of the elevation; while the clumsy minarets and crude stripes of red paint, added by the Italian Fossati during the restoration under Abdul Medjid, still further detract from its height. We find, in fact, some excuse for the Philistine who compared it to a blanc-mange surrounded by candlesticks.

It is not until one gets inside that one recovers something of the impression that inspired mediæval and modern travellers with pages of eulogies and ecstasies. I shall not compete with them; for the building has real beauty, and therefore will have something to say to each one of us. Some of us may see St. Sophia as the " great outward expression of a World Empire consecrated to the religion of Christ " at the same time as the " outward expression which man has given to the idea of God's omnipotence and omnipresence." Or we may find it the " most perfect representation that art has devised of the theology of the Christian Church," and look on the dome as " symbolizing the central doctrine of the Trinity to which all the other members contribute support and by which they are crowned and incorporated." Or we may see in it the " most splendid example of the last great gift of Hellenic genius, Byzantine architecture." Or like honest Sir John Mandeville, be content with remembering it as the " fairest church in all the world." Or like the still more honest but youthful Byron, consider it " not a patch on St. Paul's."

Whatever the effect on us of what is left of the splendours of St. Sophia, the impression they made on the earliest pilgrims was an influence for good. When Vladimir of Russia sent envoys to inquire into the Christian religion with a view to its adoption in his dominions, it was their report of a service that they had attended in St. Sophia that settled the matter.

We felt bound to believe (they wrote) that in this church one is more than elsewhere in the presence of God, for the rituals of all other countries are there entirely eclipsed by a grandeur which we ourselves will never forget.

It is a recommendation that may not appeal to all of us ; but it saved Russia in all probability from Mohammedanism.

The approach to the church was originally through a series of forecourts, some travellers say as many as seven. Some of these survived to as late as the sixteenth century, and were filled with booths for the sale of Moslem charms and relics. The original church was indeed not only the fane itself, but a whole quarter of cloisters, chapels, porticoes, libraries, hostels, the patriarchal palace, and the walled gardens for which the Byzantines were famous. There is now no vestige of the Outer Court (atrium) and Fountain (phiale), but the Outer Porch (exo-narthex) is still standing though stripped of its mosaics.

If we had been a Byzantine family attending a service in the time of Justinian we should have hurried through the outer courts when we heard the booming of the semantron, a wooden sounding-board beaten by deacons with mallets, as you can still see and hear in remote monasteries of the Levant. Before entering we should have washed face, hands and feet in the Fountain or Brazen Sea resting on the backs of bronze beasts. Round its margin was inscribed this ingenious palindrome :

ΝΙΨΟΝ ΟΝΟΜΗΜΑΤΑ ΜΗ ΜΟΝΟΝ ΟΨΙΝ
(Wash your follies not alone your face).

In the narthex vestibule we should have found a crowd of penitents excommunicated for various offences ; and the men of our party would then have passed through the centre door into the nave, the women by the less honourable side door into the galleries. At first they had been allowed to sit together, then were separated by a wooden partition down the nave ; and, as the more the Church repressed women the more irrepressible they became, the tiresome creatures were finally banished to the galleries. For the degradation of women by the hareem and yashmak, by the eunuch and the minion, from which they are only to-day being freed, was begun not by Turkish and Islamic conquerors, but by Greek Churchmen and Persian courtiers. So we find Chrysostom complaining that the galleries chatter and laugh all through his sermons, and that they egg on the men to heckle him on theological points unsuitable for public discussion.

The bronze narthex doors, nine in number, in triple attribution to the Trinity, are worked in a Greek design of classic beauty, and those on the south still show the dints made when the Janissaries hammered for admission on that day of terror when the city was taken. The circular devices in the panels, four to each panel, are magic spells in monogram form. In the three upper circles the letters on the left represent Κυριε Βοηθοι (Lord help) ; then, on the right in order from top to bottom, Theophilus, his wife Augusta, and their infant son Michael. The two lower give the date 6349 of the Creation and four of the Indiction, i.e. A.D. 841. On the lintel over the central door is chiselled an open book inscribed with a verse from St. John, " The Lord said I am the door of the sheep : By Me if any man enter he shall be saved." Over the cornice a large mosaic is dimly discernible—a Christ between medallions of the Virgin and St. Michael, said to be portraits of Theodora and Justinian. On the left is an Emperor kneeling, probably Basil II, a fine soldier, as the mosaic dates from 981.

Passing through the disfiguring Moslem curtains, embroidered with the profession of faith, we enter the church. At first sight it is difficult to appreciate the scale partly owing to the perfect proportions, partly owing to the disproportionate Moslem decorations. As a matter of fact the nave is no less than 110 feet wide, 200 feet long, and 180 feet to the apex of the dome. But we at once see that the problem of putting a round dome on a square building so as to combine the impressiveness of the dome with the spaciousness of a basilica, has been here successfully solved, and that too on a magnificent scale. The roof of a basilica was too oppressive and heavy to express the aspiration of a Christian architect. The supports of a dome had hitherto been too obtrusive and cramping. The problem was to carry the dome on as few obvious supports as possible. The solution in St. Sophia is to support the dome at either end by semi-domes carried on piers, and so to reduce the main supporting piers to four. The angles between the supporting arches being filled with pendentive vaulting provide a circular bed for the dome. Demi-semi domes are then worked into the angles to complete the design. It is this audacious and admirable use of the semi-dome and the pendentive which is the most striking feature of the work of Anthemius and Isidorus.

Æsthetically, the dome achieves the desired effect. Thus van Millingen says :

For elasticity of spring, for grace and majesty of upright flight, and for the lightness with which it hangs in air, there is no canopy like it. Poised on arches and columns, soaring from triple bays to semi-domes, and from semi-domes to central dome, culminating convergent above a circle of forty lights, through which the radiant heavens appear, it is not strange that it has seemed a canopy merged in the sky, and that men have, for more than thirteen centuries, worshipped beneath it, feeling that this is none other than the House of God—this is the Gate of Heaven.

Architecturally, however, St. Sophia has never been repeated, because its construction is unsound. The flatness of the dome, so impressive inside, so disappointing outside, causes a lateral thrust that cannot be counteracted. The first dome, with a diameter of 108 feet and an axis of only 40, soon fell. Even when the axis was increased, it was still too little. Recourse had to be had to all manner of devices, such as using an especially binding cement, mixed with the spittle of particularly holy men ; and unusually light and porous Rhodian bricks, each stamped with the initial letters of the verse, " God is in the midst of her, she shall not be moved." These bricks diminished in thickness towards the centre of the dome, and into every twelfth course was built the relic of a saint. Whether this was legitimate technique must be left to professional opinion. But we may consider it justified by results ; and a few figures will show what these early Greeks achieved. The dome of St. Sophia is 108 feet broad by 46 feet high. St. Peter's is only 139 feet broad, and as much as 190 feet high.

In spite of the strain of the lateral thrust, the structure has stood the wear of time and the tear of earthquakes very well. After the dome of Anthemius had fallen it was rebuilt by Isidorus a few feet higher than before, and the church was rededicated in 562 ; the only principal actor in the previous ceremony left alive being the aged Justinian himself. An earthquake so shook the edifice in 867 that Basil the Macedonian piled up the great north and south buttresses to prop the dome. In 975 the western semi-dome fell and was rebuilt. The eastern semi-dome also collapsed, and was restored under John V, and was rebuilt again by Murad III in 1575. Abdul Medjid in 1849 spent a quarter of a million sterling on a general restoration entrusted to the Italian brothers Fossati, when the structure was strengthened with girders and put in thorough repair, even the mosaics being cleaned and then whitewashed over again.

The only Moslem architectural additions are the minarets. A plain heavy brick minaret at the south-east was built by the Conqueror, which was raised by his son Bayazid to match another in marble that he built at the north-east. The two more graceful western minarets were added by Selim in expiation of sins to which he attributed his naval defeat at Lepanto.

Of the original glories of the interior decorations there alone remain the columns and the mosaics. The eight great serpentine columns on each side of the nave were once the pride of the Temple of Diana at Ephesus. The eight porphyry columns in pairs between the piers were taken from the Temple of the Sun at Baalbek after Aurelius had conquered Zenobia. The other twenty-four columns below of various-coloured marbles are said to be from the Temple of Apollo at Delphi and the Temple of Pallas at Athens. The sixty smaller ones above, round the women's gallery, are forty of verde antique, twenty of jasper, and seven of granite. Their travels have been most tediously retraced by the laborious Salzenberg. The capitals bear the monograms of the royal pair. Some of the marbles that veneered the wall spaces everywhere are gone ; but the mosaics still remain, though whitewashed over, like the frescoes in so many of our churches. However, by going up into the southern gallery and gazing steadfastly into the vault over the apse windows, one may still make out dimly the great mosaic of the Christ in Benediction.

The decorations to-day are of course mostly Moslem. Almost every Sultan is commemorated by some contribution. Thus, the two great candlesticks, flanking the Mihrab, are loot from a Hungarian church, and were presented by Suleiman I. The chandelier was a gift from Achmed III. The great oval urns of alabaster from Murad III, though some say they are from the Christian cathedral, and used for holding holy water. The marble pulpit, with its delicate lace-like carvings, represents the elegant taste of the age of Murad IV ; while the ornate Sultan's loge, on its seven marble pillars, reflects the luxury of Abdul Medjid.

Our Byzantine family would have seen much that is to be seen no more. Before them would have risen the great iconostasis, or rood screen, painted in panels 14 feet high, divided by gilt columns. Three doors in it admitted to the sanctuary (bema). In the middle of the sanctuary stood the altar, raised on three steps, plated with gold, and on gold pillars. Anybody touching one of those pillars was safe, even from a Byzantine monarch or a Byzantine mob. The curtains were of silk and gold brocade, into which were woven 500,000 pearls. The Emperor's chair was of gold, those of the patriarchs of ebony inlaid with ivory. From the vault hung many thousands of gold and silver lamps. The altar table itself was of gold and ivory, studded with jewels; and, deposited on it for safety, were the imperial crowns. It had a mosaic inscription which began, "Thine own, O Christ, from thine own, thy servants Justinian and Theodora," and went on, "Keep us in the orthodox faith, and increase to thine own glory the Empire thou hast entrusted to us." Which shrine of pious Imperialism had, however, eventually to be sacrificed to the exigencies of Empire finance and was replaced by a cheaper one. This the Latin Crusaders knocked to pieces and shipped off to France; the sacrilegious ship being, however, satisfactorily wrecked in the Marmara. On to the third altar Mohammed the Conqueror climbed to make the first Moslem prayer, and it was then destroyed.

Over the altar was the canopy (ciborium) borne on silver pillars, and bearing a gold cross, standing on a solid gold orb. East of the altar were the thrones of the bishops, that of the patriarch being solid silver, inlaid with gold. West of the sanctuary was the choir, separated by a gilded grille.

In Justinian's day the service of the cathedral employed 1,000 people, and its upkeep the rentals of 11,000 shops. There were 100 singing eunuchs and 200 choir boys. There was even a choir of 100 women, a concession to art contrary to orthodoxy. Three hundred musicians in crimson silk played harps, cymbals, dulcimers, mandolines, tambourines, and zithers. Ten bishops and 800 priests took part in the ritual. As late as the twelfth century a daily service was held; but, at the end, in the fatal fourteen hundreds, the resources of the Empire were unable to find even the necessary tapers and oil.

The pulpit (ambon) was on the north of the nave, a little east of the centre. It was a sort of gallery, not unlike the existing Sultan's loge, made of costliest marbles, adorned with jewels and gold enamel. Over it was a canopy plated with gold, and jewelled, bearing a solid gold cross. The pulpit was entered by two stairways, equally gorgeous, and was the scene of the coronations. Five years' revenue from Egypt had been expended on it. The southern side apse was the Treasure House; in it were twenty-four copies of the Gospels, each in a gold case weighing 200 pounds. In the Sacristy were the chariots of Constantine and Helena, made of solid silver, and such a quantity of gold plate that it took 100 porters to carry it in procession. But of greater value than all was, to mediæval eyes, the hundreds of relics, records of almost every important event in Scripture, from the True Cross and Crown of Thorns down to the Crib of Bethlehem.

But enough has been said, even in this bald inventory, to convey the idea that the furnishings of St. Sophia made it a suitable shrine for the spirit of Byzantine imperialism and idolatry.

A series of pictures of the scenes in St. Sophia would be a pageant of all Byzantine and Ottoman history. But two such pictures, though out of their proper place, I shall insert here in order to complete the story of the Church before leaving it.

On an Easter morning in April 1204, the leaders of the Latin Crusaders, fresh from the conquest of the city, are carousing in the sanctuary. A naked courtesan, sitting on the Patriarchal Throne, is conducting a mock service in a nasal chant to obscene words. A soldier is administering a mock sacrament, after mixing the consecrated bread and wine with filth and blood. The nave is full of soldiers and their women drinking and dancing, while pack animals, piled with plunder, are being driven in and unloaded. The magical and mystical power of the Great Church, that was as strong a defence of Christianity as was the military prestige of the Great Walls, have both been desecrated and destroyed by Christian robbers.

On May 28, 1453, an hour before midnight, Constantine XIII and his captains kneel before the altar in the gloom, lit only by a few tapers, and take the sacrament of the dying. For all know that either death or dishonour awaits them before another sunset. The sacrament is given to them according to the Roman ritual. For a few months before, in the hope of getting Western support against the Turks, the Emperor had accepted the spiritual authority of Rome. And since then the great church has been abandoned by the people. The Emperor rides out through the night to die upon the walls ; and before daybreak the church is crowded with refugees in a frenzy of panic. The Ottoman conqueror is already on his march through the city. In vain the trembling crowd tell one another that the angel with the flaming sword would surely stop him at Constantine's column, as foretold by prophesy. But this last hope is dispelled by a thunder of blows on the bronze doors of the southern vestibule. A mob of Janissaries rushes in, and begins at once to sort out the captives and bind them in pairs. The caste divisions of Byzantine society, built up like its walls by a thousand years of custom, collapses in a moment. Countess and kitchenmaid, courtier and beggar, monk and merchant, are hurried away in long files to be sold as slaves. A great uproar then announces the approach of Mohammed. He pauses in the porch to reprove a Janissary who was breaking down the marbles, and entered by the south door. He strides along the nave, and, in the doorway of the sanctuary, stops and calls loudly, " God is the light of the heaven and of the earth." He then orders an imam to proclaim the call to prayer from the patriarchal throne. As the last la-illa-il-Allah died away, the conqueror mounts on to the altar table and kneels in prayer. This was designed to break any mystic power that might still remain in the magic shrine of the Christians. The church will not be consecrated to Islam until it has been washed in rose-water from dome to foundation, and every Christian emblem destroyed or disguised.

One other scene from St. Sophia, and that only a vignette. A Christian workman employed in the repairs of 1849 has fallen from a scaffold, and is dying. As soon as it is dark, a priest is brought in by fellow-workmen secretly. The brief prayers are hurriedly muttered over the dying man as he lies in a dark corner ; for discovery means death for all. Thus was the Christian service held in St. Sophia for the last time—or was it perhaps for the first time.

The reverence with which the conqueror regarded St. Sophia was not merely personal. It has been shared by the Ottoman princes and by the Turkish people. The Sheikh of Aya Sofia is second only to the Sheikh of the Mosque at Mecca. The Government has spent large sums on St. Sophia, even when the mosques of the Sultans were left to fall to ruin. Moreover, Islam had soon surrounded its captive with a dense cloud of superstition. Thus, according to the popular belief of Stamboul, the prophet Elijah daily worships under the dome, but he is visible only to the pure in heart of the true faith. The dome, moreover, cannot fall, because a hair of the prophet was mixed in the mortar when it was repaired. The southern door was made from the wood of Noah's Ark, and you will never be shipwrecked if you lay your hands on it while saying two prayers for Noah. The mosaics of the Archangels under the dome are really bat-like Djinn, who have the power of prophecy. They have not pro-phesied since the birth of the prophet, because nothing after that seemed worth it. And there are tangible wonders as well. There is the Shining Stone, a piece of translucent marble in the west side of the gallery. The brighter it gleams the brighter are the fortunes of Islam and of the House of Osman. Then there is the Sweating Pillar—the most north-westerly of the columns on the ground floor. Put your finger into a hole in it, protected by a brass plate, and the damper you feel the stone, the better is your character and your chance of recovery. This is probably a Moslemized version of the miracle-working column of St. Gregory. Next comes the Cool Window. This is the most north-easterly window on the northern side. And if you feel a cool breeze there, it is not as you might suppose the usual Bosphorus northerly draught, but a breath of the pious eloquence of Sheikh Akhshems-Eddin, who always preached in this corner. Finally, there is the Conqueror's Hand—a mark something like a red hand on the south-east pier, probably the emblem of some long-forgotten secret society. The Janissaries, we remember, shared the sign of the Red Hand with our Baronet-age. Here, you will be told, Mohammed the Conqueror smote the wall in scorn as he rode his charger up over a great heap of corpses. And, if you object that he walked into the church and that no one was killed there, Christian slaves being valuable, why " How does the mark come to be so high ? "

In spite of such signs and wonders, the Moslem mind has never really felt at home in St. Sophia. No amount of rose-water or caligraphy could really convert the great church. Its orientation is not to Mecca, and the long rows of carpets have to be arranged cat-a-corner, while the worshippers prostrate themselves skew-wise. On all sides we find symbols of conquest not of conversion. Over the minber hang the two green silk flags that symbolize the subjection of Christianity and Judaism. While the Sheikh, as he ascends to preach the Friday sermon, carries a drawn sword before him as a sign of conquest. It is only in the nightly services, during the fast of Ramazan, that the cathedral becomes wholly Moslem. For the half-obliter-ated Christian symbols are then wholly obscured in the gloom, and the thousand twinkling lights show only the giant Moslem escutcheons and emblems. The eyes of the Christian watchers in the gallery see only the long dim rows of worshippers below, rising and falling in rhythmical prostrations like waves of the sea, while their ears are filled with the boom and rustle of their mass movement.

But on the eve of the great Christian festivals of Christmas and Easter, both Turks and Christians avoid the church. For then those destined to die within the year will see ghostly lights burning on the altar, pale gleamings of the ancient glories of gold and jewels and a dim congregation of long-dead worshippers. They will hear faint echoes of solemn chanting until the four angels in the dome beat their wings and the vision vanishes.

Some of us will be distressed in St. Sophia by the sight of a temple of the True Faith desecrated by the infidel. Others again may see in the great church, when stripped of its pomp and humbled to the dust, a purified symbol of the teaching of Christ. A year or two ago it seemed likely that the Western occupation would become permanent, and that St. Sophia would be restored to the Orthodox Church. That the mihrab, showing the direction of Mecca, the minber or pulpit, the ugly wooden escutcheons with the names of Allah, Mahommed, and the Six Imams, and the four minarets, would all be swept away. The escutcheons are no doubt a disfigurement, reminding one of the hatchments of the squire's family in our country churches. And one may hope that the new regime may find a more artistic assertion than they of a faith that has filled St. Sophia for five hundred years with devout worshippers. But is there not much less to offend against the spirit of Christianity in such earnest expressions of faith as are the minarets for the muezzins' daily call to prayer, or in the minber for the Friday sermon, than there is in the much-admired columns, robbed from heathen temples, and presented to the tyrant emperor by wealthy citizens for the " safety of their souls." Many of the Moslem inscriptions are beautiful in themselves, and wonderful examples of an art which, denied expression in the reproduction of natural forms, has found a strange beauty of its own in caligraphic design. The inscription that encircles the dome above the forty-four windows runs—" In the name of God the Merciful and Pitiful. God is the light of Heaven and Earth. His light is in Himself, not as that which shines through glass or gleams in the morning star, or glows in the firebrand." Is not this a more suitable inscription for a place of worship than the inscription on the north gallery : " This place is for ever dedicated to the most noble lady Theodora," that empurpled prostitute. Or than the slab in the south gallery inscribed " Henricus Dandolo," which covers the mortal remains of the old robber who caused the cathedral to be desecrated.

Perhaps the best solution would be that St. Sophia and the other churches, since converted into mosques, be laicized as

European monuments in trust of the Turkish nation. So that whatever is beautiful or interesting, whether of Christian or Moslem origin, may be preserved for the future enjoyment and education, not only of Western visitors, but of that ever-growing body of Eastern intellectuals who can appreciate beauty when it is the expression of another faith than Islam. This is a task in which the Turkish Government might properly expect, and accept, the assistance of Europe. So that the gorgeous Christian marbles and mosaics might be restored to their original glories, and the no less lovely Moslem tile coverings and marble carvings be as carefully preserved.

Before we leave St. Sophia, we may note on the south-west of the church Justinian's Baptistery, now the Turbeh of Mustapha, a domed octagon within a square building, with twelfth-century mosaics. And, on the north-east, a circular building supposed to be the Baptistery of Constantine the Great, and a survival of the original cathedral. Baptism in the early church was total immersion in puris naturalibus ; a fact which the gloomy divines of the day found awkward in their denunciations of mixed bathing. It was still more awkward for their converts when, as frequently happened in the early heresy hunting, they had to fly for their lives without waiting to find their clothes. The five Turbehs on the south side are tombs of Sultans, and four of them of Ottoman construction.

There are of course many other churches well worth a visit ; but, after St. Sophia, they would as sights be an anti-climax. We shall fit in three of the more interesting—St. John of the Studium, St. Saviour in the Country, and St. Theodosia. But the others must be left to the student, or to those who stay long enough for side-shows. Of these others the more interesting are : St. Thecla, near one of the gates on the Golden Horn (Aivan Serai Kapoussou), which is a curious revival in the ninth century of the Basilica style; St. Theodore Tyrone (Killise Djami), between the mosque of Suleiman and the aqueduct of Valens, attributed to the twelfth century, but probably older; St. Mary Pammakaristos, over the Phanar, which has a peculiar development of the Byzantine style, having the main dome supported on a drum resting on four arches, all carried on another drum resting on eight arches. It has fine mosaics, and was, after the conquest, the church of the Patriarch until made a mosque by Murad III. The fires, during the recent war, that destroyed much of the town, account for the disappearance of two ancient churches, Feneri Issa Djami, and Boudroum.

The Cisterns and New Rome

If, after St. Sophia, you have energy left for a still deeper plunge into the past, you can visit one of the two great cisterns that are close by. Both these belong to the age of Justinian. The cistern called Bin Bir Derek (Thousand and one Columns) is among cisterns as St. Sophia is among churches. When I last saw it, it was being used by silk-spinners. This industry found the damp and darkness of these ancient cisterns advantageous, and the silent figures moving in rhythmical motions in the gloom made an eerie effect. This cistern is partly filled with rubbish, and its columns are marked with the monograms of the donors, for the most part still undeciphered. The curious traveller will, however, do better to choose the Yeri Batan Serai (Underground Palace). This vast crypt was built by Justinian, under the portico of the Basilica. The 336 columns in 28 rows have all finely carved capitals. But the main interest is that the cistern still serves its original purpose of storing the water brought by the aqueduct of Valens, and still is exactly as when it was built. What we have here before our eyes is just what we should have seen if we had lived in the sixth century. And that is an experience not to be got everywhere or every day. Moreover, the long avenues of great columns, half-seen in the dim lighting, the gloomy lanes of black water disappearing into darkness, the shadows in the heavy vaulting overhead, the lovely detail of carving on some capital, all together go to make this an impressive view of the underside of Constantinople.

There are many other cisterns, some complete, some caved in. But the only other of interest is that under the foundations of the Sphendone at the southern end of the Hippodrome, which supplied the palace. The cistern of Mokios, which supplied the houses on the seventh hill, is worth a glance for its enormous expanse. Naval sham fights were held on it, and it now accommodates a small village. But this will by now have been enough for a morning's excursion. And as we cross the Hippodrome again to take the tram down to lunch in some restaurant near the bridge, we may recall another scene in the city's history with which it is associated.

Belisarius, the greatest of the many great generals of the Eastern Empire, and one of its few really great characters, had broken the Vandal power in Africa and conquered a new continent for Justinian. He consequently became suspect and was recalled; but, in deference to his immense influence with the people, he was accorded a triumph in the style of Old Rome, the first that New Rome had seen. It must have been a sight worth seeing. For, to the usual display of the treasures of the Eastern Empire was added the spoil of the Vandals, themselves for generations the spoilers of the ancient world. In this spoil were many historic relics, such as the vessels of the Jewish Temple. Behind it walked Gelimar, the handsome Vandal chief, repeating to himself as the chronicler tells us, " Vanity of vanities, all is vanity." While beside him, in plain service uniform, walked Belisarius. The captive chief and the conquering general then knelt before the throne of Justinian and Theodora. The general, before he rose from his knees, obtaining pardon and a pension for his opponent. The lesser spoils were then scattered among the crowd. With which pleasant scene of glory crowned with generosity, we can leave the golden age of Constantinople under Justinian and Theodora. She was to die soon after of cancer. He lived until 565—long enough to rebuild the edifice of Roman civil law in the Codes, Pandects, Novels, and Institutes, and to establish Orthodox dogma with interminable treatises against the Monophysites. His church has outlasted his State. The dome of St. Sophia still stands, but that overload of Imperial tyranny and taxation that he first laid on the pillars of the State has crashed for the last time in our own day.

Those of us whose time is short can now if they like go straight to the Palace of the Blachernæ in the next chapter. Those whose purse is light can take the tram out to the walls at the Romanus Gate and join us again there. While those who have a car or carriage can make an excursion with us out to the Marmara end of the walls at the Golden Gate, and so right along the walls to the Golden Horn.

We can imagine our conveyance to be a muledrawn carry-all, and we ourselves on the way to see the Triumph of the victorious Emperor Heraclius, the second Triumph in the city's history. We shall follow now the same road as then, though it will look very different. Byzantine Constantinople was a maze of crowded slums and crooked lanes with three great streets driven through it. Along them were palaces and public buildings standing in public gardens, and here or there a great square or Forum surrounded with porticoes. The Mēsē or Middle Street that we are following ran from the Milion past the Law Courts through an almost continuous line of arcades and squares. Among the many monuments that adorned it, we should have noted with approbation the life-size statue of an elephant who killed a banker who had ruined his keeper. The Emperor Severus put up this statue to the judicious pachyderm, and took him into the imperial service. A little farther on we should have passed the Palace of Lausus, one of those with which Constantine lured the Roman patricians to his new capital. But we should have found it converted into a Palace Hotel for wealthy visitors. As such it had been adorned with some of the great art treasures of the city—the Venus of Cnidos by Praxiteles in white marble, the Lindian Athene in smaragdite, the Samian Hera of Lysippus, and the ivory and gold Zeus by Phidias from Olympia. This combination of Palace Hotel and Empire Exhibition is an idea worth noting. We should then have crossed the Forum of Constantine, and should have stopped our mule-cart at the foot of the column where, safely sealed up under Christian symbols, lay the magic powers of the Palladium of Troy lately brought here from Rome. We should then have been pointed out the bronze gates of the Senate House, which were those presented by Trajan to the Temple of Diana at Ephesus. " Great is Diana of the Ephesians," we should have said—" but greater our worthy Senators." On the north we should have had a passing view of the Horse Guards Parade, where Alexander the Great reviewed his forces before the expedition against Darius, a tradition that would not have interested us much.

We should now be passing all the way between porticoes— arcades below and terraced promenades above. These promenades were adorned with statues of pagan deities, popular actresses, and the prevailing Emperor—the gift of plutocrats on the make. To keep up a proper supply of Emperors it was made an offence to replace an Emperor by an actress, and the Emperors' statues were also all made sanctuaries for slaves and criminals. The shops under the arcades all had uniform frontages faced with marble as required by the Office of Works. These arcades concealed the crowded slums of the Bakeries. Farther on, where now stands the Mosque of Bayazid, we should have come to the Forum of Theodosius. This was the University quarter now covered with the buildings and square of the Seraskierat (Ottoman War Office). Curiously enough, I write this just after reading that this old War Office has been assigned by the Angora Government to be the new Turkish University.

We should have found this Byzantine University not very unlike a medresseh or Moslem school. There were thirteen Professors in Latin and fifteen in Greek, who lectured mostly on rhetoric, grammar, and geography. Mathematics was the

study of the mystic qualities of numbers, and there was no multi-
plication table. After twenty years of teaching the professors
were retired with the ranks of Counts of the Empire, something
like an O.B.E. with a pension. The lectures often degenerated
into comic entertainments. The freshmen, known as "Tup-
pennies" (dupondii), used to be put in the fountain (Greg. Naz.
laud. Baz. 16), while the seniors fought duels and played practical
jokes on the professors.

This mystic science of numbers still exists in Constantinople,
where it is studied by various orders of Dervishes and known as
Ibn-Vifd. It is now chiefly used for drawing up Moslem prayers
in the convenient form of combinations of figures. It is a fas-
cinating game something like making up figure squares. The
Dervishes also preserve for us the mystic study of letters as
taught in our Byzantine University. Thereunder every letter
has its own genius. Thus inscriptions over doors are composed
with a view to the corps of guardian spirits that they will enlist,
and great care has to be taken to secure those who will be suitable
and who will get on together. This art is also closely associated
with astrology, and unless the inscription is drawn up in the
right phases of the moon and the right positions of the stars it
loses all force. Which all shows some real insight into the laws
of literary art. But it is in medicine that we owe most to the
city. It preserved the science that Greece took over from Egypt
until Europe could carry on the work : for example, the practice of inoculation for small-pox that was brought to England
by Lady Mary Wortley Montagu in the eighteenth century and
that became the basis of modern prophylaxy ; and the Turkish
bath that Mr. Urquhart, also of the British Embassy brought to
London in the nineteenth century, possibly the best preservative
of health in town life.

In this Byzantine University was also the Record Office,
and in 1877 a quantity of leaden seals or treasury tallies were dug
up on the site. On the west of the square we should have seen
another big hotel with accommodation no doubt appropriate to
the pursuit of learning. For, instead of the Venus of Cnidus, etc.,
its decoration consisted of brass representations of the various
vermin suggestively flattened against the façade. These were
charms of that famous wizard, Apollonius of Tyana, who was
evidently something of a health reformer running a " swat-that-
fly " campaign.

Here from our mule-cart we should admire a sight that we
can still see from our motor-car—the great aqueduct of Valens

striding across the valleys, and we may regret that the system has
not also survived by which wharf-dues were substituted for
water-rates by Theodosius II. " It would be execrable," said
that excellent Emperor (Cod. XI. xliii. 7), " that the houses of
this benign city should have to pay for their water." The
aqueduct was protected at intervals by effigies of storks, another
measure of the ingenious Apollonius to prevent these birds
polluting the water.

A little farther, just south of the present Shahzadeh Mosque,
the Mēsē, divided then, as it still does, one branch following the
ridge along the Golden Horn to the Blachernæ Palace, the other
following the Marmara to the Golden Gate.   If we take the first
we shall pass over the remains of the great bath of Constantine,
which survived into the Ottoman epoch as the Tchokhour Ham-
mam (the Sunken Bath).   It was ruined by an earthquake, but
many of its chambers still exist as walled-up cellars under the
modern houses.   We shall, however, follow the Marmara branch
through what was then a poor quarter.   The square, at the
bifurcation of the road, was the market-place entered by a gate,
over which was a measure of wheat between two severed hands
—the Byzantine punishment for giving short measure.   Here
also we should have passed one of the " Steps " or public food
stations.   There were some eighty of these, where, on presenting
a wooden tessera or food ticket, and after having it checked
against your brass plate on the wall, you got your ration of bread,
oil, wine, and meat.   The Steps were so called because, to prevent
any breaking of the queue, it was made to wind upstairs.   We
should then have come to the Forum of the Ox adorned with a
colossal brazen bull from Pergamos, used under Julian the
Apostate for the slow combustion of martyrs, but subsequently
reserved for profiteers—a judicious decoration of a proletarian
suburb.   Next we would have passed through the Forum of
Arcadius, now Avret Bazaar, and then the Et Meidan or meat
market, afterwards the head-quarters of the Janissaries.   Here
we should have seen, as we can to-day, the Column of Martian.
Its Turkish name, Kiz Tash, or Maiden's Stone, is explained by
the magical power attributed to it of blowing over her head the
skirts of any girl who had loved well rather than wisely.   It is
none the less in good preservation, but has long been enclosed
in a private garden.   Near Avret Bazaar, we can still see the
remains of the Column of Arcadius which, until 1715, was covered
with interesting reliefs.   At the foot of this column, on the capture of the city in 1453, the Grand Duke Lucas Notaras and his

sons died fighting heroically. The original Golden Gate, in the line of Constantine's walls, afterwards called the Jesus Gate, is marked by the Issa Kapou Djami. We would then probably, as we can still to-day, turn in at the Monastery of St. John of the Studium, to rest after our long drive.

The courtyard of this monastery (now Mirakhor Djami) is a pleasant spot, a shrine of ancient peace. In the shade of its trees we can reflect for a few minutes on the long story of this church built as long ago as A.D. 463 by Studius, a Roman patrician. It was but little changed until a fire in 1872 and a snowfall a decade or two ago reduced it to its present ruins. It was one of the principal monasteries of the Akoimetai, or The Sleepless Ones, so-called from their never-ceasing intercession for a sinful world—

> —religious men were they
> Nor would their reason, tutored to aspire,
> Above this transitory world, allow
> That there should pass a moment of the year
> When, in this land, the Almighty's service ceased.

The court we are sitting in is the ancient atrium, and the narthex, or porch of the church, is the remaining side of the cloister which surrounded it. The marble pillars, with late Corinthian capitals, carry a flat architrave and the characteristic art motives of classical Greek art—the egg and dart, the dentils and beads, mingled with Byzantine designs of foliage, birds, and crosses. We note that the Basilica has widened and shortened on the way to becoming a square Byzantine church. The interior hall is divided by a double row of Byzantine columns with Corinthian capitals. The triforium gallery is now gone. It divided the aisles into two stories. The columns in the lower story carry a flat entablature, in the upper they carry arches —a curious combination of the two styles.

In the fifteen centuries of its existence, this church has been a centre of Byzantine history. It was held by the most powerful monastic order of the capital. It was also a theological college, to which students were attracted from all over the world, by its reputation and by the convenient proximity of the Imperial hunting-grounds just outside the walls, which they were free to use. The tomb of one such student, Dionysius, a Russian, is still shown. Hither came unpopular Emperors seeking refuge, and hither were carried any popular icons threatened with destruction by the Iconoclasts. The Abbot, Theodore the

Studiete, carried on the campaign for orthodoxy against no less than eight successive iconoclastic Emperors. In an age of growing servility the stubbornness of the Studium was worthy of a better cause.

THE GOLDEN GATE AND HERACLIUS

We now reach the end of our drive—the Golden Gate. This was the State entrance to the city. It was built of polished marble, the gates themselves were gilt, and the gateway was adorned with reliefs. Some of the reliefs have been found nearby, having probably been taken down as the result of the efforts of Sir Thomas Roe, British Ambassador in 1621, to buy them for his patrons, the Earl of Arundel and the Duke of Buckingham. Sir Thomas was quite an enterprising burglar, and successfully corrupted the Turkish officials, but was foiled by the Greek populace. " I could not get the stones (he writes) yett I almost raised an insurrection in that part of the Cytty."

Like our Marble Arch, the Golden Gate was only open for royalty. Ordinary traffic passed through another gate between the second and third towers which also came to be called by the same name. The Golden Gate also became a great fortress, securing the Marmara front of the wall, as does the present castle of the Seven Towers, built by Mohammed the Conqueror.

If we are interested in history, we may note that the first Triumph that passed through it was that of Theodosius II, whose car was drawn by elephants. The last was that of Michael Palæologus in 1261, when the Greeks had retaken the city from the Latins. But on this occasion the triumphal car was occupied by an effigy of the Virgin. The gate was walled up on the Ottoman Conquest, and has remained so, in deference to the tradition that a Christian Conqueror would one day, through it, enter the city.

If our interests are archæological, we can investigate whether this gate is really the Golden Gate by seeing whether the rivet holes, holding the letters that once made up the inscription over the gate would correspond with the inscription that was on the Gate of Theodosius. This inscription was as follows:

HAEC LOCA THEODOSIUS DECORAT POST FATA TYRANNI
AUREA SAECLA GERIT QUI PORTAM CONSTRUIT AURO.

As the holes follow the shape of the letters—∴ for A and ∵ for capital T or V, it is quite a good game, though apparently

too heating for archæologists. On the other side of the Golden
Gate was the inscription—

He who built the Golden Gate brought the Golden Age.

But the Golden Age of Byzantium was a very different thing
from the Golden Age of Athens. Inside the Golden Gate we
should have found ourselves in a motley crowd crowding the
porticoes that lined the road and waiting for the Triumph of
Heraclius that was being marshalled outside. As observant
travellers we should at once have noticed that the simple severity
of clothing in classic Greece had given place to an Oriental
elaboration and elegance of costume. Greek respect for the
beauty of the human body had, through an unfortunate combination of Oriental luxury and orthodox prudery, turned men
and women into clothes-pegs. Every station in life had its
appropriate and elaborate costume. The Athenian or Spartan
girl in gymnastic tunic would have been driven by indignant
monks from the porticoes, where courtesans defied the Theodosian
Code by peacocking in robes of rank reserved to noble ladies.
With the loss of the athletic tradition, nakedness was driven
out of the baths onto the stage by over-careful ecclesiastics.
Though even in these Byzantine days the old Greek tradition still
survived, as appears from a contemporary " best seller," where
the heroine, a lady of title, makes the acquaintance of the hero, a
gentleman ranker, by leaving her clothes on the beach in his
charge. This author, Arestænetus, would, however, certainly
not have been approved by Chrysostom, who, to keep on the safe
side, advised that young ladies should not take a bath at all.

The characteristic dress of Byzantium for both sexes was the
long gown reaching to the ankles, heavily embroidered and furred,
which was worn over a silken tunic, with gloves, shoes, stockings,
and a cap—in fact, the complete paraphernalia of a world of tailors
and haberdashers. Every profession almost had its own costume.
Celibates of an ascetic turn assumed a protective colouring by
wearing red. Philosophers had a suitable grey. Rhetoricians
a no less appropriate crimson, and physicians blue.

Passing through the Golden Gate we should find the Triumph
marshalling outside. Here are the Emperor's guard, in green
tunics with red facings, and white gaiters over black shoes, each
with a gold ring round his neck, a long spear, and an oval shield
with a blue rim and black rays on a red ground. The captains'
shields have a yellow labarum on a green ground. Here would
be all the Court costumes as you may see them to this day in the

contemporary mosaics, carried off by the Crusaders to San Vitale at Ravenna; or more prosaically, in the paper casts at South Kensington. Here is the prefect of the city in his silver wagon, with a team of four abreast. Here are other dignitaries on white horses, covered with gold trappings, surrounded by running footmen with rods of office. Here are the great ladies behind silk curtains, in carriages gaily painted and gilded, like the Sardinian carts of to-day, drawn by white mules, and guarded by eunuchs, whose whips we should have had to avoid just as a few years ago we kept away from the eunuchs surrounding the carriages of a pasha's hareem. Here, in a canopied carriage, drawn by four white horses, as you may see on the medals, is the Emperor Heraclius himself, in the Imperial purple robes, embroidered with mystic green ducks in red circles, and with scarlet slippers. "What," we should have whispered, "is this long-nosed, weak-chinned, furtive old gentleman, scratching his beard in a characteristic gesture of indecision, the hero of the most audacious maritime and military adventure known to history? Is this the man, who, at the great battle of Nineveh, pierced the triple phalanx of the Persians on his war horse Phallas, and transfixed with his lance the valiant Rhazates right through his golden armour?" Well, well, the official eye-witness says he did it all. And yet every one is saying how he has just insisted on crossing the Bosphorus by a bridge of boats, carefully screened by boughs from any sight of the sea, and on having a carriage instead of the traditional white charger. A human being evidently this Heraclius who is suffering from a reaction after the tremendous feat of arms which has made him a hero. Does he realize, as he props up his crucifix on his gowned knees, what a hero of romance he has become for all time? And how—

A thousand swinging steeples shall begin as they began,
When Heraclius rode home from the wreck of Ispahan,
Naked captives pulled behind him, double eagles in the van—
But is that a tale for lovers on the way to Saadabad?

It is, in any case, a tale that must wait for the next chapter.

CHAPTER II

THE BYZANTINE EMPIRE

"Is it your pleasure now, Sir, to decline and to fall?"
(Silas Wagg to Mr. Boffin)

THE WALLS AND GATES

WE have now come to the most arduous stage of our long trip through Byzantine history, and of our lightning tour of the Stamboul sights : we have before us a drive of at least ten miles, and a duration of nearly a thousand years. It will be a " long funeral march with many a dying fall," to follow the Eastern Empire to its burial in the Latin and Ottoman conquests.

Our landmarks for our excursion into the Golden Age—from Constantine to Heraclius—were the Hippodrome, the Churches, and Cisterns. In the Iron Age, during which the Empire was fighting for its life against enemies without and Court corruption and civic degeneracy within, they will be no less suitably, the walls and the palaces. And it is significant that in this age the palaces are no longer " stately pleasure-domes " looking upon the circus, the cathedral, or the Marmara from open gardens and terraces, but grim castles half-buried in the fortifications and guarding the vulnerable spots in the Land walls. It is significant also that the Emperor, who was in the Golden Age the Ruler of the World and the Regent of God, becomes, at the beginning of this Iron Age, a successful general and administrator, and at its close no more than a Captain of the Gate, the leader of a forlorn hope in an isolated outpost.

The landward walls of Constantinople are one of the great sights of Europe. They are not only in themselves impressive, they are so perfectly expressive of all that the city stood for in this aspect. As we drive along the walls from the Golden Gate on the Marmara to the Wooden Gate on the Golden Horn, we can grasp, as we never could from books, the might and majesty of a bulwark that protected the culture centre of civilization from tidal waves of barbarism for ten centuries. These long lines of walls and towers rising tier above tier from sea to sea—their alternate courses of grey stone and red brick shattered here and there by earthquakes and siege engines, overgrown here and there with ivy and trees, and green under the aquamarine blue of a Constantinople sky—these walls, still grim and warlike in their ruin—their long history written on them in inscriptions and hurried repairs in the face of the enemy—they are all that is left of the military science of Greece. Here we have that science that in its youth defeated in the open field the myriad hosts of the older civilization of Persia, but in its old age took shelter behind walls to defend itself against the myriad hosts of barbarism. Had not this citadel held the isthmus between the continents, the wave of Islam would have swept Europe in the infancy of Christian civilization, and might well have supplanted it. Here the tide was checked in its direct channel, and forced to flow slowly round by way of Africa and the Spanish Peninsula. But for the protection provided by these walls during its infancy, Christianity might have been crushed in its cradle, and we ourselves might have been to-day at the same stage of development as the Turks, the Bulgars, or the Serbs. Our world might not have been a worse place; but indubitably it would have been very different.

On the Marmara the walls are flanked by a great mediæval fortress—the original Strongylon or Kuklobion (the Round Fort), dating from Zeno (480). In the ninth century it was rebuilt as the Heptapurgon (Seven Towers), which was razed to the ground by the Latin crusaders. Under the Greek Empire an attempt to refortify this point on a large scale was stopped by Bayazid I, under threat of blinding his hostage Manuel, son of the reigning Emperor John. Directly after the Conquest Mohammed rebuilt it, and probably upon the original plan, seeing that the inner enceinte is circular, and has seven towers (Yedi Kouleh). Two of these were thrown down by an earthquake in 1768. Until about a century ago each tower was surmounted by a conical roof.

The Castle of Seven Towers was for centuries the headquarters of the Janissaries, and its associations are mostly Turkish. There is no truth in the " awful atrocities " that will be told us about it by our Greek guide : " Seven Viziers hung by the neck on that hook ! "; " The pile of Christian heads overtopped that tower," etc. Unfortunate incidents there were, as was usual in State prisons of the period : the boy-Sultan, Osman II, was murdered here by his Grand Vizier in 1622, and the Hospodar of

Wallachia, Constantine Brancovano, was here tortured for five days, in a vain effort to extract from him the secret of his hidden treasure. It also served as a prison for the European Ambassadors who failed to keep the peace between their Governments and Turkey—a precedent that, like many much-criticized Turkish institutions, has much to be said for it. The inscriptions recording the inconveniences to which they were put can still be read, in Latin, French, German, Italian, and one in English.

We return now to the Great Walls proper.

Their concrete core is faced with squared stone, limestone from Makrikeui, where the quarries can still be seen. The stones are bound together by brick courses, the bricks often stamped with the donor's name. Nothing but a succession of earthquakes could have reduced the walls to their present ruinous condition, as is shown by the way in which many of the towers are cracked from top to bottom.

The Inner, or Great Wall, was the main defence. It is 30 to 40 feet high, and 13 to 15 feet thick. It carried a battlemented parapet 5 feet high, and was ascended by flights of steps running up stone ramps.

Its ninety-six towers are about 60 feet high and of all shapes, from square to octagonal. They are, in structure, separated from the wall, as required by the principles of fortification. Each tower has two floors: the lower a store-house or arsenal, the upper a guard-room. On the roof were the military engines.

Between this Great Wall and the outer wall is an inner terrace (peribolos) 60 feet wide.

The outer wall is from 3 to 6 feet thick, and about 30 feet high. The lower part forms a retaining wall for the inner terrace, the upper is an arcade, with a rampart over barrel vaults. Its towers rise about 30 feet above the terrace, and are alternately square or crescent ; variations upon these forms being the result of hurried repairs.

Beyond the outer wall, again, is the outer terrace, 60 feet wide, and sheltered from the moat by a battlement 6 feet high. In the bases of the square towers of the outer wall, below the terrace level, there are often subterranean passages, leading from small posterns in the outer terrace to within the walls. These must have served for the reinforcement, or the retreat, of the defenders of the outer terrace. Most of the hard fighting in the sieges raged round the outer wall.

The moat is also 60 feet wide, and was probably at least 30 feet deep. It is traversed by walls, and the buttresses upon one side of these walls show that they were dams to hold up the water. They were also aqueducts for filling the moat and supplying the wall, since we can see pipes within them where they are broken. That there is no mention of water in accounts of the later sieges is explained by the fact that the first object of the preliminary bombardment would naturally have been to breach these dams and empty the moat.

The Gates are alternately Military and Public: the former admitting only to the fortifications, the latter to the city highways. The Military gates were known by numbers, the road gates by names.

Following the paved triumphal way along the outside of the walls, between the moat and a continuous line of Turkish cemeteries, we pass first the second Military gate, now the Belgrade gate, and next the public gate of the Pegæ or Spring. At this gate the Greeks, under Cæsar Strategopoulos, entered in 1261 by crawling up a drain, and overthrew the Latin Empire. Inside the wall there hangs the mace of the Janissary Idris, a stone ball attached to an iron handle. A Turkish inscription extols his prowess and tells the weight. Close by, in an angle of the road, is another Turkish relic, the largest of a row of seven Turkish tombstones. Here is buried, according to the inscription, the head of Ali Pasha Tebelen, the hero of Albania and of "Childe Harold?" After his execution it was exposed on a gold plate at the Seraglio gate: the executioner refused a large offer for it from a London showman, and it was buried here by his friends.

At about the middle of the walls we reach the gate of Rhegium, or Melandesia, so called from the ancient Rhegium, now Kutchuk Tchekmedje, some 12 miles distant. It was also known as the Red Gate, after the Red Faction who had charge of it. On the north face of the south tower is an inscription "Victory to the Fortunes of our god-protected Emperor Constantine"; but the last line—"And of the Reds"—has been effaced—a curious record of the old faction fights. Other inscriptions here record repairs of the wall. The most noteworthy of these proclaims that Constantine or Cyrus, the prefect of Theodosius, here in sixty days "bound wall to wall." This has bothered archæologists unaccountably. It surely records the great moment in the construction of the Theodosian Walls when the two factions, who were building in competition from either end, met in the middle, and joined wall to wall. The damaged condition of the wall hereabouts is due to attempts to destroy it in 1868, when the Sublime Porte sold several towers to contractors at about £40 apiece. The demolition was only just stopped in time by the British Ambassador.

Next we pass the fourth Military gate, and the public gate of St. Romanus (in Turkish Top Kapoussou, or Cannon gate), where those who have avoided our longer circuit can rejoin us. The Gate of Charisius, farther on, is named after the head of the Blue Faction who built it. It was also called the Polyandrion, or Many Men, perhaps because this middle wall, the Meso-Teikion, was always made the object of the fiercest assaults, and had to be heavily manned. It was at about this point, in the valley of the Lycus, that the Turks broke in. But we shall return here later.

We have been following hitherto the triple Wall of Theodo-sius, a monument of the Golden Age—the age of wealth. But we now come to where the wall bulges out in fortifications obviously of a later date—monuments of the Age of Iron, or of war. Originally the Theodosian Walls continued along their own line across to the Golden Horn. But the military requirements of the Iron Age caused the line of the Wall to be carried forward as a salient, forming a flanking fortress even more formidable than the Seven Towers at the other end.

THE FIRST SIEGES

It was in the time of Heraclius, whose Triumph we were attending at the close of the last chapter, that the city first found itself completely invested. The death of Justinian marked the end of the epoch of imperial supremacy. Tiberius, his successor, according to a contemporary historian, Theophylactus Simocatta, was assured by an angel that the catastrophe would not occur in his virtuous reign. No doubt, in the absence of a public Press, angels expressed public opinion. Anyhow, the first sign of dis-ruption appeared in the military revolt in which Maurice and his children were assassinated. Maurice was a Conservative Emperor who was trying to reinforce the Imperial authority. Phocas replaced him, a representative of the revolt against the ruling class and the central power. In view of his radical politics, we need not be too shocked at the horrid portrait of him drawn by contemporary chroniclers. While in view of the policy of Phocas in depriving the Patriarch of Constantinople of his œcumenical rank we need not attribute the congratulations of Gregory the Great upon this bloody accession to any admiration of his personality. In any case he failed. The Persians under Chosroes advanced to the Asiatic shore of the Bosphorus, and the

Avars approached the Land Walls. The city was decimated by plague and famine, and deserted Phocas. Heraclius, ex-arch of Africa, was called in to depose the Radical. Phocas was dragged on board the new Emperor's ship, and his last sarcasm is recorded : " Wretch," said Heraclius, " how have you conserved the Empire ! " " No doubt *you* will be Conservative enough for it ! " retorted Phocas ; who was thereupon beheaded, and his party banished.

Heraclius had arrived at the Harbour of Julian, below the Hippodrome, known by the Turks as Kadriga Liman (Galley Harbour). It is said that the remains of galleys used to be visible here under the water, until the railway line destroyed all traces of the past. It was, nevertheless, several years before Heraclius, most adventurous of strategists, could gather strength enough to relieve the city. A voluntary sacrifice of church and private treasures was made for the first time. Its success was doubtless due to the new Emperor's threat to transfer the capital to Carthage. Nor was the threat mere bluff. Heraclius was a Roman, born in Africa, where the Roman language and tradition had survived with a vigour elsewhere lost. It seems singular to us to find, at the very beginning of the city's decline, a proposal being made which was not to be put in force until our own time, when, for the same reasons, the Turks transferred their capital to Angora. His resources recruited, Heraclius took the offensive, in a brilliant employment of the sea-power which he still retained. Penned in on two sides, he embarked an army for Iskanderoon, in the eastern Mediterranean, defeated the Persians decisively on that flank, and followed this up by sailing for Trebizond on the Black Sea, and, after two years of hard fighting, penetrating to the heart of Persia. By this bold raid he shattered the Sassanid dynasty and the career of Chosroes.

In the meanwhile Chosroes had been trying to end the war by capturing Constantinople. But the sea power of the Greeks retained command of the Bosphorus, and thus held the Persians passive spectators upon the Asiatic shore. The offensive against the Walls had to be left to their Scythian allies, Bulgars, Gepidæ, Russians and Slavs, under the command of the Avar Khan. Some historians assume that they actually broke through the Great Walls. But, if so, how were they ever got out again when once well inside the city ? What they probably did penetrate was an outer defence, the Long or Anastasian Wall : an entrenchment thirty miles long between the Marmara and the Black Sea, roughly represented by the modern lines of Tchataldja.

This success enabled them to ravage the undefended suburb of Blachernæ, then still outside the walls, and to launch in vain a host of eighty thousand barbarians against the Great Walls themselves.

Chosroes had siege artillery. His twelve wooden towers over-topped the ramparts, and for ten days the walls were battered and sapped. But in siege-craft as in sea-power the Greeks were still masters of the world. Their Greek fire consumed the towers, and their galleys swept the enemy small-craft from the Horn. In the end the Avars were repulsed; but for days the point of assault, where the walls end at the Golden Horn, was in great danger. Worse than this, the impregnability of the walls had been challenged. The mere sight had been enough in the past for Goths and Huns. But now this attack in 626 was to prove only the first episode in the long siege that was never again to be wholly raised until of the treasure guarded within the walls there remained nothing worth looting. The doomed city must have realized this. For no sooner had the besiegers withdrawn, than the great outwork known as the Heraclian Wall was thrown out, and the whole quarter from the Palace of the Blachernæ to the Porphyrogenitus Palace became one huge fortress, securing the Golden Horn end of the wall as the fortress of the Seven Towers secured the Marmara flank.

If we now diverge and climb up to the summit of the higher of the hills outside the Golden Horn end of the walls, and sit down among the turbaned Turkish tombstones under the cypresses, we shall be on the site of the camp of the Latin crusaders who broke into Constantinople in 1204. We enjoy from here a fine *coup d'œil* of this the most historic end of the walls; and we can read upon the walls themselves a compendium of the history of the Byzantine Empire.

That lofty inner wall, with its high towers, is the Wall of Heraclius, a monument of the rally under that New-Roman Emperor, and of the first successful defence against the Persians and Avars. The fact that it is built inside, and forms no part of the line of main defence, may remind us that Heraclius and his dynasty are more often included under the Roman Empire; and that the Byzantine Empire is then taken as beginning with Leo the Isaurian, who built the lower line of wall outside Heraclius's Wall.

The change from Roman to Byzantine, that this view of the two lines of wall suggests, is of great historical import-ance. Roman Constantinople was cosmopolitan, œcumenical, and imperial. But as the bounds of the Empire crumbled, the Greeks of Europe were driven in upon the capital by Avars and Slavs, and the Greeks of Asia by Persians and Arabs. The fall of Antioch and Alexandria, the Greek capitals in Asia and Africa respectively, swelled the Greek element in the city, filling the gaps made by war and plague. From the provinces also the Greeks flooded in, driven by the imperial tax-gatherers and tempted by the doles of free food and the lures of commercial profits and Court promotion. Greece itself became largely Arnaut and Slav. Constantinople thus became the Greek national capital, upon whose defence depended the survival of the race. The Romaioi or Romans soon became a designation for Greeks of the capital who were distinguished only by their dialect from the Helladikoi or Greeks of the provinces. The boundaries of the Empire, as restored by Heraclius, became the racial frontiers of the Greeks ; and could these have been maintained, Grecian culture would have continued to lead and leaven European civilization. But the open frontiers of western Asia and eastern Europe proved powerless to stem the succeeding inrushes of military barbarism ; and in the end Constantinople alone remained the last stronghold of Greek civilization, safe-sheltered behind its walls and its fleet.

This racial change, from Roman to Greek, was scarcely accomplished when the capital was again threatened, this time by a more formidable enemy. The Arabs, more generally known in this connection as the Saracens, were not savages like the Avars, nor freebooters like the Persians. They possessed a culture inferior to that of Greece, but adaptable, and capable of assimilating Greek ideas. They had a commerce that followed their conquests. Their creed was inferior to Christianity as a spiritual faith, but superior to Orthodoxy as an inspiring force. They came not as mere raiders, but as reformers, offering to the oppressed provincials a release from the imperial extortion and corruption. Even the provincial Churches, the first shock of conquest past, settled down almost with relief under tolerant and trustworthy Arab rulers. The Saracen power, though not yet in the full flood of its supremacy, was on the crest of its first success. The Caliph Moawiyah could command sufficient resources for the siege, and had already recognized that in Constantinople lay the key to the command of the Roman Empire. Against such progressive pressure there seemed little probability that the decadent bureaucracy and the dilapidated walls could long hold out. But another stout rally of reformers, under Constantine IV, the " Bearded " (Pogonatus), proved equal to the emergency.

In the spring of 672 the Saracen fleet arrived before the city. The walls were invested by sea and land ; but every assault was repulsed, chiefly by the aid of the " Greek fire " tubes, spurting burning naphtha. The Saracens were, moreover, unequal to maintaining a winter siege. For seven years they returned to the attack each spring, and withdrew to Cyzicus every autumn. At last they retreated in exhaustion, and were all but destroyed on their retirement through Asia Minor. So deep an impression did the city's resistance make upon the Caliph, that he made peace, and even paid tribute. It was in the course of these sieges that Abou Eyoub died ; the same who had received Mohammed in his house on his flight to Mecca. He was buried where now stands the Mosque of Eyoub, which we shall visit later.

For all this success at the walls, all was not well within the city. This is evident from the vicissitudes of Justinian II (685–711), one of the " building " Emperors. Of him Gibbon relates :

> His favourite ministers were two beings least susceptible of human sympathy, a eunuch and a monk ; to the one he abandoned the palace, to the other the finances ; the former corrected the Emperor's mother with a scourge, the latter suspended the insolvent tributaries with their heads downward over a slow and smoky fire.

After ten years he was deposed, his nose slit, and his ears cropped in the Hippodrome. But he had his revenge, in 705, when he sat with his feet on the necks of Leontius and Apsimaris, the two Emperors who had reigned in the interval. Another six years, and he was again deposed, torn with his small son from the church of the Virgin at Blachernæ, and killed outside the Palace. The Emperors had by then transferred their residence to the mighty Blachernæ Palace ; and most of the troubles took place at the Blachernæ Gate now facing us.

THE LATER WALLS AND ISAURIAN DYNASTY

This sort of thing did not strengthen the Imperial authority, and Emperor followed Emperor at the rate of about one a year, until the crisis of the Arab peril again produced real rulers and reformers in the Isaurian dynasty.

When Leo the Isaurian became Emperor the Bulgars and Slavs had overrun Europe right up to the Great Wall—the Saracens had ravaged Asia Minor right up to the Bosphorus— six Emperors had been deposed in twenty-one years, and every army opposed to the superior military system of the Saracen had mutinied. Leo was an Isaurian, that is, a foreigner of Asia Minor, probably an Armenian, and an iconoclast, that is, a heretic. But he so reorganized the administration—military, financial, and judicial—that it outlasted for many centuries contemporary Governments that have been much more advertised and applauded. It is from his reformation that we may date the Byzantine Empire. And that Empire may be subdivided again into three dynasties, Isaurian, Basilian and Comnenian, each of which is especially associated with a section of these buildings before us.

During the second period, that of the Basilian dynasty, from Basil I, the Macedonian, 867, to Michael VI, 1057, the Byzantine power is at its height, both within and without Constantinople. Its magnificence is commemorated in the strip of wall running from the end of the double Leonine and Heraclian Walls through the so-called Prison of Anemas, past the Tower of Anemas, to the adjoining Tower of Isaac Angelo, which forms the foundation and retaining wall of the splendid Blachernæ Palace. Beyond this again is Comnenian.

The walls before us thus provide us with an admirable memoria technica of the three stages in the history of the Byzantine Empire. And before we leave our bird's-eye view of them, and plunge into their labyrinth of detail, we do well to fix this scheme in our minds.

Leo the Isaurian was, however, more than a successful soldier —who " put his trust in reeking tube and iron shard." Like Napoleon, he established a new military system. The Byzantine Army that for five centuries defended the Empire without ever dominating the civil Government was a clever combination of conscript regulars, mercenaries, and native levies. The Imperial Guard or foreign legions never usurped power at Constantinople as they did in Rome. But more than that, Leo recovered the allegiance of the provinces by restoring the authority of law in the Empire. In Finlay's words :

Leo converted the strong attachment to the Laws of Rome prevalent in society into a lever of political power. . . . The Laws of Rome saved Christianity from Saracen domination more than the armies. The victories of Leo enabled him to consolidate his power and constitute the Byzantine Empire—in defiance of the Greek nation and the Orthodox Church ; but the Law supplied him with this moral power over society. . . . The torrent of Mohammedan conquest was arrested, and as long as the Roman law was cultivated in the Empire, and administered under proper control in the provinces, the invaders of Byzantine territory were everywhere unsuccessful."

Leo's true memorial lies in the Ecloga, a popular edition of the Codes that was given official authority, and thus brought the law within reach of the layman. It is unfortunate that all the records of his reign are coloured by the *odium theologicum* of the controversy between Orthodox and Iconoclast, and by the contempt of the metropolitan Greek for the Asiatic provincial. For his reformed regime rendered noteworthy service to civilization.

Leo's re-enforcement of the imperial authority did not, however, prevent his son, Constantine V, from having to fight his way into Constantinople by a *coup de main*, in 743. Constantine owes his name Copronymus, and the infamous reputation reproduced even by Gibbon, to a " bad Press "—the chroniclers of the period being all orthodox. For his moderation in success, and his Bulgarian campaigns, show him to have been an efficient sovereign. Orthodox conspiracies pursued him unceasingly ; and they were severely punished, the leader of one of them, the Patriarch Constantine, being led to execution riding backwards upon an ass. His reign, further, is marked for us by the destruction of the sea-walls on Seraglio Point when, in 763, during a winter of extraordinary severity, icebergs drove down upon them from the Black Sea ; and also by the great plague of 749, which converted the whole once populous region outside the walls into a hunting park. These catastrophes were, of course, fully exploited by the Orthodox opposition. We can find a close similarity between the scenes of panic, superstition and precaution recorded of this plague, and those of which we read in the great Plague of London. There would seem to have been less difference between the minds of men inhabiting these two capitals separated a thousand years in time than between the minds of our own countrymen living in the seventeenth and in the nineteenth centuries.

Constantine V, son of Leo the Isaurian, had married Irene, an Athenian of great beauty and ability, who took advantage of becoming Regent to attempt an Orthodox revival. To this she owes a place of honour in history as manufactured by monkish chroniclers, such as neither her character nor her career deserved. Finlay quite lets himself go about her :

When vested with the regency as the widow of an iconoclast Emperor, it required no trifling talent, firmness of purpose, and conciliation of manner to overthrow an ecclesiastical party that had ruled the Church for more than half a century. On the other hand the deliberate way in which she undermined the authority of her son, whose character she had corrupted in order to deprive him of his throne and send him as a blind monk to a secluded cell, proves that the beautiful Empress whose memory was cherished as an Orthodox Saint was endowed with the thoughts and feelings of a demon.

She was certainly unsuccessful in her foreign policy. It was during her reign, in 800, that Charlemagne revived the Western Empire, thereby raising himself to an equality with the Emperor of the East, and securing the political allegiance of the Pope. Then, too, Haroun Al Raschid, another friend of our youth, appeared upon the Bosphorus, and had to be bought off. Irene was eventually deposed by her Arab chamberlain Nikephorus. But we pass him over, as also Michael I, and come to Leo the Armenian, whose walls we are now going to visit.

Leo the Armenian, of this dynasty, built the wall we are now looking at, outside the Heraclian Wall, in 865. Archæologists differ as to why the wall was here doubled, and have attributed it to fear of an assault by Crum the Bulgarian. Crum was doubtless angry enough, having only just escaped with his life and with several arrows sticking in his back from a treacherous ambush laid for him by Leo, when he was on his way to a conference at the point where we now are standing. He would certainly have returned to the assault, had he not died before it was ready. But I venture the opinion that the double wall was constructed against a more insidious enemy than Crum. It was to secure the Blachernæ Palace against a *coup d'état* from within. The double wall, when we examine its plan, reveals itself as a double defence for the Gate, which had been three times forced in the recent dynastic disorders, with results disastrous to the reigning Emperors of the moment. It is to be remarked that, after this addition, although a coup was often attempted, it never again succeeded. The theory, anyhow, seems worth investigating.

Passing along the Golden Horn, and through an opening— once the Wooden Gate (Xuloporta)—in the ruins of a wall that continued the line of the Great Wall down to the water, we enter a city quarter called still the Aivan Serai or High Palace. This and the next beyond it, Balat (palaton), owe their names to the Blachernæ Palace, which is behind the wall on our right. As we pass through the Turkish gate of Aivan Serai, we have, on our left, the degraded ruin of a palace where once lived the daughter of Theophilus, of whom more anon. It is now one of the most unsavoury and unsafe districts of Constantinople. The vicinity of the Palace was for centuries abandoned to the gipsies ;

and as a disillusioned traveller reports—" it would be difficult to imagine any spot more unclean, infectious, and pestilential." In so far it but perpetuates, in its noisomeness, the Court corruption that it replaced.

Close by is the ancient Church of St. Peter and St. Mark (Atik Moustapha Pasha Djami). It was built in 450, to guard a most precious relic, the incorruptible robe of the Virgin Mary; whence, possibly, its prison-like appearance. In the street outside is the ancient font, which was thrown out when the church became a mosque. It is fashioned from a single block of marble, the steps worn deep by feet that only trod them once.

The Church of St. Thekla, now Thoklou Ibrahim Dede Mesjid, is more interesting in its architecture and associations. It was built in the ninth century by an invalid daughter of Theophilus, who enjoyed the distinction of having refused the grandson of Charlemagne. The palace built for her by her father can still be seen, in ruins, inside the wall east of Aivan Serai Kapou. Her church represents a return to the Basilica style; and its austere piety, reflecting that of the invalid princess, remains still apparent through all the paint of an Ottoman restoration in 1890.

Paint is a Turkish precaution against ghosts—not a bad one— and if we go through the gate of the Blachernæ, by the Emperors' private way, into the enclosure between the Heraclian and Leonine Walls, we find a secluded spot shaded by trees and haunted by many ghosts. Here was discovered miraculously the tomb of Abou Seidel, the companion of the Prophet who is supposed to have perished during the first Arab siege. If the location is correct—and who shall say it is not ?—we have here the enemy of Leo the Isaurian buried where he fell, under the wall—for it must be remembered that the outer Wall, that of Leo the Armenian, had not then been built. Mohammed the Conqueror appointed Ibrahim Dede guardian of the place; and his name was thus coupled with that of Thoklou or Thekla. For centuries all Christians were excluded from the precinct.

If we leave the enclosure between the walls, and return to the Londja quarter, we can visit the Church of St. Mary of Blachernæ. Anyone who prefers to omit this can go straight up inside the wall to the higher ground, once the Palace Precinct, and rejoin us at the Tower of Anemas.

The Church of the Holy Virgin of the Blachernæ was the most sacred, as St. Sophia was the most splendid, of Byzantine times— more sacred even than that of the Holy Apostles with its relics— so sacred, that it was largely upon its account that this quarter was first converted into a fortress and then into the royal palace. The earlier Emperors were accustomed to lead a triennial ritual procession from the original palace, across the city to this church. But Emperors of the later secluded period hesitated to face the populace upon so long a route, and since to abandon the ceremony was out of the question, they moved their residence to the Blachernæ. The only reason for the church's peculiar sanctity would seem to have been the neighbourhood of the Holy Well (Ayasma) which made it from the first a " Place of Power." Later this pagan Naiad of the Spring was given a Christian cloak by the transfer from the neighbouring St. Peter and St. Mark of the Robe of the Virgin. The all-powerful Virgin of the Blachernæ was in fact a canonized reincarnation of the " Fairy of the Fountain." It was the Well and not the Robe that counted. Thus, as soon as the official service was over the Emperor went to the Chapel of the Well, the eunuchs took off his royal robes, and dressed him in the leution, or gilt bathing costume. He then prayed before the icons, and bathed in the fountain; and, upon leaving, he presented gold to twelve water-carriers. We have here, in fact, a pagan ceremony.

It was this Fairy Virgin who helped Michael the Drunkard to defeat the Russians. And when in 1434 some young nobles, chasing their pet pigeons, burned down the church, the city gave up hope, knowing that their fairy queen had abandoned them to the Genii of the Mussulmans.

After the Conquest the site was razed, and divided up among private owners ; but for the Greeks it still retained its traditional sanctity. Finally, the Guild of the Furriers bought the land, and pious Greeks erected the present reproduction of the ancient chapel. The floor still preserves the ancient porphyry pavement, and in the shapeless mass of masonry close to the gate on the left we see all that remains of the ancient church. In this admission by the Ottomans that it had proved all in vain to try and Islamize the site, and in the fact that this restoration of a religious shrine is the only one that they ever permitted, we have proof of the vitality of a nature cult that thus survived a thousand years of idolatry, iconoclasm and Islamism.

The chapels and castle built to consecrate the spirit of the spring are in ruins all round us, but the spell of the fairy still charms this quiet corner for a weary tourist. Here we may make a halt under the trees or upon one of the towers overlooking the Blachernæ quarter, and consider for a moment what this great controversy was, between Iconoclast and Orthodox, which prevented, in effect, the Eastern Empire from taking firm root in the Greek race, as the Western Empire rooted itself in the German race. For had a reforming regime, such as that of the Iconoclasts, succeeded in enlisting the mental superiority and racial solidarity of the Greeks, it would have established a Greek national state that could have resisted the Turks.

Iconoclasm was spiritually a Puritan and rationalist reformation, inspired by the long association of the southern Armenians, the Isaurians, etc., with the Moslem monotheistic revolt against idolatry. It was politically a struggle between Priest and Prince such as takes place in all communities at a certain stage of their development. And it was socially a rivalry between the Romaioi and the provincial Helladikoi, between the national and the imperial Greeks, such as has always been the bane of the Greek race. Thus we find Leo the Isaurian at one time ordering all sacred pictures to be hung out of the reach of idolatrous worship, at another breaking the hold of monks and bishops upon imperial finance—and being violently attacked by John Damascene, the last of the early fathers, from his safe refuge at the Caliph's Court. And at yet another time forced to fight a fleet, sent against Constantinople by the Greeks of the Peloponnese. Iconoclasm was not mere image-breaking for the sake of a demonstration, but a determination to break a priestly power injurious to the public welfare, put in force at first with all possible deference to public prejudices. The Byzantine iconoclasts actually did much less material damage than the British Independents. It was not they, but the Latin Crusaders, the representatives of a Church that upheld Orthodoxy against Iconoclasm, who robbed the Eastern Church of its reliquaries and relics, its treasures of art and artifice.

The controversy grew steadily more embittered, and reached its height under Copronymus. But the duel between Leo the Armenian and the powerful abbot, Theodore the Studiete, whom we have already met, was marked by the great moderation of an Emperor, who had no intention of creating "martyrs." His position reminds us of that of Charlemagne, who published the so-called Caroline Books on the subject.

Leo the Armenian was an excellent Emperor, but his Orthodox opponents had public opinion behind them in the matter of idolatry. One conspiracy succeeded another, and in an evil moment Leo pardoned, on the petition of his wife, one Michael the Amorian. "You may have saved my soul," said Leo to her, "but you have sacrificed my life." The following night,

Christmas Eve, a midnight service was held in the Palace of the Blachernæ. On his way to it Leo visited Michael's cell, and found him asleep on his jailer's bed, with the door unlocked. But Leo's piety postponed action until the service should be ended. On so solemn an occasion the palace chapel-choir had been increased, and the assassins entered among the supernumeraries. It was dark and cold, and both the Emperor and his chaplain wore heavy furred gowns with hoods, so that it was not until Leo's deep voice was heard joining in the chant that the conspirators could identify and attack him. He seized a ponderous gold cross, and defended himself; but he was soon cut to pieces. Michael, still in fetters, was then brought from his cell, and proclaimed Emperor.

Michael proved a better Emperor than this beginning might warrant. But when the Orthodox found that, although he recalled Theodore the Studiete, he would not restore image-worship, they made him in his turn the subject of libellous legend and dubbed him the Horse-jockey, the Heretic, or the Stammerer on account of his bad Greek. Before long he was engaged in a nine years' Civil War with a rival—the incongruously named General Thomas. The large fleets and forces engaged upon either side are significant of the wealth of the Empire.

If we move on to the southern end of this Leonine Wall, we shall see the marks of the hasty repairs effected by Michael when General Thomas was advancing upon the city. There is also an inscription recording that this wall was repaired by Michael and Theophilus—this being the first occasion when a son's name is found associated with that of the reigning sovereign. The date $+\sigma\tau\Delta+$ you will no doubt recognize at once as " A.D. 822." General Thomas tried an assault with rams and scaling-ladders. But Leo's Wall frustrated Leo's avengers, even as it foiled every other attempt to carry it.

THE BLACHERNÆ PALACE AND THEOPHILUS

This obscure inscription is the first record in stone of Theo-philus, whose epitaph might be that he tried to be a perfect Emperor and succeeded in being an imperial prig. It was Theophilus who first established the custom of riding weekly to this Church of the Virgin to give his subjects an opportunity of presenting petitions. He did not altogether give up the public appearances in the Hippodrome; but he preferred to appear there as a simple charioteer of the Blue faction. For the weekly public procession to church had the advantage of seeming more democratic in character, and of exposing the Emperor to less danger. The practice, it may be remarked, was continued by the Ottoman Sultans down to our own time.

Theophilus had been educated by the most learned man of the age, John the Grammarian, who afterwards acted as his ambassador to the Caliph. His justice and discretion remain apparent even through the opprobrium of his Orthodox chroniclers. His only fault would seem to have been a certain Puritanical priggishness. His regard for the democratic tradition of the Iconoclast dynasty compensated for his failures in the field which earned him the title of the Unfortunate, and has left us a store of pleasing legend characteristic of the period. Thus Petronas, his own brother-in-law, was accused by a poor widow of breaking the law of "ancient lights," by raising his house high above hers : a serious matter in the overcrowded city, as we can realize still to-day. Theophilus, finding that his injunction to lower the house had been disregarded, ordered its demolition, and sentenced Petronas to be flogged publicly, which shows how completely the traditional Greek pride of person had disappeared. It had become no more a dishonour to be bastinadoed by imperial order in Byzantium than it was in Bagdad. To be beaten by the Emperor's own hand was even regarded as an honour ; and we have its survival in our own ceremony of Knighthood. Petronas not long after became Governor of Chersonnese, and, later, commanded victoriously against the Saracens. On another occasion, as Theophilus was riding out at this Blachernæ Gate, a man stepped forward and claimed the Emperor's horse as stolen goods. The Emperor held a "Court of pie-powder" from the saddle, and on the claim being established, dismounted and proceeded on foot. Another anecdote gives us a picture of the transition in royal marriage customs, from the practice of the early Emperors, who made either love-matches or political alliances, to the hareem of the last decadence. Theophilus, an elderly widower and philosopher, had no use for a hareem, and conditions in the East had cut off the supply of foreign princesses. His mother accordingly invited the most suitable candidates to a fête in the Blachernæ. After appropriate entertainment, they were ranged in rows, and Theophilus reviewed them, a golden apple in his hand. The Court betting had been all in favour of Eikasia, a leading beauty and *bel esprit*. The Emperor stopped in front of her, and led the conversation up to a quotation, no doubt prepared before-

hand, which we can render by the lines from " Paradise Lost "
(IX. 900)—

> He never shall find out fit mate, but such
> As some misfortune brings him or mistake."

The lady responded promptly, in the hexametre jingle then
displacing the classic metres, with lines probably from a popular
song, something like this:

> It's always the girls who bring
> Whatever is good—and bad:
> They can make a cad into a king
> And can make a king into a cad.

But it was trying Theophilus too highly. He passed on,
and without further remark handed the apple to the demure
Theodora—a choice that was to prove disastrous after his death,
but possibly had its recommendations during his life. Eikasia
went into a convent, and took to writing hymns, by which she
became more renowned in her lifetime, and after, than she would
have been as Empress. A sense of humour is less dangerous
in a hymn than on a throne. Theophilus and Theodora lived
happily ever after; but she must have found him trying at
times. For instance, merchants had discovered that by taking
members of the Royal family into partnership they could evade
the customs duties. This became a scandal; and Theophilus,
having heard that the Empress was interested in a large lading,
arranged to be with his Court on one of his rebuilt towers when
her vessel sailed past Seraglio Point, flags a-flying and horns
a-blowing. A few seemingly irrelevant questions gave him the
information he expected; whereupon he ordered that the cargo
be escheated as belonging to nobody, seeing that an Empress
in trade is a juristic impossibility. The story is thoroughly
characteristic of Theophilus.

Of the great palace built by him on the Asiatic shore in
Moorish style, to plans brought by John the Grammarian from
Bagdad, nothing remains. But his name will be found on many
of the Towers of the Sea Wall. His last act was to secure his
son's succession by having the head of his old comrade-in-arms
and brother-in-law, Theophobus, brought to his bedside. Thirty
days after his death Theodora finally ended Iconoclasm; and
the images were restored on February 19, 842, a date ever
afterwards observed as a festival of the Orthodox Church. John
the Grammarian, tutor of Theophilus, an inventor and thinker

well ahead of his age, was blinded and banished—a symbolic sentence.

Theodora followed the example of Irene, and sent her son Michael the Drunkard to the bad. The condition of the Court can be realized from the ease with which a handsome Macedonian groom, to whom Michael had married one of his mistresses, made his way to the throne, as Basil I, and founded the Basilian dynasty. This decadence of the Court, however, had not yet extended to the city. Constantinople was never more peaceful, prosperous, and, within limitations, more progressive than during the epoch we are now entering. The bed-chamber plots and camarilla policies of the Blachernæ concerned the city little. The Emperors emerge from the Palace purlieus, strut their brief hour in the Palace porticoes, and pass on into the Palace prisons. The Empire, raided by invaders and ruined by taxes, steadily declined. But the city piled its wealth ever higher. Certain events in this epoch illustrate the power of its wealth. The Bulgars became so impressed with the city and their commercial intercourse with it that they embraced Christianity, while the magnificence of the embassy of John the Grammarian to the Caliphate, increased by his artifices, secured peace for the eastern frontier. There was another incident, little noticed by historians, but even more significant. The seaboard cities of the West were being sacked and the growth of Western civilization checked by Norse sea-robbers. We can see (in Skylitzi's History, Vol. II, p. 30) a contemporary picture of these Norsemen and their Long Ships, looking, in their beards and fur caps, just like to-day's caricatures of " Bolshies." So little do times change or we change with them. In 860 such a raid, under the Varangs, who had taken command in Russia, descended upon Constantinople. But the Long Ships were repulsed so decisively that a victory which it seemed difficult to attribute to the leadership of Michael the Drunkard was ascribed to the intervention of the Virgin of the Blachernæ.

THE PALACE PRISONS AND BASILIAN DYNASTY.

We can now visit the actual site of the Blachernæ Palace. The two centuries during which the Basilian dynasty occupied it in splendour were happy in having no history of interest to tourists.

The changing character of the age is exemplified by its three leading Emperors. Basil, the Macedonian and ex-groom, distinguished himself as a jurist, and his " Basilica " is the last and most elaborate revision of the Roman Law, the foundation of the city's prosperity. It is not improbable that his legislative activity was a legacy from the hard-working Theophilus, the product of the labour of Commissions set up by him. Leo VI, the Wise, was a philosopher, and wrote a treatise on civil administration and military organization. Constantine Porphyrogenitus is best known for his great work on Court ceremonial.

Basil the Macedonian is generally remembered for two episodes. A wealthy widow of Patras, Danielis, was the founder of his fortunes. On his accession she journeyed to visit him in a State litter borne by slaves, with an almost royal retinue. She presented him with a hundred youths, a hundred maidens, and a hundred eunuchs, all of course slaves ; with a hundred pieces of tapestry, a hundred of wool, a hundred of silk, a hundred of cambric so fine that it would pull through a reed, a hundred pieces of gold, and a hundred of silver plate. She sent orders from Constantinople for silk carpets to cover the whole pavement of a church Basil was building ; and crowned her benefits by dying soon after her return, and leaving him the greater part of her immense fortune accumulated in the Patras silk industry. He thus became proprietor of eighty villages, and of so many slaves that his successor, Leo, released 3,000 of them. The story gives us a picture of a provincial society as rich and as deteriorating as that of the capital. It is not well with a country when capricious old ladies are able to put the lives of thousands at the mercy of a handsome young parvenu. The other incident took place near the end of Basil's life. A stag had the audacity to charge the Emperor, get its antler under his belt, and unhorse him. He was in some danger, until an attendant drew a knife and cut the girdle. Basil immediately had the man decapitated, the penalty for drawing a knife near the Sacred Person. We cannot regret that Basil died soon after, from the shock to his nerves.

Leo VI the Wise justified his nickname by reigning for a quarter of a century without worse trouble than Palace plots, and the destruction by the Saracens of the second city in the Empire, Salonica.

Alexander, who reigned after his brother Leo for a few months, believed that his genius inhabited, not inappropriately, the bronze boar in the Hippodrome. The boar accordingly received gold tusks, jewelled eyes, and much reverence in religious ceremonies.

Of Constantine Porphyrogenitus we have a more amiable picture. He aspired to excel in mathematics, astronomy, architecture, sculpture, painting and music. He was however really quite human, and would only transact public business with the help of his youngest daughter Agatha, who sat by his knee, read the reports of his ministers, and told him what to minute on them in purple ink. His book on administration is largely occupied with diplomatic devices for preventing foreign sovereigns from getting copies made of the crowns, robes, purple boots, and other Imperial paraphernalia. They were to be told, for example, that these objects were inhabited by powerful genii, who would not respect the wearer unless worn according to the mystic rules of Court ceremonial. He mentions the sad end of Leo IV, who, having put on the wrong crown, died of brain fever. Constantine, however, was no fool. He knew the meaning of prestige in a world where the power of mind expressed itself through magic, not mathematics.

The only other Basilian worthy of mention is Basil the Bulgar-slayer (Bulgaroktonos), the hero of all modern Greece. By a series of campaigns and with cold-blooded cruelty he broke the rising Bulgar power in Eastern Europe, and reasserted the Imperial rule as far as the Adriatic. By so doing he destroyed a bulwark that might have held back the Latin raiders. He was buried in the chapel of the Hebdomon Palace, which was formerly identified with the Porphyrogenitus Palace, but is now known to have stood on the Marmara, at Makrikeui, two miles outside the walls. Two centuries later the Palæologi reoccupied it, during the ejection of the Latins, and found among the ruins his tomb recently violated but still containing his embalmed body. Some robber had taken the sceptre from the hand of the stern old warrior, and replaced it by a shepherd's pipe. But it was too late then to remind the Byzantine Emperors that the shepherd's pipe was as " good magic " for a monarch as the mystic sceptre.

By this time the wealth of the Empire consisted, indeed, mainly of middleman-profits accumulated in commerce. Industry and agriculture, dependent on slave-labour, were dead or dying under extortion, in depopulated provinces. The Basilian dynasty died out in an epileptic, Michael, a Paphlagonian soldier who reached the purple by way of an intrigue with the Empress Zoe, wife of Romanus III (1028–1034). He was deposed and followed by a " Monstrous Regiment of Women," the joint rule of Zoe and Theodora, with the assistance of Constantine X (Monomachus) the third husband of the reprobate Zoe.

Finally, under Michael VI, a bureaucrat, the army at last revolted, and raised the general Isaac Comnenus to the purple. He reigned only two years, and then retired to the Studium Monastery. The grim old soldier came into collision with the

monks ; and especially with the Patriarch, who proclaimed himself the Emperor's equal. " I made him and can unmake him ! "
was his war-cry. The Patriarch's appearance, however, in the
veritable Imperial boots of purple led to his arrest and banishment
by the Varangian Guard. Isaac could deal with the priests ;
but the cleansing of the Palace was beyond him.

But we must now see something of this Palace that ruined an
Empire. As we walk southward inside the wall, towards a mosque,
Aivas Effendi, or proceed up a flight of steps behind the Church
of St. Mary Blachernæ, we pass through the remains of the
northern wall of the Blachernæ citadel or palace precinct. The
fragments of massive ruins in the outer city wall on our right
(the so-called Tower of Anemas) are all that remains of the
magnificent palace itself. Until the site is cleared and excavated,
we can only imagine what it once was like from the impression it
made upon travellers such as Luitprand and Benjamin of
Toledo. Here the later Emperors passed their luxurious lives,
in an ever-increasing seclusion : on one side the city mob held at
bay by the palace walls ; on the other the comparatively tame
boars and bulls of the kunegetion or hunting-park outside the
walls. Of this great game-preserve Niketas writes bitterly,
" The game wardens, who guard the mountains and the forests
for the Emperor's hunting as carefully as the angels guard the
gate of Paradise, threaten to kill any official who orders timber
to be cut for the fleet ! "

It is an ideal site for a palace ; looking out one way over the
hunting-park, and the other over the city—a vista of domes and
towers—between the Golden Horn and the Marmara. Convenient
also ; for in this wooded country at their gates the Emperors
always held the " key of the fields," while they could keep an
equally close watch on the Blachernæ Gate, the " key of the
walls."

The city wall here is double, and the two lines are connected by transverse walls, which break up the space into vaulted
chambers. The chambers are connected by arches pierced in the
transverse walls, and divided into three floors, the lowest being
cellars, the upper lit by loopholes in the outer wall. Possibly
these cellars were used as prisons ; but to speak therefore of the
structure as the " Prison of Anemas " is as it were to entitle
Windsor Castle the Prison of Perkin Warbeck. Anemas was an
obscure and futile conspirator against Alexius Comnenus, and
owes his undue prominence to the space given him by Anna
Comnena, the historian princess. These cellars are now accessible

from inside. Formerly it was necessary to enter by a postern in the outer wall, in the angle made by the Tower of Anemas; and thence climb a ladder and crawl on all fours through a filthy hole, continuing until stopped by a grating in the pavement of the courtyard of the Aivas Effendi mosque, a grating which was used for the discharge of refuse. If this feat—which is better left to athletic archæologists—is safely accomplished, we may feel, like the learned Papoulos, that we are standing "with unutterable exaltation in the prison of the highborn Anemas." Or we may, if we prefer, identify this winding way with the "Ladder of Acheron" in Scott's "Count Robert of Paris," where the dainty Anna Comnena met the gallant Howard. But the substructures are half-filled with rubbish, a cesspit in fact, and until they are cleared we may from outside examine what the more visible "prisons" really are.

The inner wall is pierced throughout by a corridor, lit by loopholes on either side. This is the original city wall and the retaining wall of the Blachernæ terrace. At some unknown date it was strengthened by the outer wall and the transverse buttresses, probably when the terrace was piled higher inside and palace buildings erected upon it. We have here, then, the subterranean world of the original palace, similar to that which we see on the Palatine in Rome; where the parasites, slaves and retainers festered and swarmed, and from which now one now another child of fortune, such as Basil, emerged into the splendours of the upper stories.

THE ANGELO TOWER AND COMNENI

Outside these substructures there are twin towers, that to the south known as the Isaac Angelo Tower, that to the north as the Anemas Tower. Neither of these names have any historical importance. Isaac Angelo was one of the later Comneni; and an inscription with his name is to be seen in the tower; but it means little, since it is, in any case, a hurried and haphazard construction. The projecting pillars built into the wall carried balconies overlooking the open country, and the upper story was obviously a belvedere of the palace towards the end of our epoch. In the Anemas Tower we see one of the fortified stairways leading from the palace to outside the walls. The more regular structure noticeable here, of squared stone and brick laid in courses, places the date at least as far back as the Basilian epoch, when the city was still comparatively secure from outside attack. Later this pleasure-portal was built up and converted into a bastion.

From the tops of the twin towers we can survey much that reminds us of the decline of the Byzantine Empire, and of its fall at the Latin conquest. Looking southward, it is not difficult to detect the line of the old wall, of which some ruins remain. It runs straight across to the ruins of the Porphyrogenitus Palace. But another line of wall, also marked by ruins, returns from inside the Porphyrogenitus Palace, at first in a more easterly direction to a point now marked by a fountain, and then westward again, to join the Prison of Anemas. The space thus enclosed, on the spur of the Sixth Hill, was the precinct of the palace. So we can see that the palace buildings originally abutted on the city wall for all this part of its length. Splendid it must have looked, with its colonnades and balconies and its pyramidal pavilion piled above the grim wall and moat. An idea of it may be obtained from the bird's-eye view on p. 126.

As the Empire declined, and the enemy closed in, this position became too exposed. And for this reason we find Manuel Comnenus throwing out a new wall, in the wide bend south of where we stand.

The section of this wall in the salient nearest to us is a still later structure, and belongs to the last period of all, that between the Latin and Turkish conquests. Its small square towers and fashion of construction, if we compare them with the great circular towers and the wall 15 feet thick of Comnenus, mark it as built by the Palæologus dynasty.

Looking now northward, back over the Leonine and Heraclian Walls, from our eyrie on the Comnenian Tower of Isaac Angelo, we can review the first scene in the last act of the Byzantine drama.

The Byzantine ruling class were by now living laxly and luxuriously, leaving all fighting to the army. The demoralization of their art and architecture is obvious. Music alone of the arts seems to flourish better in surroundings of aristocracy than of democracy. Vice is less deadly to music than vulgarity. The sacred music of the Byzantines, which is preserved for us in the noble choirs and chants of the Russian Church, excited a more spiritual admiration in travellers of this period than the paintings and pageants of the contemporary graphic and plastic arts. The invisible organs that perpetually filled the chambers of the palace with soft music may have been trying at times. But they must have been less tiresome than the golden plane tree, whereon innumerable jewelled birds twittered and fluttered, or the vulture that screamed and flapped its wings over the royal gate, or the golden lions that reared up and roared on either side of the throne. Yet on such toys were the great talents of Leo the Mathematician and John the Grammarian expended. However, they served to please simple provincials like Luitprand, who came in 948 with a present of eunuchs from Verdun. Even so did the Turk in " Eothen " marvel at the mechanical wonders of the West, and exclaim, " Whirr—whirr—all by wheels ! whizz—whizz—all by steam ! "

But it would be as unfair to judge of Byzantine art by the Blachernæ as of ours by Buckingham Palace. There are frescoes of this period still in Constantinople ; although none, so far as I know, nearer then Mount Athos are on view. They combine a realistic technique with a taste for ugly imaginings. Their favourite subject, the tortures of the damned, does not imply a cruelty of character ; for a people that paints cruelties *in terrorem* is less likely to inflict them. It was a lightning-artist turn in this *genre* on the part of the missionary Methodius that frightened the Bulgars into submission. Again in illuminated manuscripts Byzantine art set a standard never surpassed. But, thanks to the Crusaders, in order to see specimens of this art we have to go as far afield from Constantinople as the works of St. Gregory Nazianzen, in the Library of Paris, or the Menologium of Basil I in the Vatican. In the South Kensington Museum there are some beautiful ivory reliefs ; while the typical jewellery of the East, the large round flat earrings, and its ornaments, feathers, fans, etc., are borrowed from Byzantine models. In mosaics, however, was its supreme achievement ; and one of the best examples is to be seen in the Church of St. Saviour in the Country, which is close by us, within the wall. The church therefore can be conveniently dealt with here.

THE MOSAICS

St. Saviour's stands in the low ground behind the wall south of the Porphyrogenitus Palace. Its Greek name was Khora, its Turkish Kakhrieh. It was first built—at a safe distance from the town—as a shrine for the martyrs of Diocletian's persecution. Justinian rebuilt it with some splendour. But the present church dates from the period of the Comneni, when the Bulgar princess Mary Dukaina reconstructed it. Mary married her daughter Irene to Alexius I, Comnenus—of whom more anon—and was herself as good as she was beautiful. The church thus forms a lovely memorial of a lovable woman. In plan it exemplifies the latest development of the Byzantine style. It is almost square.

The lateral thrust of the dome is met by the device—then novel—
of setting it upon a drum.   Eight of the sixteen windows have
been closed.   The chapels adjoining were built later, under the
Palæologi.   The lower walls are still sheathed with marble slabs
in a variety of colours and designs, a decorative feature of
Byzantine architecture surviving scarcely anywhere else.   But the
mosaics are the glory of the church, and have gained it the name
by which it is known, the " Mosaic Mosque."   Within the church
they are obscured by whitewash ; but, oddly enough, outside
they have been left untouched, and the Moslem imams take a pride
in their beauty.   In the outer porch, exo-narthex, they have been
badly damaged ; but in the inner porch they can be seen in their
pristine brilliance.   In date they are probably all of the last
period, that of the Palæologi.   The lifelike forms, the flowing
draperies and harmonious grouping reveal a new departure.   The
old convention of a rigid religious symbolism has been replaced
by a free search after beauty.   Whether the change was due to a
new Greek inspiration, or was a concession to Italian influences,
matters little.   It was a new birth in Byzantine pictorial art,
just before the destruction of the city brought ancient convention
and new inspiration to a common end.

These mosaics reveal to us a living art lost to the world,
through Latin and Ottoman looters—a new life of more value than
most ancient objects of art or *vertu*.

In the outer porch is Christ Pantokrator (All-powerful) with a
cruciferous nimbus, the left hand holding the Gospels, the right
hand giving a benediction.   Above on the right is the Miracle of
the Loaves and Fishes ; and on the left, the Marriage at Cana.
This is the conventional choice of subjects symbolizing the
Eucharist.   The other subjects in this porch deal with the
Nativity and early life.   The Massacre of the Innocents, unfortunately damaged, is particularly realistic.

In the inner porch over the central portal we have again
Christ in benediction, and the mosaic is dated for us by a portrait
of Theodore the Metochite, who first restored the church (1321).
He wears a huge spreading striped cap, a mark of favour from
Andronicus II.   We find this same shape of cap among the
costumes of the Ottoman Court ; which shows us how far, even
in detail, the Turkish regime reproduced that of the Byzantine.
Theodore on his knees is presenting a model of the church.   On
either side are portraits of St. Peter and St. Paul.   These must
have become objects of suspicion to the Moslem ; for they are
partly concealed.   This porch is concerned with the history of

the Virgin. Joachim and Anna are seen with their fair-haired child. The Virgin, with other girls, receives skeins for tapestries. Her skeins turn to imperial purple at her touch, as evidence of her high destiny. This last is illustrative of the character of this art, wherein religious feeling is finding its expression in a reproduction of the life of the day. Thus another, the Healing of the Sick, is a scene such as daily took place in the porches of the hospitals, which were the pride of Byzantine civilization.

In all these mosaics the expressions are lifelike, and have the plaintive melancholy of an art that knew itself, alone, to be alive in a dying age.

Inside the southern dome is another Christ in benediction, surrounded by the thirty-nine Patriarchs, according to the genealogy in St. Luke.

In the four pendentives are four healing miracles—Peter's wife's mother, the two blind men, the dumb and blind demoniac, and the woman with the issue of blood.

In the northern dome the Virgin holds an infant Christ, in a medallion, and around her, in two rows, are his twenty-seven Hebrew progenitors.

Inside, towards the apse, there is, under the whitewash, a colossal Christ on the left and a Virgin on the right. These mosaics were cleared for the inspection of Kaiser Wilhelm II, and afterwards re-whitewashed.

The church was not converted into a mosque until 1511. In the eighteenth century it fell almost into ruins. It was restored in 1875 by Sultan Abdul-Aziz; and again, in 1889, by Abdul-Hamid for the benefit of the German Emperor. It would be a fine undertaking for the Turkish Republic to restore it wholly to view.

We return to our historical survey from the Tower. After a period of confusion there emerged a ruler, Alexius Comnenus. In 1081, when Nicephorus III was Emperor, Alexius had fled with other conspirators from the Palace—possibly by the very stairway where we are standing. There were horses waiting below, and an army of adventurers not far away. The walls remained impregnable to him; but not so the Byzantine army. German mercenaries in charge of the Charision Gate were bribed to admit his army of rebels, who at once dispersed to plunder. Alexius arrived almost alone in the Hippodrome, and the old Emperor Nicephorus with his faithful Varangians could easily have crushed him; but he lost his head, and took sanctuary in St. Sophia. Alexius entered the Palace; and the city was given over to the adventurers and the mob. The Slav mercenaries of the rebel Greek nobles, Comneni, Palæologi, and Dukai, then took a bloody revenge for the atrocities of Basil Bulgaroktonos.

The first mortal blow to the Empire of the Greeks was, thus, administered by the Greeks themselves, and on the suitable date of All Fools' Day. From this date the supremacy of Constantinople as a civic and commercial centre declined. Wealth alone remained the object of life ; and it was to be sought solely in the city. The sense of imperial prestige was lost. The Hippodrome and the Court might be as full of display as ever ; but the frontier fortifications were left to crumble, the naval and military organizations were neglected. Alexius might submit to the penance of sleeping on the floor with a stone pillow, and of living on dry bread and water for twenty days, but the Greek race after a thousand years is still doing a harder penance for his—and their own—treachery to the great trust. They had opened the way for the conquest by the Latins.

The Crusaders and Palæologi

The Latin-Normans had by now become the superiors of the Greeks in enterprise and endurance, and all but their equals in experience. As *conquistadors* they had failed in their persistent efforts to reach Constantinople by way of Macedonia, from their base in Italy. But they had better fortune as Crusaders, the leaders of immense hosts in a holy war against Islam. Dependent as they were upon chartering Venetian shipping, they could not transport by sea the vast hosts of the first Crusades. The only route, therefore, was by land through Constantinople. Although the slow advance of the Turkish power in Asia Minor was steadily absorbing strip after strip of the imperial territories, yet the Greeks of Constantinople looked upon the Latin allies of the Cross against the Crescent with distrust that soon became detestation. In fact they very much preferred the Turks, who were at any rate no nearer than Smyrna and with whom they were on tolerable terms, to having their capital occupied by these hordes of un-disciplined barbarians, who as heretics were more odious than infidels. The nephew of Alexius became a Mussulman, and his Prime Minister was a Turk. The Emperor found it far more difficult to maintain good diplomatic relations with the Crusaders than with the Caliph. The description left to us by Anna Comnena of the negotiations with the First Crusade, of which she was a witness as a girl, reads not unlike an account of a collision between one of the imperial bureaucracies of to-day with an army of Bolsheviks.

Princess Anna was a journalist of merit. Here is her " story " of the reception in the Blachernæ Palace of a deputation of the First Crusade—then encamped just outside the walls at the Cosmidion, a fortified monastery overlooking the Golden Horn. On the deputation were Peter the Hermit, Godfrey de Bouillon and Bohemond, as to whose manners Anna is very contemptuous. " They were indeed a mob and would in no way allow themselves to be represented through the Nine Ceremonial Introducers." The Emperor by much diplomacy manœuvred them into taking an oath of allegiance. But hardly was this accomplished when, as Anna writes : " One of their Counts had the impudence to seat himself beside the Emperor on the throne. The Emperor kept his temper and said nothing, knowing what these Latins were like." Count Baldwin stepping forward pulled him away by the hand " and reproved him." "And he made Baldwin no reply, but staring rudely at the Emperor, muttered something in his own gibberish which was interpreted to me as, ' Faith ! he is a boor to stay seated when better men stand.' The Emperor asked what he was saying, but on hearing made no remark—only when all was over he called up that boastful and unblushing Latin and asked him what was his lineage and where he came from. ' I,' said he, ' am a Frank of pure blood and good breeding. And where I come from there is a church at a cross-roads, and whoever wants to meet another in fair fight makes his peace with God and there abides the encounter. Long have I myself tarried there, but the man bold enough to brave me found I not yet.' " To which the Emperor replied : " If it is fighting that thou desirest thou shalt soon have it and to spare. But take my advice and do not get separated from thy fellows, but keep in the line, for I know how the Turks fight."

We can see how absurd to the accomplished Greek was the Frank with his ideas of one gentleman being as good as another, and of war being a sort of gentlemanly game. But Alexius was a man of the world and all might have been well if only all the Crusaders had been gentlemen, or under the control of gentlemen like Raymond of Toulouse, who alone refused Alexius homage and eventually alone won his goodwill. Unhappily they were for the most part either fanatics, who looked upon Orthodoxy as only a degree less damnable than Islam, or freebooters like Bohemond, to whom the Golden City seemed a more profitable bird in the hand than the Holy City far away across the wastes of Anatolia.

Nothing could better show the superior statecraft of the Byzantines than the success with which Alexius passed these disorderly hordes through his capital in 1017, and profited by their campaigns against the Turks, whether successful or otherwise. Thus, in the first campaign, in Asia Minor, Alexius left the hard fighting to the Crusaders, and employed his own army in consolidating the reconquest of Smyrna, Ephesus and the other Anatolian cities, which were returned to his Empire under the treaty. It was natural, on the other hand, that the Latins should have grudged their spoils to the Greeks ; and should have attributed to Greek treachery the destruction of the second expedition under Hugh of Vermandois and the Count of Toulouse. This last was a bitter blow to Western chivalry ; and all the more so because hundreds of noble ladies, who had accepted the escort of these armies so as to rejoin their husbands already ruling in Syrian cities, were thereby doomed to slavery in Eastern hareems. The regret of the Greeks was perfectly polite but perfunctory. For the second expedition had been passed through Constantinople with even greater difficulty than the first. The Italians, of whom it was mainly composed, had even refused to leave the city ; and when Alexius used force had then attempted to storm the Palace Precinct, with a want of success which we can the better understand after our survey of the Blachernæ fortifications.'

The complete rupture between Greeks and Latins came as the result of a dispute over Antioch, which was annexed by Bohemond. The Norman-Latins landed an invading army in Albania ; and the Empire was only saved because they could not challenge Byzantine command of the sea. In order to escape the cruisers of Alexius, Bohemond, when he wished to pass from the Syrian to the Albanian front, was compelled to sham death, and hide in a coffin, accompanied by a very defunct cock, to give a convincing atmosphere—a device that wrung an unwilling tribute to Latin resolution and resource from the contemptuous Anna Comnena.

We may look upon these early successes of the Greeks over the Latins with a sympathetic eye, not only because it was the success of sea power, but because it was due to our own ancestors. When the Norman-Latins invaded Albania and Macedonia from their bases in Sicily and South Italy, they were held in check by the Varangian Guard. A whole corps of this guard was composed of English, who, as we have already related, had sought in the Byzantine service the liberty lost at Senlac. Historians allow us to suppose that in one combat at least, on the Egnatian Way, the same combatants who had opposed one another at Senlac tried conclusions again, and with a different result. The failure of the descent of Bohemond upon the Empire—comparable to that of William on England—shows that the resources of a failing imperialism were still superior to those of an infant nation.

Alexius had staved off the Latin threat ; but it was at ruinous cost. Venice had an old connexion with Constantinople, and remained loyal to the Empire long after other Italians had asserted their independence. The Venetian merchants were as eager to share in its pretentious titles as in the profits of its trade. In order to secure the Venetian alliance and its maritime support against the Latins, Alexius was forced to permit them trading privileges that made them ruinous rivals of his own subjects. For instance, the rate of 10 per cent. on imports was reduced in their favour to 4 per cent., and arrests of Venetians had to be notified to their own colony. These privileges mark the first appearance of the exemptions and extra-territorial rights of foreigners in Constantinople, which were respected or revived by the Ottomans, and were only recently abolished in the Treaty of Lausanne. It speaks well for the tradition of law in Constantinople that a regime of privilege established a thousand years ago should only have been ended in our own time. It is also interesting to find the Comneni playing off one alien interest against another even as the later Sultans had to do. When preferential rates on customs duties threatened to throw the whole imperial trade into Venetian hands, Manuel Comnenus called in the Genoese and Pisans to compete with the Venetians. And it is noticeable that the quarter assigned to the Genoese was the Galata suburb, which afterwards became, under the Sultans, the foreign quarter. Greek trade would, even so, have gone under quicker than it did, but for the reservation of the Black Sea to the imperial flag, and of the whole grain trade to the imperial state. The ground also was retained in State ownership, and the shop rents therefrom continued to provide most of the imperial revenue. These three provisions may well give those of us who are politicians food for thought.

It was moreover overlooked during the wordy warfare at Lausanne that the regime of the Byzantine chrysobulum, of which the Ottoman capitulation was only the modern counterpart, in no way originated in any administrative incapacity of the Turks. It was an international institution, dating from the first establishment of foreign colonies in the capital ; and it was presumably found indispensable to its function as an international commercial centre. Alexius, that cunning and conciliatory diplomat, we

may feel sure would not have missed such a propitiatory present-
ment of his case as this, had it fallen to him to be negotiating
at Lausanne. It was indeed unlucky that Comnenus did not
hold what Comnenus held any better than Curzon did. For
these privileges granted to the Italian colonies, combined with
the Latin conquest of the commercial centres in Greece, Syria,
and Palestine, did more than anything else to hasten the end of
the Byzantine Empire.

The Second Crusade that descended upon Constantinople in
1147, in the reign of Manuel Comnenus, was a more respectable
enterprise than the several expeditions of the First Crusade. A
German army under Kaiser Conrad, a brother-in-law of the
Emperor, came first. Then a French army, under Louis VII.
Both came to grief in Asia Minor, mainly owing to their own fault,
but in part owing to the falsity of the Greeks. For their treachery
the Greeks, this time, had no excuse ; for, in spite of the incite-
ments of the Bishop of Langres against the heretics of Constantinople, Louis and the French commanders had followed the
good example of the Germans in respecting the capital and the
other imperial cities. Yet the Greeks provided guides who
misled them ; the flour was adulterated with chalk ; and the
Crusaders' bills were cashed in a depreciated currency specially
coined for the occasion. The extermination of these well-
equipped expeditions, of which the survivors only saved their
lives by embracing Islam, was a blow that Europe never forgave
to the Empire.

Delivered from the Second Crusade, Manuel succeeded in
restoring his authority over Dalmatia, and in thus threatening
the Venetian Republic itself. This encouraged him to take up
again the matter of the privileges of the turbulent and predominant Venetian colony. A faction fight of Venetians against
Lombards gave him his opportunity. He ordered all Venetians
to confine themselves to their own quarter and to take the oath
of allegiance. Some complied ; but a riot broke out again,
during which the Lombard warehouses were sacked. Manuel
then put the whole Venetian colony under arrest, and sequestrated
its property. Venice retorted by sending a force, in 1172, that
reconquered Dalmatia, and a fleet that occupied the Greek Islands.
But this fleet, decimated by pestilence, was destroyed by the
Byzantine galleys ; so that a Venetian embassy had to be sent
to sue for peace. The conditions were not such as to induce the
Court to mitigate its usual arrogance towards foreign ambassadors;
and the Venetian envoy, Henry Dandolo, was to enjoy thirty

years later an opportunity of avenging petty slights, such as touchy diplomats must often since have envied. So ill received was the embassy, that the Venetians assassinated their Doge in disgust, and unsuccessfully besieged Ancona. But Manuel was by then engaged in Asia Minor, and peace eventually restored the *status quo ante bellum.*

In Asia Minor Manuel showed the same blindness to the real peril threatening his Empire, the steady growth of the Turkish population and prosperity. He broke down two useful bulwarks against them by attacking the Armenian kingdom of Cilicia and the Frankish principality of Antioch, and wasted strength on a futile expedition to Egypt. After ten years' peace with the Turks a successful campaign opened to him their capital, Koniah ; but he preferred to invite their Sultan, Kilidj Arslan, to Constantinople. Another ten years of peace followed, and then in 1176 he led an enormous force to total destruction at the hands of the Turks at Myriokephalon, a defile in Asia Minor. In 1180 he died, the last Emperor to attain a position of world-importance.

By breaking with the Venetians Manuel had created a competitor to the Greeks in sea-power. And this mistake he aggravated by disorganizing his own navy. Like our fleet in Elizabethan days, the Greek navy had been composed of a number of government ships at the capital and of local squadrons, maintained by other commercial centres. Manuel forced these local centres to contribute instead to the navy, and then neglected to defend them. Again, in place of organizing the army, as before, in strategic training camps, he billeted the troops out in cities, where their discipline was soon demoralized. It was an attempt to imitate the feudal system of Western Europe which, like subsequent " reforms " under the Sultans, only succeeded in disorganizing an existing system better adapted to the real conditions. The dispersed Byzantine garrisons degenerated into something not unlike the shop-keeping janissaries of the Ottoman regime.

Manuel's worthless successor, Alexius, was deposed by Andronicus ; a circumstance only of importance because the local Latins, who supported Alexius, were massacred by the Greek supporters of Andronicus. Gibbon relates :

" The Latins were slaughtered in their houses and on the streets ; their quarter was reduced to ashes ; their clergy burnt in the churches, and their sick in the hospitals ; and some estimate may be formed of the slain from the clemency which sold over four thousand Christians into perpetual slavery to the Turks. The priests and monks were loudest and most active in the destruction of the schismatics ; and they chaunted a thanksgiving when the head of a Roman Cardinal, the Pope's Legate, was fastened to the tail of a dog and dragged through the city."

It was, in fact, an early " Eastern atrocity," an eruption of racial and religious hatred, not without a political purpose. It is curious to read the comment of Saladin upon this " atrocity " in a letter to Nachir-Jedin-Illah of Bagdad : " Thus has Allah punished the so-called soldiers of the Faith. For this and many other benefits am I thankful to Allah ! "

From this time on the Greeks and Latins of Constantinople were at feud, and often engaged in bloody fighting. And the growing weakness of the Byzantine fleet allowed the Frankish pirates to ravage the Greek coasts with impunity.

The contempt into which the Court had fallen became evident when the Third Crusade, under Frederic Barbarossa, passed through. This expedition was the best equipped and best commanded of all ; and quickly overawed the opposition of the Emperor Isaac and his armies in Thrace. Barbarossa might easily have captured the city ; he was within striking distance, and his fleet of Genoese and Italian vessels was far superior to the Greeks. But he was content to exact a passage of the Dardanelles unmolested, forcing Isaac to take an oath publicly to observe the treaty. Isaac had to console himself with boasting in a letter to Saladin that he had at least delayed the Latins. Isaac Angelo was the type of Emperor for whose long life his enemies did ever pray. When besieged by Branas he pledged his plate with the churches to raise a defence loan ; but when Branas was defeated, he was not above reclaiming the plate without repaying the loan.

Under his successor, Alexius III, the sanctity of law, the foundation of imperial 'prestige was finally ruined. Alexius sent vessels into the Black Sea in 1195, nominally on a salvage expedition, but with secret orders to seize any vessels found. The Court profited largely from these piracies ; but the courts were besieged by ruined merchants clamouring in vain for justice. They even stood in rows with tapers in their hands along the Emperor's private passage to St. Sophia. But only the subjects of the Turkish Sultan of Koniah received any redress. The Sultan's energetic diplomacy not only secured them compensation, but forced Alexius himself to pay an annual tribute.

The Orthodox Church, although ready enough to make a stand in the interests of idolatry, would not intervene for an ideal of equity. For example, a banker Kelmodias was kidnapped by a gang of courtiers, and held to ransom. A delegation of merchants appealed in vain to the Patriarch, a brother of the Empress Euphrosyne. It was not until a mob assembled and threatened to throw him out of the window of his palace, that at last the Patriarch became convinced of the claims of justice, and the Court brigands were foiled. As neither person nor property in the city had now any security, the Italian colonies had no longer any commercial interest in upholding the Empire. And so at last came the ominous alliance between the Venetian sea-power and the Frankish land-power.

THE LATIN CONQUEST

When the Fourth Crusade assembled at Venice, it was found that they could not pay the extravagant cost of Venetian transport to Syria. But the alternative land-route through Asia Minor had been shown by the fate of the previous two Crusades to be hopeless, in view of Greek policy. The old Doge Dandolo accordingly proposed that they should pay expenses by capturing Zara on the Adriatic. This was done ; and the Venetians, who had still a claim outstanding against the Empire, for reparations under a treaty with Manuel, proposed, with the support of the Lombards and Belgians, and in spite of the opposition of the Pope and the French, to convert the Crusade into a plunder-raid upon Constantinople. Their pretext was the restoring of the deposed Isaac. In April 1203 the Fourth Crusade sailed from Zara, and disembarked on the Asiatic shore of the Bosphorus.

Only twenty imperial galleys were by this time fit for service. The Latins commanded the Straits and crossed to the European shore. They had become proficient in combined land and sea tactics, and the instant their transports drew up at the Bosphorus quays, the " brows " were dropped, and the cavalry, ready-mounted, dashed ashore, and drove the disconcerted defenders in rout behind the walls of Galata. The Golden Horn, from the citadel on Seraglio Point to the great flanking tower of the Galata fortifications, was closed with a chain, the remains of which can be seen in the Museum. But like other defences of Constantinople the chain must have been a symbolical rather than a material barrier, for it was easily broken by one of the heavy transports, armed with a ram and bearing the Aquila or Eagle. In later historians the " Aquila " has been interpreted as signifying that the transport was helped by the north wind or " aquilo." The Venetian fleet then entered the Horn.

Meanwhile the land-forces had occupied the Marmara end of the land-walls facing the Blachernæ Palace. They could not

invest the whole wall; and therefore chose this point, actually
the strongest for defence, induced by the same curious fascination
which tempted so many besiegers to attack the Blachernæ citadel
—only to their undoing. The golden domes gleaming above the
wall seem to have acted once again like the candle upon the moth.
Villehardouin, who saw it all, relates in his Norman French:

God wot it was a fine thing to see how that Constantinople having
three leagues of front across the land the whole host could not besiege but
one of its gates—et moult estoient perillosement que onque par tant poi
de gent ne furont assegiés tant de gent en nulle ville.

A double attack was delivered almost immediately. Archers
and crossbowmen in the fortified tops of the Venetian vessels
drove the few defenders from the single Sea Wall; while other
vessels, fitted with towers, came alongside and dropped draw-
bridges on to the parapet. The old Doge, in full armour, directed
the storming parties; which won the wall, but got into difficulties
in the narrow streets behind it. The city was practically taken,
when Dandolo was forced again to withdraw, in order to defend
the land-camp, which had been threatened in the meantime by
the failure of the land assault and by the Greek counter-attack in
that quarter.

Their land attack on the Leonine Wall was also successful at
first, the Crusaders getting a footing on the wall. But a charge
of English Varangians armed with battle-axes swept them off
again. It is pleasant to recall that even at this early date it fell
to us to strike a blow for civilization against barbarism. The
wall was cleared; and the defenders sallied out and deployed
outside. Had Alexius then led them straight against the
Crusaders' camp, the day would have been won. But he did not.
And either from cowardice or under compulsion from a cowardly
Court, he fled that night, bearing with him what treasure he could
hurriedly collect. In the hope of a peaceful compromise, Isaac
was, as hastily, restored, and the gates were opened to the
Latins.

But neither the old blind " Sursac " (Sieur Isaac), as Villehardouin calls him, nor his blackguardly son, Alexius IV, could
deal with so desperate a situation. They were in the power of
the Latins; and the payments they made to the leaders and the
provisions they supplied to the troops purchased them scarcely
any respite. The treasure left by Alexius III, the private fortune
of his dowager Empress, the imperial plate, even the Church plate,
were sacrificed; and still the Crusaders postponed their departure

in hopes of more. Dandolo, who alone could have unravelled the complication of claims as between the Venetians, the Crusaders and the Empire, was only waiting for a pretext to annex the city and partition the Empire. The Latins had been withdrawn to Galata, and their soldiery was only allowed to visit what is now " Stamboul " in small parties. But a collision was sooner or later inevitable. In August 1203, while Alexius [IV was away in Thrace, fighting Alexius III, some Flemish soldiers, who had been carousing with the Flemish merchants, began plundering the warehouses of the Turkish quarter. The Greeks drove them out, and pressed them so hard that they set fire to houses as they fled, in the hope of checking the pursuit. For two days and nights the fire raged right across the richest part of the city, from the Horn to the Marmara, and it but narrowly missed St. Sophia. An immense possession of public and private buildings was destroyed. In the result the whole Latin population left Stamboul for ever, and took refuge with the Crusaders in Galata.

After this calamity the Empire had no other resources left but to strip St. Sophia and other churches of their ornaments, and even of their shrines and reliquaries. And a further treaty was imposed upon Alexius, enforcing the acceptance of Papal supremacy by the Orthodox Church. A racial and religious revolt of the Greeks resulted, in January 1204. It was led by Alexius Dukas Murtzuphlos or the " beetle-browed." Alexius IV was strangled ; and Alexius V proceeded to prepare a desperate defiance of the Crusaders. He restored the confidence of the imperial troops by successful skirmishes that cut off the Crusaders from their supplies. He re-established order in the city, patrolling it himself, mace in hand. He repaired the walls, and reinforced the artillery on the Sea Walls, so as to prevent attacks by means of the flying bridges. He refilled the treasury by confiscating the private fortunes of all the treasury officials, the tax-farmers and the government contractors. Murtzuphlos, in a word, effected the beginnings of a Greek nationalist revival ; but of the Greeks of the capital, murderous enough in a mob, he could not make soldiers.

The Crusaders, meanwhile, were engaged in the congenial but contentious occupation of apportioning the plunder and partitioning the Empire—in anticipation. A secret treaty of partition was drawn up, its dispositions so ill-drafted and its delimitations so ill-described that it is as difficult now for modern historians to penetrate the true purpose of these French and Italian freebooters as it may be seven centuries hence for

historians to understand the real policy of the Foreign Offices in
those treaties partitioning Turkey, in which the ideals inspiring the
crusaders of our Great War were translated into terms of " Great
Britain obtains——", " France obtains——", " Italy obtains——"
Crusades that began by—

> in glorious Christian field
> Streaming the ensign of the Christian Cross
> Against black pagans, Turks and Saracens—

would appear all too often to end in this way.

By April 9 the Latin Crusaders had made things ready for
another assault. It was concentrated this time upon the Sea
Wall. But the artillery arrangements of Murtzuphlos prevented
the former boarding tactics ; and when the crusaders landed on
the quays, and tried to storm the Sea Walls with scaling ladders.
they were repulsed with heavy losses. The seamen were, however, as always, men of resource. They lashed vessels together,
and upon this foundation erected wooden works strong enough
to withstand the artillery of the city. From behind their shelter
other lines of shipping swept the wall with missiles. By these
tactics, and with the help of a strong north wind, they succeeded in driving the *Pelerine* and the *Paradise* alongside one
tower, and in throwing a party of Venetians and Crusaders over
a boarding-bridge into it. An " eye-witness," Monokes, Bishop
of Tournay, describes the attack—

> Mais anchois y eut grant assaut
> Car li mur ierent fort et haut
> Par devers la mer furent pris
> Et desbarete et soupris.

Before the defenders could rally, four towers had been seized,
a gate thrown open, and the knights were landing their horses.
Dandolo himself, then eighty years of age, bore the banner of
St. Mark up the breach. At this critical moment the reserves
of Murtzuphlos in his camp at the Monastery of Pantepoptes
refused to counter-attack, and retired on the Bucoleon. The
Crusaders seized the Blachernæ citadel, and the city was won.
Even so the Crusaders thought it necessary to burn a large part
of what was left of the city, to obviate the inconveniences of
street-fighting. They might have spared it. The Greeks were
cowed, and Murtzuphlos fled.

Should we wish later to visit the place where the entry was
made, we shall find it near the tower in the wall to the east
of Yeni Aya Kapou, in the Petrion citadel, now the Phanar,

which was the space enclosed between the two walls, the only place on the sea-front where the wall is double. The chroniclers say it was a tower of the Petrion that was taken, and if you look at the base of the walls between Yeni Aya Kapou and Aya Kapou, you can see water-worn blocks of stone, showing that here the harbour came right up to the walls. So that, at this spot, the Venetian ships could have got near enough to throw bridges on to the parapet.

The capture of the city was followed by scenes of sacrilege and outrage, contrasted by the Greeks with the clemency shown by Mussulmans in their conquests. The desecration of shrines and the violation of nuns shocked a civilization accustomed to the usual horrors of a sack. This all the more that the offenders were Crusaders, bound by their oath to live in chastity and abstinence, and to shed no Christian blood. Pope Innocent III, who is not free from suspicion of complicity in the campaign, was horrified by excesses which he recognized defeated his policy, the union of the Churches. The Latin clergy were among the most rapacious of the robbers, and their convents everywhere eager receivers of stolen goods. Well might Pope Innocent deplore " that the Greek Church, afflicted by such persecution, would scorn to re-enter into obedience to the Holy See—would see in the Latins workers of betrayal and works of darkness, and would deservedly detest them as worse than dogs."

Niketas the chronicler leaves us a picture of his experiences: his palace guarded by a friendly Venetian of the colony disguised as a Crusader—then five days of terror—then the household escaping on foot through the still burning streets, disguised as poor refugees, the younger women, with blackened faces and bundled in old clothes, huddled in the middle (even as I have myself seen refugee families hurrying through the streets of Galata). In spite of all precaution, a young girl of noble family is carried off. Niketas, with great courage, follows her captor, and appeals to all Latins whom he meets. He is fortunate enough in the end to secure the help of a friendly Crusader, who rescues her. He reads it as the end of the world and something unbelievable; but we need not go back to chroniclers of seven centuries ago to learn that civilization, of itself, affords no security.

It was a misfortune that the savagery of the Crusaders drove from Constantinople the Court and the Greek upper class. Had the aristocracy and bureaucracy remained, to compromise themselves by a coalition with the alien and infidel invader—even as they did during our more humane occupation which put an end to the Ottoman Empire, the city might have made a new beginning as capital of a Greek progressive State—even as it may now become the capital of a progressive Turkish nation. For the imperial idea that races and religions could live together in unity had broke down then, as it has again recently, and as hopelessly. The Flemish, Italian, French and German partners in the capital of Christian civilization had been cheated again and again by the Greek managing directors. So they liquidated the enterprise, and realized such assets as they could for the benefit of their own national group. And these assets were worth having. The new Belgian Emperor, the Belgian Baldwin, estimated that the total spoil dispersed was greater than the whole wealth of the rest of Europe. Three hundred thousand marks were divided locally—of which the Venetians received a half—and a further fifty thousand as freight. Writers console themselves with the reflection that what survived of the works of art, of the books and experts, was scattered over Europe, and served to inspire the Western Renascence of art and learning. But, had Constantinople not been destroyed, there might well have been another Greek Renascence of art and learning ; and the question may be left open as to which would have proved the greater gain.

After this liquidation of the Empire, Constantinople could obviously only revive again as the capital of a united Greek nation. The Greek race had still time to reconstruct its State, recruit its military strength, and recover its commercial stability, profiting by the commanding position of the city between Europe and Asia. For a time indeed the loss of the capital did prove as good a purgative to the Greeks as it has done in our own time to the Turks. The audacious adventure of little Theodore Lascaris in the mountains of Bithynia suggests a national movement as lively as the Turkish Renascence under Mustapha Kemal. If you want an interesting example of how history recreates itself and yet never repeats itself compare what you can read of the Greek national Renascence with what you remember of the Turkish. You will see that the reason the Greeks failed and the Turks may succeed is the different attitude of the two nations to Constantinople. The Greeks, driven from Constantinople, remained under the influence of dynastic disputes which divided them into three new States, the " Empires " of Trebizond, of Nicæa, and Epirus. The geographical split might have been avoided, but for the political ambitions of the Court cliques surrounding different claimants to the throne. None of these three areas could get clear of Constantinople. No sooner did the Nicæan Empire begin to prevail, than the *émigré* aristocracy and bureaucracy there resident, in place of concentrating upon the reconstruction of the State, worked only for the reconquest of the capital and of their own privileged position. You see the indomitable little Lascaris, beset on every side, dashing hither and thither; at one time meeting the Latin Emperor Henry in the field, and forcing him to make terms; at another running a tilt against Khaikosrou, the Seljouk Sultan. The Sultan unhorsed him and pinned him with his lance, but Lascaris equalized matters by slashing the legs of the Sultan's horse, bringing him to the ground, and running him through. The gallant little " Emperor " could claim a large share of his little " Empire's " success in asserting its claim to the national capital, and its right to be considered the Greek national government. But when, after sixty years, the Empire of Nicæa became the Greek Empire at Constantinople, the first thing the reinstated ruling class did was to exterminate the sturdy Greek mountaineers of Bithynia, to whom they had owed their restoration.

Meantime, for half a century, the Latin Empire held sway at Constantinople. And the period is only important because it showed how futile was the Crusaders' dream that they could rebuild a Christian Eastern Empire on a foundation of Western feudalism. The Latin Empire was never more than a foreign occupation, living on such financial and military support as it could borrow from the West. The provincial administration of the feudal freebooters, who gathered like vultures round the carcase, was ruinous. Everywhere little Courts sprang up, wasting the country in perpetual rivalry. In the city itself the Latins showed their administrative incompetence. Their neglect of the public services and of the sanitary system alone made what remained of the city uninhabitable. Their way of living disgusted the Greeks. Having plundered everything portable or pawnable in the city, the Latins were reduced to stripping the copper roofs off the public buildings and to melting down the bronze ornaments in order to make a currency. Soon the only trade left to the sometime commercial centre of the civilized world was the export of its relics, which were sold or given in security for loans. The Baldwins, the Flemish Emperors, spent most of their time abroad, trying to raise loans or levies, at first with the fruitful assistance of Pope Gregory IX. But at last Baldwin II was reduced to pledging his only son to the Venetian bankers ; while what was left of Constantinople became in effect a Venetian protectorate. Those who may still believe to-day that Constantinople could be made an international capital, combining the philanthropic ideals of the League of Nations and the financial interests of Big Business, cannot do better than study the failure that resulted from this association of Frankish crusaders and Italian capitalists.

The Greek Reconquest

The failure of the Latins left the empty shell of the city open for the occupation of whichever local national community came to the top in the welter of paltry principalities and imperial pretenders into which the Empire had dissolved. And it became clear that the " Empire of Nicæa " was to win. Its young prince, Michael Palæologus, one of the inner clique of the ruling clans of Constantinople, had come to the front during the campaigns which secured for the Nicæan "Empire" control of the European territories of the former Byzantine Empire. He was a worthy representative of the qualities that distinguished the Byzantine ruling class. His charm of manner and candour of mind inspired confidence in a character that was wholly corrupt and false. The first story told of him is characteristic. He was suspected, on good grounds, of treason, and ordered to submit to the ordeal by fire, which meant holding a red-hot ball without becoming burnt. This he humbly declined, saying he would submit to the ordeal by battle, but was too great a sinner in other respects to be able to hope that Heaven would work a miracle for him in this one small matter. The Bishop of Philadelphia reproved his want of faith. Upon which Michael observed : " Holy father, would I were as strong as thou art in faith and innocence ! But take thou the ball from the furnace in thy hands and I will receive it from them in dutiful submission ! " The subtle Greeks were of course delighted at this diplomatic exposure of the inaptness and ineffectiveness of Western institutions—when imposed upon the Greek intellect.

In 1259 Michael was raised upon a shield—an adoption of a Frankish coronation ceremony singular in the circumstances—though the oath which he took to abdicate when the legitimate heir should attain his majority was wholly Byzantine in its character. For he was a representative Byzantine Greek ; and there is no doubt that his usurpation of the throne, as the result of the intrigues that surrounded the minority of John IV, who was the legitimate Lascaris, was a misfortune.

The administration of the later Lascaris Emperors of Nicæa had been distinguished by a national rather than an imperialistic motive. They had been the fathers of their people, had husbanded the resources of the State, had restored agriculture, and even to some extent industry. When the Empress of John III (Vatiscos) complained that she had no crown, John replied that he would see about it—if she would start a poultry farm. And before he died he presented her with a crown out of the proceeds of the sale of the eggs.

But Michael VIII, the first of the Palæologi, inaugurated a more imperial rule. He recovered Constantinople; but he wasted the revenues in buying the allegiance of the noble families and of certain factions. With disastrous shortsightedness he consumed his armies in attempts to subdue the prosperous independent Greek communities.

His recovery of that sucked orange, Constantinople, proved an easy matter. Baldwin II was at the end of his borrowed resources and the Venetians were engaged in a desperate fight with the Genoese for supremacy at sea. By 1260 Michael was in Thrace, outside the walls. He was in touch with the Greeks who had settled there, on the imperial hunting-ground, and who had, for their own protection, formed a militia of " Voluntaries." He was also in treaty with the Genoese; who had in the meantime repudiated the obligation imposed upon them and on the Venetians in 1238, by Gregory IX, never to ally themselves with Greeks against Latins. Michael promised them a monopoly of the Black Sea trade, and the property and old privileges of the Venetians at Constantinople. The Genoese, in fact, to cite a recent parallel, played the same rôle in the recovery of Constantinople by the Greeks from the Latins and Venetians, and for the same reasons, as the French played in its recent recovery by the Turkish national State, from the Greeks and British.

Michael in this way held all three keys to the capital—an army, organized support from the local Greeks, and command of the sea. The Venetian fleet embarked most of the garrison, and went off into the Black Sea; nominally to retake Daphnusia, actually to avoid being caught by the superior Genoese fleet. The Latins, moreover, trusting to the fact that the Greek army under Strategopoulos was too small and ill-equipped to storm the walls, even neglected to man them adequately. Strategopoulos and Koutrizakes, the leader of the Voluntaries, scaled the outer wall, crawled under the inner wall through one of the subterranean sally-ports that had fallen into disuse as a drain, and approaching the Gate of Pege from inside, broke down the wall that blocked it. It was not the first or the last time that a sewer, actual or moral, proved the road to imperial power in Constantinople. The army entered, and at dawn defeated the Latin garrison which was hurrying up from the Palace. Baldwin fled to Greece, in such haste that his crown, sceptre, and sword were left on the quay. The Greeks, or a mere handful of them, for most of them had gone off pillaging, arrived before the Bucoleon Palace. The Latins and Venetians that remained were still numerous enough to have overpowered them. But the Greeks began to set their houses on fire, while leaving their escape to the shipping open. A truce was concluded, which permitted a peaceful evacuation by the whole Latin population.

Michael Palæologus, who had been engaged in collecting troops for a siege, was informed that the surprise had been successful; and returning, he made his solemn entry through the Golden Gate, walking behind a sacred picture of the Virgin. He as solemnly inaugurated the dynasty of the Palæologi by blinding the rightful Lascaris, John IV, a little boy of eight; claiming credit for himself because the operation was performed after the most humane of the six recognized methods. His next task was to seek to restore the former splendours of the capital. But this was more difficult, and beyond the strength of the new national State. The effort, together with the peculations of the returned *émigrés*, soon reduced the provinces and the peasantry again to ruin and revolt. Historians, following the Court chroniclers, tell us that " the recovery of Constantinople restored the Greek nation to the position of a first-class power." But the depressing story of the reactionary rule of the Palæologi shows on every page that Constantinople was proving the ruin of the renascent Greek race. Poor little John Lascaris, blinded and in bondage at Nicæa, was the true type of the Greek nation. The rascally Michael Palæologus, ravaging from the Blachernæ Palace, was equally the true type of the Greek Empire. With his coming to Constantinople the future of the Greek nation passed from it to Athens.

One monument of Michael still survives: the part of the wall south of where we stand. Its small square stones date it from the Palæologi. He also ran an outer entrenchment across outside the Great Wall, to guard against surprises. With a fleet manned mainly by " Gasmouls " (Græco-Latin cross-breeds), he recovered command of the narrow seas; and the "Turco-pouls," Græco-Turk hybrids, held a similarly prominent position in his army. From among the soldiery, it is noticeable, the pure Greek element disappears. We find Michael unhorsing his excellent Greek cavalry in order to mount Alan mercenaries, and losing a battle against the Turks as a consequence; and he revived the law which prohibited Greeks who paid taxes from bearing arms. It would seem that, once back in Constantinople, the Emperors no longer dared to allow their subjects any training in arms.

"The century and a half"—to quote Finlay—"during which the Empire of Constantinople was ruled with despotic sway by the dynasty of Palæologus is the most degraded portion of the national annals. Literary taste, political honesty, patriotic feeling, military honour, civil liberty, and judicial purity, seem all to have abandoned the Greek race, and public opinion would in all probability have had no existence had not the Greek Church placed itself in opposition to the imperial government and promoted a spirit of partisanship on ecclesiastical questions." The Emperors, being no longer able to rely on the Greek nation, were forced to seek support abroad, and pay for it with the surrender of Greek interests and ideals. The first of these surrenders was the concession by Michael to Pope Gregory of the Union of the Latin and Greek Churches in 1274. The achievement of unity in the Church, by the submission of the Orthodox Patriarch to Papal discipline and dogma, might at first sight seem a gain to the Christian cause. But it was not so. After the failure of the Crusades, the defence of the Christian Church in eastern Europe and western Asia against the creed of Islam depended upon the development of a Greek nation; and the Orthodox Church was the only institution upon which the national ideal could concentrate. Every other expression of this ideal was frustrated by the dynastic wars or alliances with national enemies, and by internal strife. When the Orthodox Church submitted, many Greeks left the city for the national principalities of Achaia and Trebizond rather than accept the united Church.

Yet another of the payments made by Michael in order to prop the Empire was the concession, fatal to national interests, of further trade privileges to the Italian colonies. He played off the Genoese against the Venetians, even as the Sultans in the days of their decline played off the French against the English, and he bought the protection of both against the Latins and even against the Pope, who in reprisal excommunicated the Genoese, but did not dare to do the same to the Venetians. Under these treaties the Italians were exempted from revenue control, and allowed " free port " privileges for their factories, as well as judicial " extra-territoriality." These constituted complete " capitulations," equivalent to those that survived to our day. The monopoly of the internal as well as of the external trade of the Empire passed into Italian hands. The Greek cities, commercial centres before the Italian cities existed, found themselves prohibited from trading one with another, except through foreigners. The recovery of Constantinople, so far from reviving Greek commerce in the city, killed it.

In industry it was the same story. The taxation imposed with the object of supporting the parasitic population, from the Emperor down to the meanest slave, had before long annihilated the infant industries born during the Nicæan national regime.

Andronicus II (1282–1328), who succeeded Michael, made an attempt to reform the Church, with the help of the Patriarch Athanasius, a hermit of austere reputation. Bishops who passed their time in political intrigues were ordered back to their Sees. Monks who, as the confessors of noble families, ambled on sleek mules from palace to palace wangling and wire-pulling, were shipped off to monasteries ; and the corrupt connexions between Church and Court were broken. Great was the to-do in Constantinople. But to a corrupt government any reform is the worst of menaces. Andronicus, fearing an increase in ecclesiastical authority, forced Athanasius to resign after four years in office. Before he departed to his monastery, Athanasius took an unkind revenge. He drew up with much care a " curse." This he sealed up in a jar, with his patriarchal seal on the lid to keep it in, like a " Djinn," and hid it among the carvings over one of the galleries of St. Sophia. Years later, it was found by some small boys who were pigeon-hunting. They broke the seal, and let out the curse. The result was a panic in the city. Messengers were sent post-haste to the aged Athanasius in his monastery, and he generously called the curse off. But it worked all the same. The attempt at reform had clearly failed, and exultation over the recovery of Constantinople henceforward changed to apprehension over an impending catastrophe. To use a modern formula, we might say that public opinion had realized that with the lost opportunity had vanished the last chance of constitutional reform and of a more democratic regime. To Constantinople of the thirteenth century it was clear that the "curse" of Athanasius could not be got back again into the jar.

The first calamity was the descent upon the city of the Catalan Free Company, a Spanish association of Western adventurers, in character more like the buccaneers of a later age than like the feudal Crusaders or freebooting conquistadors. Their elected leader was a German, Richard Blum, who blossomed out as Roget de Flor, and started in a small way as a pirate. In 1303, having offered his services to the Emperor, he arrived at Constantinople with a fleet and a small army for a campaign against the Turks. The Turks had by this time advanced almost to the Straits. There followed the usual troubles, due to Greek treachery and Latin turbulence. The Companions lived at free quarters on the Greeks and levied contributions ; and soon Roget was scheming to set up a Spanish " sphere of influence " in Asia Minor. In vain Constantinople was laid under contribution to pay his extortionate demands and get rid of him. The Spaniards fortified themselves in Gallipoli, and proceeded to pay themselves. The Emperor did not mend matters by having Roget de Flor assassinated in the apartments of the Empress and his escort of three hundred cavalry exterminated by the Alan guard. Further, the mission of protest sent by the Catalans under safe conduct from Andronicus was murdered by Greeks at Rodosto, and all the Spaniards in Constantinople were massacred. After which the Catalans, in alliance with the Turks, waged a war of extermination on the Greeks right up to the walls. Those Greeks who escaped the sword were sold as slaves to the Turks. Finally, in 1310, the Catalans withdrew, ravaging Thrace as they went, and entered the service of the Duke of Athens. They left Constantinople a citadel in a desert.

Such calamities, combined with the fact that the Greek nation was dispersed under various governments, left the Empire no match even for its neighbouring enemies. None the less it proceeded to lapse into bitter civil wars. They began between Andronicus II and his son Andronicus III, who besieged Constantinople in 1328. They continued between the second Andronicus' premier, Cantacuzenes, and his widow Anne, who was regent for John V, then a minor ; and they concluded with John's final success in 1355.

In the intervals of civil war the dominant dynasty found time to attend to the independent Greek colonies, in the hope of annexing them to the moribund Empire. The Greek Emperors paid their Turkish mercenaries in slaves, delivering their own Greek subjects to be carried off to Asia Minor to strengthen the Turkish State. Even the Albanian and Epirot mountaineers were raided and reduced to slavery by Turks in the pay of the Greek Emperor. Under Cantacuzene the army consisted principally of these Turkish mercenaries, and to satisfy them he embezzled the contributions sent by orthodox Russians for the repair of St. Sophia, damaged in the earthquake of 1346. When this was exhausted, he robbed the churches of their plate. The Turks, also, were welcomed as residents in the city, and given the usual privileges. And all this at a time when the Turkish advance in Asia Minor had brought their armies right up to the Straits, and absorbed the whole Greek race upon that shore, and at a time when their simultaneous ravages in Thrace had still further reduced the remnants of the Greek population in Europe.

The Porphyrogenitus Palace and the Greek Empire

Our excursus into history has been a long one. And as the Palace of Porphyrogenitus occupied a prominent place in these last gloomy annals, let us, for a change, move southward and inspect its ruins.

There is somewhat more to be seen of this most important of Byzantine palaces than we found on the bare Blachernæ site. But there is very little to be said about it. It is not even known for certain who built it. The Turkish name, Tekfour Serai, means no more than The Crowned One's Palace ; although the Greeks, with their customary polemical ingenuity, wish to derive Tekfour from τοῦ κυρίου. Its identification with the Palace of Porphyrogenitus, otherwise the Palace of Constantine, seems moderately certain ; and in this case it must have been one of those built by Constantine Porphyrogenitus. Even as a roofless shell it remains a good specimen of Byzantine domestic architecture ; and we may well visit it on our way to the Gate of Xylokerkas, and the last scene of Byzantine history. It must originally have had three stories, the second story being on a level with the wall. The façade, as we can still see, was decorated with mosaic designs in brick and stone. The windows were framed in marble, and opened upon marble balconies. In order to screen the western side from missiles, a large tower was built, partially blocking the Xylokerkos Gate. Over the windows can still be seen the monogram of the Palæologi which, being interpreted, means " *Βασιλεὺς Βασιλέων Βασιλεύων Βασιλεύουσι,*" and is, under the circumstances, a fine example of " thinking imperially." The traveller Tavernier, visiting the Palace in 1688, moralizes over the ruin in a language that I hope will not be impenetrable to any intransigent Imperialist : " Squalet turpitas haec Imperatorii operis majestas . . . et non absimilem cum tempore rebus similibus, utcunque floreant, internecionem minatur."

Since we are in the Palace, and some of us may wish for a picture with which to fill the empty shell, here is a scene taken from the civil wars of this period. In 1345 Constantinople was ruled by one Apokaukos in the name of the Regent Anna. While Apokaukos and Cantacuzene were "fighting for the crown," Stephan Doushan, the great Serb, was making a strong bid to secure Constantinople as capital of a South Slav Empire. As Finlay says, " It is always the policy of a prime minister in a despotism to treat even a moderate and legal opposition as rebellious sedition." Apokaukos accordingly interned a considerable number of the leading Greeks in the court of this Palace. He himself lived near by at the arsenal on the Horn, where, as Grand Duke of the Fleet, he had at command a force of a thousand half-breeds. Having had prisons built in the Palace precincts he was rash enough to enter the yard to inspect them without enough escort. One of the prisoners, a Palæologus, felled him with a log, and the others finished him off with the masons' trowels and picks. His head was cut off with an adze and set over the doorway. Whereupon his retainers massacred the prisoners and pillaged part of the city. Cantacuzene, his rival, consequently made himself Emperor, in 1347 ; the arrangement having been made with the Empress-Regent Anna, that her son John V should marry Cantacuzene's daughter Helena, and the whole family be crowned together. The Throne, with three Empresses and two Emperors seated upon it, must have been a bit crowded ; but no doubt the public were delighted at seeing " Kings and Queens a-settin' all of a row." But in other ways the show was not what it had been, and the chronicler Nicephoras Gregoras regretted it should have been generally known that " the jewels in the crowns were glass, the robes not cloth-of-gold, but tinselled, the plate only brass, and all that looked like rich brocade merely painted leather." But by then the Empire was itself *postiche.*

The Empire was, moreover, again in pawn, and this time to the Genoese, who had taken possession of the fortified quarter of Galata. The Genoese collected the imperial revenues as security for their loans, keeping 200,000 byzants for themselves and remitting only 30,000 to the Empire. On Cantacuzene effecting a partial repudiation that restored some rights to the Greeks, the Galata Genoese attacked Constantinople in 1348, and burnt the Greek fleet. Cantacuzene retaliated by promoting a war between the Genoese and the Venetians. He and his Greeks supported the Venetians, and eventually were joined by a Catalan fleet from Achaia. In 1352 a big sea-fight took place off the Prinkipo Islands in full view of the Sea Walls; and in this the Genoese prevailed. "The Roman Empire," Gibbon says, "sunk to a travesty of the name, might even have sunk into a province of Genoa, if the ambition of the Republic had not been checked by the ruin of her freedom and naval power," for, as we remember, the struggle of a century and a half between Genoa and Venice ended finally in the victory of the Venetians. For the moment peace was patched up at Constantinople, at the cost of the Venetian colony; and, after another interlude of civil war between Cantacuzene and John V, it was with the help of the Genoese that Black John captured Constantinople and restored the Palæologian dynasty.

John got into the city by a truly Greek ruse. On a stormy night in December, a large merchant vessel came driving down on the boom across the port of Heptaskalon, in the Marmara Sea Wall, making signals of distress. The sailors cried to the guards that they were sinking, and the boom was opened. Before it could be closed, two galleys dashed in and landed troops. The town rose, and Cantacuzene shut himself up with his Turkish Guard in the Blachernæ citadel, not having had the time to throw himself into the new circular fortress which he had built for such an emergency at the Golden Gate. Thence he retired to a monastery; and occupied himself with writing a story of his own times that should induce posterity to do him justice. In spite of frequent references to his own "almost incredible virtue," the history condemns him as patently as any of his longsuffering subjects could have desired. The long reign of "Black John," now become "Beautiful John" in contemptuous allusion to his amours, covered the period from 1341 to 1391, and with it the closing scene of the Greek Empire. In 1382 the battle of Kossovo, and in 1396 that of Nikopolis, established firmly the Ottoman power in Europe, and reduced the Eastern Empire to a mere *enclave* round Constantinople, which was already tributary to the infidel. When, towards the end of his reign, John, in anticipation of the inevitable siege, tried to strengthen the citadel of the Golden Gate with the solid marble blocks stolen from the church of the Holy Apostles, which we remarked upon as we passed there, Sultan Bajazid ordered him to desist, threatening, as we may remember, to blind his son Manuel, whom he held as a hostage at Broussa. Beautiful John, now become a wretched old reprobate, thereupon destroyed his work, and soon afterwards died.

The city itself, long shorn of its splendour, now survived as little more than a quarry. For years the courtiers and the ruling classes had been living upon the sale of its marbles, its tessellated pavements and mosaics, to the Italian colonies, who exported them for the decoration of the cities of Italy. That the last fall of the curtain was so long delayed can be attributed to no vigour or vitality among the Greeks, but only to the dissensions among the Turks themselves and to their temporary difficulties with the Tartars. The darkness now gathers so heavily over the doomed city that little light is thrown for us by history on life in it during this last phase. But two incidental side-lights give us an idea of the depth of its degradation. Under a treaty with the Empress-Regent, the Sultan Othman had acquired the right to use the market-place at Constantinople for the sale of Christian slaves. It was a shrewd move ; for the slaves were thus often ransomed at prices above their market value. The imperial historian, Cantacuzene, gives us a description of such a mart, rows of young men and naked girls—even priests and nuns—exposed for sale, and sometimes flogged in public in order to stimulate the charitable. Such a recital, by an Emperor of " almost incredible virtue," leaves us a picture of the Empire devoid almost of human decency. But it still clung to its inhuman decorum. Thus a French traveller gives another glimpse—of the Empress riding back from St. Sophia to the Blachernæ.

She appeared attended only by two ladies, three old officials and three eunuchs. A bench was brought, and when she had mounted it, one of the old officials took her mantle, passed to the off-side of the horse, and held it as high as he could. She then set her foot in the stirrup and bestrode the horse like a man. The old minister then wrapped her round with the mantle, and placed on her head one of those long, pointed hats ornamented at one end with three golden plumes. She wore broad flat earrings heavily jewelled, especially with rubies. She seemed young and handsome, and I should have found no fault in her had she not been painted—assuredly without need. The little company then went on their way to the Blachernæ.

That prim little Empress (with her hat in the latest fashion) and her prudish old courtiers would have to pass the slave-market on their way home. We can see her and her ladies turning away their eyes and some old courtier supplying an explanation that emigration was for the good of the Empire: "They will be better off where they're going, we can't feed them here," and so forth. Thence they pass into oblivion, and with them we will let the Greek Empire pass charitably into oblivion too.

For the last scene of desperate defence belongs, not to the dying moments of the tawdry and tainted Greek Empire, but to the resurrection of a Greek nation.

The view more generally taken of the Turkish conquest of Constantinople is that it transformed the capital of Western culture and Christian civilization into the capital of Islamic inertia and of an oriental intrusion upon Europe. But the change implied no sudden subversion of Europe by the East. Those who have read the previous pages may see in it rather the logical culmination of a long course of developments. And they may be prepared for the view of it which is taken here, that it marked the commencement of a new chapter, a chapter in which the nations both of eastern Europe and of western Asia were eventually to emancipate themselves from an effete imperial system. Before the fall of Constantinople both the city and the Greek communities outside it had long been tributary to the Turks. The later Palæologi were vassals of the Sultans. The last, resolute defence of the city emerges, even in its failure, as the first of a long series of unsuccessful efforts made by a new Greek nation to throw off the yoke of Asia with the help of Europe, and to issue, purged as by fire, from the Byzantine corruption and imperialistic impotence that had proved their bane.

This view has at any rate the merit of allowing us to witness the tragedy of the last siege without undue depression. With it in our minds, to balance our sympathies, we shall not be misled by our just admiration of the last struggle of the Greek Empire, and by our equally just abomination of the ultimate throes of the decadent Ottoman Empire, into overlooking the indisputable advantage to the Eastern world which resulted from this substitution of competent Turks for corrupt Greek governance at Constantinople.

THE OTTOMAN CONQUEST

The causes of the decline of the Greek Empire can be comprehended even in a summary. The Greek Empire fell because the ruling class at Constantinople developed, owing to its wealth, into a Court caste, out of contact with the community and without roots in the race or in the religion of the country. In a despotic atmosphere the imperial prestige, based upon Roman law, and the intellectual progress, due to Greek enlightenment, could not be maintained; and the Body Politic died.

But it is more difficult to account for the development of the Ottoman Empire within the scope of a guide-book. The Turks, at first sight, would seem to have been an association of barbarous tribal communities, united by a feudal military system for the purposes of a fanatical crusade. Why, we may ask, should their feudalism and fanaticism have succeeded in establishing an Ottoman Empire in the city where Christian feudalism and fanaticism had just hopelessly failed to establish a Latin Empire? The explanation, put in as few words as possible, would seem to be this: firstly, the structure of the Ottoman State until the last century, although it appeared to be despotic in its façade, was democratic in its foundations; and secondly, the Turkish character, by temperament, training, and tradition, was more equable and equitable than the Greek or the Latin. I shall be returning again to this explanation of the Ottoman supremacy, with additional evidence of its correctness; and I shall be concerned to show you how in the end Turkish capability and character were corrupted by Empire— or, if we desire a concrete term, by Constantinople.

It is sufficient for the present, however, to note that the Ottoman Empire, which early in the fourteen-hundreds decided that Constantinople must become its capital, represented a form of government superior to that of the Greeks. It embodied a long tradition of civilization, a combination of the culture of the Turks at Koniah, of the Greeks at Philadelphia, of the Syrians at Antioch, and of the Arabs at Bagdad. Its dynasty had justified itself by providing a long succession of leaders and lawgivers. The justice of Othman became proverbial. His son, Orkhan, is described by Finlay as the greatest original legislator of modern times; and certainly the early Ottoman codes compare favourably, in respect of honour and humanity, with the Byzantine. It would seem that this small Ottoman clan succeeded in reviving a racial respect for justice which contact with more sophisticated civilizations had weakened among the Seljouks; and, further, in making its rule representative of that respect. Alike the ready allegiance given to the rule of the clan by its co-religionists, and the ready acceptance of it by Christians, were due to its recognition of responsibility for the administration of justice. And it may be remarked in this context that the general respect for equity, and not alone for law, does produce in Eastern communities a " Christian " relationship between individuals, such as is often lacking socially in Western communities.

But, besides this, Orkhan arrived, possibly by accident, at an arrangement for the association of subject races in political power ; and this without weakening the executive. He established a ruling class, composed of two castes—one military, the other civil—recruited by conscription from the subject races. In modern language this is described, and much censured, as the " tribute of blood." The " tribute " children thus obtained were educated either as soldiers, the " Janissaries " or new soldiery, or as civil servants. Both divisions obtained not only education at the public cost and emancipation from all the evils of poverty, but also the opportunity of elevation by merit to power.

Under the Byzantine Empire there had been a career open to talent—of a sort. Narses the eunuch became a great general ; Cantacuzene the chamberlain became an Emperor. But as a rule power was strictly reserved for one class—this restriction applied eventually even to the Church—and the exceptions were limited to promotions among the parasites of that class. On the other hand, the tribute child from Albania or Greece or Trebizond got as good an education for public responsibility as he would have had on the charitable foundations of Eton or Winchester. In its cold-blooded purposefulness the training can only be compared—so far as my experience goes—to that given in the orphanages of the Russian Communists. When the system was abolished, in 1685, the Janissaries alone represented a " tribute " of 12,000 young men. The excellence of the early Ottoman administration is evidence also that, on the civil side, the system was no less a success.

Fortified by this rough acquaintance with the structure of the early Ottoman Empire, we can approach the siege of Constantinople more dispassionately, and see in it something more than the mere onslaught of barbarism upon civilization. Greek sources themselves bear witness to the admiration felt by enlightened Greeks for the Turks—an admiration that, unhappily, found expression in Constantinople only in the aping of Turkish fashions. Among the populace exhibitions of Turkish archery and horsemanship, held in the Hippodrome, were at this time as popular as Wild West Shows have been with us.

The Greeks of Constantinople lost more than one opportunity of escaping from Turkish vassalage. They ignored the opportunities given to them by the Tartars in the East and by the Hungarians in the West. John VI even avoided taking any part in a revolt against the Turks, headed by his brother the Despot of Sparta, who afterwards became Constantine XIII. In such contempt did the Sultans hold an Empire, now reduced to little more than the city of Constantinople itself, that when Constantine XIII was crowned at Sparta in 1449, Sultan Murad did not even trouble to veto the accession of the rebel. But the pacific Murad died in 1451 ; and he was succeeded by the ambitious and youthful Mohammed II. Of him the Byzantine envoy and historian, Phranzes, relates that he was a talented youth, well educated, and speaking five languages other than Turkish. His Court at Adrianople was a brilliant political centre, both for Eastern Europe and for Asia Minor ; and since territorial expansion in other directions could only be expensive, it was inevitable that he should soon turn to the easy and culminating conquest of Constantinople. The wily voluptuary, John VI, might have been able once more to postpone the crisis by diplomacy ; but Constantine brought the blow upon himself at once. He summoned his Suzerain to increase the subsidy paid him for acting as jailer to a Turkish claimant, another Orkhan. At this folly even the Grand-Vizier Khalid, who was supposed to be in Greek pay, threw up his brief ; and Mohammed took the first hostile step.

He began by building the Castles of Roumeli and Anatoli Hissar on the Bosphorus. These controlled the Strait, cutting off Constantinople from all supplies and supports from the north, and thereby reducing by half the advantage of its sea-power. For the Venetians favoured the Greeks, and they were as strong at sea as the Turks were weak. Constantine protested : only to be reminded that he was a vassal of the Sultan. There ensued skirmishes. The Greeks tried to stop the Turks from pulling down a church, and from taking the harvest from the reapers. The Turks thereupon declared war ; and Constantine set to work to put the city in a state of defence. But the Greeks had by now lost the habit of bearing arms ; and their orthodoxy was ill-disposed to support a " Uniate " Emperor, preferring doubtless even the Infidel Mohammed to the Schismatic Constantine. The Grand Duke Notaras declared he would prefer to bow to the turban of the Sultan rather than to the tiara of the Pope. The Latins, on their side, would not fight for a Greek Emperor. The Pope, in response to an appeal, sent Cardinal Isidore with a small force and some money. Constantine, in return, celebrated his union with the Papal Church on December 12, 1452, in St. Sophia. From that day the Cathedral was deserted by the orthodox, who, says the historian Ducas, looked upon it thenceforth as a den of devils. One Scholaris led a religious revolt; the same man who subsequently, as the Patriarch Gennadius, effected the union of the Orthodox Church with the Ottoman State.

The walls had fallen out of repair. The monkish overseers had embezzled the money; and some of it was found by Janissaries years afterwards hidden in one of the towers. The supply of gunpowder was short; and as the towers would not stand the shock of heavy gun discharges, the Greeks had to fall back upon the old stone-throwing apparatuses. Upon the Italians, on land as by sea, rested the main burden of the defence. Of the twelve sectors of the defensive lines two only were commanded by Greeks. The defending force comprised only 9,000 men, of whom half were Greeks; and the fleet consisted of three Venetian galliasses and twenty galleys.

Mohammed spent the winter in drawing up with his own hand plans for the siege, down to the last detail. He had the better artillery, and had secured the services of Urban, a Vlach, formerly in Greek service, who had mastered the art of casting monster cannon. For Roumeli Hissar he had made a gun that could hurl a stone ball across the Bosphorus; and he now made another of 2½ feet calibre, wherewith to batter the walls. An Ottoman historian describes this gun with pride. It was drawn by 100 buffaloes, served by 500 cannoneers, took two hours to load, threw a ball of 1,200 pounds, and—he might have added —burst at the fourth discharge. The transport of this and the other siege artillery delayed the arrival of the army before the walls. It was not until April 6, two months after leaving Adrianople, that Mohammed II encamped on the Crusaders' Hill outside the Blachernæ. But the panic created in the city by the powers attributed to the great guns was worth the delay. Mohammed had with him an army of 70,000 foot, of whom 12,000 were Janissaries, and 20,000 horse. His fleet of 320 vessels consisted chiefly of small coasters, all of them inferior to the Venetian vessels.

The first action was a naval engagement between the Turkish galleys and some Italian ships bringing supplies. These latter, being what our naval ancestors termed " high-charged " ships, ran down the low galleys, and dropped rocks through their bottoms. Mohammed witnessed this defeat from the shore. He rode saddle-deep into the sea in his excitement, lost his temper, and struck with his mace at his admiral, Balta-oglou. He even ordered him to be impaled, but this the Janissaries refused to allow; and the Janissaries represented a political power that Mohammed, even in a battle-crisis, had to respect.

The siege on land at first went no better. The monster gun burst. But the terror it had inspired survives in the name " Top-Kapou," the Cannon Gate; and the two stone balls now over the gate of St. Romanus were inserted by Mohammed's orders as a memorial to it. The great siege-tower also was captured and burnt in a sortie led by Justiniani, the Genoese commander. And Johann Grant, a German engineer, responded to the bombardment of the Ottoman cannon and siege-engines with counter-battery fire, and countermined the saps.

But the defence was in difficulties, owing to the walls suffering greater damage from the shock of their own guns than from any battering inflicted by the enemy artillery. And a daring manœuvre finally turned the tide of war in favour of the Turks. It was obvious that the light Turkish galleys could not hope to face the Venetian ships under sail and in the open sea. But within the Golden Horn, sheltered from the wind and protected by the shore batteries, they might well be more than their match. Mohammed's difficulty was to get into the Horn, past the Venetian squadron and the chain that barred the entry. Now the Venetians had not long before startled the world by transporting galleys from the Adige to Lake Garda. This precedent inspired the Sultan to try and convey his galleys five miles across the upland behind Galata. To his engineers who had conveyed the monster gun through Thrace this problem presented little difficulty. Wooden causeways were laid down and well greased; and over these the galleys were hauled by windlasses and buffalo teams, with their sails set, their flags flying, and the bands playing. The first squadron made the trip in a single night and appeared afloat on the Golden Horn in the morning, to the dismay of the defenders, who now had five more miles of Sea Wall to man.

The Venetian squadron in the outer port at once sailed up the Horn under cover of night. But the flagship was sunk by a stone-shot, and the rest drew off. The men from the sunk vessel who swam ashore were made prisoners by the Turks and decapitated next morning in sight of the defence. The garrison retaliated by beheading upon the walls over 200 Moslem prisoners.

The same ill-fortune attended a raid of Venetian fireships on the following night. In these enclosed waters the Turkish artillery was not to be braved with impunity ; and as soon as its superiority was established the Turks constructed a pontoon bridge, floating upon great jars used in Galata for storing oil and wine, to serve as another avenue of attack, and to bar any further approach to the inner port.

Simultaneously, and with the help of the Hungarian envoy, who showed the Turkish gunners how to direct their fire so as to cut the wall into sections, a breach was effected at the Gate of Romanus, and the moat was filled up. Justiniani, in command there, appealed to Notaras for more artillery. But that orthodox bigot refused to take any suggestion from a Latin, and Constantine himself could scarcely restrain the two from coming to blows. The imminence of defeat seems indeed to have loosened such central control as may have existed over the twenty or more leaders of the different contingents. During the four days which the Turks devoted to preparations for their great assault, the Greeks would seem to have occupied themselves principally with squabbling.

Of the last night before the assault there are several accounts by eye-witnesses, all deeply impressed by the solemnity of the occasion. In them Constantine, an uninspiring personality, plays this last act like a hero. The day before he had refused the very reasonable offer of the Sultan to let him retire to a principality in the Peloponnese. Had he accepted it, he might have saved his own and thousands of other human lives : he might even have accelerated by several centuries the emancipation of Greece. But he declined. And, as the first Greek Emperor to prefer death to dishonour, this foolish, elderly failure deserves to be remembered by us, not as the last of the Palæologi, but as the first of the Pallikars.

The historian Phranzes was with Constantine all that last night, and we can almost live it again ourselves with him. First we see the Emperor kneeling in St. Sophia at midnight, and receiving the sacrament for the dying in a darkness made gloomier by a few smoking torches. From the cathedral we can follow the little party through the lightless and silent streets, where the torches glinted from behind barred windows and barricaded doors, and a restless murmur from within told of the townsfolk making their useless preparations against the dreaded dawn. So on to the Blachernæ, a dark and deserted citadel, and to the walls.

Earlier in the evening the Turks had been holding the solemn celebrations customary with them the night before a battle. The whole upland and port without the walls had then been a blaze of light. There were lamps hung before every tent, lanterns on every mast, and countless scattered bonfires reddening up the sky. An illumination all the more ominous for the strange silence, interrupted by no sound more warlike than the muezzin's melancholy call to prayer:

> —a sad and solemn task to hold
> The midnight watch on that beleaguered wall.
> The heavy clouds were as an Empire pall;
> The giant shadows of each tower and fane
> Lay like the graves. A low mysterious call
> Breathed in the wind, and from the tented plain
> A voice of omens rose from each wild martial strain.
> For heaven, earth, air, speak auguries to those
> Who see their numbered hours fast pressing to the close.

But by the time the Emperor reached the wall, the silence had been broken: the preparations for the assault were already well advanced. We can still accompany him, and, unlike the prudent Phranzes, we can stay to witness the assault from the best vantage-point—the great circular Tower of Kaligaria. This stands at the salient of the Comnenian Wall, outside the Xylokerkos Gate and the Palace of Constantine.

From this tower we have on our right the Kaligaria Gate, so called after the boot-makers' shops inside. It is also called Charsia Gate, and by the Turks Egri Kapou, both meaning Crooked Gate. This Gate was defended throughout the siege by Johannes Grant, the German engineer. On our left we look along the Mesoteikion, and the sector of the main Ottoman assault. "When we came to Kaligaria," Phranzes tells us, "at the first hour of cockcrow, we dismounted and ascended the tower. And we heard a murmur of much talking and a mighty tumult outside. The guards told us that all night it had been so—for the Ottomans were making ready and dragging up their siege machinery for an assault on the walls—and they were already at the moat."

And so upon our tower the Emperor leaves us, and rides on to his death, at his post by the Romanus Gate, hard by the Great Breach.

We need not aggravate our sense of the tragedy by lending

credence to an opinion expressed by certain historians that if the defence had only held out a little longer it would have had a chance of ultimate success. The relieving ships from Italy, which were held up by northerly winds at Chios, could not have affected the issue. The Ottomans were prepared to keep up the succession of assaults until noon; and there is no evidence to show that the Sultan had any intention of retiring even if he had failed that day. Constantinople was doomed irrevocably, and had been doomed for a number of years.

The assault was delivered at dawn, against the northern half of the Land Wall, and against the western half of the Sea Wall along the Horn. For two hours the defence held out gallantly. Then it crumbled; and collapsed at the last so suddenly that there is still a controversy, based upon a conflict of evidence, as to whether the Turks broke in first over the Sea Wall at Aivan Serai, or through a neglected postern in the Comnenian Wall, or over the Wall in the Lycus valley, or through the Great Breach at the Gate of St. Romanus. But it is the assault at this Gate, where both Constantine and Mohammed were personally engaged, which has always attracted most attention. One of the great guns first breached Justiniani's barricade. The first assault, by light troops (Azab), only served to bridge what was left of the moat with dead bodies. The second assault, by Anatolian regulars (piade), was thrown back likewise; but its vigour had driven the defence to extremities. Justiniani himself, severely wounded, had to retire to his ship—where he died a few days later. Some of his Genoese deserted, and the remainder lost heart.

At the third assault a party of Janissaries, led by a giant, Hassan of Ulubad, stormed the breach. They were all killed; but further waves of assault pouring up overwhelmed the defenders. The Emperor Constantine was killed in the mêlée, near the Gate of St. Romanus, by an unknown hand.

Another Turkish storming party forced the postern in the wall between the tower on which we stand and the Xylokerkos Gate, and so took the defenders of the Crooked Gate in the rear. This Gate had not been walled up, so as to allow of sallies by the defenders. It was now, therefore, thrown open by the successful storming-party. The Blachernæ citadel thus lay exposed to the inrush of the besiegers, and all resistance came to an end.

At first the victorious Turks as they hurried inward through the streets slew all they met. But as soon as it became evident that the city had fallen the slaughter ceased. The Grand Duke Notaras and the Greeks defending the Sea Wall surrendered.

The sack was much less cruel than that which had followed the taking of the city by the Latins. But the sight of rich and poor being sorted by age and sex irrespective of their rank, and driven away in files as slaves, seems to have shocked the chroniclers more deeply than outrage and massacre. To the Turks, indeed, the principal booty offered by the impoverished capital was these slaves. The Latins had already taken the very stones and the bones. The Turks took what alone was left, the life itself, and reduced the Christian population of the city from a possible 100,000 before the siege to a probable 10,000 after it. Some few inhabitants escaped in the shipping. The Cardinal Isidore, disguised as a soldier, was ransomed by one of the Genoese of Galata, who had held himself neutral. The bailo of the Venetians and the consul of the Catalans were put to death, with their families. So also was the Grand Duke Notaras and his children. The large section of the population represented by the slaves of course merely changed masters ; and the deliberate expatriation of the remaining free inhabitants into slavery suggests that the Turks were desirous of re-populating their new capital with a more vigorous stock. In pursuance of this policy, no sooner had they established themselves than they began drafting in picked groups of all races, who were accommodated in the various quarters of the city as fast as they could be rebuilt. A sturdier Helladic stock was in this way grafted upon what little was left in the city of its Romaic population ; and that that little was greater than the chroniclers, or for that matter than the Turks themselves would have us believe, is suggested by the fact that the names of practically all the leading Byzantine Greek families survived in the Phanar down to our own time. These Phanariote families, we may remark here, became one of the two important elements in the eventful re-establishment of the Greek nation.

But our knowledge of what happened immediately after the siege is obscured, on the one side, by the necessity of discounting the usual Greek accusations of " atrocities." And on the other by the worthlessness of the Turkish chroniclers, who had adopted a blend of Persian phraseology and of the Frankish rhymed chronicle, in its effect both ludicrous and exasperating. Here is a specimen from S'ad-ud-Din, reproducing something of its arrhythmic jingle :—

When by the aidance of the One beyond gainsay—the fortitude of the defenders of the castellated city was passed away—and the happy tidings " Verily our hosts the conquerors are they "—were become the support of the victory-crowned array—and " enter in peace " sounded in the ear of the army of the Fay. With leave from the Threshold-of-the-World-Conquering King to plunder and spoil did those avid for booty into the city sweep—where laying hand on their families and wealth they made the worthless misbelievers weep—Acting on the exalted order " Slaughter their elders and enslave their youth,"—those unprofitable properties which in the days of old—through years untold—had been controlled—by the hand of profligacy, became the portion of the Champions of Truth. And so that spacious land—that city great and grand —from being the Seat of Antagonism became the centre of the Currency. And from being the nest of the Owl of Shame—became the Portal of Splendour and Fair Fame.

If we can imagine such a sample of history being written in a shorthand without vowel-points and constructed for a different language—which is the general effect of writing Turkish in the Arabic character—we shall cease to wonder that the Turks are not a race of readers. We ourselves can take refuge even in Gibbon's periods with relief.

But for Gibbon as for modern historians the real meaning of the fall of Constantinople is obscured by its dramatic but irrelevant incidents. The moving scene in St. Sophia, and the spectacle of Mohammed riding up through the Great Breach over a barrier of dead bodies, with among them, unrecognized, that of the last Emperor—these and others have contributed to isolate the event, and cause it to be treated as a new departure. It was, as we have seen, a long-overdue development. Internationalism at Constantinople can only be maintained upon the foundation of a vigorous local nationalism. It was inevitable that the strong Turkish nation should replace the weaker Greek. And it was no less inevitable that when the Turkish control became infected in its turn by the tradition of Byzantine imperialism, it should have been reduced to the same ineffective level. It is open to us to think that when Khalid, the sagacious Grand-Vizier of the young Mohammed, did his utmost to prevent the attack on Constantinople, and, when that failed, subsequently spread through the camp false rumours of relief, he was not influenced by Greek bribes—for the Greeks could offer little and Turkish Viziers of that age were not corrupt; but that he recognized what all Young Turks to-day have realized, that Constantinople was a plague spot, and that he acted in prophetic fear of what its possession might involve for the future of his people. Be that as it may. The State entry of Mohammed II appeared to the moralist of that day as the triumph of Islam over Christianity, of evil over good. To the moralist of a later day it came to mean the triumph of justice and reform over oppression and rascality, of good over evil. But to us it may present itself neither as the one nor as the other, but as the inevitable substitution of the sound Ottoman social system for the decayed Greek imperialist ideals and interests.

Our long excursion round the walls ends with the fall of the Greek Empire. With the same fall ended the long part which the walls had played in the history of the world. For centuries the Turks kept them in repair. But the improvements in modern artillery, and the reclusion of the city within the heart of a great military system, deprived them of all further interest other than as picturesque ruins.

CHAPTER III

THE OSMANLI EMPIRE

He sailed east, he sailed west,
  Until he came to proud Turkey;
And he viewed the fashions of that land,
  Their way of worship viewed he.

("Ballad of Lord Bateman")

THE GREAT MOSQUES AND SULTANS

THE story of the Byzantine Empire in Constantinople is built into the walls. That of the Osmanli Empire is bound up with the mosques and bazaars of Stamboul. For convenience I shall make a distinction between the mediæval Osmanli Empire, based upon Christian slavery, and the modern Ottoman Empire, with its theoretic basis of equality.

The order of the Sultans [1] also admits of the same convenient grouping. There were ten great Sultans of the rise of the Empire. Of these five ruled before the conquest of Constantinople. Mourad II (1421–1451), as we remember, tried to take it ; Mohammed II (1451–1481) succeeded. The last of the great ten was Suleiman the Magnificent (1520–1566). The following twenty or so, beginning with Selim the Sot (1566–1574), were unimpartant Sultans, of an epoch of stagnation. Lastly came five Sultans of the decline, beginning with Mahmoud the Reformer (1808–1839), and ending with the revolution against Abd-ul-Hamid (1876–1908). These last five will be treated of in a separate chapter, under the heading of the Ottoman Empire.

The story of Osmanli Constantinople is best told through the lives of its Sultans and their memorials in mosques and mausoleums. Of the open-air cemeteries spired with cypresses we have

---

[1] Osman I took the title of Sultan : the proper Turkish title was Khan. Originally all the members of the direct line were entitled to be called Sultan. The women put it after their name, as Fathmah Sultan, Besma Sultan. The word Sultana is a Western invention. Gran' Turco and Grand Signor are of Italian origin, and now disused. Padishah was the Turkish for Sovereign, and is also used for foreign royalties.

already seen something on our circuit of the walls. They extend for miles about Constantinople, in both continents. But these unknown dead have no story for us, although almost every tombstone tells its tale. By the shape of the turban you can tell what any important man was and almost when he lived—until the coming of the fez makes all equal. A turban slightly askew, for instance, tells of a career cut short by the axe or bowstring. A shell or a leaf ornament marks a woman's grave.

Even the cypresses are memorials ; for one tree used to be planted for each new household admitted. You are in a world where everything has a symbolic significance. If you meet a funeral you will see it hurries along almost at a run, and you will be reminded that the soul of the Mussulman, like that of the ancient Greek, can find no rest until his body is buried.

Of minor mosques (Mesjid) there must be nearly five hundred in Constantinople ; some of them little more than a room. All are supported by charitable foundations (Wakf). Most of these are doomed to disappear under the reformed regime, the Ministry of Education having better uses for the revenues. In fact, the good work that Gladstone's Charity Commission did for us is already well under way in Constantinople.

The Imperial mosques (Djami), however, are likely to remain one of the principal sights, both as historic and as artistic monuments. It will not be practicable to visit them all in chronological order. I shall therefore give you a route which will bring you to those best worth seeing in their proper order ; and deal with the others incidentally as we arrive at their several dates—leaving you to fit in visits to them, if you want, as best you can.

Our first mosque must obviously be that of Mohammed the Conqueror. It was completed, as an inscription over the central door records, in the month of Redjeb, year of the Hedjaz 875, that is, in A.D. 1471. It was restored after an earthquake in 1768. It has been argued that its " semi-Italian style " dates only from the restoration, and that the original character of the building was then lost. I hold it, on the contrary, to be as exact a reproduction of the original design as is certainly the Djehanghir Mosque, rebuilt in 1764. For at the time Turkish taste was conservative, and the Treasury still capable of satisfying a sentiment that would naturally desire to reproduce faithfully an edifice so sacred. The " Italian " effect is not due to any later imitation of baroque, but to the Latin alloy inherent in the late Byzantine style.

Mohammed's Mosque was built by a Greek, Christodoulos, and is clearly a copy of St. Sophia, reproducing even the cruciform ground-plan. The Greeks will tell you that the architect was afterwards impaled, so as to prevent his building a rival structure for any successor; while the Turks will tell you that he had his hands cut off, because he shortened the pillars so that they should not outrival those of St. Sophia. The Turkish legend continues that the maimed Christodoulos appealed for justice to the Cadi, who summoned the Sultan before him. The Sultan would have seated himself beside the Cadi on the bench, but was sternly ordered to stand in the dock. He was then directed to plead guilty; which he did; and sentence was passed upon him. After which the Cadi rose, threw himself at the Sultan's feet and did homage. As he bent, a dagger fell from his sleeve. " What is this ? " said the Sultan.

" To stab you with, dread Padishah," said the Cadi, " had you defied the law ! "

" O righteous judge ! " said Mohammed, producing a battle-axe from under his cloak, " and this would have struck you down had you unjustly acquitted me ! "

These legends are worth recalling as characteristic of the Greek and Turkish attitudes of mind ; but both are fictions. Christodoulos was handsomely rewarded with a grant of the Church of the Virgin of Moukliotissa, and the neighbouring streets; and he died a rich man.

The dome is the highest in the city. Both outside and inside the mosque makes an impression of austerity, which is heightened inside by the severity of the black and white arabesques. The incongruous gold inscription on a blue tablet is the traditional prediction of the Prophet : " Constantinople shall be subjugated. Happy the Prince, happy the army that shall achieve that subjugation." Such associations make this mosque an object of especial veneration and admission used to be difficult. It is well to keep always in mind that although a Mussulman community may treat its mosques as social and even as commercial centres, their forecourts as bazaars, and their floors as playgrounds for children, mosques are none the less the shrines of highly sensitive sectaries ; and in the case of this mosque additional attention to avoid giving any offence is probably still advisable.

The atrium, or cloister, of the Byzantine church has in the mosque become the forecourt, with a marble pavement, a canopied fountain, and a red granite and verde antico colonnade taken from the Church of the Holy Apostles. It is a pleasant place, with pretty Moslem children chasing each other up and down the marble steps or playing hide and seek in and out of the dappled sunshine under the trees.

The outer court is less peaceful, but even more picturesque, shaded by the trees beloved of the Turk, plane, acacia, cypress, ilanthus, and mulberry. It is crowded with parti-coloured fruit-sellers, fakirs, hadjis from Mecca, faith-healers who cure with a magic hand-wave, water-carriers, itinerant cook-shops, charm-sellers, letter writers, turbaned Ulema softas, idiots, beggars, barbers, porters, *et hoc genus omne*, in an omnium-gatherum of infinite variety.

Round the court are many-domed buildings, which house the dependencies of every mosque of importance : schools (super-seded now by the secular schools of Young Turkey), seminaries, hostels, hospitals, almshouses, an asylum, baths, a public kitchen and a library.

The service of every mosque requires an Imam or Mullah, who corresponds to our Parish Priest, whose qualifications are some slight knowledge of the Koran. Also a Muezzin, or Clerk, who chants the responses and intones the " call to prayer " from the minaret. The " call " runs, " Alláhu akbar,"—God is great (five times) ; " ashadu an lá Iláha ill'Allah,"—I testify there is no God but God (twice) ; " ashandu anna Mohammadan ras úl-ullah,"—I testify that Mohammed is Prophet of God (twice) ; " haya alla 's-saláti,"—Come to prayer (twice) ; " Haya 'alál-halah,"—Come to salvation (twice) ; " Alláhu akbar " (twice). When the nasal intonation that spoils all oriental music for our ears is lost in the height of a minaret or in the depth of a fine voice, the long-drawn cadences of the " call " can be very impressive. Too often it is a thin wail, or a jackdaw-like squawk-ing. The Khatibs or preachers earn a living by going from mosque to mosque on engagements, or on regular provincial tours. A few still draw good audiences ; but their exhortations are devoid of interest. The clock-winder (Moakhit) is an ad-junct of most mosques, since the five daily services are regulated by a combination of the Moakhit and the moon—more compli-cated than our Golden Rule for finding Easter. Finally, there are the mosque boys, who divide their time between the mosques and the Hammams, and who are nothing like so ingenuous as they are ingratiating.

A feature of the courts of all imperial mosques is the col-lection of mausoleums, or turbehs. Each turbeh generally accommodates a number of tombs, those of the family or of favoured viziers and generals of the builder. Since for two centuries no fresh turbehs have been built, the later Sultans have been accustomed to make their choice as to which of their predecessors should afford them hospitality—with consequences chronologically confusing. The bodies are buried only a foot or two under the pavement. The site is marked by a catafalque, shaped like an Ottoman coffin. This is sometimes of gigantic size, to suggest the importance of the dead. As in the cemeteries, the men are distinguished by a turban, and after the Reform by a fez; a Sultan by heron's feathers. The guardianship of the turbeh is a hereditary benefice, and is still in many cases held by the descendants of the original nominee. In some turbehs you will see a pathetic crowd of children's tombs nestling round that of a Sultan or Valideh (queen-mother), and you may perhaps feel sorry for parents seemingly so afflicted. But you must not be too ready with sympathy in the Near East. See how many of the little turbans on these tombs have an ominous tilt to one side. The deadly disease that raised infantile mortality in the seraglio was the bowstring.

Near the Mosque of Mohammed, on the east, is the turbeh of the Conqueror himself, a ten-sided, two-storied and domed building of white marble. From the marble steps you are now allowed to look in at the catafalque of the Sultan, surrounded by a mother-of-pearl railing, and covered with a velvet pall. The Conqueror lies alone; no successor having ventured to intrude upon his rest. His tomb is the shrine of very sacred relics: one, a Koran copied by himself, which you may look at; and another, the tooth lost by the Prophet at the battle of Ohud, which you may not—or possibly you may by now, if you want to very much.

You should certainly pay a pilgrimage to two of the tombs of royal ladies in this court, for each enshrines a romance. Beside the tomb of Goulbahar Sultan, wife of Mohammed, is that of an unknown and unnamed princess. The English guide-book will probably tell you that this is the tomb of Mohammed's mother. But this is an "official version"; for his mother was a notability, the daughter of Charles VI of France and the sister of Isabella, wife of our own unfortunate Richard II; and she is buried at Broussa. Who then is the nameless lady? The Turkish mullah in this more tolerant age may confess to you that her name was Irene, and that she was a beautiful

Greek with whom Mohammed was deeply in love. But, since she was a Christian and refused to abjure her religion, Mohammed, in a rage at the reproaches of the Sheikh-ul-Islam and the mullahs, summoned Irene before them all, unveiled her, and said : " This woman I love as I do my life ! but my life I give to Islam ! " and forthwith beheaded her. Whereupon, moved by the tragedy, the Ulema granted the luckless beauty the unprecedented honour of this burial as a Moslem. Another rotunda-like turbeh, farther east, belongs to a later age. It is that of Nach'shadil Sultan, wife of Abdul-Hamid I, and mother of Mahmud II, the Reformer. She was a French Creole of Martinique, Aimée de Rivery, cousin and companion of Josephine de la Pagerie, who, we may remember, after escaping the guillotine which eliminated an uninteresting husband, became the Empress Josephine. Aimée was rescued from a shipwreck as she was returning from her convent school at Nantes, only to be captured by an Algerine corsair, and exposed for sale at Algiers. The Dey bought her, and sent her as a present to the Sultan. There is a double romance for you ! These two little girls, starting from a remote island on the far side of Africa, became, one by way of the Terror, the other by way of the slave-market, the one Empress of the West, the other Empress of the East.

But we are roaming off our route. The next mosque in order of date is the Mosque of Mohammed's son, Bayazid II. It stands off the line of our tour, outside Seraskierate Square, between the Grand Bazaar and the tram, where you will pass it and can visit it at your leisure. It was built by a second Christodoulos, a nephew of the first. The Greeks, of course, have a yarn about him too. Bayazid asked of him whether he had " done his best." The architect, exasperated by the Sultan's parsimony, replied that he had " done his best—for the money." Whereupon he was beheaded. But the Turkish legend is again the more attractive. The mosque is haunted by multitudes of pigeons. These, say the Turks, are the descendants of a pair given by a widow, who in giving them gave her all to God. Since the Sultan had only given what he could spare, it is consequently her name, and not his, which is inscribed in heaven as the donor ; while, on earth, the mosque is known not as the Bayazidieh but as the Dove Mosque. The pigeons have, in the course of centuries, considerably dimmed the resplendance of the exterior.

The building has nothing very distinctive about it. The

cruciform ground-plan has become confused; and the flower-frescoes on the vaults do not appeal to every taste. The fore-court, however, is striking, with its three-sided portico and multi-coloured marble columns, its great canopied fountain, and its marble and porphyry pavement.

The Turbeh of Bayazid stands here in a little garden, a lovely octagon building. An undistinguished sovereign, he seems to have thought it necessary to assert his importance by an extra size of catafalque and enormous candlesticks. Bayazid was a mystic and his personality remains a puzzle. He was the first Osmanli Sultan who did not make himself personally prominent in the field with his victorious armies. But he kept the dust brushed out of his clothes when on campaign, had it made into a brick, and buried here with him. You can give Bayazid and his brick a miss if you like. For he was too modern a character for the mediæval Turks. He was deposed by his son Selim and the Janissaries; and died, with suspicious promptitude, three days later.

The mosque of Bayazid's successor, Selim the Cruel, in the Phanar, can be taken in by a detour after that of the Conqueror, or it can be left out altogether. Its gloomy mass, dull without and dark within, is a suitable memorial to the tyrant; and it would be remarkable that Suleiman the Magnificent should have built such a testimonial to his father unless he too had appreci-ated its fittingness. The ugly forecourt and plain minarets are all in keeping. Guide-books praise the " propriety of its pro-portions." But perhaps its chief interest is that it is said to be built of the material used by Constantine when he started, a thousand years before, to build in the Troad the Capital which he afterwards erected on the Constantinople site.

Selim " the Grim " was a parricide and fratricide; but his cruelty was characteristic of his age. A picturesque " poetic justice " in his punishments appealed to public opinion. He was not unpopular, and he is known to Turkish history as " the Just." Corrupt judges, for example, were required to condemn themselves to death. During the eight years of his reign he decapitated seven Grand Viziers; and a "vizierat of Selim " long survived as a proverbial term for any remunerative but risky job. He was a poet, and wrote chiefly in flowery Persian; but his more simple Turkish verses have a note of true pathos. Even in a rough rendering the lines suggest what a French critic would term " chose vue et vécue." It is the voice itself of imperial Constantinople.

Every morn my hosts of fancies ride o'er streams of tears to war:
  O'er the one-piered, two-arched bridge my brows have builded, forth
    they fare.
Veiled in airy webs, bespangled with each good and evil star:
  Every evening fickle fortune winds me in her wanton hair:
Still alone, a lonely stranger, in strange lands I roam afar,
  While around me march the sullen guards of grief and pain and care.
Till I've read life's riddle, emptied its nine pitchers to the end
Never shall I, Sultan Selim, find on earth a faithful friend.

After reading this we can better understand the poet Selim sobbing over the verses addressed to him by his brother before he was bow-strung, or listening hysterically to the strangling by his deaf-mutes of his little nephews. His cruelty suggests calculation, even convention : it is not the perverted or political savagery of Mohammed who, when drunk, could murder the whole family of Notaras because he would not surrender his son to the infamy of the seraglio, could flay princes alive, have antagonist leaders sawn in two, or massacre whole populations after their conditional surrender. But to the professional wars, and peaces, of Byzantine times succeeded now an age of wars of racial and religious extermination. The weapon of persecution, which was merely misused by such monsters as Vlad the Impaler, a Wallach tyrant, could achieve its political purpose, as Selim proved when he completely extirpated the heretic Shi-ite population of Asia Minor. He was seriously thinking of applying the same policy to the more tolerated Christian infidels, and was only prevented by the courageous Mufti Jamali, who alone of his Court had any influence over him. Jamali appeared, leading the Patriarch by the hand, and boldly reminded Selim of the Christian "privileges." The Sultan challenged the Patriarch to produce the Hatti Sheriff, which conceded them. The Patriarch could only tremble and mutter that it had been burned. Things looked very black ; but no Greek is ever taken at a loss. Three aged Janissaries were produced in time, who had been present at the siege, and were prepared to swear to the document's having existed. "The oldest inhabitant" has always been a trump card in Eastern lawsuits ; and once again it took the trick. But it did not save the Christian churches. Up to that time they had been allowed complete liberty of worship, and there had been only eight mosques in Stamboul. Now, with one exception, that of the church attached to the Venetian Embassy, they were all desecrated, and converted into mosques.

Selim before he died had doubled the extent of the Empire

by his conquests in Persia. By his conquest of Egypt he acquired the Caliphate for the House of Othman. When he died he was making immense preparations for some further military emprise, probably the conquest of Rhodes. But one secret of their strength was that the Sultans could prepare for years without having to disclose their plans. " If one hair of my beard knew what the other was doing I would pluck it out ! " said Mohammed. "Whither next should the Holy Caliph lead the Faithful?" they asked the grim old Selim on his deathbed, in the hope of discovering what his plan was. " To another world ! " said Sultan Selim, and turning his face to the wall found at last his " faithful friend."

If you leave out the Mosque of Selim, you can go straight from that of the Conqueror to the Mosque of the Shahzada (Heir Apparent), on the main road back to the town. The fore-court, when I last saw it, was a wild thicket, threaded by paths and dotted with turbehs half-buried in trees and shrubs. The mosque was built in 1543 by Sinan the great, the only Turkish architect. The beauty of its elegant minarets and exquisite tile-work is too apparent to call for analysis ; and we can turn at once to the story attached to it. Suleiman the Magnificent, successor to Selim, was a first-rate general, a good administrator and lawgiver, a patron of the arts, and a student of Aristotle. An Italian contemporary describes him as a tall thin man, with a " smoked " complexion, fine black eyes, long nose, a thin mouth with long moustaches, and a forked beard. His Turkish title, " Lord of the Age," was a bold claim; for his contemporaries included the great rival Charles V, Francis I, Henry VIII, and Elizabeth, Pope Leo X, Sigismund of Poland, and Akhbar the Great Moghul. It was an age of great sovereigns ; and yet Suleiman holds his place with them. His reign represents the culminating point of the Turkish Empire ; and, since his power was unchallenged, it was unstained by the violence of his predecessors. Even though he laid waste the Austrian border with a barbarity that makes us welcome, in his failure to capture Vienna, the turning-point of the flood of Turkish conquest to its long ebb, yet his personality is sympathetic, and his private character compares favourably with that of his predecessors and successors.

He was the first and last Sultan to raise a slave to the position of Queen-regnant. The only other occasions when a Sultan even went through a form of marriage was when Orkhan II allied himself with the Greek Princess Theodora, and Abdul-

Medjid with the Egyptian Princess Besma. Here is a notice of the event, from the archives of the Bank of St. George, at Genoa, the oldest banking-house in Europe; which has preserved its correspondence with Galata since 1346:

> This week there has occurred in this city a most extraordinary event, one absolutely unprecedented in the history of the Sultans. The Grand Signior Suleiman has taken to himself as his Empress a slave-woman from Russia, called Roxalana, and there has been great feasting. The ceremony took place in the Seraglio, and the festivities have been splendid beyond all record. There was a public procession of the presents. At night the principal streets are gaily illuminated, and there is much music and feasting. The houses are festooned with garlands and there are everywhere swings in which people swing by the hour with great enjoyment. In the old Hippodrome a great tribune is set up, the place reserved for the Empress and her ladies screened with a gilt lattice. Here Roxalana and the Court attended a great tournament in which both Christian and Moslem Knights were engaged, and tumblers and jugglers and a procession of wild beasts, and giraffes with necks so long they as it were touched the sky. . . . There is great talk about the marriage and none can say what it means.

We can now safely say that it meant ruin to the House of Othman. For Roxalana "Ghourem," the Joyous, acquired an absolute ascendancy over Suleiman, which she used ruthlessly in the exclusive interests of her own children. Finally, she committed him to a crime; one which was to cost the Empire dear, and which was commemorated by this Shahzada Mosque.

The Shahzada by right, at this time, was Moustapha, son of Suleiman by a Georgian who had died in childbed: a fine fellow capable of carrying on the line of the great Sultans. Roxalana, herself, had three sons, Mohammed, a weakling, Djeanghir a cripple, and Selim, afterwards the Sultan and Sot. On the strength of her own superior status Roxalana induced Suleiman to disinherit Moustapha. The little Mohammed soon afterwards died; and the general view that this was a divine judgment did not lessen the grief of the parents, who erected this Mosque of the Shahzada in his memory. Nothing daunted, Roxalana so intrigued against Moustapha, that the young man was summoned to his father's tent while on campaign, and incontinently strangled. The little crippled Djeanghir, now the Heir, was, however, so devotedly attached to the handsome and gallant Moustapha that on hearing of his death, he pined and died. The succession accordingly passed to Selim the Sot; with consequences from which the Empire never recovered. For as a result there followed, first the regime of the Sultanas, and then that of the Kopreli Viziers; while the figures of the Sultans themselves fade into the Hareem.

There are other smaller mosques, which have more cheerful associations with this family. One is the Mihrima Mosque, built also by Sinan, for Suleiman's favourite daughter. This laughter-loving lady insisted that the great architect should build such a mosque that the worshippers within it should not feel that they were indoors. It is indeed a marvel of lightness and a miracle of lighting. It stands high on the summit of the Sixth Hill, on the site of the ancient Monastery of St. George, overlooking the walls. For this reason it came to be used for the solemn service attended by a Sultan about to lead an army out to war through the Adrianople Gate. In Turkey beauty had no higher mission than to serve war.

The other mosque is that of Mihrima's husband, the Grand Vizier Roustem Pasha. It is the exact converse of the Mihrima Mosque, dark, over-decorated, and on a low-lying site. In it Sinan has expressed a sharply-contrasted personality, that of the stern worldly husband who was never known to smile. Roustem thriftily insisted on the lower story being arranged for shops, whose rents should maintain the mosque. He also built into it his unrivalled collection of Persian tiles. The enormous fortune which it commemorated even more than it did the founder was dispersed on his death. For it is indicative of the democratic foundation of Turkish society that the fortunate did not " found a family." Accumulations of wealth were generally annexed by the autocracy.

Another mosque, the Sultanah, was a surprise present from Suleiman to Roxalana. She had, it is said, a fancy for coloured marble columns, both to look at and to stroke. And so we see here no less than sixty, collected for her by Suleiman. He also added to the mosque charitable foundations for women, including a hospital open to all women of any country or creed.

Of Roxalana herself, the one and only Ottoman Empress, we can now form a clearer opinion, since the portrait painted by Bellini and given to Sir H. Layard by Abdul-Aziz, has passed into possession of the nation. We see her in profile, her red hair hanging down her back in two braids. On her head is a high crown over a silk cap, and there are several rows of large pearls round her neck. The face is a clever—and a cruel one.

The great Mosque of Suleiman, our next point, is the most costly and conspicuous example of Ottoman architecture. It commemorates the capture of Belgrade and Bagdad. The general effect is disappointing. It is said that Sinan was cramped by his orders to copy and outclass St. Sophia. Certainly the same structural weakness in the support of the dome has here, too, disfigured the exterior with clumsy buttresses. The aspect from outside is also injured by the crowding of the dependent institutions ; and from inside it is not improved by the raffle of cords and wires. The ten galleries of the minarets remind us that Suleiman was the tenth of the dynasty, and was born in the first year of the tenth century of the Hagira. The proportions of the interior are impressive, and the colouring pleasing. There are two rose-windows of great beauty, from Persia. The columns were looted indiscriminately from Classic Temples and Christian churches ; of interest are two gigantic porphyry columns from some pagan temple.

In the white marble pavement of the Court-yard is one porphyry slab, which it has been said was intended for a place of honour inside, before the mihrab. But a Greek mason secretly carved on it a cross, hoping thereby to convert or confound the infidel. All he achieved was his own decapitation on the stone he had desecrated ; which is now placed, cross undermost, where the faithful may tread it under foot.

The turbeh of the Sultan is a beautiful piece of decorative stone-work. The Cashmir shawls affected by Suleiman, and the huge white turban of his own design, are worth noting.

It was under Suleiman, at the apex of the Empire's development, that the first signs of its decay appeared. After the capture of Belgrade and Rhodes, Suleiman ventured to divert the energies of the Empire for two years into ways of peace. But the Janissaries mutinied at this, and the Sultan, after killing the ringleaders with his own hand, found himself forced to undertake new campaigns against Hungary and Austria. His failure to take Vienna, and his disastrous retreat, although veiled in vain-glorious proclamations, marked the turn of the tide. The defence of Vienna, and of Szegedvar, where he died, showed that Christian races no longer welcomed the Turks as a relief from worse rulers. They had begun to prefer death to the disastrous subjugation by a Sultan. The change manifested itself suddenly. While Hungarian peasants were still emigrating in order to enjoy the improved tenure obtainable under Ottoman rule, Hungarian citizens were blowing themselves up rather than accept Ottoman administration.

Suleiman, known to Europe as the Magnificent, was known to his own people as the Legislator. During his reign a Commission was sent from England with a view to reforming our judicial system on the lines of his. And yet, only fifty years later, we find Christopher North advising merchant venturers to employ false witnesses for preference in Turkey, because they knew their business. Roustem, Suleiman's Grand Vizier, seems first to have made a system of selling offices to the highest bidder. Later this was extended to the army and navy. Ibrahim, his other prominent Vizier, was the first conspicuous instance of another growing evil, the elevation to responsible positions of personal favourites or palace functionaries. This, Ibrahim, a Greek, had abilities; others so promoted by later Sultans had not. For instance, Mourad, grandson of Suleiman, wandering in the Bazaars, heard a cook complaining of the local government. Pleased with the answers of this man Ferhat, Mourad shortly afterwards promoted him to Grand Vizier. Mourad, we may mention here, was a miser. He kept the money produced by the sale of his offices under his bed. The horde being on an imperial scale, he soon had to sink a well there; and every night he poured in the day's takings until the well held nearly three millions, all in gold coin.

Kotchi Bey, a contemporary Turkish historian, attributes the Ottoman decline to yet another custom instituted by Suleiman. He ceased to preside openly over the Divan; but listened to its proceedings from an adjoining room, behind a curtain. "This ended," says Kutchi Bey, "in the curtain taking the place of the Caliph!" But in view of the inferiority of Suleiman's successors, this gradual abdication of authority in favour of the Grand Viziers may have had its recommendations.

Suleiman, greatest of Sultans, died; and this was the manner of his death, before Szegedvar.

"The city which had defied Suleiman, and which he had sworn to capture, was taken; but Suleiman himself knew nothing of it. For two days his lifeless corpse with staring eyes and rouged cheeks had sat in his tent propped on the divan. No break was allowed in the usual routine: reports were made to the dead Sultan, meals served, messages sent. The moment Szeged fell the royal tent was struck, and the royal carriage with the Emperor still upright inside hurried to Constantinople." So Suleiman, dead, travelled that road which he had made so many travel with death in their hearts. Busbequius, returning from an embassy to his Court, was no sooner outside the walls than he met wagon after wagon loaded with boys and girls, on their way from the frontier to the slave-market in Constantinople. The less valuable were driven in herds or tied in a long chain. "Beholding this woeful sight, I could not forbear weeping at the unhappy state of Christendom." This Busbequius, too, had humour. When he wanted to send a secret letter, he put a sucking pig in the dispatch bag ; and the Turks, hearing the squeaking, were restrained from touching the unclean receptacle.

Selim the Sot succeeded Suleiman, thanks to Roxalana. In a few months the Caliphate from being the wonder of the world became the joke of the Bazaars. Turks have a strong sense of primitive humour ; and a drunken Caliph appealed to it. Barbaro, the Venetian ambassador, remarks : " Whoever saw his face inflamed with Cyprus wine and his short figure corpulent with indulgence, could respect in him neither the warrior nor the ruler of warriors. Nature unfitted him to be the Head . . . of that warlike State." A catchword was started, " Who will stand us a drink to-day, the Khodja (priest), the Kadi (justice), or the Kalif." Though contrary to the Koran, drinking had become very prevalent. Busbequius, again visiting the city in 1553, tells us :

"I saw an old man who, after he had taken up a cup of wine to drink, used first to make a hideous noise. I asked his friends why he did so. They answered that by this outcry he did as it were warn his soul to retire to some secret corner of his body, or else wholly to emigrate, that she might not be defiled with the wine he was about to guzzle."

Perhaps it was as well that authority had passed from the Caliph to the Viziers. The necessity of keeping the army and navy busy led to war with Venice, and to the capture of Cyprus. A naval league was formed against the Turks, and they were utterly defeated by Don John of Austria at the battle of Lepanto. They had fallen behind in shipbuilding ; and the big Italian ships carried guns that crushed their galleys at long range. A contemporary Portuguese ballad reports :

> The balls of the Christian cannon
> Were of great battery :
> But in the Turkish galleys
> Was light artillery.

Great was the panic at Constantinople. Selim II could think of nothing better than to return to the policy of Selim I ; and ordered a general massacre of the Christians. The Grand Vizier, however, postponed its execution. The same danger threatened the Christians in 1593, after the Spaniards took Patras. A new era had evidently begun. The Turkish aggression had leagued all Christianity against it ; and, being forced on to the defensive, it proceeded to treat its Christian subjects no longer as partners, whose profits might tempt other Christians to invest in the Empire, but as prisoners and hostages.

THE LESSER MOSQUES AND SULTANS

The Sultans following Suleiman are symbolical of this decaying initiative. Of the twenty, about half came to an untimely end. Four were murdered and five deposed, of whom three were subsequently done to death. Their personal decadence is partly attributable to the practice, begun under Mohammed III, of imprisoning the heirs in a carefully guarded building in the old Seraglio, the Kafess or Cage. They were thus denied any experience of government. The first victim of the Kafess was Akhmet.

During his fourteen years of reign (1603–1617), Akhmet conferred two benefits on the city. He wrung from the mullahs a withdrawal of their prohibition of tobacco, which had been the cause of constant riots; and he built the noblest mosque in Constantinople.

For the mosque of Akhmet we return to the old Hippodrome. It stands on the finest site in the city, side by side with St. Sophia : the masterpieces of the two Empires in contrast. It commemorates no victory; but its erection coincides with the Treaty of Sitvatorok, the first of a succession of pacts disastrous to the Empire. Next to Eyoub it is the most sacred of the mosques, probably because a fragment of the Black Stone of Mecca is built into the mihrab. It is the only mosque with six minarets—the number until then reserved for El Haram, the mosque at Mecca. Akhmet had to build for the latter a seventh minaret before Mecca would accept of this usurpation by the Caliph. The young Sultan worked at the building with his own hands; and the clothes which he wore while at work can still be seen in his turbeh near by. With the strenuous picture of Akhmet which they suggest, we may compare the account of him given by Knolles :

The Padishah was in rich cloth of gold embroidered with perles and diamonds ; his turbant covered with fine plumes of black heron's feathers enriched with great diamonds, and a chain of the same stones about the lower part of his turbant ; on his little finger he had a diamond of large bigness and inestimable price that gave a marvellous great light. He was proudly mounted on a goodlye horse richly caparisoned, the sadlle embroidered with perles and diamonds, the stirrup of pure gold with diamonds, and on the horse's mane great tassels of them ; before him on his saddle-bow a Leopard covered with cloath of gold; with a great number of Pages very beautiful, chosen from among the tribute children and appointed for the pleasure of their masters.

The mosque has been generally chosen for official celebrations; and has been the scene of more than one crisis in Turkish history. The last and gravest was when Mahmoud the Reformer destroyed the Janissaries in 1826. The Sacred Banner was then planted over the mihrab, and the faithful were adjured to rally to the Caliph. The issue was long in doubt, but was decided in the spacious forecourt of the mosque. On the great sycamore the dead Janissaries hung in rows, as the Turkish historian says, " like the black fruit of a tree of hell."

The beautiful Fountain of Akhmet, close by, is perhaps the finest of the many public fountains. The very elaborate inscriptions, besides their decorative purpose and obscure meaning, have each a cryptic significance. For instance, the characters are so arranged that an addition of their numerical values gives the date of the erection. Such fancies were dear to this descendant of Othman. One other innovation connected with Akhmet's name must be recorded. He first departed from the traditional practice of murdering a score or more brothers upon his accession. But since the Caliphate had to pass to the eldest male of the house, the succession to it, as a result of his action, ceased to pass any longer in the direct male line, a further cause of intrigue and confusion.

The last mosque of interest is the first you will have seen after crossing the bridge, the Yeni Valideh Djami, or New Mosque of the Sultan's mother. It was begun by Machpeikér Sultan (the Moon-faced), favourite wife of Akhmet, and a lady who played an important part in history. The daughter of a Greek priest, she was one of the leading Sultanas of the period of the Hareem rule; that lasted for the life of seven Sultans, and for seventy years. Her mosque was unfinished when Achmet died; and during the subsequent two reigns Machpeikér was a prisoner in the seraglio. But with the accession of her son, the warlike Mourad IV, she returned to power, and retained it during his reign and that of her son Ibrahim. Upon Ibrahim's death, and the accession of Mohammed IV her grandson, her authority was challenged by Tarkhann Sultan, his mother, with results ultimately fatal to the older lady. Thereupon Tarkhann finished this mosque, nearly fifty years after its foundation.

Built entirely of white marble, even though dingy with dirt, this mosque is still a most beautiful building. The minarets have a slender and unsurpassed elegance, and the building is grouped round and graded up to the dome with masterly skill. The blue tiling, the lacework carvings, and the opalescent stained-glass are in themselves worth a visit. One column, of a peculiar rose-pink, was a present from Cyprus, sent, upon its capture, by Kapoudan Pasha Yousouf, the handsomest man of his time. But neither the present nor his good looks could save the Admiral from eventual decapitation. The mosque with its interrupted history, remains a very lovely memorial of the reign of the Sultanas, the "Monstrous Regiment of Women."

The later Sultans were many of them mosque-builders; but their mosques may be left in obscurity, like their memories.

A few, however, of earlier or later date, which have some special feature of interest, may be briefly mentioned here.

The Mosque of Nouri Osmanieh (Light of Osman) is a last effort to experiment in a new design. Mahmoud I, in 1746, told his architects to make originality their chief object. The result is more eccentric than effective. All the conventional features of mosque-construction are there, but unpleasingly distended or distorted.

Another curiosity is the Mosque of Davud Pasha, on the seventh hill, which has the distinction of having been built sixty years before the Conquest by the Turks. It was, therefore, a capitulation granted *to* the Turks, and not by them. Bayazid I asked Michael Palæologus for leave for the Turkish residents to have their own mosque and law-courts like other colonies; and Michael readily granted it. But this earliest local mosque is now deserted and in ruins. If tradition be correct, an even earlier mosque would be the so-called Cellar Mosque (Mahsen Djami), in Galata, near the Custom House. This would seem to be a mediæval vaulted cellar. But the Mussulmans claim it to be the most ancient mosque in Europe, where the Arabs interred their leaders who fell in their attack on the city in 718. This interesting identification was effected with the help of an angel early in the seventeenth century.

Last, and least, is Mahullah Djami, near the Column of Constantine. It is a mosque in miniature, complete with minarets, gallery, etc., and not more than 12 feet across.

THE OLD SERAI AND THE SULTANAHS

We now leave the mosques, and our next visit, to the Old Seraglio, will enable us to get an impression of another two centuries of the history of the city.

The word seraglio is as hybrid as the institution. A Persian word " serai," used for the Byzantine Palace as rebuilt by the Ottomans, reaches us as " seraglio " through the Italians, who were the first link between the Empire and Europe. The first plan of the Turkish seraglio can be seen in the engraving facing p. 126. It may at once recall to us the tent and stockade of a nomad khan. But with passage of time it grew more and more like the old Byzantine Palace quarter. Thus, the outer precincts were public, but the inner quarter became again a Forbidden City, jealously guarded. As late as 1634 a Venetian was hanged for inspecting it with a telescope from the windows of his house. The irregular battlemented wall with square towers, under which we pass in the tram, fortified it from the city. It was constructed as a summer palace for Mohammed the Conqueror, and known as the " New Palace." But the seat of Government, under him, remained the Old Palace (Eski Serai) in the centre of the town— the big enclosure seen in the engraving. Suleiman first made the Seraglio the seat of the Government. And it remained so until 1839, when Abdul-Medjid withdrew to a new palace on the Bosphorus. In 1865 the Seraglio was badly damaged by a fire, and since then it has only been used for annual ceremonies.

Many of the historic kiosques within it, such as the white marble Yali Kiosque, have disappeared. Of those that remain the first we shall see is the Aläi Kiosque, built into and looking over the wall near where the tram reaches it. From it the Sultans could see something of their humbler subjects, especially when undergoing execution down by the Horn. Here it is said Mourad IV used to sit with a crossbow, practising on the passers-by, until the Ulema limited him to ten heads per diem, as the bag allowed to a Caliph.

The four gates still remain : the Iron Gate, the Gate of the Cold Fountain (Soük Tchesme Kapou) which we pass in the tram, the Gate of the Rose Palace, and the Sublime Porte (Bab-i-Humayoun). Before passing through this last, we may note the niches on either side, very convenient for the exhibition of the heads of Grand Viziers on silver plates. Above it is the inscription set there by Mohammed I : " God shall perpetuate the builder's glory—God shall uphold his work—God shall make fast his foundations." But the imperial irade no longer runs in Constantinople, or anywhere else. Even before the end the outer Court had suffered a loss of dignity. The railway had entered it, and market gardens had encroached upon it. The avenues of plane-trees and of cypresses, leading to the kiosques, make pleasant vistas still, but the historical associations are now the principal attraction.

The Court inside the Sublime Porte was the stamping-ground of the Janissaries. Here, when the moments approached to depose a Sultan or behead a Vizier, they upset their kettles, or great round cooking-pots, beat them with their wooden spoons, and by much rushing about and shouting worked themselves up to the requisite violence.

In front is the huge old plane-tree of the Janissaries, from whose boughs they themselves and their victims have, alternately, hung in rows. On the left the Church of St. Irene. In the Armoury of St. Irene there are a few rarities to be seen, and, as usual, much rubbish. The sword of the Conqueror, another of Skanderbeg, who was the great Arnaut patriot, an armlet of Tamerlane, the keys of conquered cities, some beautiful chain mail, and probably by now other objects of interest. The crusading armour is interesting. So are the good collections of mediæval Turkish arms. Up in the galleries is a very interesting collection of costumes made by Abdul-Medjid in the middle of the last century before Europeanization had quite ended the old picturesque Orientalism. This collection is a great help in getting an idea of the look of life in Osmanli Constantinople. We see here, for example, groups representing the Sheikh ul-Islam, the Viziers and Pashas, the Commander of the Janissaries, with their respective subordinates, a grim little group of the delivery of a death sentence, the Chiefs of the White and Black eunuchs, examples of the distinctive dresses of the Esnafs or Trade Guilds, and many other models of the highly-coloured Ottoman life which ended a century ago with the reforms of Mahmoud II. The story of Constantinople is indeed a costume-drama, and dress plays as large a part under the Ottomans as under the Byzantines. Many of the strange Turkish costumes are actually copied from the Byzantine. For example, that of the Peïks, or Running Guards—helmets of gilt bronze with a black crest, and gilded halberds; or that of the Sinistrals and Silahs, the Life Guards, with gilt headpieces and tall plumes—their officers in fur-trimmed robes of green velvet.

The Chief of the Black Eunuchs (Kizlar Aghassy), one of the most important State officials, was in charge of the women of the Palace. The Chief of the White Eunuchs (Kapou Aghassy) was in charge of the " pages." The first had the rank of a Pasha of Three Tails, the second that of a Pasha of One Tail. The Tugh, the Tartar symbol of dignity, was originally a yak's tail;

but after the Turks left Central Asia horse-hair was necessarily substituted. The Sultan headed the table of precedence, with Seven Tails.

If we had visited the Old Seraglio in 1542, in company with the writer of this letter, preserved in the archives of the Bank of St. George, this is what we should have encountered first :

You enter the first Court-yard surrounded by arches like a cloister. This is where the white eunuchs live, and you will generally see a number of them walking about dressed in their strange costume of pointed turbans and flowing robes of silk. They look for all the world like mummified old women, very thin and shrivelled. They attend on the Grand Signor and keep order among the white pages, Christian boys stolen from their parents to the number of 300–400 a year. Some of these boys are very handsome and magnificently dressed. Their cheeks are plump and their eyebrows painted. Strange things are told about them, but such matters are common here and little commented on. Next you pass into another Court, where dwell the black eunuchs. Of these there are several hundred, unlike the white, monstrously fat. They are regular savages. They keep watch over the women of the Sultan, who live in small but very beautiful palaces each under the management of a Court lady.

European whites, though preferred as pages, never became eunuchs : only the Asiatic whites from the Caucasus. The black eunuchs were mostly from the tall Soudanese tribes. Many of these giants can still be seen about the Bosphorus Yalis (villas), identifiable by their squeaky voices. Making mutes of them proved a failure. The whole Palace soon learned to converse in the sign-language of such omnipotent officials.

In the Seraglio were trained those of the tribute children selected for the " Civil Service." They constituted a sort of college or cadet corps. The early training was very severe. Bastinadoing by eunuchs and bullying by seniors were the daily portion of the itchoglou. In the presence of seniors they kept silence, and stood with eyes downcast and arms folded. After six years a select number passed on into the Second Chamber ; the rest being sent back to the fighting Janissaries. In the Second Chamber they were carefully educated in languages, open-air games, etc. They were then safe for employment in the Second Division, as Treasury clerks or Palace curators. A still smaller number passed on thence to the Third Chamber, where they were further educated in the highest accomplishments, such as valeting, calligraphy, the care of pet dogs, etc. These last then became eligible for posts about the Sultan's person, and thereafter for provincial Governorships and Pashaliks. In its steps, and in the succession of qualifications it imparted, the ladder corresponded to our more modern training for Government posts, with its boarding-school, university and private secretary-ship.

We have a description of this school by an Englishman, Dallam, who brought out the present of an organ from Queen Elizabeth to Mohammed II.

I came in directly on the Sinyori's righte hande but he would not turn his head to look at me. He satt in greate State yet the syght of him was nothing to the traine which stood behind and made me almost think I was in another world. I stood dazzling my eyes with lookinge on his people the which was 400 in number. 200 were his principall padgis apparaled in ritche clothe of goulde in gowns to the midlegg, upon their heades litle caps; great saches of silk about their waistes; on their legges red cordovan buskins. Their heades all shaven, saving behind their eares a locke of hare like a squirrels taile. Very proper men and Christian borne.

The third hundred were Dum men, who could neither heare nor speake, in clothe of golde, their caps of violet velvett, the crown like a letter bottell, the brims in five peaked corners. Some had hawkes on their fistes.

The fourthe hundred were all dwarfs bigbodied but low of stature, everyone with a simmetare.

It can be seen that the population of the Court was imperial in the Byzantine or worst sense of the word. The " outside " Court, which only came in when " *de service*," might be mainly Turkish; but the " inside " Court was alien, save for the Sultan himself, and his brothers or nephews immured in the cage. But it was the inside Court that governed the Empire; and the avenues to power, such as this school, were accessible to aliens only. The circumstance contributed to maintain the curious Ottoman tradition of a blended tyranny and equality. Thus the Sultan drew pay as a private of Janissaries, and yet remained an object of religious reverence. He combined, in fact, the attributes and authority of a Turkish chief, a Greek city tyrant, and a Persian God-King.

At the inner end of the outer Court of the Seraglio is the battlemented arch, with two conical capped towers, of the Middle Gate (Orta Kapou), or Gate of Peace (Bab-el-Selam), which leads to the inner Court. The chamber on the left of it was fitted with all conveniences for executions. Viziers and pashas could be drowned in the cistern underneath, then beheaded, and the heads exhibited by the Janissaries at the Sublime Porte. Eventually heads came to be exposed there for sale by the executioner, whose perquisites they were.

Before entering the inner Court we may visit the Tchinili

Kiosque (Tile Kiosque), under the north wall on the left of Orta Kapou. One of the oldest Ottoman buildings, built in 1466 by the Conqueror, its function as a museum has been taken by a new Museum, built in 1891, when the discovery of the Sidon Sarcophagi stirred national pride to see to their proper preservation. These old and new Turkish Museums imitate, oddly enough, the one the form of a Byzantine church, the other that of a Classic temple. For Tchinili Kiosque reproduces in a secular Turkish building the cruciform shape, the dome, pendentives, apse and portico of the church ; so strong was the Byzantine spell upon architecture. Although the tiles are nearly all gone it is still a beautiful building, and an ideal summer palace.

All these kiosques are roofed with lead. This is not, as we might suppose, due to the ease with which lead can be worked so as to take the curves of the concave eaves and convex domes. In this as in everything there is an inner meaning. Since Byzantine times a roof of metal has been a royal prerogative. One dethroned Sultan protested bitterly when the rebels, in the rush of a revolt, shut him up in a building with a roof of clay tiles. The propriety of his protest was at once admitted ; and, for the remaining few days of his tenancy of any earthly dwelling, a kiosque with a leaden roof was assigned to him.

The Museum collection was begun in 1850, and during the reign of Abdul-Hamid II acquired importance owing to its energetic administration by a painter of merit, Hamdi Bey. It was he who asserted the right of Constantinople to receive the finds made by the various foreign archæological enterprises, in spite of the opposition of the Powers. Apart from the sarcophagi and the classical exhibits already described (v. p. 22), the objects that concern the Empire, such as the furniture of Selim I, call for no comment, and can be left to the catalogue obtainable in the Museum. Hamdi Bey himself had an interesting history. In 1825 the Greek Community of Chios, at that time the centre of Greek culture, was massacred. Among the women and children sold into slavery was a boy of 12. He was bought by Mahmoud the Reformer, who became fond of him, and had him educated at Paris. He afterwards became Hilmi Pasha, one of the best of the Grand Viziers of the reformed Empire. One day his old mother appeared as a beggar at his gates, and was at once acknowledged and given precedence as head of the hareem. Hilmi's son was this Hamdi, who through the dark days of Hamidianism kept alive the torch of Turkish culture, and proved a benefactor of the archæological world.

Admission to the Inner Seraglio, the " Sacred Residence," the " Celestial Abode," the " Ineffable Coronation of Destiny," used to be a costly and complicated matter, but is now comparatively simple. Passing through the Orta Kapou, we have on our left the execution chamber, and on our right the ante-chamber for foreign envoys. The Turkish sense of humour doubtless enjoyed keeping Ambassadors waiting, sometimes for whole days, in surroundings calculated to correct any undue sense of their own importance. The want of solidarity and the servility of the Christian envoys earned them no better treatment; and as the authority of the autocracy waned its arrogance waxed. When at last it pleased the Sultan to admit the Ambassadors the summons was conveyed to the gatekeepers in the loud announcement, " Let the dogs be fed." The party was then conducted across the Inner Court to the Hall of the Divan, the building with a belfry on our left. There the Ambassador dined with the Grand Vizier, while his suite picnicked in the portico on leather carpets. The " scanty dishes," as one dissatisfied diplomat described them, were served in the green-tinted crockery reputed to neutralize poison. Several thousand Janissaries filled the Court, and to these, upon the appearance of the foreigners, were served kettles of rice. If they fell upon the rice and devoured it with normal ferocity, all was well. If they ate slowly and sullenly, a revolt was brewing. If not at all, it was on the boil. If they upset the kettles—the fat was already in the fire. After the meal the Ambassador received the regulation robes of honour : twenty-four for the French, sixteen for the English, twelve for the Venetian. In return he handed over his offerings, which were hurried off for the Sultan's inspection before the audience. Knolles, a British Ambassador of the sixteenth century, thus describes an audience of Selim the Sot :

All things now in readiness and the Embassaders sent for they set forward with their train, and came to the Third Gate which leadeth into the Privy Palace of the Turkish Emperor, where none but himself, his eunuchs, and the young pages his minions, have continual abiding. . . . Being entered in at this Gate, the Capitzi by whom they were conducted suddenly caused them to stay and set them one from another about 'five paces in a little room all curiously painted over ; on both sides of which room, when all things were whist and in deep silence certain little birds were heard to warble out their sweet notes and to flicker up and down the green trees of the gardens as if they alone had license to make a noise. . . .

Selymus himself in great majesty sat in an under-chamber, parted only with a wall from the room wherein the Embassaders followers attended whereunto he might look by a little window. The Embassaders were led single to make their reverence to the Great Turk and in the meantime certain of the Capitzi with the presents in their hands fetching a compass about mustered them in his sight before the window. All this while not the least sound in the world being raised. The Embassader's followers placed one after another as aforesaid were not aware that the Great Sultan was so near. Howbeit they were set in one after another, neither could he that came after see his fellow that went before but suddenly as one was let out another was advanced forward to the door where the Capitzi-Basha and the Oda-Basha taking him by both arms and by the neck and so leading him apace, by the way felt softly his wrists lest peradventure he might have some weapon in his sleeve.

Thus rather like men carried to prison than to the presence of so mighty a monarch they were presented; he sitting upon a pallet covered with carpets of silk as was the whole chamber. The Sultan sat gorgeously attired in a robe of cloth of gold all embroidered with jewels when, as the Embassaders followers by one and one brought before him and kneeling on the ground a Turk with all reverence taking up the hem of his robe gave it them in their hands to kiss. Selymus himself all this while sitting like an image without moving and with a great state and majesty keeping his countenance deigned not to give them one of his looks. This done, they were led back again, never turning their backs towards him but going still backward out of his presence. The Embassaders then delivered unto Selymus their letters and briefly declared their message, when he, answering in four words, as " that they were to confer with his Bashaws," presently they were dismissed. And so coming out of the two inner gates they mounted on horseback and took their way being accompanied by the whole order of the Janissaries with their captains. Among whom were certain of their religious called Hadji, who continually turning about and in their going singing or rather howling out certain psalms for the welfare of their Sultan gave occasion to wonder that they either left not off for weariness or fell not down like noddies for giddiness. Beside them many more on horseback, in regard whereof the Embassaders when come to their lodging to requite their greedy courtesy, frankly distributed among them above four thousand dollars and yet well contented them not.

Such " frog-marching " of foreigners before the Sultan was said to date from the assassination of Amurath by Milosch Kabilovitsch, after Kossovo. The arms and horse-armour of the assassin are to be seen in the Armoury at St. Irene, and their excellence explains how the desperado all but fought his way to freedom in the confusion. The " Embassaders " at least, we note, had by this time freed themselves from the indignities inflicted upon their suite, who were, doubtless, mostly Levantines.

Knolles, the Ambassador, was a Fellow of Lincoln, and a man of insight. His history, published in 1610, gives us an idea of how darkly loomed the Turkish peril over Europe in that age. In it he deplores " the declining state of the Christian Common wealth, the desolation of the Church militant here on earth, the dreadful danger daily threatened unto the poor remainder thereof." And little wonder when such communications were being received as the following " Letter of the Great Turk to all the Kings and Princes of Christendom." Therein Sultan Akhmet, a boy of nineteen—" Shadow of God on earth, Baron of Turkey, Lord of the Upper and Lower Seas, Beloved of Heaven," etc., etc.—calls on the Great Champion of Rome (i.e. the Pope) and his confederates the Princes of Christendom to submit themselves to his will. If they will " open their Towns and Gates " they may " retain their faith and accustomed ceremonies." Otherwise let them expect "nought else but mortall wars and firing of cities, with great occision and death both of old and young." The Sultan's armies are " even now marching through Hungarie to invade all Germany and the countrie of France," and will " soon capture Rome, whose gorgeous temples shall be used as was the Temple of the Holy Sophie."

Such was the Eastern Question in the spacious days of Elizabeth. To our forefathers Constantinople was a word of terror. Akhmet's summons to the Powers is still a long way from the " Identic Notes " of the Great Powers to the Porte in the nineteenth century. Not until the reign of Mourad III did the Sultans treat with Christian Princes as equals. Until then the Viziers addressed foreign sovereigns as " brothers."

The entrance to the innermost seraglio is along a path bordered with cypresses through the Bab-i-Sadet, or Gate of Felicity. The Hall of the Divan or Throne Room is in a graceful pavilion, but the apartment is modest in view of its immense importance. The throne is in the shape of a four-post bed, encrusted with gems, but not otherwise interesting. Here met the Council of the Nine Viziers. The Grand Vizier sat cross-legged on the dais, and above his head was a gilt grill with silk curtains, behind which sat the Sultan, invisible. In the lobby without waited the tchaouses, the ministers of doom. When the Grand Vizier had affixed his seal to a document he handed it to the kapuji. The kapuji kissed his hand, took it, and bore it shoulder-high from the room to the Sultan. On returning with it, now sanctified with the " toughra," he held it above his head, and all the Viziers rose and bowed as he passed. The Grand Vizier received it reverently, kissed it, pressed it to his forehead, and then read it to the Council. In this room and with this Byzantine ceremonial Councils debated the fate of peoples and the fall of dynasties. Here, for example, in 1525, came Queen Elizabeth's Ambassador to beg Mourad II for help against the Armada.

Outside and opposite us upon the right are the Nine Kitchens, funnel-roofed buildings. They range from the first, for the Sultan, and the second for the chief Sultanas, down to the seventh for the pages, the eighth for the scullions, and the ninth for the secretaries of the Divan—a significant order of precedence. Crossing a flower-garden, and passing through courts which were the quarters of the pages, you will come to the Library. It is contained in a small kiosque, with a fine bronze door, built by Moustapha III. The 5,000 manuscripts, mostly in Arabic, Persian, Turkish and Greek, the relics of the Byzantine Empire, have been repeatedly catalogued, and again recently by the Englishman, Stephen Gaselee, the German, Jacobs, and the Russian, Ouspensky. It is unlikely, therefore, that the travellers' tales of undiscovered treasures will now come true. Moreover, the Library was almost entirely destroyed by fire towards the end of the sixteenth century.

Beyond the Library is the Treasury. Treasuries are apt to enjoy an ephemeral brilliance. In the last decade of the Empire this Treasury could not compare, for example, with the Aladdin's Cave which the Russian Communists made of the Imperial Museum outside the Kremlin. Possibly the Turkish Republic, by the time you will see it, will have transferred what there is left to their Museum also. At all events the solemn and senseless ceremony that used to precede the opening of the door has been discontinued. Within there is a good deal of costly gear, jewelled harness, arms and plate. The most valuable *objet d'art* is the Persian throne looted by Selim I. Another exhibit, both ugly and unique, is a gigantic emerald. Some of the armour has associations, notably that of Mourad IV ; and there is a capital collection, arranged chronologically, of the costumes of the Sultans. Their varied taste in turbans is intriguing. Were they following a fashion of the day, or setting a new one ? Are the peculiarities of folding and finish personal, or of the period ? When Mahmoud adopted the fez, was it because the turban was symbolic of reaction, or only because he found it heating to his head ?

A discovery made here in 1680 has ever since given to the romantic hope of new finds. A box was opened, and found to contain a golden casket. In this was a mummified hand, on which was written, " The hand that baptized Jesus the Lamb of God." Undoubtedly this was the relic preserved at the Monastery of St. John Prodromos, and the very casket which Anna Comnena had made for it. The Sultan gave it to the Knights of Malta, and the Knights to the Tsar Paul in 1797.

The Seraglio was, as you can now realize, an institution, a whole palace quarter, like Whitehall Palace, or its own Byzantine predecessor. A warren of alleys and pavilions, gardens and gates, stables and kitchens, scattered haphazard, full of picturesque corners and pleasant courts, often sordid, splendid only in patches. Sandys described it in 1610 as " goodly groves of cypresses with plaines, delicate gardens, artificial fountains, all varieties of fruit-trees, and what not rare ; luxury being the steward and treasure inexhaustible." Beauty there is still in the Old Serai, but for palatial pomp we shall have to wait until we cross to Dolma Bagtche.

The Kiosque of Bagdad, for example, a copy ordered by Mourad IV of a pavilion he saw in that captured city, has beauty. So also has the Kiosque of Abdul Medjid, and the enjoyment of its view will probably be no longer lessened for the foreigner by the necessity of making polite conversation and of absorbing rose-leaf jam.

THE CAGE AND MOURAD

The Kafess or Cage, the State prison, may now be accessible. I myself have never seen that " ominous row of two-storied buildings, with windows only on the upper floor, covered with fine tiles and filled with splendid inlaid furniture." But I believe it still exists. In the Cage for two centuries the Heirs were entombed, as shadows under the shadow of death : in the company only of deaf-mutes and of odalisques who could never be mothers. Othman III passed fifty years in the Cage, and when he emerged had all but lost the power of speech. Suleiman II passed thirty-nine years there, copying and illuminating Korans. The poor saint through the thirty months of his subsequent reign begged continually to be restored to the peace of his prison. Selim III, after being buried in it for fifteen years, plunged so recklessly into revolt against the whole imperial system that he fell a victim to it. Even after Mahmoud II had modernized the Empire the practice continued. Mehmed Reschid, who succeeded Abdul-Hamid in our own day, lived a life of close imprisonment in a suburban villa.

We should see the Kafess, if only to provide a background for our memories of the historical scenes that took place there. Such a scene, for example, as followed the death of the murderous Mourad. It was Mourad who, succeeding at the age of fourteen, had broken with a rod of iron the regime of the Sultanas and the soldiery. When he was twenty-three the Sipahis revolted, murdered his Grand Vizier before his eyes, and called for his deposition as a sure prelude to his death. Mourad by his bold bearing quelled the revolt, facing the mob alone, like our Richard II. He took also a very Richard-like revenge; first in secret assassinations of the Janissary and Sipahi leaders, and, as he grew stronger, in an indiscriminate Terror. In one year, 1637, he executed 25,000 of his subjects, many with his own hand; and his total "butcher's bill" is estimated at 100,000. Having thus restored discipline to the army, he employed its activities in the reconquest of Bagdad, where only 300 of a garrison of 20,000 escaped extermination. He was the last Sultan who, after commanding in the field, made a triumphal entry into Constantinople. Rycaut, who was in Constantinople during his reign, has left us a picture of him:

When in his cups he is insupportable. The Pachas of greatest note he puts to death, and confiscates their estates. . . . He takes singular delight to sit in a Kiosk by the sea side, and from thence to shoot at the people with his bow and arrows as they row near the banks of the Seraglio, which has caused the boatmen ever afterwards to keep themselves at a distance from the walls. He likewise takes pleasure to row in his barge from one garden to another on the Bosphorus, so, if he observes anyone so bold as to put forth his head to see him pass, he commonly makes him pay the price of his curiosity by shooting him with his carbine.

Moreover, Mourad used to patrol the taverns at night with an Italian renegade, Bianchi, and if he caught anyone smoking, he first declared himself, and then cut off the offender's head. He at least succeeded in putting the fear of authority into a lawless society; and it was said—with doubtless an unconscious irony— that "the roads of the Empire under Mourad were as safe as the streets of Constantinople." But if Mourad drowned the Empire in blood, his brother and successor Ibrahim dragged it in the mud. Ibrahim (1640–1649) had been in the Cage from the age of two, with no other education or experience than those which wine or women could provide. His portrait, with turban tilted tipsily on one side, shows us a face amiable but bleared. He had survived two accessions; but the bow-stringing of royal brothers, though no longer *de rigueur*, was still *à la mode*, and he lived in hourly expectation of the executioner. The virile Mourad, it was known, was resolved to let the dynasty die, rather than leave the throne to his demoralized brother. Mourad fell ill at twenty-eight; ordered Selim's execution; and died with a grin on his face on learning from his mother Machpeikér, the Sultana Validéh, that Ibrahim was "dead." But Machpeikér had no intention of

depriving herself of the chance of recovering despotic power for
the hareem.　Ibrahim was dead—almost—with terror, but otherwise none the worse.　For, no sooner is Mourad dead, than all the
palace rushes tumultuously to toady to the new Sultan.　In panic
terror Ibrahim and his women pile the furniture against the door.
It is broken in, and Ibrahim, crazed with fright, can only see in
the protests of loyalty traps set to get a pretext for his murder.
As nothing will convince him, the corpse of Mourad is hurriedly
fetched and tumbled into the room.　Ibrahim, translated in a
moment from the tomb to a throne, dances with delight round it,
yelling " The Empire Butcher is dead—is dead ! "

But Ibrahim had not done with the Kafess.　Some Heirs seem
to have emerged from it tolerably sane, and made tolerable rulers.
Not so Ibrahim.　During the calamities of the hareem rule of
Machpeikér, we have occasional glimpses of him, spending hours
in weaving jewels into his straggly beard, throwing gold sequins
to his goldfish, or receiving every Friday from his mother the
fattest of fair ladies—for Turkish taste has always inclined to
embonpoint.　Meanwhile hareem rule was proving disastrous.
" Our people are ruined.　The Infidels besiege our towns.　Their
fleets blockade the Straits."　So ran the proclamation of the
conspirators who overthrew Ibrahim.　For the Turks, who could
tolerate the homicidal maniac Mourad, could not endure his
harmless and henpecked brother.　And so within nine years he
was again sitting in the Kafess, waiting this time for the hurried
footsteps that might announce his restoration.　At last he hears
the steps coming and flings the door open.　But on leaving prison
he had been imprudent enough to provide the House of Othman
with a male heir, who was now seven years old.　His own mother,
the Sultana Validéh, with the prospect of a yet longer regency
during a grandson's minority before her, had abandoned him.
And, this time, it was the bowstring.

But hareem rule was not to survive him long.　Tarkhann,
mother of Ibrahim's son the little Mohammed IV, contested the
authority of Machpeikér ; and a duel resulted.　Once more
Constantinople became the scene of one of those faction fights
which Court rule under the Greek Empire had made familiar.
Tarkhann, who as Queen-mother had the better constitutional
claim, was supported by the Vizier and the Sipahis, or Horse
Guards : Machpeikér, the old dowager, by the Janissaries or
Foot Guards, the Palace and the Clergy.　Paul Rycaut, secretary to the Embassy sent by our Charles II, thus describes the
Palace war :—

The Vizier had given orders to all the Pashas and Beylerbegs and others his friends that without delay they should repair to the Seraglio with all the force they could bring, bringing with them three days' provisions, obliging them under pain of death to this duty. In a short space the gardens of the Seraglio, the outward courts and all the adjoining streets were filled with armed men : from Galata and Tophané came boats and barges loaded with powder, ammunition and other necessaries : so that in the morning by break of day appeared such an army of horse and foot in the Streets, and Gallies in the sea, as administered no small terror to the Janissaries : of which being advised they thought it time to bestir themselves.

Hearing the tumult Machpeikér naturally supposed it was her friends the Janissaries overthrowing their soup-kettles and rising in her aid ; and discovered her mistake only in time to hide in a cupboard. There the old dowager was found, dragged into the street in deshabille, and strangled with a curtain-cord at the Orta Kapou—an outrage on decorum that was felt as an imperial disgrace. After the Vizier on the one side, and the Agha of the Janissaries on the other, had been killed, peace was made. But hareem rule under Tarkhann endured only for a short time longer and gave way to the regime of the Köpreli Viziers (1656–1702). Our ideas of the regime of the Sultanas are derived principally from Racine's " Rival Queens." Racine got the story of the Hareem War from De Cézy, the French Ambassador. But " Machpeikér " and " Tarkhann " seemed to his ear names unsuited to polite verse. So he rechristened them " Roxane " and " Atalide " ; and thereby communicated to many others the confusion that probably existed in his own mind between Roxalana and Machpeikér.

Now that the Sultanate is no more, the Kafess is possibly on view. But the end of the Caliphate is not likely to have made it more easy to get admission to the Hirkai Sherif Odassi, the Chamber of the Sacred Mantle. This was closed even to all lay Mussulmans, except the Sultan and a few great dignitaries. For relic-worship, contrary to the direct command of the Prophet, was too traditionally a part of the atmosphere of Constantinople for the Turks not to be seduced into it in their turn. The Chamber contains the Five Relics of the Prophet— all objects of idolatrous veneration. The principal one is the Sacred Standard, which tradition asserts to have been the tent curtain of Ayesha, the Prophet's favourite wife. It is said to be of wool, 12 feet long, and green, with no device. It has not been unfurled since 1596 ; although " unfurling the sacred standard " is the phrase for a proclamation of war. It is wrapped in a banner of the Caliph Omar, and preserved in a case of wood inlaid with mother-of-pearl and studded with precious stones. The last time it was in the field was in 1683, which is approximately the date we have now reached in our history.

THE GREAT VIZIERS AND RELICS

During the latter half of the seventeenth century the Empire was ruled by the able family of Köpreli, to the entire eclipse of the incapable Mohammed IV, Akhmet II, and Moustapha II. The Köpreli formed the only exception I know to the rule that in Turkey public office is not hereditary. They were, also, the most eminent of the Albanians who have so often provided rulers for the Empire. At the age of seventy Mohammed Köpreli, who had begun life as a scullion, was given full powers to save the State if he could. Blood-letting was the remedy of the age for all ills alike. During his five years of office, accordingly, his executions averaged 5,000 a year. Before he died (1661) he had repressed and reconstructed the army and navy, recovered command of the eastern Mediterranean, and restored confidence in the government. His son Akhmet, an even abler administrator, in like manner reformed the civil and judicial systems. But his efforts to revive the military supremacy in Europe failed. The nations of Central Europe were by then too fully grown to be overthrown by a Levantine Empire already enfeebled. Akhmet, in turn, was succeeded as Vizier by one Kara Moustapha, a boon companion of that jovial huntsman Mohammed IV. It was he who undertook the second siege of Vienna in 1683.

Benetti, the Venetian dragoman, saw the start of this army, and has left us a lively account of it. First came the Sacred Standard borne by an Emir, with a dervish shouting " Hawa, Hawa ! " and other dervishes in hair-coats dancing. Then the Stamboul Effendi and the two Kadi Askers (supreme judges), with turbans so large that a man could not embrace them. Next the Grand Mufti (Primate) in white. Then pages, leading wolf-hounds, wearing gold-laced coats with red-spiked collars ; and four horsemen carrying hunting leopards. Two camels, one carrying the Koran, the other a piece of cloth from the Prophet's tomb. A hundred Janissaries bearing their kettles, their cooks in black leather aprons riding on laurel-wreathed horses. Then the archer-bodyguard in great helmets ; Delhis in tiger and panther skins ; pikemen in mail with green and yellow cloaks, on armour-plated horses. Four silk banners with eighty Aghas. Twelve Chavushes with black staves and silver chains. The Horse-tails, on white-wired poles with silver ornaments. A military band of kettledrums, cymbals and trumpets. (We should note that our military bands were borrowed from the Turks.) The Grand Vizier, resplendent. The Page Corps in shining mail with gold caps. Then Mohammed—himself a hunched, haggard little man—riding on horseback, in white robes embroidered with flowers and diamonds, with a fur-lined hood, a small turban and diamond spray. Following him the fine young Shahzada, more pages, the Sword-bearer, the Turban-bearer. And, behind, the six carriages of Sultanas; that of the favourite drawn by eight white ponies, the others by six. These carriages were covered by round canopies painted with arabesques and closed by red and green silk curtains. Yet other ladies in horse litters. And then, buffalo-wagons and miles of marching troops. Through all the procession back and forward ran the dervishes, naked but for little green aprons and tall felt caps, shrieking fanatical cries and blowing cow-horns. So went the Sword of Islam on its last great Jehad—to its greatest disaster. For if, in 1529, Suleiman had failed to take Vienna, but had suffered no serious defeat, in 1683 the Ottoman armies were so decisively defeated that they ceased for ever to be a menace to Europe. Thereafter their European frontiers receded more and more swiftly eastward. Sobieski annihilated the Ottoman army, claiming even to have captured the Sacred Standard itself among the hundreds of other banners. This, however, the Ottomans deny; and as no one then or since has ever seen the " Sandjak Sherif," we may assume that it is still, if anywhere, in its case in the Seraglio.

Another relic in the Chamber is the black camel's-hair mantle of the Prophet. This also used to be called out on military service; and is said to have won the battle whenever the Sultan wore it. It has now lost even its civil function, of being solemnly kissed every Ramazan by the Caliph. After which ceremony, the mantle was washed with water from a golden dish, and the water bottled in tiny phials. These were distributed to the most favoured of the faithful, who then broke with the water their Ramazan fast.

Other relics are the Prophet's beard, yet another tooth, and another footprint. They are all contained in hermetically sealed bottles, decorated with gold filigree and jewels, and enshrined upon an altar in the middle of the room. There are also the silver key of the Sanctuary at Mecca, and Korans copied by the Caliphs Omar and Othman.

THE HAREEM

If the power of the charms and taboos contained in the Hirkai Sherif Odassi is almost gone, that of the Imperial Hareem of the Serai is gone without leaving a vestige. The revolt against the hareem in public life, which was achieved under the Köpreli, has now been realized successfully in private life. The revolution of 1908 not only swept away a rotten system of government, it also threw open the doors and windows of Turkish family life. The marble Gate of Felicity was, it is true, an open road to imperial power for one or two women favoured of fortune. But this power was bought at the price of slavery for all their sex. It was a glorious gamble, no doubt—that of drawing a winner and being thrown the handkerchief, or drawing a loser and being drowned in a sack ; or, as in most cases, just drawing a blank and living a long life of barren boredom. But now that the hareem is everywhere disappearing, the Turkish language will have to find some word for " home."

The hareem was the hub of Empire and Holy of Holies of the Seraglio. We have seen something of the part it played. As a political institution it can best be understood as the feminine counterpart of the Janissaries. Certainly in the end these " tribute girls " recruited from the subject Christian races proved as fatal to their Turkish masters as did the " tribute boys " from whom the Janissaries were drawn. If the Janissaries were highly organized, so also was the hareem. Its ruler was the Sultana-mother (or Validéh). Her Prime Minister was the Chief of the Black Eunuchs, and there was a Lady Comptroller (Kyahya Kadin), and a Treasurer (Khaznadar Usta). The " Council of State " were the four Kadins or Consorts, who took precedence in order of merit : first the Royal Queens, or mothers of sons, next the Royal Ladies, or mothers of daughters. Below them ranked the Gediklis, or personal odalisques of the Sultan, of whom twelve were in a specially privileged position. From this class were chosen the Ikbals, or favourites ; but they obtained no improvement in their position thereby, unless they bore a child. The next class, or " Ustas," were ladies-in-waiting on the Kadins and the Queen-mother. The " Shagird " class was for children, still novices. The Jariya were servants only. The whole female population amounted to some five or six hundred generally, but latterly to more. When Abdul-

Aziz left the Old Serai there was a hareem of twelve hundred women. Little wonder the privy purse required two million sterling a year.

Three hundred years ago, had you bribed your way through the Bab-i-Sadet, and come as far as you have to-day, you would have been in very great danger. Had a party of ladies appeared guarded by eunuchs, instant decapitation would have been your fate. One party of visitors only saved their heads by throwing themselves flat on their faces, like the gardeners in " Alice in Wonderland." Very few men ever caught a sight of the Sultan's ladies—and lived to tell the tale. Dallam, the Elizabethan organ-builder, was one of the few. He had made many friends in the Palace, and was one day led to a small grille in a wall and told to look through, although his guide dared not himself do so. On looking, he saw into a garden beyond, where some twenty persons were playing ball :

> Atte the first syghte of them I thoughte they had been younge men. But when I saw their hare hung doone on their backs platted with a laste of small perles and by other plain tokens I did knowe them to be women and verie prettie ones indeed. They wore a litle capp, faire chaines of perles and juels in their ears, coats like a souldiers mandilyon some of red sattan and some of blew, britches of fine clothe made of cotin wool as white as snow and fine as lawne. Some did weare fine cordovan buskins and some had their legges naked with a goulden ring on the smale of her legge. I stoode so long loukinge upon them that he which had brought me began to be verrie angrie and stamped with his foote to make me give over loukinge ; the which I was verrie lothe to dow, for the sighte did please me wondrous well.

A day in the Serai then was anything but dull for visitors. One day Dallam had his organ in pieces on the floor of the kiosque, when his Turkish workmen suddenly bolted.

> I called after my drugaman, asking him the cause. He said the Grand Sinyori and his conquebines weare cominge and we must be gone on pain of deathe. Before I gott out of the house they had run over the greene quite out of the gate and I ran as faste as my legges would carrie me after. And four neagers or blackamores came running toward me with their semetares draune ; if they could have catched me they would have hewed me all in pieces. When I cam to the gate there stood a greate number of Jemoglans praying that I mite escape the handes of those running wolves.

He was lucky to get off with a fright that made him ill, and lasted until he was safe back in England.

But the Sultan himself did not always find the hareem a Gate of Felicity. Knolles tells us of a domestic trouble of Akhmet :

The day after the marriage the Grand Seignior did cruelly beat his Sultana, the mother of his daughter whom he had married to the Captain Basaw ; he stabbed her with his kandjar or dagger through the cheeks and trod her under his foot. The reason was because she had strangled a favourite of his which was one of his sister's slaves, whom the Grand Seignior having seen sent for her. The Sultana hearing thereof caused her to be brought to her lodging, where she stript her of her apparell, strangled her, and put her clothes on one of her own slaves whom she sent to the Sultan instead of the other, and, at her return, strangled her also ; as she had done many others when they appeared to be with childe by the Grand Seignior.

After this one can face with more equanimity the tales of wholesale " noyades " of these ladies. Ibrahim, for instance, had the happy idea in one of his debauches of starting his hareem all over again. All his hundreds of women were accordingly tied up at midnight in sacks, and thrown into the Bosphorus. On several other occasions some hundreds were drowned at once. The private dock can still be seen from which so many of fortune's favourites passed to a cruel fate.

The furniture and flunkeys of great institutions survive their death. Possibly the Gate of Felicity may be still guarded at the time of your visit by a melancholy eunuch in a fez and a Stambouli frock-coat ; although for nearly half a century there has been nothing within to guard. Even as a sentry used to be set daily to guard a grass plot in the Park at Tsarskoe Syelo to prevent passers-by from picking the ghost of a wild lily that had once been admired by a Tsar over a century ago. You can meditate, at all events, upon the inscription over the Gate : " Believers enter not the doors of the Prophet without permission ! " or you can moralize as one modern traveller does :

They entered the Bab-i-Sadet, those women of unearthly beauty, languor and grace, those rarest of human flowers. They passed within that blank and mocking wall, they flitted from room to room, and yet on earth none of them is even a shadow now.

In other words, " Where is that party now ? " and my own fleeting glimpses of the unearthly beauties of the hareem did not so much suggest " flitting flowers " as the more solid associates of Hans Breitmann.

Up till now the Seraglio Hareem and the Hirkai Sherif Odassi remain two of the very few places on earth that no Anglo-Saxon or American foot has as yet trod. As the Pole used to be for explorers—as Everest still is for mountaineers— so have the Sultan's Hareem and the Hirkai Sherif been for tourists. Go to Constantinople and you may be the fortunate first to see them.

THE GALLEYS AND EUNUCHS

Leaving the inner seraglio, you may note on your way back to the Bab-i-Sadet, a relic of the Roman Empire, the altar set up in the centre of the inner court. Turning to the right outside the gate, you can enter the seraglio garden, which is now open, and visit another memorial, the Column of Claudius Gothicus (*v.* p. 21). If you then cross the garden, toward the Iron Gate (Demir Kapou), and turn down right-handed, inside the wall and towards the harbour, you will come to the last kiosque, the Kaik Khaneh, or Boat-house, standing where the Serai wall reaches the Golden Horn. Here are, or recently were, some fine examples of the kaik, a craft that has only become extinct in our own time. Also a very interesting naval prize, a mediæval galley, of which the history would seem to have been lost. Not improbably it may be one of those which Busbequius saw towed in after a sea-fight with the Genoese :

In the month of September (1560) the victorious navy of the Turks returned to Constantinople bringing the Christian captives with their Gallies, a joyful spectacle for the Turks but a sad one for the Christians. That night it lay at anchor over against Byzantium, so as to enter port next day in pomp. Solyman came down into an apartment in his gardens near the Sea side that from thence he might see the prisoners. Don Alvarez de Sandi was in the stern of his admiral's galley and with him Don Sancho de Leyva and Don Bellinger de Requesne, one Commander of the Sicilian, the other of the Neapolitan galleys. The captive galleys were all despoiled of their ornaments, pennons. . . . The prisoners were afterwards brought into the Seraglio, but so miserably hunger-starved that some fell down in a swoon. Others had arms put upon them in a jeer, in which posture they died.

The fate of such captives as lived to become galley-slaves was almost worse. A noble Hungarian, Wenceslaus Wratislaw, whose descendant was recently British Consul-General in Asia Minor, has left us an account of his servitude. His Ambassador had been rash enough to intrigue with the hareem against the Grand Vizier Sinan. His Embassy was accordingly raided, and he himself disappeared for ever. His staff, after years of hardships and hairbreadth escapes, were released at the instance of the first English Ambassador, Sir Edward Barton. Wratislaw's account of his life in the galleys was written in 1599, and translated by his descendant the Rev. A. H. Wratislaw :

We were conducted on board the galley under guard and Achmet, the Reis or captain, a Christian born in Italy who had become a Turk, ordered us to be chained to the oars. The vessel was fairly large, and in it five prisoners sat on a bench, pulling together at a single oar. It is unbelievable misery to row in the galleys—no work in the world can be harder. They chain each prisoner by one foot under his seat, leaving him so far free to move that he can get on the bench and pull the oar. When rowing you can on account of the heat only pull naked with nothing on but a pair of linen drawers. When a galley goes out through the Dardanelles iron bracelets or rings are put on the wrist of each captive so that he may not rise against the Turks. Thus fettered hand and foot he must row night and day, unless there is a gale, till the skin of his body is scorched like that of a singed hog and cracks with the heat. . . . Yet give way you must, for if the overseer sees you taking breath he beats you naked as you are with the galley scourge or a wet rope dipped in the sea until you are all bloody weals.

Often some jackanapes of a rascally Turkish boy amuses himself with beating the captives and laughing at them. . . . For food nothing but two small cakes of biscuit . . . when we rested a day or two by the shore we knitted gloves and stockings of cotton and bought food which we cooked ourselves in the vessel.

Near to the Boat-house are the dilapidated remains of the Sebetjilar Kiosque. In this the Sultan received the Kapoudan Pasha before naval expeditions started ; and from it he reviewed the fleet drawn up off shore. From a silver throne set up outside, so as to be seen from the shipping, he gave the expedition the blessing of the Caliph.

By the date which we have now reached upon our tour, the middle of the seventeen-hundreds, the Empire had become so enfeebled that enemies were once again threatening the walls from the sea ; while within them the state of affairs was truly Byzantine. The archives at Genoa give us this contemporary description :

Such is the unsafe condition of the city that people dare not go even the length of the street without armed servants. At night it is quite impossible to make a step outside without risk of a disagreeable adventure. There are no lights but lanterns, and the pavement and roads are so dreadful that no one who has not seen them could believe that human beings could bear such filth. The other morning I saw a heap of human heads on the left side of the Seraglio Gate. Most of them looked like ugly old women. I heard later they were fifty white eunuchs who had offended the Sultan. At the Seven Towers a number of prisoners, among them Christians, were thrown over the parapet of the Tower next the Torture Chamber, and you can see from the road naked and still living men caught on long hooks where they will stay until delivered by death.

The regime of the Köprelis had been followed by a period of prosperity. Houssein Köpreli had died in 1702, and Nououman Köpreli, who died in 1710, had been a failure. The Sultan Akhmet, who succeeded Moustapha, had been spared the Kafess, and showed capacity during a long reign of twenty years. He was pacific in policy, and successful for a time in war. Peter the Great in an attempt to expand his empire found himself, in Moldavia, at the mercy of Akhmet's Grand Vizier Baltadji (Wood-cutter), a palace servant promoted by a hareem intrigue, and had to buy himself off by a humiliating peace with the help of the English Ambassador. In 1715 the Morea, the home-land of the Greeks, was conquered from Venice by Coumourdji Damad (the Cucumber-seller), the Sultan's son-in-law. His siege of Corinth is now remembered as the subject of a poem by Byron. Though you would scarcely have guessed it from the poem, the Greeks of Corinth, as a matter of fact, welcomed the Turks as deliverers from the hated Latins.

This was the period of Greek ascendancy in the Osmanli Empire. The Phanariote families, who had survived the Turkish Conquest, were now supplying Governors for the European provinces, where they were as heartily detested by their fellow-Christians the Slavs and Vlachs as were the Venetians by the Greeks. On the Danube the Turks were less successful:

An Austrian army awfully arrayed
Boldly by battery besieged Belgrade,

and under Prince Eugène broke the Turkish armies at Peterwardein and Belgrade. The Treaty of Passarowitz freed Hungary for ever. Thereafter, but for a short favourable Persian war, the Empire, under Akhmet and his then Vizier, Ibrahim Damad, had peace until 1730.

The Janissaries then mutinied; and Akhmet, to save himself, flung to his wolves the bodies of his Kapoudan Pash, of his Kiaya, and of his son-in-law and lifelong friend, Coumourdji Ibrahim Damad. This did not, however, save him from deposition, and from succeeding his brother and successor Mohammed I in the Kafess, where he remained for the rest of his life. Upon this change the power passed from the ephemeral Viziers to Bashir, the Chief of the Black Eunuchs. This Bashir was an Abyssinian, bought for 30 piastres, who ruled the Empire for thirty years, and left a fortune of thirty millions. He negotiated the Treaty of Belgrade, which recovered Belgrade, Serbia, Bosnia, and Wallachia. He also introduced a Spy Terror, similar in character to that which signalized the reign of Abdul-Hamid.

The vivacious Lady Mary Wortley Montagu was much impressed by it :

> The Grand Signior with all his absolute power is as much a slave as any of his subjects and trembles at a Janissary's frown. Here is indeed a much greater appearance of subjection than amongst us ; a minister of State is not spoke to but upon the knee ; should a reflection on his conduct be dropped in a coffee-house (for they have spies everywhere) the house would be rased to the ground and perhaps the whole company put to the torture. . . . But when a minister here displeases the people in three hours time he is dragged from his master's arms. They cut off his hands, head and feet and then throw them before the palace gate with all the respect in the world ; while the Sultan (to whom they all profess an unlimited adoration) sits trembling in his apartment. This is the blessed condition of the most absolute monarch on earth who owns no law but his will.

Under Othman II, the hunchback, and Moustapha, who had been fifty years in the Kafess, the Empire was governed by another Chief Eunuch, through the Greek officials. In the meantime the Empress Catharine of Russia had developed her " Oriental Project." This was nothing more than the traditional Russian imperial policy, which Peter the Great had unsuccessfully inaugurated, and which was only abandoned in our own day. Its aim was to make Constantinople a port of the Russian Empire. And from this time on the history of Constantinople has to be dug out of secret treaties and diplomatic despatches —a form of reading even less alluring than the most flowery Turkish historian or the driest Greek chroniclers.

The policy of the Oriental Project was simply the incitement of the European provinces to revolt against the Empire. In 1770 a Russian fleet appeared off the Morea. It was nominally under the command of Alexis Orloff, brother of Catherine's favourite of the day, but it was navigated and fought by British officers under Admiral Elphinstone. The Morea rose ; but the fleet was powerless to prevent an imperial force of Albanians from devastating the country and massacring 15,000 of the insurgents. The Anglo-Russian fleet meantime defeated the Ottoman navy off Chios, but lost its flagship, blown up by a corsair, Hassan of Algiers. In return Lieutenant Dugdale steered a fire-ship through the Ottoman fleet while at anchor, and destroyed it. Elphinstone advised taking advantage of this, and forcing the Dardanelles forthwith ; but Orloff hesitated until the Turks had blocked the Strait with batteries. Having tried to establish a base at Lemnos, and been driven thence by a force landed by Hassan, who had now become Kapoudan

Pasha, the fleet withdrew to operate in Syria. But it had achieved its purpose. In the Treaty of Kainardji, signed in 1774, while the territorial terms were unexpectedly favourable to Turkey, on its side " the Sublime Porte promised to protect constantly the Christian religion and churches, and allow the minister of Russia at Constantinople to make representations on their behalf." Russia thereby procured an unlimited right of intervention, and a fulcrum for intrigue in the internal politics of the Empire. Russia in return could readily afford to restore to the Empire its lost provinces, in which the renascence of national feeling was already making headway against imperial incompetence. And Russia also agreed to withdraw the Russian fleet from the Mediterranean, but kept this clause secret so that the insurgent movement should suffer no discouragement.

Catherine made no secret, however, of the fact that her Oriental Project aimed at reviving a Greek puppet Emperor under Russian protection. She called her second son Constantine, and had him taught Greek so as to qualify him for the post. When the Crimea was annexed in 1784, she and Potemkin met the Emperor Joseph there, concerted with him a war against the Ottoman Empire, and drove with him in state through an arch inscribed " To Byzantium." The war that followed seemed likely at first to lead her there.

Early in 1790 a deputation of leading Greeks had presented to Prince Constantine an address asking for Russian assistance " in delivering from the hands of barbaric Moslems an imperial capital which they had usurped " ; to which Constantine had replied in suitable Romaic. Phanariote merchants had also fitted out a fleet which had sailed to attack Constantinople, but was intercepted by Turkey's Algerine auxiliaries. But the Russian advance on the Danube continued and the victorious Suworof was soon able to send his famous rhyming report to the Empress—

> Slava Bogou slava Vam
> Krepost bzyali i ya tam

as he pressed on his march for Constantinople. But

> Another Lion gave a louder roar
> And the first Lion thought the last a bore.

Neither for the first time nor the last that golden apple of discord, Constantinople, set the Powers by the ears. Pitt, abandoning our traditional policy of supporting Russia, asked Parliament

for means to send fleets for the defence of the city, to the Black
Sea and to the Baltic. But the Greeks had enlisted the sympathies of a Parliament inclined to look on them as the descendants of Leonidas and on the Turks as the reincarnations of
Timour and Attila. Moreover Parliament, in those days, was
more conservative than to-day as to continuity in foreign policy.
Fox headed the opposition ; Pitt dropped his war policy ; and
the century-long duel, which then first began, between Russian
military and British naval imperialism, was postponed for the
moment. Russia, as it fell out, was diverted to the partitioning of Poland ; and Constantinople was left to be fought for
on another occasion.

If, however, a pragmatical princess like Catharine and a
practical premier like Pitt could agree in thinking a proposal
to restore a Greek Empire sufficiently serious to justify a war
between Russia and England, the Greeks at Constantinople
must have considerably improved their position there, since
we saw them being marched off in slave-gangs by the Conqueror.
The centre of Greek politics was the Phanar. And since we have
done with the Seraglio, which was the centre of Osmanli politics, the Phanar may well be our next point of pilgrimage.

The Phanar is the old fortified enceinte of the Petrion, on
the Golden Horn, where the Greek survivors of the Conquest
settled. There they were joined by the Patriarch, after he had
been ejected successively from the Church of the Holy Apostles,
the Church of the Virgin Pammakaristos, that of the Vlach
Serai, and that of St. Demetrius.

THE PHANAR AND THE GREEKS

There is not much to be seen now in the Phanar, but there is
something to be said about it if you are to oversee the past
history of the city, and understand its present condition. The
ill-treatment of the Greeks in the crisis of the Conquest was
only an episode. Mohammed needed their help in restoring the
population and the prosperity of his capital ; and he wished to
avoid their dispersal into their provincial centres, Epirus, Trebizond, or the Morea. He brought in at once 15,000 European
Greeks ; and, after the conquest of Trebizond, he transferred
the whole of its upper- and middle-class population to his capital.
He also exempted the Greek residents in the city from the conscription of children. Since, therefore, the Turks took no interest in trade or industry, and the capitulatory privileges

granted to foreign colonies by the Greek Emperors had been abolished, the growing Greek population prospered and soon began to amass large fortunes.

Mohammed, moreover, greatly feared the political power of the Pope, and in order to dissolve the Union of the Greek and Latin Churches, he gave the Greeks an autonomous administration under their own Patriarch. Mohammed had no difficulty in bribing the bigots of Orthodoxy to accept the Padisha as the protector of their Church rather than the Pope. Gennadius, the fanatical monk who had incited the Churches against Constantine at the time of that Emperor's last attempt to save Constantinople for Christendom, was now prepared to accept from the Moslem Conqueror investiture as Patriarch, and ennoblement as a Pasha of Three Tails. Such excessive conformity naturally exposed the Patriarchs to criticism. Dionysius for one was charged with having conformed to the extent of circumcision, and having triumphantly shown in full Synod that the charge was false, was summoned before the Divan and rated, as a " dog "—and worse, by the Grand Vizier. The Orthodox prelates had indeed benefited considerably by the Conquest. Previously the Greek Emperors by virtue of their divine right had exerted some authority over them. The Sultan had formally conceded to the Patriarch not only a spiritual supremacy, but temporal power as a Tributary Prince. He crowned him himself, gave him a diamond-studded sceptre as symbol of his temporal power, escorted him to the gates of the Palace, and presented him with a special guard of Janissaries and a Court of Justice, all complete with prison and torture-chamber. The Patriarch might levy taxes for his own community (millet) and control his own police.[1] In return for these concessions the Orthodox clergy exhorted their provincial countrymen to respect the divine right of the Padisha, and render unto Cæsar such things as were Cæsar's—including the tribute of their children as Janissaries and odalisques.

Servility so demoralizing was not likely to cure the two defects inherent in Greek government, conspiracy and corruption. The Œcumenical Patriarchs have seldom enjoyed for long an undisturbed succession. Between the Turkish Conquest and

[1] The Armenians at Koum Kapou and the Jews at Balata received somewhat similar privileges. But the Latins were left to the Italian colonies—the Venetian section of them near the Burnt Column, and the Genoese at Galata. Under Suleiman the protection of the Latins was assigned to the French.

the present year (1924) 22 died natural and 6 violent deaths, 27 abdicated, 105 were deposed and the last two were deported. Faction so distracted Joasap, the second Patriarch, that he threw himself into a well, from which he was rescued, only to be banished for refusing to sanction the marriage of a Christian girl to a Vizier. Under his successor, Marcus, simony became rampant, and ecclesiastics bid openly against each other for the support of Turkish Pashas in their candidature for the Patriarchate or the bishoprics. In part we can trace the growing prosperity of the Phanar by the increasing prices paid for the Patriarchate. In 1461 the Trebizond interest bought it for 1,000 ducats a year. Only to be outbid the following year by the Constantinople clergy with 2,000. In 1583 the prelates protested at having to appoint an unlettered monk whose wealthy brother had paid the Turks 12,000 ducats, with the result that they were fined 3,000 ducats. Next year they bought the monk's deposition with 24,000 ducats. The wealthy brother then bid 40,000 for the monk's reinstatement. But the clergy " saw " the bid—and kept the Patriarchate. Again, a century later, Lucaris was deposed by the Jesuits for 40,000, and reinstated for 180,000 ducats. These sums were, of course, raised by the Patriarch from the prelates on appointment ; by them in turn from their priests ; and by the priests again in tithes and fees from the people—the people in question being not only the Greeks, but the Slavs, Vlachs, Arnauts and other Christian races of the Empire. In a word, just as the late Empire had been Greek under Turkish suzerainty, so now the early Phanar was functioning as a continuation of the Greek Empire under Turkish sovereignty. In every sense it was an *imperium in imperio*. But its growth was not undisturbed. In the sixteenth century the Osmanli Sultans, no longer afraid of Christians either within or without the frontiers, oppressed them cruelly. Selim I and Suleiman, as we may remember, even considered exterminating them. In the seventeenth century again the rivalry of the Latin Church, headed by the Jesuits and protected by the French, threatened their ecclesiastical administration ; and, simultaneously, the business rivalry of the foreign colonies, who had obtained new capitulations, began to challenge their commercial exploitation of the Empire.

The Orthodox Church had its one great opportunity when Cyril Lucaris became Patriarch in 1620. He had been educated in Germany under Lutheran influences, and in 1629 he published, in concert with English and German divines, a Confession of Faith, that was intended to be the manifesto of a reformed

Orthodox Church. But both the Phanar and the Jesuits bitterly opposed him. Five times he was deposed, and finally he was thrown into the Black Tower (v. p. 265), and murdered. He is now best remembered for having presented Charles I with the Codex Alexandrinus. But his career deserves study by those idealists of to-day who are concerned to associate the Anglican and Orthodox Churches. In this context an anecdote without a moral may be excused. I was reading the lessons in the Embassy Chapel at Pera, when a tall Greek Papas marched up the aisles, and much embarrassed me by glaring in my face across the lectern. Fortunately the Chaplain was better versed than myself in ecclesiastical politics and knew that, since the two Churches recognize each other's Orders, their clergy are mutually entitled to seats in the choir within the rood-screen. The Papas had been sent to test whether the Embassy would recognize this right, so one of the young ladies was bustled out of the choir-pew, and the not over-clean Papas installed in her place, with most incongruous and inharmonious results.

But, before we leave these grey solid houses of the Phanar, one word more as to the period of Greek predominance that they recall. A revival of prosperity for the Greek community came with the reforms of the great Viziers at the end of the sixteen-hundreds. The tribute of children had ceased for ever; the taxation of the rayahs was reduced for a time; and the provincial Greeks were free to begin their training for the national renascence as Klephts and Armatoles. Our concern, however, is not with these Pallikars but with the Phanariotes of the city. These Palæologi, Mavrogordati, Ypsilanti, Karadja, the old aristocratic families of Byzantium, with a leavening of Italians, the Moroussi, the Giuliani, the Rossetti, and a strong element of nouveaux-riches, were just the men whom the deteriorating Turks needed, to help them in governing provinces where the feudal regime of the Timariotes was breaking down. Accordingly, in 1669 we find the Grand Vizier, Akhmet Köpreli, creating a new office, " Dragoman of the Porte," for his secretary, Panayoti, who, as an honest Phanariote, became known as the " Green Mouse," also an unusual animal. Under his successor, a Mavrogordato, this post became practically that of Foreign Minister. Soon after a Greek was appointed to administer the Islands, and entitled " Dragoman of the Fleet." And by 1716 the European provinces were all under the governance of Greeks, who were called Hospodars, a Slav word meaning " Lord." So it came that by the middle of the eighteenth century Christian Turkey was all in the hands of Greeks, either civil or clerical. The Hospodars were re-creating Greek social life in local Courts of princely pomp. The Patriarch and bishops were conducting what was in effect a governmental system ; while centres of education and culture were growing up at Kuru-Tchesme on the Bosphorus and at Cidonia near Smyrna. The revival of Greek language and literature, initiated by Rhigas (1753–98) and Caraes (1748–1833), although centred abroad, inspired even the Phanar with new intellectual life. It was in a literary renascence that the revival of the Greek national feeling first found expression, and initiated, but ultimately wrecked the renewal of a Greek imperial ideal. Just as, at a later date, the national movement that brought down the reformed Ottoman Empire had its beginnings also in a literary movement. The Turks instinctively sensed the danger at once. Rhigas was extradited to them by the Austrians, and executed at Belgrade—the first casualty in the Greek War of Independence.

I have more than once called Constantinople Babylon—and you will still find it a Tower of Babel. Most native-born inhabitants express themselves with equal ease in four or five languages, not so difficult a feat as it may seem in view of the ideas to be expressed. Turkish being impossible as an international tongue, Greek has always been used as the currency of the petit commerce, which is in Greek hands, and Levantine French as the language of big business and of the international bureaucracy. Greek, then, is the current small change. And like small change long in circulation, it has been worn down, defaced, and even alloyed until it is very unlike its original classic designs of inflexions or syntax. The rich diphthongs, for example, have all been blended into a single monotonous squeaking. The Hellenic sentence, " οἱ υἱοὶ ἔχοιεν τὴν ὑγίειαν," becomes in Romaic " Hee heehee heehee-en teen eeheehee-an." You can read the Hellenized modern Greek of a newspaper without difficulty if you have had the benefit of a classical education. But the Romaic recitative of your cabman will sound a meaningless Morsing on one note. On the other hand, the importation of foreign words has given Romaic a flexibility agreeable to every one but to the scholar. The inscription, " Omniboi pros ton Terminon dia olous tous Trenous," is intelligible, whereas its Hellenic equivalent would defeat a Senior Classic. Romaic is easily picked up by ear, not so easily by the eye. It would be a calamity for the traveller anxious to get into touch with local life, if this useful medium of exchange were to be driven out of general use by the Turks, even as they have driven out the Greeks themselves.

This last expulsion, however, belongs to the story of the rise
and fall of Greek nationalism, which follows in a later chapter.
We are still concerned here with the abortive revival of Greek
Imperialism, as conceived by the Oriental Project and confirmed
in the Treaty of Kainardji. Under it foreign Ambassadors,
Consuls and their dependents became responsible for their co-
nationals, and the Porte was unable to prevent the Powers
obtaining such " berats " or charters in favour of large numbers
of merchants and others willing to pay for them. A whole
population of Greeks, Armenians, and Jews were thus withdrawn
from the Ottoman jurisdiction, and the only remedy left to the
Porte was to give its own subjects berats on better terms. The
Greeks, merchant venturers *par excellence*, benefited under this
system. The commerce of the Levant and of the Black Sea
passed into their hands, and their branch agencies in European
capitals rapidly grew into important concerns. Their accumu-
lating profits they generously devoted to the promotion of the
" megali idea "—the restoration of the Greek Empire.

By the end of the eighteenth century Constantinople was
again an international capital. The Sultan was somewhat in the
position of one of the Iconoclast Emperors, asserting his authority
through an army not always amenable. Indeed, the Varangian
Guard and the Byzantine regulars had been more reliable than
were the Janissaries and Sipahis. The Greeks under their
Patriarch and Phanariote families were more powerful and
prosperous than in the days when these authorities had overthrown
Christian Emperors of Asiatic race and heretic religion. If
Russia had been allowed to oust the Turks and restore a Greek
Empire, we cannot doubt that within ten years the Empire would
have ousted the Russians, and the rest of the story of Con-
stantinople would have been told in Greek.

THE BAZAARS AND THE POWERS

But enough of history, with its might-have-beens and hadn't-
ought-to-be's. We have still Stamboul, and still its Bazaars, to
visit.

The Bazaars are not what they used to be ; probably they
never were. But what remains of their picturesqueness belongs
to this same highly coloured epoch at the close of the eighteenth
century. Their arms and ornaments and silks and embroideries
are, or profess to be, the products of that last outburst of colour
and costume before our drab period of ready-mades and reach-
me-downs. And how even we English did enjoy dressing up and

showing off in those days! A Constantinople resident records in his diary in 1810:

We were interrupted in our debate by the entrance of a stranger whom on the first glance I guessed to be an Englishman but lately arrived. He wore a scarlet coat richly embroidered with gold . . . with two heavy gold epaulettes. On entering he took off his feathered cocked hat and showed a head of curly auburn hair which improved in no small degree the uncommon beauty of his face. He was attended by a Janissary attached to the British Embassy and by a professional Cicerone.

You will say that was just the sort of thing that you would expect from Byron—for of course it was Byron. But clearly it was just the sort of thing that the writer expected from any young " Englishman lately arrived." A century ago you and I in Constantinople would be making such contribution to the general gaiety of nations as our fancy dictated and our purse allowed. A century before that we should have had to disguise ourselves as Turks. Even nowadays a protective colouring is an advantage in Constantinople and highly advisable anywhere outside—a warning colour scheme like the wasp, or a hinting of gorgeous backgrounds, like the dragonfly. I myself used to make as careful a toilet for a day's ride in Macedonia as for a royal garden-party, and a traveller once traversed Anatolia *en prince* on the strength of an address in Prince's Gate.

The Bazaars, although they alone now suggest the East, are not an oriental institution. The covered markets which we call " Bazaars " should properly be named " Tcharshi." But the foreigner has forced his misnomer upon the native, since they continue to exist mainly for his benefit. The covered arcades also are a Byzantine institution, and these Bazaars belong to a time when Greek customs had again prevailed over Turkish in the local commercial life.

The Missir Tcharshi (Egypt Bazaar), for the sale of drugs, gums, and spices, was built by Tarkhann Sultana, the successful supplanter of Machpeikér in the Hareem War. It is a barrel-vaulted building, over a hundred yards long, where the salesmen sit picturesquely among their baskets, boxes, and bags. The attraction of the place was, however, its oratorio of odours. One came out of it feeling armed and embalmed against the deadly stenches of Stamboul on a summer's day. And if to-day the aromatic Missir Tcharshi is not what it was, yet thanks to Young Turkey the stenches also have lost something of their vigour and variety.

The Grand Bazaar is a more complicated structure. It has

a circumference of about a mile, and five miles of covered arcades radiate from its hub, the Bezistan.   It is a walled and gated city within a city, and one where you can easily get lost.   It claims, poetically, to contain 7,777 shops, but 3,190 would seem nearer the prosaic mark.   The Bezistan, a rectangular building fifty yards long of solid masonry, is clearly Byzantine, although the Turks ascribe it to the Conqueror.   A one-headed Byzantine eagle, over the Booksellers Gate, places the building before the tenth century, after which time the eagle became two-headed. The gates are called after the quarters to which they admit, the Goldsmiths, the Embroidered Belts, etc.   The wooden gallery round the top is for police supervision, and smoking is prohibited on account of the value of the wares.   For the Bezistan used to be the tourist's Mecca.   Here were damascened armour, silvered pistols, inlaid guns, musical instruments, gems, seals, and coins. Within the dark little booths, in the dim light filtering through the dirty glass of the vault, sit the vendors spider-like.   Once within the web of their urbanity and you will get your money's worth—of atmosphere.   And what matter if, once outside that enchanted twilight, the cold eye of day proclaims your ancient arms Brummagem, your Broussa silks from Lyons, and your Persian carpets made in Germany?   They will none the less remind you of that happy hour in the Bazaars where you got a glimpse of the gorgeous East.   That's what we all go to Constantinople to see—and if we saw there only the genuine East we should feel far worse swindled.   The bearded old Armenian pirate sitting cross-legged on the little dais before his booth—or the handsome young Jewish rover who captures us as we pass and tows us into port—are at least providing us with an Arabian Nights entertainment.

Of course, you must bargain—that is part of the business and a social duty—and the more politely and pointedly you can depreciate the goods the better friends you will make and the better treatment you will get.   In Athens you can still hire a peripatetic philosopher to argue Ethics with you.   And in the Bazaars you will profit by some very real gems of courtesy and comedy, given away with your more dubitable purchases.   If authentic " business " and not simply atmosphere be our object, we may go to the antika shops of Pera.

The flood of Russian exiles, following the Russian revolution, and the flight of Greeks and Armenians out of the city, following upon the Turkish restoration, have at the moment put in circulation a quantity of valuable family treasures.   The best of these are not to be found in the Bazaar booths. But the patriarchs of the Bazaar can put us on the track of this big game if they recognize us as a customer who is a real connoisseur. Do not go on such a hunt, however, if your courage or cunning are likely to fail you at a pinch. Walking up tigers in thick jungle is a safe sport compared to it. And the lifelong regret over missing a prize because you weren't bold enough at the higher bid is almost worse to bear than to " return from the ride—with the smile on the face of the tiger " ! I speak from sad experience. On my second afternoon in the near East a seedy individual produced from its wrapping of rags for my inspection a small and beautiful marble head of a girl. Supposing this to be a common incident of street-hawking east of the Balkans, I put him off until I could post myself in the current prices for works of Praxiteles. But I never saw the head again, or anything like it, in twenty years of antika-hunting.

For those who cannot afford big bids and don't want bric-a-brac there is the Bit Bazaar (Louse Fair). Here, as in the Caledonian Road, good stuff can sometimes be found, mixed with rubbish and rags. But if the eye of the buyer must be no less keen here, his nose must be even blunter. In the East, before anything can qualify for the rag-market, it must have lived a life crowded with experiences.

The book-stores, near the Mosque of Bayazid, on the site of the Chartopratia, or Paper-market, of Byzantine Constantinople, used to be well worth a visit, and may be so again. Here, in an old Byzantine portico, survived until the War one of the principal arts of the East. Turbanned and gowned old gentlemen, with reed pen and colour-box, and gold leaf and burnisher, laboriously filled page after page with exquisite script and elaborate designs. The script was the strange calligraphic art imposed on the Moslems by the restrictions of their religion. But the illuminations in colour and design were Byzantine. Since Turkish rule has been restored, it may be hoped that some of these artists may have returned.

Near Mahmoud Pasha Kapou are the attractive booths for jewellery, silks, carpets, and other wares. Ouzoun Tcharshi (Long Market) has perfumes, pastry, and sherbet. The Slipper-market possesses, as one of its attractions, one of the charming fountains put up by Mourad III to his bootmaker, which records that his boots always fitted, and were sent home on time—a testimonial more moving than that of the Royal Arms with its " By Special Appointment." The Sandal Bezistan used to be the centre of the silk trade. But the Turkish silk industry was killed at about the date we have now reached in our historical survey (1790–1810), by the commercial privileges conceded to the Western Powers as the price of their support of the Empire. The rents of the stalls here were worth in 1800 ten times what they had fallen to by 1850. The deserted and decaying Sandal Bezistan has now for over a century stood as an eloquent monument to the folly of trying to maintain imperial prestige at the cost of national prosperity.

The empty Sandal Bezistan will serve, therefore, as an appropriate illustration for an account of the commercial decline of the Osmanli Empire. In a two-thousand-year story, such as that of Constantinople, history may be allowed to seem at least to repeat itself. We have seen the Greek Empire, less afraid of the foreign colonies becoming powerful than of its own subjects, ruin itself economically by concessions to the Venetian and Genoese colonies. And now again, the Porte, alarmed at the prosperity of the urban Phanariotes and the power of the provincial Pallikars, preferred to ruin them and itself by again entrusting the economic life of the Empire to foreigners rather than reform its own system.

It is an ill wind that blows nobody good, and the break-up of an old prosperity is the bargain-hunters opportunity. The Ægean Greeks used to carry on a thriving trade with the Dutch, and their returning vessels brought furniture and pictures for the Greek family homes. Once, sailing among the Islands, I came upon the yacht of a Levantine merchant-prince piled high with this Dutch eighteenth-century furniture obtained from Greeks ruined by the Hamidian regime. Now probably you would be able to buy this same furniture as a bargain from a British Levantine family ruined by the Treaty of Lausanne.

And just as we saw earlier the different partners in the Byzantine Empire dissolving partnership and realizing such assets as they could, before setting up on their own, so, once more, we find the minor partners in the Osmanli Empire, the Greeks, Slavs, Roumanians, and even the Albanians—for long the most loyal servants of the Empire—involved in the same process. Only the Jews remained, permanently loyal to any Empire that might exist, and our own time has provided even this most imperial of races with a national home. The partnership between Turks and Greeks by which the Greeks administered the Empire and exploited it economically, and the Turks defended it, was an impossible dualism : bound to end in a struggle between the two races and religions, and in the secession of the defeated race as an independent nation.

There was a further reason for the failure of the Turk to maintain his predominant position in the partnership. Why, it may be asked, were all the efforts to reform the Osmanli Empire, so as to check secessions, unsuccessful ? For these efforts were both genuine and thorough. The answer is clear enough, but it has not hitherto been given. The Turkish movements for reform were the outcome of a revived national feeling, just as the Greek movement had been. In fact the Turkish national movement began almost simultaneously with the Greek at the end of the seventeen-hundreds. But the Turks being at the moment the dominant imperial race, their national renascence wasted its energies for a century—even as the Greeks had done—in attempting to galvanize a moribund imperial system. With this explanation we can the better understand the sensational incidents that accompanied the early Ottoman reforms at Constantinople and account for their ultimate failure.

The Osmanli Empire, like the Byzantine Empire, rested on three pillars—autocracy, justice, and the imperial guard. Ottoman justice had by now fallen so far from its pristine integrity that all the foreign colonies and Christian communities had " contracted out," by capitulations and customary law. The imperial guard, the Janissaries, had moreover lost nearly all military value and become a sort of ruling class. They were more concerned with exploiting their privileges to fill their pockets than with fighting on the frontiers. They were no longer recruited from the flower of the Christian peasantry, but had become an hereditary caste and trade guild. Their reconstruction, had it been possible, might have procured the Empire an extended lease of life. But they were recalcitrant to all reform, and military reconstruction had to confine itself to making efficient soldiers of the mediæval cavalry, the Sipahis, and of the infantry, the Piade, who were not Imperial and were recruited from Turks alone.

Under Moustapha III (1757-74), the French Ambassador, with the help of Baron de Tott, had started a new Turkish army on modern lines. Selim III (1789-1807) carried on this policy; until he came into collision with the Janissaries. The first round in the contest was won by Selim. But it was at the cost of his Serb provinces, where he had encouraged the Christian rayas to revolt against their tyrants, only to find the victorious Christians, with Russian support, thereafter defying the Empire altogether. A Turkish army was defeated by Karageorge, and Servia became free.

Constantinople, meanwhile, had become involved in the Napoleonic wars. France was playing the part taken by Germany a century later. She controlled the Turkish army, and her envoy, Colonel Sebastiani, was dictating an anti-Russian policy to Selim. Our Ambassador delivered an ultimatum, requiring the Porte to join the Anglo-Russian alliance against France; and then sailed in a frigate for Tenedos, where lay the British fleet under Admiral Duckworth—seven battleships and two frigates. On February 19, 1807, this fleet forced the Dardanelles with little damage, and, appearing before the city, demanded the surrender of the Turkish fleet and submission to our conditions, under menace of bombardment—an anticipation of the situation of a century later.

But the Ambassador and Admiral allowed themselves to be drawn into negotiations; and during the fortnight that they lasted the whole city worked feverishly at the fortifications. By the time that a thousand guns and a hundred mortars from the French arsenal had been mounted, the Admiral realized that he was outmatched. On March 1 he weighed anchor. But the Dardanelles defences had also been strengthened. The huge stone balls took effect, two frigates and 600 men were lost, and the fleet narrowly escaped destruction. It was a lesson that such blows can only be effective when they are delivered suddenly, and sharply driven home—a lesson that was forgotten by a century later.

THE JANISSARIES AND STAMBOUL

The guns of the reformed regime had saved the city from all but a fright. But it was the regime that had to suffer most from the effects of that fright. Most of the Janissaries had been sent to the Danube, but the remainder rose against the next reform measure, which proposed to enrol the youngest of them in the regular army. The reactionary Ulema supported them; and the Grand Mufti readily gave them a fetva deposing Selim, on May 7, 1807. Selim had been unwise enough to keep no force of his own at hand, and to save his life he sent for his cousin, Moustapha III, from the Kafess, and took his place there.

But the provinces knew that reform was the one chance for the Empire. Moustapha Bairakdar (Standard-bearer), Pasha of Rustchuk, with 40,000 Bosnians and Albanians, marched on Constantinople, bringing with him the Sacred Standard. On

July 28, 1808, he appeared outside the Seraglio, and demanded Selim. Moustapha III, to save his own life, gave hasty orders for the assassination of Selim and also of Mahmoud, almost the only surviving members of the house of Othman. The mutes, after a desperate struggle, succeeded in strangling Selim while Bairakdar's followers were breaking their way into the Seraglio. But Mahmoud, hidden in the furnace of a bath, could not be found. The body of Selim was thrown out to Bairakdar in the hope he would then accept Moustapha as Sultan. Bairakdar none the less forced his way into the Throne Room. Moustapha was dragged from the throne, and sent to the Kafess, and his women, who had been rejoicing over the death of Selim, were sewn into sacks and flung into the Bosphorus. Mahmoud was found, and proclaimed Sultan, and Moustapha was soon afterwards put to death. Mahmoud, after strangling Moustapha's only son, and drowning another five women of his hareem who seemed likely to give birth to rivals, remained the sole representative of the dynasty—a circumstance to which he owed his life in the counter-revolution that followed.

For, no sooner had the Bosnian levies left the capital, than the Janissaries and Ulema rose again. Bairakdar was blown up in a tower which he had fortified, and the artillery joined the rebellion. The Janissaries now ruled the Empire, and they inaugurated a complete reaction. They terrorized the capital, and in the provinces followed any ambitious Pasha who chose to make himself independent. Mahmoud's new troops were disbanded, his French *corps de ballet* was dismissed, the new schools, the printing-press and the libraries, all disappeared. Constantinople became again rigorously Mussulman and mediæval, and the Turkish renascence was checked.

In 1808 Stratford Canning, afterwards the Great Elchi, came on a Mission and reported the Empire moribund. It seemed inevitable that in the general turmoil of the Napoleonic wars the decayed edifice must collapse, and that it would have to be rebuilt on its original Greek foundations. To Canning as much as to Mahmoud, the Ottoman Empire owed its additional century of life, no less than the fact that it has, in our time, fallen a prize to the Turkish and not to the Greek nation. As early as 1809 he could write, " The Government is radically bad, and its members, all alive to its effects, have neither wisdom nor courage to reform it." It was a typically diplomatic estimate of the situation.

The first part of Mahmoud's reign had been spent in success-

fully restoring imperial authority over and imposing a central
government on the ambitious provincial potentates. But after
his first failure in Constantinople it was all eighteen years before
he could again recover control of his capital, and subdue the
imperial corps of the Janissaries. Mahmoud, a small man of
aquiline features, soon showed that he had both the wisdom
and courage required to reform the Empire. He had two enemies
to deal with, the Greek rivalry for Empire and the reactionary
Janissary regime. He crushed his Christian rivals with Moslem
fanaticism, and then countered Moslem bigotry by a Turkish
national reform movement.

He had no easy task. The Greek revolutionary movement
might indeed have succeeded before the end of the Napoleonic
wars, and a Christian Empire would then have been re-established,
but for the same difficulties that prevented its establishment in
our own time, the first being that the Powers could not agree
as to which of them was to have Constantinople, and the second
being that the Greeks could never agree among themselves.

It was the future of Constantinople and the dispute it caused
at Tilsit, between Napoleon and the Tsar Alexander, which saved
Europe from a most unholy alliance for the partition of the world
between the two military despotisms. When the Tsar's insistence
upon the Russian annexation of " Tsargrad " would no longer
brook prevarication, Napoleon told de Meneval to bring in the
largest-scaled map of Europe. Long he studied it, and then
he exclaimed, " Constantinople ? Never ! It is the Empire of
the World."

The second difficulty also was then, as always, present. The
Greeks were still as divided among themselves as when their
Empire fell. They had one centre in Constantinople under the
civilized but unmilitary Phanariotes ; one centre in Epirus, under
Ali Pasha, and yet another in the Morea, under the wild Mainotes.
There was nothing, obviously, to prevent them being all three
overpowered in turn. Only the last-named centre, with which
we are not dealing here, proved unconquerable even in defeat,
and survived as the Greek nation.

The Phanariote movement, and its organization the Hetairia,
as also the uprising under Ali Pasha and its relations with the
Janissaries, had a Greek Empire as their object. The Phanariote
policy was a more or less peaceful penetration of Constantinople,
to end in a substitution of Greek for Turkish authority. The
Turks, finding the Greeks were becoming the predominant
partners, fell back on violence and were encouraged thereto by

the Greek independence movement in the Morea. All possibility
of a Turkish and Greek partnership in Empire ended in a war of
extermination that broke out in 1821, a war which found only
its final sequel in the wars of expatriation in our own time.
The Greeks began by massacring all the Moslems in the Morea.
Mahmoud retorted by encouraging a Turkish massacre of the
imperialist Greeks in the Islands and the city. He began by
banishing all the Greeks not engaged in trade, filled the city with
troops, and armed the Moslems. Seven Greek bishops were
imprisoned, and many prominent Greeks executed. At dawn on
Easter Day, 1821, the Patriarch Gregorios was offering the
Eucharist in his cathedral church, when he was summoned from
the altar by Turkish officials, and hailed before the Synod in
the Phanar. He was declared to be deposed, and within a few
hours was hung from the gate of the Patriarchate, with a paper
pinned to his breast accusing him of traitorous conspiracy with
the Hetairia. His body was given to the Jews, with orders to
drag it through the streets and throw it into the sea. The
Greeks will tell us that it floated alongside a Greek vessel,
miraculously, next morning. Actually it was quietly surrendered
by the Jews to the Greeks; who buried it at Odessa with the
honours due to a saint and a martyr.

Thus encouraged, the Janissaries broke out into a massacre
of Christians, tolerated by the Sultan. The Greek ecclesiastical
and educational centres, the Phanar and Kourou-Tchesme, were
sacked. The model university town of Cidonia, built with the
price of the jewels which the Phanariote ladies had sold to the
hareems, was razed to the ground. The Greek notables were
assassinated and whole communities, men, women, and children,
slaughtered. The Russian Ambassador left Constantinople in
protest. But Great Britain and France were pro-Turk and
Mahmoud prosecuted his " plan of thorough " until the Phanariote
movement was utterly crushed. For a century there was no
further question of a Greek Empire at Constantinople.

Mahmoud then found himself free to deal no less faithfully
with his second enemy, the Janissary reactionaries. Year by
year he had weakened them by eliminating their leaders. Stratford Canning relates : " I remember that frequently, crossing
the Golden Horn, I observed loose mats floating here and there,
and enquiring, was told in a mysterious manner they had wrapped
the bodies thrown after private executions into the harbour."

Any doubts Mahmoud may have had as to the advantage of
substituting a modern Turkish army for the imperial Janissaries

must have been removed by the success of the modern Egyptian troops sent by his ally, the Pasha of Egypt, to suppress the Greek national revolt in the Morea. By April, 1826, Missolonghi had fallen. And in June of that year Mahmoud summoned the chief functionaries of the Empire and the Aghas of the Janissaries to sign the new regulations which incorporated one-fourth of them into his new corps, under military discipline. On June 12 this new regime came into force. On June 14 the kettles were overturned, and the revolt began. Mahmoud immediately filled Stamboul with troops, and set up the Hirkai Sherif, the Green Standard, in the Mosque of Ahmed. The populace rallied to the reforming Sultan at the At-meidan. The Janissaries assembled in the Et-meidan, in the western quarter, and advanced as far east as the Square of Bayazid, whence they were driven back without difficulty to the Et-meidan. They had no chance against disciplined troops, which included 14,000 trained artillery. Stratford Canning, sitting at lunch that day in the British Embassy, in Pera, saw from the window " two slender columns of smoke rising above the opposite horizon." He was told that the Sultan had fired the barracks of the Janissaries. Four thousand Janissaries perished from the fire of the guns or in the flames. On June 17 the corps officially ceased to exist. But Mahmoud was ever one to ": mak' sikker " ; and Canning reports what followed :

> The mere name of Janissary . . . operated like a sentence of death. A special commission sat for the trial, or rather the condemnation, of crowds. Every victim passed at once from the tribunal into the hands of the executioner. The bowstring and the scimitar were constantly in play. People could not stir from their houses without the risk of falling in with some terrible sight. The Sea of Marmora was mottled with bodies. Nor was the tragedy confined to Constantinople and its neighbourhood. Messengers were sent in haste to every provincial city where any considerable number of Janissaries existed, and the slightest tendency to insurrection was so promptly and effectively suppressed, that no disquieting reports were conveyed to us from any quarter of the Empire.
>
> The Sultan's Ministers are still encamped in the outer Court of the seraglio, where frequent executions take place under their eyes. This afternoon my informant saw to his astonishment a body of Turks in various dresses, but armed with muskets and bayonets, arranged in European order, and going through the new form of exercise. . . . He says the men acted by word of command, both in marching and in handling their arms. The Sultan . . . descended after a time and passed the men in review. His Highness was dressed in Egyptian fashion, armed with pistols and sabre, and on his head in place of the imperial turban was a sort of Egyptian bonnet.
>
> Rank, poverty; age and numbers are alike impotent to shelter those

who are known as culprits or marked as victims. . . . Whole companies
of labouring men are seized and either executed or forcibly obliged to quit
Constantinople. The entrance to the seraglio, the shore under the
Sultan's windows, and the sea itself, are crowded with dead bodies, many
of them in part devoured by dogs."

For months the poor of the city preferred to starve rather
than eat their staple food—fish.

Blood-letting, and to spare! But in spite of it, the war
between reaction and reform went on for all the rest of Mahmoud's
reign. In 1834 the issue of a new currency, stamped in defiance
of the Prophet's precept with the Sultan's head, caused a revolt.
Four thousand paid for their scruples with their lives. But the
currency was called in, and thereafter the " toughra " or Sultan's
cypher was substituted for the ruler's head on Turkish coins.
The bridge, also, that Mahmoud built between Galata and Pera
was interpreted as symbolical of the Sultan's breaking down the
barriers of the faith. It soon became an accepted road to
martyrdom to seize his bridle as he rode over it, and shout,
" Ghiaur Padishah ! " Never did Iconoclast or Uniate Emperor
suffer more than this reforming Sultan from the bigotry which
has always characterized Constantinople.

Historians make almost as great a mistake in representing
Mahmoud as the first creator of a reformed and, in so far, new
Ottoman Empire, as did the journalists who labelled Moustapha
Kemal as its last reforming ruler. If we study the Eastern
Question from Constantinople itself—always the only key to its
mysteries—we can see that the " reforms " of Mahmoud did no
more than break up the Empire as then existing, and resolve it
into a group of nations inspired by the crudest and most uncom-
promising " Chauvinism." With Mahmoud's reforms disappeared
the last remains of the old imperial institutions which kept the
Empire together—the Janissaries and the religious autonomies
(millets). Under such institutions alone could the European and
Asiatic races, the Christian and Mussulman, have continued as
partners in Constantinople, subject to the Ottoman presidency.
But Europe was not yet prepared to allow the Turks to exterminate or expatriate their Christian partners : a course which
offered the only alternative solution of the problem.

For a century the Turks continued the struggle to Turk-ify
the Ottoman Empire, with the single result, as we have indicated,
of delaying for a century the renascence of a Turkish national
State. They did not even succeed in Turk-ifying Constantinople.
They only so enfeebled that Circe of cities that, in the end, all

the nations of the East, including Turkey, have been enabled at last to break clear of her spells.

Before we leave Stamboul, and follow the last century of the story of Constantinople from the modern suburbs of Pera, Galata, and the Bosphorus, we may well climb the Seraskierate Tower, and take a last look at the mediæval metropolis of the East.

From the walls to the sea little has altered in this view since the time of the Osmanli Conquest. The fire-swept region of the city, destroyed during the war, covers much the same area as the tract which was swept by the fire that followed the entry of the Crusaders. The lofty domes and minarets of the mosques are still pre-eminent, with beneath them here and there a lower-domed Christian church. The great stone Khans—some of them well worth a visit—those hostelries that once received travellers of the Golden Road to Samarkand, the great Bazaars where the wealth of all the East was displayed, the long harbour crowded with coasting vessels—all still are there as monuments of the greatest of mediæval Marts. The cupolas of the Baths, with their bull's-eyes of coloured glass, the grim stone dwellings of the Phanar, the rambling galleried wooden houses of the Turkish quarters, the gardens of the Seraglio, seen over its walls, the pleasure-gardens that mark the wealthier quarters, still from this kindly distance show a city where reign luxury and leisure. But look closer and you will see how the barren wastes and burnt-out areas with the general dilapidation and decay show the end to which all luxury and leisure inevitably lead, while above the general ruin there towers foursquare one great Bastille of massive masonry. A prison you will assume—and a prison of a sort it was—that Administration of the Ottoman Debt. The Debtors' Prison, where the extravagances of the Ottoman Empire immured for half a century the young Turkish nation.

CHAPTER IV

THE OTTOMAN EMPIRE

Are you ready for a fight—for we are the English !
Yes, we're ready for a fight—for we are the Roman soldiers !

(Nursery Game)

I HAVE reserved the Gallicized form " Ottoman " for the history of Constantinople during the nineteenth century, the period during which repeated efforts were made to convert Constantinople into the capital of a Constitutional Empire, with autonomous states and parliamentary institutions on the model of the British Empire. This story can be conveniently combined with a tour of Galata and Pera. Constantinople proper, that is Stamboul, retreated into the background for the space of this century, from the reforms of Mahmoud to the revolution of the Young Turks. It was Pera-Yildiz that provided the scenery for the last act ; and this Europeanized suburb remained the political centre of the Empire until a few years ago. When the capital of the new Turkish State was established at Angora, the Pera Embassies and the Bosphorus Palaces, in their turn, became as much memorials of the past as are the Old Serai and the Blachernæ Palace.

GALATA AND THE COLONIES

The word " Galata " is not improbably derived from the Greek word for " milk." Galata was the original Byzantine milk-market, although it long since lost its rural innocence. It is at once the nearest and the most ancient of the suburbs of Constantinople. Not long ago the lower quarter of Galata along the quays and the Golden Horn was as picturesque as —and even more picturesque than—Stamboul itself. But commercialization has killed the colour in all but the remoter corners of the Jewish quarter, Hasskeui. Unhappily commercialization has been less successful in cleaning out what has been for centuries a cesspool of the Levant. New white marble banks of

184

Attic-American architecture stand backing on filthy alleys which shelter what Murray dismisses as "the most depraved population of Europe." After dusk these back streets of Galata near the docks are not places to venture into at all. They have, however, a certain interest as revealing that side of European civilization which has most offended the Turk and the Moslem. The austere little hill-town of Angora represents the Turkish protest not only against the futilities of the Chanceries of Pera and the fanaticisms of the Medressehs of Stamboul, but against a social system that can tolerate the association of the banks and brothels of Galata. The modern Turk is not conspicuously moral, nor yet especially high-minded. But he has energy and enthusiasm ; and he has learned that if the shops of the Grande Rue de Pera display one side of the medal, the slums of the Grande Rue de Galata conceal its reverse. An Ottoman Empire ruled in the last resort from the heights of Pera would soon sink to the moral level of Galata. We cannot deny that the Turk has had justification for this view. In my own recollection the comparative decency of the back streets of Galata under the despotism of Abdul-Hamid, and under the discipline it imposed upon the cheaper criminals, compared favourably with the licence allowed under the Allied occupation. Even before the war, foreign influences enabled high-class swindlers to escape justice as easily in Constantinople as elsewhere. The great local boom of the '90's, for example, was engineered, I regret to say, by two Englishmen, one of whom still holds a public position. To-day the return of the Turk and the flight of the Greek has given Galata a chance of setting its house in order. If the new regime really succeeds in its efforts to create a new human species, a business Turk, resembling the business Tartar of Baku, there may some day be a purified Galata taking the place of the iridescent Galata of the past. For the present the current of business in Constantinople is as completely choked up as in Petrograd, and what colour there is is that of the stagnant pool.

The Galata walls were sacrificed to utility in 1857 ; but here and there a fragment remains, and the line of the mediæval walls is marked by Hendek or Ditch Street. There are also some old Genoese palaces left to remind us of the Genoese origin of the town. In the Pershembe Bazaar, is the Palazzo del Podesta (Mayor's Palace), an obviously Byzantine building. Near by is St. Peter's, with a dominican Friary, the earliest Latin church remaining. The church preserves a sacred picture of the Virgin, clearly an early example of Byzantine art, which is said to be the miracle-working picture once belonging to the Pantokrator Church, and transported here at the Conquest. Another tradition, however, maintains that that particular picture was torn up by the Janissaries, who wore the shreds as talismans.

An old Franciscan Monastery near by was at one time the French Embassy, as is shown by the fleur-de-lis. Later the Ottoman Bank occupied it, until the bank was transferred to its new palace.

The Church of St. Francesco, asserted by the Latins to have rivalled St. Sophia in magnificence, was burnt down in the sixteenth century; and its ruins were rebuilt as a mosque by the wife of Mohammed IV.

St. Giorgio al Monte, rebuilt in 1677, and St. Benoit, in the Lazarist Monastery, are not without interest.

The Church of St. Paul, with an Italian campanile, was converted into a mosque in 1535, for the use of a colony of Spanish Moors exiled from Spain. They were established in Galata to counterbalance the growing Christian cosmopolitanism of the city.

These churches appear principally in history as the scenes of the fierce fights for precedence between French Ambassadors and their colleagues. As an instance: On May 15, 1592, the French Ambassador, M. de Germigny, going in State to the Church of St. Francis, found the front pew usually reserved for him occupied by the Venetian Ambassador, Morosini and his suite. A squabble ended in a scuffle, in which de Germigny got his face smacked. "Nothing," wrote the insulted dignitary, "but the sacred character of the place prevented my utterly losing my self-control (for I was suffering considerable pain) and ejecting the said Venetian Bailie and Ambassador by force." On a later occasion the French came off better; for their Ambassador, de Lanscome, "a very violent person," by coming early got the seat of the imperial Ambassador, and held on to it through the row that followed. The scene was so scandalous that the Grand Vizier closed the church until the Ambassadors "shall have learned better manners." I myself remember a great fuss in the British church, because the French Ambassador had been given a seat in a pew, instead of the more prominent position that the French Republic—then, by the way, engaged upon expelling the Catholic Orders from France—claimed as the protector of the Eastern Catholics. A chair was hastily brought, and M. Constans installed in solitary state on the chancel steps.

Great, too, was the sensation in 1906, when, on the reopening of the Church of St. Antonio in Pera, the Franciscans flew the Italian flag in place of the French, and thereby transferred the allegiance of that influential Order in the Near East from France to Italy. Their example was followed by the Dominicans and their schools; and almost at the same time other Orders and churches claimed the protection of Germany.

These squabbles were but the surface signs of the struggle for local supremacy between the French and Italian influences; a struggle that had its part in the final fall of Constantinople from being the capital of the Eastern Empire to becoming no more than the commercial port of a Turkish Republic. One of the main reasons for that fall was, as we have seen, the fatal mistake made by the Ottoman Empire in reviving the privileges which had been conceded by the Byzantine Emperors to the foreign colonies in the capital. These privileges, first accorded to the Italians and to the Turks themselves, had been all abolished at the Conquest, with the exception of those held by the Genoese in Galata. For under the Byzantine Empire, the perpetual faction-fights between the Venetians and Genoese had led to the Genoese being expelled to the suburbs across the Golden Horn. There they rebuilt the walls, including the Galata Tower (Tower of Christ)—which still exists—and the great Harbour Tower which once carried the chain that closed the port. Since they thus held the key to the Golden Horn, they soon came to play a more notable part in the story. They opposed the Venetians, who were financing the Latin conquest of the city by the Crusaders, and so suffered a temporary eclipse. Upon the restoration of the Greek Empire they re-emerged, and succeeded to the predominance which had been held by the Venetians. This policy of preferring the Genoese to the Venetians was continued by Mohammed the Conqueror. In the Adriatic Capitulation, two years before the Turkish Conquest, he had confirmed the Genoese in their possession of Galata. This secured the neutrality of the colony during the siege. Genoa itself, as we may remember, looked upon the neutrality of its colonists as disgraceful; and the contingent which the city of Genoa sent, under Justiniani, proved the mainstay of the Greek defence. Nor did the Galata Genoese profit noticeably by their desertion of the Christian cause. All the well-to-do fled when the Turks entered. Their last Podesta reports, in June 1453:

The Sultan walked all over the city (Galata), and inspected everything. He ordered that after an inventory of their contents had been made, seals should be affixed to the doors of the shops and houses of those who had fled. Of these inventories he gave me copies for delivery to the Genoese on their return—if that should be within three months—otherwise they should be sent back to him for confiscation.

I might myself describe, in almost identical words, the procedure followed by the modern Turks on their re-entry into Galata after the armistice of Modania.

The Podesta was replaced by a Turkish official, and the affairs of Galata and Pera after the Conquest were administered by a sort of Vestry of twelve, the Serenissima Communita di Pera e Galata, which met in the Sacristy of St. Anne. About the middle of the seventeenth century, the foreign Embassies left Stamboul for Galata, only the Persian Ambassador remaining. The Venetian Embassy also did not migrate until the beginning of the eighteenth century, when it built the palace in Pera, which became the Austrian Embassy on the fall of the Venetian Republic, and has now become again the Italian Embassy. The Lion of St. Mark is still visible in the Great Hall, and the fine old building is plainly of Italian inspiration.

The old Genoese houses of solid stone have withstood the periodic fires which have swept away the wooden-built quarters of Galata, and many of them are left. In one of these were born André and Joseph Chenier, sons of the French Consul by a Greek; of whom one was to be immortalized by his poem written under the shadow of the guillotine, the other by the Chant du Départ.

By the eighteenth century Galata had become cosmopolitan. The rivalry for the profits of the trade of Constantinople was no longer between the Genoese and Venetians, but between the Italians and the French, with the English as runners-up.

The French owed their position as protectors of all the Eastern Latin Christians to Sultan Suleiman. Suleiman, the son of a Frenchwoman, was not likely to overlook their claims when he desired to find a counterpoise to the Italians. But the privileges he gave them made a disastrous departure from precedent. For he accorded them directly to a foreign Government, and no longer only to a Constantinople colony of foreigners. They were also more than usually derogatory to the imperial sovereignty; both generally, in that he recognized Francis I as protector of the Latin Christians, and specifically, in that he granted the French such exceptional privileges as a restriction of customs duties to 5 per cent., and a tax-exemption for five years. It was, of course, not long before other foreign States made good their claim to like commercial privileges; while the French political protectorate became restricted in practice to a formal patronage of the religious Orders.

The foreign colonies at Galata, and their Ambassadors above in aristocratic Pera, although rivals among themselves, naturally soon learned that their interest lay in making common cause against Ottoman authority. A concession once gained by one was claimed alike by all, and all joined in repelling any attack upon one. In this way the Capitulations were built up, a body of extra-territorial privileges that practically internationalized the foreign colonies and the foreign commerce of Galata; which is as much as to say—of Constantinople. We shall hear more about them again when we come to their abolition at Lausanne.

The effect of these privileges was to concentrate all the commerce in the hands of the foreign colonies and their co-religionists. When the Greeks suffered eclipse in the persecution that accompanied the War of Independence, their place was taken by the Armenians. When the Armenians in their turn became suspect and were suppressed, there were Jews, Syrians and Levantines galore in the purlieus of Galata to compete for their jobs. Only the Turks were cut off by their own action and with their own assent from the Galata gambling-dens. They sat at the receipt of custom in the Sublime Porte, the Custom-house, and other toll-gates on the road to riches. Yet even these gleanings were grudged them by the ungrateful Ghiaour, who spoke scornfully of " corruption." " Why should I be ashamed of accepting a mejidieh," said an Ottoman Customs-officer to me once. " I never get my proper pay, and if a tra-veller smuggles because he has paid me, it is he who is corrupt, not I ! " On the other hand, I shall not easily forget the cour-teous scorn with which an officer of my escort in Macedonia waved aside the proffered honorarium: " I am an officer of zabtiehs—not a Constantinople Pasha ! " he explained. But Constantinople Pashas are no more ; and the Customs-officer now may be as likely as not an ex-officer from Angora. So it may be as well to leave any matter of bribing to your hotel dragoman, who will make no mistakes.

The back streets of Galata—it may strike us at once on our round—with their Greek population and remains of Byzantine buildings, are very like the Phanar. It was an alliance between the foreign colonies of Galata and the merchant princes and the Patriarch of the Phanar that the Turkish reform movement had to fight. The Phanar had its aristocracy, Cantacuzenes, Palæo-

logi, Callimachi and Hypsilantis; and they were allied with
Italian nobility, such as the Giuliani, Morosini, and Rosetti,
who had been educated in the new Greek schools that sprang
up during the eighteenth century, and who had grown rich on
the profits of administration and commerce. The Phanariote
families could outbid the Embassies in gorgeous display; and
their bizarre Byzantine dress—long robes and turbans—with their
Oriental customs, such as the separation of the sexes on different
sides of the room, did not interfere with the gaieties of life. So
there was a constant going and coming of kaiks between the
Phanar and Galata.

The old British Consulate, in a side street behind the present
office, provides us with an illustration of the colonial life of old
Galata. Here, early in the present century, in a corner of a
cellar where they had been walled up during some political
crisis, were found the archives of the Levant Company—that
curious institution which looked at one time as though it might
develop into a British Ottoman Empire, even as its contemporary,
the East India Company, grew into our Indian Empire. If we
did not succeed in penetrating the Empire of the Turks as we
did the very similar Empire of their cousins the Moghuls, it was
because Constantinople gave to the Near Eastern Empire a centre and a solidarity that the Moghul Empire, for lack of such
a centre, never acquired. In India we could fight our French
competitors as well as the native despotisms, province by province. But in Constantinople the French and British dualism
never came to an open duel. The French reconstructed and
controlled the new army. We reconstructed and controlled the
new administration. But an open civil war, in which we should
have backed the Greeks, and the French the Turks, was prevented by the local circumstances. For in Constantinople British
imperialism was never more than a superstructure, imposed for
a time upon the top of the imperialism of the Greeks, the Turks,
and the other foreign colonies. It could not, as in India, lay
the foundations of an Empire by opening trading factories in
one native state after another, and by imposing an imperial
control upon rajah after rajah. Above all, it could not, issuing
as it did only from Galata and Pera, strike any real root in the
soil. I remember passing this old Consulate the last time I
was in Constantinople, and, walking behind a party of school-
children, I counted five languages in their chatter. " Children
of three years old," says Lady Mary Wortley Montagu, " often
speak five languages in Pera." Pera and Galata are parasitic.

Strong races, like the Turk, Greek, Slav or Armenian, may accept alien imperial rule for a time. But not through the medium of Pera.

Close behind the Consulate is the Galata Tower. The foundations of the Tower of Christ are Byzantine ; the lower tower dates from 1348, just before the Conquest, and the upper part was rebuilt a century ago by Mahmoud the Reformer. It is in itself, therefore, an epitome of the Empire. The height is 150 feet, and there are 200 steps to climb. But there is no need to go beyond the Chamber of the Fire-watchers, with its fourteen windows. The watchmen and a map will tell you all you want to know about the details of the views to be seen from each window. You should also get them to show you the curious old clock, said to have been brought from St. Sophia.

In a town where whole quarters are destroyed by fire every few years, these watchmen have an important function. To reform the fire-service was one of Mahmoud's first cares, and nothing speaks more eloquently of his difficulties than the fact that a few years ago you might still have seen the weird spectacle of the touloumbadjis going to a fire.

First came, from far overhead, the long-drawn wail from the Galata Tower, " Yangheen Vaar," followed by the name of the quarter where the fire had been spied. A few moments later followed, to the upsetting of the passers-by, a rush of tall men in a little mob, running swiftly over the cobbles, and naked but for a loin-cloth. Ahead of them dashed their leader, carrying a metal staff with a head decorated either with a pair of horns or with a sort of metal top-hat. In the middle of the mob six men, who were relieved at short intervals as they ran, bore upon their shoulders a large brass-studded tray, with something resting on it that looked like a big pair of grocers' scales. This was the fire-engine. The others were armed with hatchets and immensely long poles with hooks at their ends. A party of savages on the warpath, you might have said, and not been far from the truth. For the touloumbadjis did not believe in leaving anything valuable, or otherwise, to be burned. All the same, they knew their business. I recollect once, when a village on the Bosphorus was well alight, we landed a party of bluejackets from a cruiser to help. But they could do nothing. Pumps were useless ; hatchets could only chop ineffectively. Dynamite cartridges only blew holes in the ground, and made a great noise—until a telegram from Yildiz put a stop to that, for Abdul-Hamid could not abide dynamite ! At last a party of touloumbadjis arrived.

Their fire-engine was at once put carefully aside, together with the top-hatted staff, in a place of safety. The long poles were then raked through the windows of the tall wooden houses until the hooks got a purchase-hold somewhere inside. Thereupon clusters of the naked wild-men tailed on to each of the poles, swung them with loud yells, and levered upon them, until the whole house collapsed with a crash.

From the watch-chamber and the gallery of the Tower of Christ we can look out over the whole of Constantinople, and the contrasted periods and styles under our eyes are singularly suggestive of the whole contradictory relationship between East and West—a relationship which was transformed a century ago under Mahmoud, and which was being even more rapidly reconstructed when I last climbed the tower during the time of the Lausanne Conference. We may well think, as we look out, that if only the representatives of Europe in the Embassies below us could have surveyed Constantinople and its problem from a height as remote as this above the commercial echoes of Galata, they, too, might have detected the menace of fire as swiftly, and proclaimed the danger as clearly, as these keen-eyed and loud-voiced watchmen. How much of the devastation and misery upon which we are looking out might then have been spared! How many millions would be alive that now are dead! Some such thought must have been in the mind of the British diplomatist who designed the book-plate of the Embassy.

It was an evil day for the Turkish race when the Crescent replaced the Cross over the dome of St. Sophia. When their feudal chieftains entered the palaces and private mansions of the Byzantine Greeks, the simplicity and severity of their society became exposed to an infection it could not resist. Just as the American Indian tribes were exterminated by our drinks and diseases, the Turkish tribes fell victims at once to a luxury of which they had had no experience. After but two centuries the Ottoman society was no longer Turkish. It was Levantine, or rather Byzantine, with an Eastern in place of a Western orientation.

The process began at once. The Turkish ladies adopted the Byzantine fashions—the diaphanous Yashmak or veil, the wooden chopines, and the rest of the Byzantine wardrobe. We can see in the Greek Tanagra figures a Yashmak pinned, just as it is still pinned in Turkish Anatolia; or a shawl held in the mouth, just as is still the habit of unveiled Turkish peasant women. The Hareem was reorganized on the exact model of the Gynæcea of the Empress Helen. The palaces were built, and the courts

modelled after the Byzantine fashion. The Kanoun-Namé, or
Code, of the Conqueror, with its chapter on the Constitution, on
Ceremonial and on Commerce, might have been issued by any
Byzantine Emperor. The chapter on the Constitution, with its
concentration on the mystic number Four—the four Viziers, etc.—
is inspired by the Greek magical art of numbers. Little wonder
that, when in the eighteenth century the Greeks were again
advanced to the position of a deputy ruling race, it appeared as
if the imitative process was on the point of culminating in the
substitution of a Greek Emperor for a Turkish Sultan.

The reforms of Mahmoud, accordingly, were directed against
a condition of affairs in Constantinople wherein the supreme
authority had come to be distributed between three centres—
none of them in any sense Ottoman. There was the Seraglio and
the Janissaries—which had grown very like a Byzantine Court
and its Imperial Guard. There was the Phanar—with its wholly
Greek elements. And lastly, there were Galata and Pera—with
their revived privileges, foreign colonies, and ambassadorial
authority. We know already how Mahmoud dealt with the
Janissaries and the Greeks. But the Ambassadors were too
strong for him. All that any Sultan could do was to divide Pera
against itself by accepting the protection of the Power that
seemed the least exacting at the moment. The French had their
turn first, under Mahmoud. During the reigns of Abdul-Medjid,
Abdul-Aziz, and Mourad, the British people paid the piper, and
the British plenipotentiary could call the tune. Under Abdul-
Hamid the Germans took first place.

PERA AND THE EMBASSIES

The British Embassy then should be our next point. From
Galata to Pera there is a variety of routes; by the funicular
railway, by walking up the ancient Step Street (Yuksek Kalderim),
which will give us a good idea of old Pera, or by the tram, through
the Petit Champs des Morts. The last is prosaic, but it is perhaps
the best if we wish to get a general idea of the town. The tram
winds up from the Galata bank buildings, with an outlook down
over deserted cemeteries to the Golden Horn, until it passes on
the left the Constantinople Club, and next door to that the
Pera Palace Hotel. Beyond follow less pretentious hotels,
mostly with good views, and then the walls and gate of the
British Embassy. This was built in 1870, in Italianate style, and
belongs, therefore, itself to the period of the decline of British

influence rather than to that of its development with which we are dealing.

In the Embassy chancery is an interesting coloured print of the presentation of Stratford Canning and his suite to Mahmoud II in 1810. The Sultan is dressed in full Oriental costume, for this was before his reform epoch, and is seen squatting inside a grated alcove. For the Seraglio had for many years cultivated Byzantine seclusion, wherein the Sultan remained sheltered from all infidel eyes.

Mahmoud, however, soon after this broke out through those bars. The son of a French Creole, whose adventurous life-story has already been told, he was more likely to make things move than the sons of fat Circassian slaves. His sister also, Habibullah Sultan, was a poetess, and as Miss Pardoe tells us, a woman of great beauty and brilliance. Her poems, often reprinted, have much merit, especially her last, " Song of Death." The mysterious allusions to poison you find there may have some connection with her own mysterious death, in her " Yali " on the Bosphorus, where she had been confined by her brother for interfering in politics.

But on the occasion commemorated in the engraving, Canning was evidently impressed by the barbaric splendour of the Ottoman Court. He writes :

The courteous ceremonies of Turkish etiquette were not yet divested of their antique forms. A long procession on horseback, interrupted by a row across the harbour in boats of Turkish fashion, led to the Seraglio. . . . The pageant began at a very early hour, and took up the greater part of the day. The Sultan's throne, which resembled a four-post bedstead hung with cloth of gold and studded with jewels, almost filled the dark room in which he received the Ambassador . . . near him at one side was a rich casket, on the other a drawn scimitar. The chief officers of State, in their splendid costumes invented from those seen in a dream by Suleiman the Magnificent, were ranged on his right.

In the last chapter we encountered a fellow tourist, Lord Byron, doing the grand tour. In Canning's report of this first audience we find that scarlet coat again :

We had assembled for the first audience in the hall of our so-called palace, when Lord Byron arrived, in scarlet regimentals, topped by a profusely feathered cocked hat, and coming to me asked what his place (as a Peer of the Realm) was to be in the procession. I referred him to Mr. Adair, and the upshot of his private interview was that as the Turks ignored all but officials, any amateur, though a Peer, must be content to follow in the wake of the Embassy. His lordship then walked away with that look of scornful indignation which so well became his imperious features. The next day the Ambassador, having consulted the Austrian Internuncio, wrote to apprise Lord Byron. Byron's reply gave assurance of the fullest satisfaction, ending that the illustrious penitent would attend the next audience in His Excellency's train, and humbly follow " his ox or his ass or anything that was his."

You will probably agree that Byron had the best of it.

Fifteen years later, when the audience took place which began the reign of the Great Elchi over the Ottoman Empire, from the British Embassy, we find that much that was picturesque had already passed away, with the Janissaries and the Phanariotes :

This time His Majesty was dressed more or less like a European General, in a dark blue frock-coat, richly embroidered, white cashmere trousers, black shoes and a fez. The former stately surroundings had disappeared, and instead of sitting in his bird-cage-like throne, the Padishah occupied an arm-chair and actually permitted the Ambassador to sit in another side by side with him."

By 1842 we find Canning writing about—

The extraordinary change which is daily taking place in the manners of the people. . . . Very few years more and not a turban will exist. Grand Vezier, Reis Effendi, Ulemas, now wear the red cap, Cossack trousers, black boots, and a plain red or blue coat buttoned to the chin. No gold embroidery, no jewels, no pelices. . . . The Sultan has paid a visit to Madame Hubsch and been bear shooting at Belgrade, for which he borrowed Black's gun, and in fact behaved so unaccountably that Cartwright cannot account for it but by believing him to be cracked.

Mahmoud was no more " cracked " than was Peter the Great. He was pursuing his policy of modernizing the Empire with persistence and some perspicacity. In quick succession followed newspapers, steamboats, naval and military colleges, orders of merit, quarantines, balls, sidespring boots, and even portraits of the Padishah—each innovation a worse shock to the orthodox than the last. " Such resolution and immovable firmness, such patience, are rare among Princes," was Canning's tribute to him on his death, in 1839.

He was succeeded by his eldest son, the gentle and generous Abdul-Medjid, who at once, under the influence of the British Embassy, declared himself on the side of the angels in the " Hati-Sherif of Gul-Hané " : Gul-Hané is the semi-circular little kiosque outside the southern corner of the inner wall of the Seraglio. This profession of faith in liberal principles made a great stir at a time when Western Europe was still in reaction. But it had little result, for the liberal Vizier, Raschid, who was responsible for it, was overthrown, and replaced by the reactionary Riza. In spite of Canning's efforts, a Mussulman reaction began, and the newly-won rights of the Christians were suspended. It became apparent that the remodelling of the Empire as an association of autonomous religious communities was not going to prove feasible. Islamic orthodoxy had collided with Greek orthodoxy, and dissolved the political partnership between the Porte and the Phanar. Islam was not yet prepared to accept equal citizenship as between Mussulman and Christian, in a Constitutional State. Before that junction could take place, religion and politics would have to be divorced.

In dealing with the religious side of this difficulty Mahmoud and the reforming Sultans made one serious blunder. They suppressed the Dervishes, and broke the momentum of the movement which they represented. As the tekké of the Whirling Dervishes is in Pera, near the head of the Funicular, and the tekké of the Howling Dervishes is at Kassim Pacha, in the valley west of the Embassy, we may suppose ourselves to be on the way to witness a performance, and consider the significance of the dervish movement as we go.

The dervishes were no doubt closely connected with the Janissaries. The Janissaries were founded under the auspices of the Bektashi sect. And these monastic orders were also like the Janissaries, in that they could have been developed into an imperial institution, " a pillar of Empire." Moreover, unlike the Janissaries, they not only progressed themselves, but were prepared even to give a lead to public opinion. They had much in common with the preaching Friars in Europe, and they embodied a protest—as did our early Dissenters—against the deadness or demoralization of an established orthodoxy.

The Islamic hierarchy was at this time capable of development. The Imams, or parish clergy, had no spiritual activity, or even priestly authority. They lived on the fees obtained for circumcizing, marrying, and burying, eked out by keeping shops or schools—wherein the Koran was learnt by rote. They were quite illiterate and often immoral. But, at the same time, the Imams were very influential with their congregations. The Mullah, who is often confused with the Imam, belonged to the Ulema class. Now the Ulema were a class learned in the sacred law and the Koran. And since all relations in life had, legally speaking, to be referred to the Koran as the sole Civil Code, the Ulema formed a theocracy of great legal and spiritual authority. The Sheikh ul-Islam was their head, and the Sheikh could even depose the Sultan—unless the Sultan, representing the Sword of the Caliph, could manage to decapitate the Sheikh first. The

Mufti or Kadi, the Justice of the Peace, was one of this Ulema class, qualified by some special training. So also were the three Judges of Appeal, Kadi-ul-Asker, for Anatolia, Roumelia and Constantinople respectively, who ranked next to the Grand Vizier. Finally, the lowest grade of this hierarchy, the Seminarists or Softas, were always ready for action—or rather reaction. Because the hierarchy was, of course, in every way conservative.

THE DERVISHES AND THE PALACES

Not so the dervishes. Dervishism, which originated in Persia, and soon became dominant in Bagdad, was based upon mysticism. Its twelve Orders embodied most of the varieties of religious enthusiasm known to the mediæval or the modern world. Since all the Orders were at one in asserting the right of any Mussulman to interpret the Koran for himself, it was natural that the dervishes should combine an immense amount of magic, mumbo-jumbo, and immorality, with genuinely religious points of view and political principles of breadth and even of depth. We, as good tourists, are more interested in the picturesque and peculiar side of the dervish ceremonies. But there is another side to dervishism. Contrast, for example, with Mohammed's view of the future life this view of the Mevlevi dervish :

> You say " the sea and its waves." But in so saying you do not mean two different things. For the sea, rising and falling, makes waves—which, when fallen, return to the sea. So it is with men, the waves of God : who, after death, are made one again with Him."

Under Abdul-Hamid you might still have met dervish ascetics wandering naked through the streets. But the Turlaki, the most fanatical Order, have disappeared from Constantinople, and the Santons, or Holy men, rarely appear there. Until the war these fakirs were fairly common in the neighbouring villages, shrivelled old men in filthy rags, hung about with charms and amulets. We cannot, however, read about the Orders without realizing that they were a revolutionary element in Islam, which might have been used not only for religious reform but for political reconstruction—even as our Dissenters were. For the rebels of one generation become the Radicals of the next ; and, finally—if rightly used—the reformers of another. But, from Suleiman onward, the more reforming the Sultans were, the more they repressed the dervishes—until Mahmoud II completely suppressed a movement that might have saved the Empire.

If Islam is ever revitalized, the impulse will not come from any Puritan reaction, such as Wahabism. It will be due to some new spiritual inspiration emanating from one of the dervish Orders. It is this thought, the thought of the mystical meaning behind the ceremonies, that we should bear in mind when we attend one of their singular services.

The Bektashi are the most important of the Orders. Their religion was no more than a tacit recognition of a Supreme Being; their ritual only the invoking of the name of Allah 1,001 times, with the dropping of a pebble on every ten repetitions. But their political position was more definite. In association with the Janissaries they played, during the eighteenth and early nineteenth century, much the same part in the Ottoman reform movement as did Freemasonry in European reform movements. They were, in fact, affiliated with French Freemasonry. Fazil Bey, a friend of Voltaire, remodelled the Order, so that it remained the organization of the Young Turkey movement for over a century. Its activities were philosophical, literary, scientific, and political, all with a national *arrière-pensée*.

Under these circumstances it is not surprising that they were suspect to the despotism of Mahmoud, while that of Abdul-Hamid banished them from the capital. Their only tekké when I knew them, was at Roumeli Hissar, in a modern villa close to the American College.

The Bektashi are obviously something very different from the felt-capped fanatics that the word dervish suggests to us. Do not think that the members of this or any other of the dervish Orders are limited to those that you may see on the streets wearing the distinctive dress. The upper classes of the Bektashi only put on the woollen cloak and the conical cap when indoors. If you are invited to lunch by a smart young officer and are received on arrival by a weird-looking wizard, you will be safe in assuming that your host is not a fanatic but a free-thinker.

The Whirling Dervishes (Mevlevi) are less political and more picturesque. They wear a yellowish or white felt cap, with a turban round it: that of the Sheikh, or prior, of the tekké being usually green, since he is almost always a Seyyid, or descendant of the Prophet. The Sheikh of this Order is the only dervish dignitary with an official position. He ranks next to the Sheikh ul-Islam, bears the title of Mollah-Hunkiar, or princely priest, and used to invest the Sultan with the Sword of Osman on his coronation.

Foreigners are admitted to their peculiar services after the opening prayers. They are expected to stand, and remove their shoes. The ritual is generally in the evening, and takes place on a highly polished platform. The public stand round, and there is a latticed gallery for the hareems. The orchestra, in a gallery, consists of a few musicians, playing—in defiance of the Koran, on stringed and other instruments of interesting antiquity, tabors, dulcimers, one-stringed fiddles, lyres, etc. For an account of the ceremony I quote first from " Turkish Life," by Mrs. Garnett :

The *devr*, or exercise of the Mevlevis differs entirely from that of the other Orders, and is accompanied by instrumental music. The service begins with the recitation of prayers and passages from the Koran, followed by a pleasing performance on the flutes, zithers, and tiny drums, of which the orchestra chiefly consists. The brethren, who have meanwhile been seated on the floor round the circular central place, now rise, throw off their cloaks, and advance in single file, with arms crossed on their breasts and downcast eyes, to the Sheikh. Bowing to right and left of the prayer-mat on which he stands, they kiss his hand, and in return receive from him a kiss on their tall sugar-loaf hats. This done, they immediately begin to spin round, balancing themselves on the left foot, while maintaining a rotary motion. Gradually the arms of the devotees are unfolded and extended, the right hand raised with the palm upwards, and the left lowered with the palm downward ; the eyes are closed, and the head is inclined towards the left shoulder. Mentally reciting the invocation of " Allah ! Allah ! " they whirl round the " Hall of Celestial Sounds," the faces of even the youngest neophytes wearing an expression of devout serenity as they revolve to the sound of the reed-flutes, a music which appears to have an entrancing effect on those who understand its mystic language. For to the dervish ' lovers of Allah ' it is said to express the harmony of His creation, in which they circle like the planets of the empyrean detached from the world in a rapture of spiritual love and communion with the Eternal.

The ceremony varies somewhat in different tekkés, and here is another description :

Although the space is circumscribed the Whirlers never gain upon one another, as they continue for some five minutes their machine-like twirl. Their pale and passionless faces remain the while entirely unmoved ; and their whirling, inflated garments create a keen draught through the chapel. At the end of that period, whenever the name of the Prophet occurs in the intermittent chant from the gallery, they pause simultane-ously, fold their hands on their breasts, and bend reverently at the sound ; their ample robes winding about them, at the sudden check, in the fashion of mummies. An interval of prayer follows ; and the ceremony is repeated twice. At the end of the third dance they all fall prostrate. Those who have remained spectators fling over them their cloaks, and a dervish kneeling on the Sheikh's left rises and delivers, rapidly and solemnly, a long prayer, prolonging the last word of each sentence with a ' Ya hu ! Ya hu ! ' This prayer is offered for all in authority ; and at each name they all bow their heads. When that of the Sultan is reached, they fall once more flat on the ground, howling dismally. Then they rise to their feet, bow to each other, and retire.

The ceremonies of the Whirling Dervishes are graceful and inoffensive. But those of the Howling Dervishes, though interesting, are repulsive.

The Sheikh, in a bright crimson robe, comes in and squats in front of the mihrab, on either side of which burn two small braziers, occasionally fed with incense. The musicians assemble, and sit in a circle. At the other end of the room a number of the congregation and the Order arrange themselves in a row. The Sheikh begins the office. The musicians bang on the cymbals and tambourines, crying out as loud as they can, " Allah Akbar ! Ya hu ! " The dervishes lolling against the wall also begin to bellow in cadence, beating the measure with their feet and swaying their bodies to and fro. Louder and louder they roar, until their excitement rises to frenzy. Their eyes start from their heads, they foam at the mouth, and in about an hour several of them are rolling on the floor in epilepsy. While the excitement is at its height, several mad men and women are brought in and laid gently before the Sheikh, who tramples upon them very lightly with his feet. Children are brought in and receive the same pressure. A spruce young officer prostrates himself, and is similarly treated. By this time the dervishes at the upper end of the room have lost all control. The tambourines and drums clash and boom. The whole frantic congregation is screaming, as if possessed, " Ya Allah ! Ya hu ! "

It is an unpleasing exhibition. But it is mild compared with what may be seen up-country, where these Rufai dervishes still wound themselves with red-hot knives and pokers—such as can be seen, though not now used, in the Constantinople tekkés.

If you visit a dervish tekké you will find it is much like any other monastery—picturesque and peaceful. An arched gateway admits you to a cloistered court of trees, surrounded by cells, refectory, and offices—a building only of one story. In the centre of the court is a square chapel, with a cupola and a fountain, the haunt of pigeons. Beyond are flower and fruit gardens with cypress avenues and tanks shaded by plane-trees. Here the mystics may be seen, pacing slowly, and telling their beads. For them every act of daily life has its mystic meaning, and they seem for the most part to have achieved a tranquillity of mind and of charitableness towards all men often conspicuously lacking in the Orthodox monasteries. Besides the brethren, who may, but very rarely do, abandon the conventual life, there are dervish lay-brothers. They are associated to the Order, but continue to

live their ordinary lives, and only don the garb in the privacy
of their homes. Not long ago the number of such lay Bektashis
amounted to nearly 100,000.

Oriental mysticism, as it expresses itself in the dervish Orders,
is an enthralling subject, but it requires a volume to itself.
What I have said about it may be enough to show that dervishism
is not a mere pantomime turn.[1]

On our way from the tekké we may, as a contrast, visit the
rather beautiful English church on the heights of Pera. It was
built as a memorial to the thousands of brave men who fell in a
crusade as misdirected as any that ever fought for Constantinople—
the Crimean War.

Abdul-Medjid was the type of self-indulgent ruler who, in
the seventeenth century, would have been ruled by his hareem,
and in the eighteenth by his Vizier and Greek ministers. In
the nineteenth century such a Sultan had to be ruled by foreign
Ambassadors. From 1842–58 Stratford Canning defended Constantinople against France and Russia. France had been supporting Mehemet Ali of Egypt, who had been rapidly conquering
the Empire from the south, and had acquired the Turkish fleet.
When France threatened us with war in 1846, and we defied the
threat, bombarded Beyrout and broke the power of Mehemet, the
prize really at stake was Constantinople. The weakness of
France, and the support of Russia, saved us from actual war,
and Canning was thus enabled to throw his whole authority and
ability into fortifying Constantinople for ever against Russia.
And he almost succeeded.

His diplomacy was that of an age when foreign envoys were
cut off from constant communication with their Governments,
and conceived and carried out their own policy. He has been
called our greatest Ambassador. Like Palmerston, he achieved
sensational results by using modern machinery with mediæval
recklessness. He made himself ruler of Turkey by enlisting
English moral prestige and military power in support of an
obsolescent imperial system. He worked for the reform of
Turkey and for the greater glory of England. But his policy
cost both Turkey and England dear, and, in the end, neither had
anything to show for it.

Early in 1853 the Tsar Nicholas said to Sir Hamilton Seymour,

---

[1] As I revise this I read that the Turks have followed the example of
Western republics in abolishing monastic Orders. So the dervishes no
longer exist—at least legally. It is quite possible, however, that loss of
property may purify and revive the movement.

our Ambassador in Petersburg: "I tell you plainly that if England thinks of establishing herself one of these days in Constantinople, I will not allow it. I am equally disposed to undertake not to establish myself there—as proprietor, that is—for as to occupier I do not say." On February 20 he added: "If your Government has been led to believe that Turkey retains any element of existence, your Government must have received incorrect information. I repeat to you, the sick man is dying."

At the same time Prince Menschikoff, a rough soldier, was sent as Ambassador to Constantinople to replace British patronage by a Russian protectorate. Canning, who had resigned in 1852, was re-appointed, as Lord Stratford de Redclyffe, to counteract him. Menschikoff's methods were brutality and bribery, and our able Ambassador had little difficulty in manipulating the issues so as to get French support against Russia, just as a decade before he had obtained Russian support against France. But he found that Louis Philippe had, when it came to the point, drawn a very sensible distinction between threatening war over Syria and engaging in it. Nicholas did not. He considered Constantinople worth a war.

The diplomatic exchanges that led up to the collision are so remote from the real issue—the possession of Constantinople—that we many of us still believe that the Crimean War was fought about nothing in particular, and might have been avoided. But the war was fought for this definite prize, and it had this not unusual sequel that, having won the war, we then lost the prize. We have forgotten to-day that the Crimean War was accepted as a holy war by British public opinion. A generation had elapsed since the Napoleonic wars. The notion of war as a purgative had had time to revive. Under the guidance of the great Elchi and of that inspired intriguer, Urquhart, English upper-class opinion was ready to accept Russia as the enemy, although the middle class remained more suspicious of France, especially after the *coup d'état* of Napoleon III. Urquhart is only remembered to-day as the adventurous diplomat who introduced the British public to Turkish baths and the Russian bogy; and the policy of the great Elchi, for a rejuvenated Ottoman Empire under British protection—was probably only dimly realized then, as it is indistinctly recollected now. But, no sooner had the Russian armies crossed the Danube and the British naval and military forces garrisoned Constantinople, than the war became manifestly a struggle between the leading sea Power and the leading land Power for command of the strategic and commercial centre of Eastern Europe and Western Asia—in fact, a " holy war." The British were defending their communications with India and their commerce with the East. The Russians were defending their only outlet towards the south. The Crimean campaign was no more than an outpost combat in the defence of Constantinople by the British against the Russians.

So far as the military results went, the war should have confirmed our protectorate of Constantinople and of a reformed Ottoman Empire. In effect, it put an end to our whole imperial Ottoman enterprise. The British people had been easily worked up to war-fever, but as usual the reckless expenditure of men and money, which so often characterizes our war-making, cooled them off as rapidly. They were, also, not without an instinctive suspicion of a crusade to prevent the Holy Places from falling into Christian hands, and to preserve the divine right of Asiatics to oppress Europeans. They grew disgusted with the Near East. That generation, at least, ceased any longer to see in Constantinople the capital of Christianity, or the commercial centre of the nearer East, or a Levantine copy of the British Constitution. They saw only the hospitals at Scutari, their dark disaster faintly lit by the Lady with the Lamp. Over in Scutari you can still see Florence Nightingale's rooms in the hospital. And you can still see there the well-kept cemetery—the only relic of a British domination which might have developed into a British dominion.

From the English Memorial Church we can go down to Beshiktash and take a boat or steamer across to Scutari, the most Asiatic of the townships which compose the Capital. From the bridge it is only a short trip across, in which we pass, upon an island off Seraglio Point, the absurdly named " Leander's Tower." The tower, now used as a lighthouse, is the remains of a Byzantine fort repaired by Mahmoud II. On an island nearer the Asiatic shore is another tower, called the " Maiden's Tower " (Kizkuleh), after the monument to Damalis, wife of Philip of Macedon, who was buried there.

SCUTARI AND THE CRIMEA

Scutari, the ancient Chrysopolis, a suburb of Chalcedon, is named after the Byzantine infantry (Scutarii Shield-bearers), who had their quarters here. It was Moslem long before the Conquest of Constantinople ; and it has always been expected to remain so, long after all Moslem footing in Europe may have been lost. Until modern times it was the mart of the Asiatic trade of Constantinople. Here Xenophon and his Ten Thousand sold their booty ; and here still stand the remains of the great Khans or caravanserais, where the traders from all Asia ended their long journeys of months or even of years. In the fine mosques and in a number of dervish tekkés we shall find that the rituals of the several sects are being observed in Scutari with greater strictness than across the water in Pera.

The older streets and the cloisters of the mosques are picturesque and Oriental in character. Otherwise Scutari is a city of the dead rather than of the living. Pious Turks have always, when possible, arranged for their bodies to be borne across the Bosphorus for burial, rather than leave them on the other side exposed to the risk of passing under the dominion of the Christians. They lie here, under the cypress trees, in the vast wilderness of cemetery. Here, also, above the bay of Haidar Pasha and the terminus of the Oriental railway, is the burial-ground founded by Florence Nightingale for those of our countrymen who died in the Scutari hospitals during the Crimean War. Her own head-quarters were in the square yellow buildings of the Selimyeh barracks, which stand behind.

In the north-west tower, to the left of the main gate, were Miss Nightingale's rooms. It came to be called the " Sisters' Tower." The sisters' quarters consisted of a large kitchen, with smaller rooms opening off it. From this modest centre the " Bird|"—name of terror to the dug-outs of the day—laboured to introduce some order into a confusion so dense and so insanitary as to seem to us insane. There were medical stores, which were accumulated in the Custom-houses for want of means of conveyance to the hospitals. And yet more stores, which kept travelling backward and forward between Constantinople and the Crimea, for want of an order from some official for their unloading. The hospitals were pest-houses, where the sick and wounded died in hundreds, of diseases evitable or curable— gangrene, dysentery, erysipelas, and exhaustion. It had been after the Battle of the Alma, October 12, that " The Times " had published the famous dispatch beginning, " It is with feelings of surprise and anger that the public will learn that no sufficient preparations have been made for the proper care of the wounded." The indictment that followed had led to an agitation, of which the practical results were a " Times Fund " and—within the fortnight—the mission of Miss Nightingale, a personal friend of the War Secretary, Sidney Herbert.

Of the work of the Lady with the Lamp, as administrator

and as nurse, I have to limit myself to one or two pictures. Her first task was to establish a moral authority that should override " red tape." If an orderly refused to put a hot-water bottle to the feet of a patient in collapse, she would walk herself—at two in the morning—over to the General Hospital, wake a Chief Surgeon, and get the order, in the interests of discipline. If some " fossil " of the Peninsular War refused to build a laundry or a delousing apparatus, she drew a cheque of her own. The Inspector-General objected that a whole new Service Regulation would be needed to provide against one patient being given at a meal nothing but fat, another nothing but bone, and a third all the meat. So she had Alexis Soyer, the world-famous *chef* of the Reform Club, sent out to cook for her hospitals. " Going to Miss Nightingale," became the last resource of any local administrator hampered by red tape. Even as " Sending for Miss Nightingale " was the last privilege of the soldier, dying of the evils that red tape had bound upon him. Her memory is immortalized by the statue in Waterloo Place, and by the poem of Longfellow. The two passages from which the poet took his inspiration deserve to be remembered. The first was written by " The Times" Commissioner : " When all the medical officers are gone for the night, and silence and darkness have settled down on these miles of prostrate sick, she may be seen, with a little lamp in her hand, making her solitary rounds." And the second is from the letter of a soldier, which was quoted by Sidney Herbert in November 1853 : " What a comfort it was to see her pass even. She would speak to one and nod or smile to another. She could not do it to all, you know—we lay there by hundreds—but we could kiss her shadow as it fell."

" I wish we had her at the War Office," wrote Queen Victoria to the Duke of Cambridge. What the Duke, then Commander-in-Chief, said of the suggestion is not on record. But in the hope that the suggestion may some day take effect in favour of a future Miss Nightingale, let us take leave of the Lady-in-Chief.

In this quiet sanctuary, with its lovely view over the Marmara, we may reflect on the strange contradictions that have marked our own connexion with the story of Constantinople. For the Englishmen who lie here fought for a policy that aimed at keeping the Russians out of the city. While, at the farther end of the Marmara, are the cemeteries of those who fell for a policy that aimed at putting the Russians into the city.

The British were not unwilling to continue the war, but peace was forced upon them by the French. Napoleon had entered into secret negotiations with Nicholas. The Treaty of Paris, in consequence, was a French victory ; for by it the Russians were kept out of Constantinople, and the British position there was made untenable. Our only justification, to ourselves and to others, for our protectorate in Constantinople had been that the reformed regime depended upon it. But the Treaty, while embodying the Hatti Humayun, a proclamation of the principles of liberty, equality, and fraternity among all Ottomans, also contained, in spite of British opposition, this clause : " that it (the Hatti Humayun) cannot give the Powers the right to interfere either collectively or individually . . . in the internal administration of the Empire." " I would rather," said Lord Stratford later, " have cut off my right hand than have signed that Treaty." Lord Eversley (Shaw Lefevre)—still, happily, alive when this was written (1924)—discussed the treaty with the great Elchi himself at Therapia, at the time of its negotiation. He tells us that Canning considered that it was " the death-blow of the cause of reform in Turkey, that England had been betrayed at the Congress of Paris, and that the Ottoman Empire was doomed." The following year Lord Stratford retired. But, true to his principles to the end, he refused to withdraw his savings from the Turkish funds, and died a poor man. He was succeeded by Sir Henry Bulwer, who, in Lord Eversley's words, " allowed himself to be put under an obligation to the Sultan which destroyed his influence." The British protectorate vanished away.

Before we pass on, however, one or two names deserve honourable mention. A Mr. Black, who died in 1828, headed a dynasty of British merchant-princes who, before the Crimean War, held almost a monopoly of the foreign commerce of Constantinople. The tradition was ably carried on into our own time by the Whittall family. The first Constantinople bank was founded by the family of Hanson. It only failed late in the last century. During the latter part of the century the commerce of Turkey was passing steadily from British into German control.

Abdul-Medjid was the last Sultan to die before he was deposed. With the succession of the handsome spendthrift, Abdul-Aziz (1861–76), the reformed Empire rattled down into ruins. Gorgeous buildings are generally accepted by later generations as evidence of prosperity. They are quite as often symptoms of decay. The British Embassy, built in 1870, and the Palace of Dolma Bagtche, built in 1853, date the decline of their builders.

Dolma Bagtche can be reached by either of two routes : one by Taksim, the other by Nishantash and the Kuchuk Iklamour Deressi (the little lime-tree valley). Dolma Bagtche (the embanked garden) stands on the site of a port where the Turkish galleys lay during the siege, and whence the Conqueror had them hauled up along the Little Lime-tree Valley over to the Golden Horn. The port was filled in, under Suleiman, by the labour of 16,000 Christian prisoners captured by Barbarossa after his Mediterranean raids. Here, however, and in the neighbouring Tcheragan Palace, the reforming Sultans came—and went.

The earliest of the buildings at Dolma Bagtche is the mosque. It was built by the Valideh, the mother of Abdul-Medjid, a washerwoman with whom the formidable Mahmoud had fallen in love one day. She remained to the end of her long life a woman of the people. Many stories are told of her, and we shall meet her again.

In the adjoining Palace Abdul-Medjid gave his Armenian architect, Balian, absolute freedom in expenditure and in expression ; only stipulating that it should surpass any other palace of any other potentate. The results, certainly, are difficult to appraise. It is worth seeing, whether we like it or not. And we may see in it, if we choose, the embodiment of a class of ideas from which the Turkish Republic is a revulsion, and to which Angora is the natural antithesis. What can be done with it all now—the Throne-room 150 feet long, with Corinthian columns in groups of fours and French frescoes ; the bath-rooms in carved alabaster ; the huge tables of malachite and lapis lazuli ; the largest plate-glass mirror ever made ; the candelabras with their mystic number of 333 silver sockets ? Yet some day visitors may read the list of these splendours as regretfully as we now read of the departed glories of the Blachernæ. The Throne-room was the scene of the last pageants of the Empire. The official reception at Bairam was still maintained by Abdul-Hamid, after his government had degenerated into little more than a monstrous system of secret service. On a settee throne at the north end sat the Sultan, in a crimson, silk-tasselled fez, and a black coat girt with a gilt sword. The Grand Vizier then headed a slow procession of the functionaries in single file along the side of the room. When he was on a line with the Sultan, each of the file in turn left the queue, and moved slowly towards the throne, crouching always lower as he advanced, until he arrived practically crawling. Then he kissed the fringe of a broad green and red silk sash hanging over the settee, pressed it to his forehead, and slipped hurriedly away backward. By the end of the century the ceremony had probably become more abject and austere than in the days of the genial Abdul-Aziz.

Under Abdul-Hamid the proper expression was one of cringing terror on the part of the subject, of remote indifference on the part of the Sultan. But once, when I was there, there came a reassertion of human nature. The procession had just got as far as the salutations of military and naval officers, and I was remarking with interest that the foreigners in Ottoman pay were even more servile in their attitudes than the Turks, when an earthquake shock shook the heavy dome and columns. In a second the slow march past was shattered into a kaleidoscope of portly Pashas bolting like rabbits through the colonnades. For once the Diplomatic Corps stood not upon the order of its going. The doorway was immediately and hopelessly jammed; so I turned to see what was happening below. Abdul-Hamid, the solitary figure left in the great hall, had half risen from the settee. He was looking wildly round for a refuge. All his majestic impassivity was gone; and he looked like a panic-stricken old Jew, grotesquely got up in a black coat, side-spring boots, gilt sword and crimson fez. The noise of the military band outside had by now given place to the clamour and rush of a frantic crowd. Slowly I saw dawning in Abdul-Hamid's face the realization that he was safer where he was, even under that rocking roof; and he subsided again upon the settee. I left him there, alone in the swaying hall—the last and most detestable of the despots that for fifteen centuries ruled in Constantinople.

But this is to anticipate : we have still something to see before we have finished with the Sultanate.

Beshiktash (the Cradle Stone) we can reach direct from Pera, by way of Shishli and the Buyuk Iklamur Deressi (large valley of the lime-trees). It commemorates a rock landmark, known to history as the Petron Thermastis.

The ruins of the Tcheragan Palace remind us that the handsome Abdul-Aziz, although he flirted with reaction during his brother's reforms, did nothing on coming to the throne but spend money. He pensioned off the multitudes of women in his brother's hareem, and promised economy even to the point of

THE OTTOMAN EMPIRE 209

monogamy; but he soon had accumulated 900 women and 3,000 eunuchs. The palace he built was almost as costly as his brother's; and his expenditure upon the immense marble foundations of the unfinished mosque was enormous. The paper reforms had given the Empire an equally fictitious paper credit in London and Paris, and the borrowings of the two spendthrifts were imperial. If earlier Sultans had maintained their State by impressing Christian bond-slaves, these two succeeded in doing so by imposing upon Christian bondholders. Abdul-Aziz even made a State visit to London, and was given the Garter; but nevertheless the British bondholder began to revolt. A Commission of Europeans under Fouad Pasha reported the finances of the Empire to be in a hopeless condition. The result soon appeared in the introduction of foreign financial control, in the Ottoman Bank and in the Public Debt Administration. So it came that power passed from these marble palaces and mosques to the grim Bastille which we have already seen dominating Stamboul. Abdul-Aziz, overlooking these financial fore-closures, may have supposed the Golden Age would last for his time. It did not quite do so.

Tcheragan, which was perhaps the only beautiful Bosphorus Palace of the Age of Borrowings, was destroyed by fire just before the War.

If we want more palaces we can take a boat and cross the Bosphorus to Beylerbey. The village was celebrated even in Byzantine times for its succession of fine palaces. That built by Abdul-Aziz in 1865 and used for the reception of foreign royalties is sufficiently imposing. While Abdul-Aziz was building it, he remarked that "it must be pleasing to Allah because the work was favoured with such fine weather." To this Serkis Bey, an Armenian, retorted courteously, "Oh no, Majesty! Allah only favours poor men. He *flatters* your Majesty!"

The Voltairean Dervishes have already introduced us to the Young Turk party. They had been organized under Midhat Pasha into a political party, with a programme of Turkey for the Turks. Young Turkey started as both reactionary and revolutionary. It was opposed alike to reforms that would pawn the Empire to foreign finance, and to reforms that would put it under the power of its own subject races. Like all nationalist movements it was chiefly literary in its first manifestations. Zia Bey, with Shinassi and Kemal, created a new Turkish literature, on Western lines. Zia was one of the first rebels against Byzantinism. In his

" Zafer-namé," a satiric poem with a mock-learned commentary in the style of Belloc, he writes :

The ways of God are dark, and His covenant is not clear.
We are taxed by Armenian Beys ; we march for a Greek Mushir.
We shall yet salaam to a gipsy whom He has made Grand Vizier !

Oddly enough, had Zia Bey lived to see the success of the Young Turk movement, after the revolution of 1908, he might have salaamed to Talaat, the Grand Vizier of the Young Turks— a Pomak gipsy ! Such are the ironies of politics.

In the early stages of the movement its policy was simple enough. Fouad's death having removed the last restraints, the mad extravagance and general maladministration ended, on October 6, 1875, in imperial bankruptcy. In one year Mihri Hanoum, a Circassian slave, got a million sterling out of the Sultan. In vain Midhat protested. The old Validéh, the ex-washerwoman, was in power, and the Sultan had shut himself up in Dolma Bagtche, and only appeared on Fridays. Moreover, the Vizier, Mahmoud Neddin, was notoriously in the pay of Ignatiev, the Russian Ambassador.

The report of the murder of the French and Russian Consuls at Salonika gave the signal for the City to rise. Thousands of Softas (students) and other Young Turks gathered outside the Palace, waiting for the Sultan to go to the Friday service. For the first time in the history of the dynasty the Sultan did not appear. The next day the mob gathered again, this time with arms, and demanded a change of Vizier. Young Turk leaders were appointed, and a tussle ensued between them and the Queen-mother (the old bath-woman Besma) with the Circassian favourite, in which the two latter kept their hold over the indolent Sultan. The reformers then obtained a fetva of deposition from the Sheikh ul-Islam, moved the guardships away from the Palace, and brought over Mourad, the Sultan's nephew, from Prinkipo. One of the Young Turks had managed to get admittance to him disguised as a tailor, and while showing him patterns gave him a message to read, " You shall be Sultan to-morrow." Mourad was so upset that the tailor narrowly escaped arrest.

On the evening of May 29, 1876, all was ready. At midnight thirty conspirators entered the Palace gates and took command of the guard, whose officers had accepted an order to remain in their quarters. Redif Pasha and the conspirators then made their way to the Throne Hall. It was lit only by moonlight, and full of slaves sleeping on their carpets. One of these waked the

Chief Eunuch, who appeared at the foot of the stairs—a giant Nubian in a white nightgown, holding a torch. Redif pushed past the apparition, and made his way to a small sitting-room in the private apartments. While he was lighting a candle the Sultan appeared from the hareem in pink pyjamas. He towered over the intruder, and in his thundering voice demanded the meaning of the insolent entry. Redif bowed, and briefly notified him of his deposition and of Mourad's order that he should proceed to the Old Seraglio. The Sultan was about to close with him, when the Circassian favourite rushed out in her nightgown and clung round the Sultan with bewailings. The old Queen-mother showed more spirit, and attacked the officers. Redif, however, convinced her that her cause was lost, whereupon she calmed the other two and advised compliance. In silence the little party passed through the ranks of silent slaves and embarked in the moonlight for the Old Seraglio. Next day Abdul-Aziz was transferred to Tcheragan, and three days later he was found there dead on a couch. Although he was mentally deranged, and some trouble had been taken to set the stage for suicide, he was probably murdered. No reliance, however, can be placed upon the " confession " made three years later by a Greek wrestler and a gardener, which implicated Midhat, as by then Abdul-Hamid was anxious to remove Midhat.

A few days later Mihri Sultan, the fair Circassian, died " in childbirth." Her death excited great sympathy, and she was buried in an ornate coffin covered with a Cashmir shawl and strewn with roses, followed by an enormous crowd. Her handsome brother, or lover, the all-powerful young adventurer, Hassan, the Circassian, showed a proper sense of the dramatic. Suddenly appearing in the Council Chamber, where all the new Government were assembled, he opened fire—not upon the Young Turk rebels, but upon those of the original Government who had joined them. He first shot Hussein Avni, a fine old Turk. While he was finishing him with a yataghan, Midhat and the rest bolted, with the exception of Rashid Pasha, who was paralysed with fear, and the Minister of Marine, Akhmed Pasha, who attacked Hassan, but was wounded and fled. Hassan then shot Rashid dead, and battered on the door behind which the Council had taken refuge, shouting, " Give up the Minister of Marine. Open the door. I won't hurt anyone else ! " The Ministers, however, replied judiciously, " Not now, my son, you are too excited ! "—and put their backs against the door. Hassan forthwith fired two shots through it, and brought down the Grand Vizier. Suddenly

Midhat appeared behind him with two officers. Hassan shot the two officers, but only wounded Midhat. Before he was finally overpowered Hassan had killed another officer, wounded seven more men, and badly frightened an enterprising English journalist. He passed his last night singing the tenor arias from " Lucia di Lammermoor," and was hanged in the morning from a tree in the garden of a café overlooking the Seraskierate square, in the presence of his numerous admirers in the Imperial Hareem.

Constantinople has lost much of its picturesqueness, but it still retains a vivid element in its politics. Mourad went out of his mind, under the strain, and was deposed before the end of the summer. Right on into this century he dragged out an interminable life, in his ill-omened palace of Tcheragan. Besma alone, the old bath-woman and Queen-mother, was none the worse for the tragedy. She lived happily until near the end of the century, always mindful of her origin, and adored by the people. When she built her mosque, she was entitled by etiquette to two minarets, but she could only afford one. The Sultan, her son, offered her the money. " No," said she, " one minaret is enough for the Call to Prayer, the other would be for my own pride. The poor need a fountain ! " So the price of the minaret was spent on a fountain. We must always regret that Besma, in place of building mosques, did not write her memoirs.

Meanwhile, another tragedy had been taking place off the scenes. The victims were less prominent, but the tragedy had greater political consequences. In April 1876, a rising of Bulgars in the Rhodope had resulted in " atrocities." Sixty villages were fired and 1,200 women and children were burned in a church at Batak. With this as ammunition, Gladstone in his " Midlothian campaign " fulminated against Disraeli's pro-Turk policy. British opinion, however, was for the moment divided, and for the following reason. Serbia and Montenegro, in the interests of their compatriots in Bosnia, had declared war on Turkey; but, being defeated, had appealed for help to Russia. The scene, therefore, seemed once again to be set for the old duel between England and Russia for Constantinople. With the anti-Russian feeling to swing public opinion to his side, Disraeli appeared as the Protector of the Porte, and ordered the Fleet to Besika Bay. It only remained to raise war-feeling in England by preaching a " holy war " against Russia, as in 1854, and the " atrocities " would have been forgotten and England pledged in support of Turkey. But things did not go according to plan. Gladstone produced in September his famous pamphlet, " The Bulgarian Horrors " :

THE OTTOMAN EMPIRE 213

> Let the Turks now carry away their abuses in the only possible manner—by carrying off themselves. Their zabtiehs, and their mudirs, their bimbashis and their yuzbashis, their kaimakams and their pashas, one and all, bag and baggage, shall, I hope, clear out from the province they have desolated and profaned.

So deep was the impression made, that even the aged Lord Stratford adhered to the Liberal party, and Disraeli tried in vain to laugh his opponent's heroics out of court. For once his sarcasms fell flat ; and his call to arms against Russia, in the speech at Aylesbury, found no response. The most he could do was to induce his Foreign Secretary, Lord Derby, to warn the Russian Government (October 30) that the feeling in England against the Turkish atrocities would give place to a very different sentiment, if it were believed that Constantinople was threatened and the Suez Canal in danger. To this the Tsar gave a reassuring reply. But Disraeli followed up, on November 9, with a provocative speech at the Mansion House, declaring that he would protect the Christian subjects of the Porte by independent action if necessary. It looked, then, as if another Anglo-Russian war for Constantinople had become inevitable.

Under these conditions a Conference met at Constantinople on December 23, 1876, to contrive some administrative arrangement for the protection of the Christians. Abdul-Hamid at once took action. On the arrival of the delegates they were greeted by the thunder of guns saluting the new Ottoman Constitution. The Constitution countered the demand for self-government of the Christian provinces by granting self-government to the Empire, and the Conference found the ground cut from under its feet.

Nor was this only a mere diplomatic device, as it has often been represented. It was a genuine move in the direction of democracy. The Young Turks had had a superficial success in their revolution. Abdul-Hamid II, who had acquired reputation as a reformer, had been made Sultan. The new Constitution was a practical application to the Empire of the principles of liberty, equality, and fraternity. It gave equal rights in a representative Parliament, with popular sovereignty. The early sessions of the Assembly in the Throne-room at Dolma Bagtche revealed a real determination to have a thorough spring-cleaning. The Conference, meanwhile, was stultified. The Sultan met all pressure by pointing first to the Constitution and then to the clause in the Treaty of Paris which forbade foreign interference. He had confidence also that our Conservative Government would support him, in any case, against Russia. As soon as the Conference broke up he dismissed Midhat. The Powers, in April, having submitted a protocol demanding reforms—which the Sultan had rejected—he had now become the national champion against the foreigner, and he felt himself strong enough, in May 1877, to close the Chambers. Midhat was tried for the murder of Abdul-Aziz, on suborned evidence, and condemned to death. The sentence, on British intervention, was commuted to exile in Arabia. But as soon as it was safe, that is in 1882, Midhat was strangled, and his head sent to Abdul-Hamid.

Russia now saw the way clear for action; and declared war, in a dignified denunciation of Turkey on behalf of Europe. The division in British opinion persisted, and Turkey was left to fight alone. After desperate fighting at Plevna, Kars and elsewhere on the two fronts, Turkey was defeated, and a Russian army advanced upon Constantinople through Thrace. On January 31, 1878, an armistice was signed. The British fleet at Besika Bay was at once ordered to the Dardanelles. Thereupon the Russians pushed forward a force to San Stephano, just under the walls. The British fleet came up to Prinkipo, just opposite. The House of Commons was asked to vote six millions for war purposes. The music-halls sang:

We don't want to fight, but, by jingo, if we do,—
We've got the ships, we've got the men, we've got the money too—

and thundered the chorus:

Russians shall not have Constant-i-noople.

If we do not owe Jingoism to Constantinople alone, we owe to it the term. Constantinople was saved. So that, a generation later, we might fight—to give it to Russia. The Treaty of San Stephano, of March 3, 1878, observed all the Tsar's engagements, and left both Constantinople and Adrianople to Turkey. But this settlement did not suit Disraeli's ideas of what was due to British prestige. So it was replaced by a very inferior settlement, the Treaty of Berlin. This Treaty gave us Cyprus, and pledged us to a protection of the Armenians which we have never fulfilled. It cut down Greece and Bulgaria to spite Russia, and thereby provided a contributory cause to every subsequent European war; and it left Turkey to the tender mercies of Abdul-Hamid. Disraeli proclaimed that he had got " peace with honour." But Lord Salisbury, our other delegate, lived long enough to admit that we had " backed the wrong horse."

YILDIZ AND ABDUL-HAMID

On the hillside beyond Beshiktash lies Yildiz-Kiosk, the Star pavilion, so called after a favourite slave of Abdul-Aziz. Yildiz shows us at once the reaction of the Hamidian regime. It is a return to the old Byzantine palace of scattered pavilions and guard-houses. The Palaces of the Reform stand boldly up between the water-front and a great thoroughfare, with ceremonial halls and modern state apartments. Yildiz retreats within shrubberies, a cluster of summer-houses and villas. You can see Hamidian reaction still written everywhere—in the dingy dilapidation from which the city has never recovered. You cannot read the face of the Constantinople of to-day unless you have some idea of what the rule of Yildiz was for a whole generation.

Yildiz, now a public park, is not unlike a badly developed suburban building estate, with its fantastic villas dispersed among the summer-houses, artificial ponds and gravel walks beloved of suburbia. In character, however, it is a revival in ugly modern form of the ancient Forbidden City, like the Old Serai or the Byzantine Great Palace or, older still, like the Cretan Palace of Minos, the original Labyrinth. It follows no architectural plan, but has grown up anyhow, to house a lot of people huddled together for a life without system or significance. The labyrinth was only a palace of which the intricacies were the best defence of its inmate. The object of Yildiz was to provide the Sultan with a hiding-place, from which he could direct in safety his government by secret service. The outer cordon of blockhouses and barracks covered all strategic points on the land side. Inside this, most of the land had been bought up and built over for trusted dependents. Inside this again were the ugly yellow barracks of the Albanian, Arab, and Turkish guards, flanking a great double screen of wall, miles in circumference.

The weak side of the Yildiz fortress was towards the Bosphorus, where the Tcheragan Palace, with its mad prisoner, occupied the water-front. For the Sultan never dared trust a warship to guard it. His distrust was one of the reasons why during his reign the Ottoman navy became a joke. I remember how a new cruiser was once bought at an absurd price as part of a deal for the settlement of British claims. The moment it arrived the Sultan had essential portions of the machinery removed to Yildiz. That he should have mistrusted the navy, as likely to become Liberal, and relied upon the army to maintain reaction, is characteristic of Abdul-Hamid's political insight. Any ambassadorial threat to move warships towards the Straits was always effective but never forgiven.

The Court at Yildiz parodied the pomps of the Old Seraglio. The Grand Vizier, once magnificent, as Canning saw him, in his official robes of white satin lined with ermine, with a great egg-shaped turban ablaze with jewels, had become a cringing old person in a kind of German civil uniform and a fez. The Kizlar Agha and his black eunuchs, horrific in their oriental garb, had become merely hideous in black " stambouli " coats, like curates. A few shrivelled white eunuchs still survived. The Pages' Corps had, as one writer observes, " now almost entirely lost its peculiar Asiatic character," and become a corps of boy-messengers. The Court was still a swarm of parasites, a mess-roll of some seven or eight thousand persons and some seven or eight hundred slaves ; but they had lost any redeeming picturesqueness. Even the palace tortures and assassinations had sunk into a lower key. Tortures by twisted cords or matches between the fingers could be made as effective as flayings alive or hangings on hooks ; and they could be kept more private. The palace official responsible for drownings was a perfectly presentable Pasha—who no doubt thought it hard when he was hanged by the revolutionaries for having held his onerous and disagreeable post. The evidence at the inquiry after the Sultan's deposition established the use of torture in the palace, but not in the Sultan's presence. An officer testified that he had been driven by the screams from a kiosk adjoining that in which Armenians were being examined as to the bomb incident of 1905.

The Hareem maintained it shierarchy, but had broken up into a number of little Courts (dairas) round the leading ladies. The Validéh Sultan, the foster-mother of Abdul-Hamid, was an able woman with old-fashioned ideas. She upheld a rigid etiquette, and all the old ceremonial: even that of presenting the Sultan with a twelve-year-old slave-girl on Kourban Bairam. But this, too, had become bowdlerized, and the child was sent off at once to school at Scutari. Whenever a new concession to the times had to be made, a new ceremonial was invented to cover it. Thus, when European doctors came eventually to be admitted, their patient was hidden behind a black curtain, and the lady's tongue and pulse were inspected through a hole in the curtain, under supervision of a eunuch. The Hareem was still recruited with Georgians and Circassians, and included over fifteen hundred women. But many, indeed most, of these were married to Court officials ; others were married to Pashas, and only came to Court when "in waiting." The four Kadines, or official Consorts, who might be either consort-mothers (Khasseki), or not, still remained. But in other respects the Court was not very unlike the Court of Petersburg in its last phase.

One other striking resemblance between these two Courts of Byzantine origin was the power of holy men of most unholy character. The Sultan was much under the influence of his astrologers and dervishes. Towards the end of his reign the support of the Astrologer Royal was the best worth buying. After him the chief of the Black Eunuchs, another permanent official. For the Necromancer General and Somnambulist General, like law officers, changed with the Government.

The Constantinople of yesterday was sunk in stagnation, while, within Yildiz, the Sultan sat year after year, spinning his spider-web of intrigue. The Constantinople of to-day appears to be changing its features, even its foundations, in a swift succession of volcanic eruptions. The reason why the progress made towards a national Turkish government in the revolution of 1876 was followed by so long a reaction will be found in the character of the Sultan. Abdul-Hamid was not a Turk by temperament. His mother was an Armenian, and, if scandal be true, his father was an Armenian doctor of the Hareem. Certainly the Hareem regime under Abdul-Medjid admitted of such a possibility. It is strange that it should have been this Armenian who began the deliberate destruction of the Armenian race. But the strength of his rule did not rest wholly upon his Armenian astuteness. Adbul-Hamid was strong because he stood for the supremacy of the Turk and the solidarity of Islam. The new Constitution had looked well on paper ; but it had no foundation in fact or feeling. It proclaimed the equality of all Ottoman races and religions, and the sovereignty and indivisibility of the Ottoman people. But there was no such thing as an "Ottoman," and never could be. There were Greeks and Slavs, who clung to religious autonomies until the moment when they could hoist the flag of independent States over their Ottoman houses. There were Arab and Albanian Moslem, who hated the Osmanli as oppressors. There were Osmanli Moslem, who would only accept Christians as fellow-subjects if they were kept in a servile class. There were Osmanli Turks, who already saw the only hope for their race in the extermination or expulsion of all other races from so much of the imperial territory as could be claimed by a Turkish nation. None of these could either express their motives or give effect to their movements through the medium of imperial parliamentary institutions. So it followed, inevitably, that the Parliament in the Throne-room at Dolma Bagtche disappeared, and the Porte itself decayed ; while all real power centred, once again, in the Palace.

Before long every important Government Department had its counterpart in a bureau secluded among the Yildiz shrubberies. These bureaux received their orders from some secretary in the Sultan's household, and transmitted them in turn to the Departments. Thus a Palace junta of military favourites administered the army ; a Palace bureau of translators replaced the Foreign Office ; and the Sultan's secret service was the real home government. For a quarter of a century the Empire was ruled through espionage. The greater part of the Sultan's time was taken up with the daily " djornals," and the reports of his spies, of his super-spies, and of his spies upon spies. The secret service always got its pay, while the civil service starved. About one and a half millions a year went in this way. When the revolutionaries seized Yildiz piles of important official despatches were found unopened, while the stacks of " djornals " were all docketed and minuted.

The effect upon the Government Offices proper was to make them, during the Hamidian regime, very depressing places. Half of those upon the pay-roll never came at all—and they were the least useless. Nine-tenths of the remainder did nothing but sit upon divans round the wall in a state of apathy, at intervals emitting heavy sighs. Occasionally one would be summoned to some Pasha's room, where he would squat down and scribble to order some hieroglyphics on a scrap of paper spread upon his left palm ; which the Pasha would then sign by smudging with his thumb. Most of these teskeres were destined for a big sack bulging in the corner—the only apparent archives. All real business was transacted by telegram from the Palace. By the end of the reign the Porte was little more than an Unemployment Bureau, where the dole was months in arrear. At festivals the newspapers announced that so many weeks' arrears of pay would be distributed. And yet this degrading existence became the highest ambition of the Osmanli.

In the army he had more work, and even less pay. So he gradually ousted the more efficient Armenian and Jew from the Civil Services.

We have curious glimpses of the Sultan's life in Yildiz. You see the evil-looking old Fagin shuffling along the winding gravel paths through the shrubberies with only a sinister secretary in attendance, and the cafedji-bashi with the portable coffee-apparatus. Suddenly, round a corner, he comes upon a gardener, who is surprised into a swift movement of salaam. Instantly the Sultan, only half seeing him through the leaves, shoots him through the head. On another such day, he is dozing in a summer-house. His favourite little daughter, finding him there, wakes him with a playful push. The Sultan fires as he wakes ; and the little girl falls dead. Over all these trim gardens and banal villas brooded the shadow of fear. Revolvers lay everywhere ready to hand ; and even hung on each side of the bath.

Yildiz was the dark and dreaded corner where the old spider brooded over the web of wires which he had woven all over the Empire. For one strength of the regime was the combination of the telegram with the spy. To every provincial centre the Sultan had his private wire. Access to the remoter end of this, which was confined to the super-spies, meant access to the Sultan himself, and this was the acme of power.

It is a relief to think that wireless has probably made such a system for ever impossible : future tyrants will no doubt rule by broadcasting.

In a short space it is difficult to give an adequate impression of life in Constantinople under the Hamidian system—of the repression of every form of public expression of opinion which it implied. It was dangerous for any Turk to be seen talking to a foreigner. One young officer who relied upon his personal position and ventured to be friends with us at the Embassy, was ambushed by soldiers when riding with us, and subjected to indignities that made him an outcast. Soon afterwards he disappeared—I never knew how or where. It was unsafe to talk politics in any public place, even with friends : and it was safe to assume that of any three people gathered together one at least would be a spy. Sir W. Ramsay relates (" The Revolution in Constantinople," p. 170) how an ex-English officer, who had drifted into Turkey to live, invited two liberally-inclined Turks to dinner. Turks are by temperament frank, and found the spy system all the more irksome. Being therefore in the company of an Englishman, these two spoke their minds. Fortunately for them the secretary responsible for preparing the " djornals " was their personal friend. Next day he warned them that the Englishman had ruined them, and advised them at once to denounce him in a counter-" djornal." He then showed their counter-report to the Englishman, who protested that it was false. " That's what they say of yours ! " said the secretary ; " and they are

two to one !" The denunciations were then both withdrawn.
The Turks joined the Young Turk party, and the Englishman
was expelled from the Club.

It was sufficient to be "suspect" to be removed. Ismail
Kemal, the Albanian statesman, relates in his Memoirs how
another Albanian was employed to assassinate him :—

One of the agents used by the Sultan was Ghazi Bey, brother of
Essad—Pasha of Tifana—to whose influence this latter owed his successful
career. This Ghazi Bey had several crimes to his account, including
several mysterious assassinations. Among them was the murder of a
young Greek demi-mondaine supposed to be the favourite of the Sultan's
heir, Mahmoud, and suspected of acting as intermediary between him
and certain foreigners. She was murdered in her own house, with her
servant and little dog. A similar fate befell a young Italian girl, whose
father was employed at the Palace, and who became similarly suspect. . . .
The Sultan called Ghazi into his private room, and told him he wanted
to get rid of certain people. The first of them was myself !

The censorship was of a kind that, even with our war experience, we can hardly imagine. And yet news somehow got published—in some form. For example, a popular captain of the
English "stationnaire," the small cruiser which protected our
colony, was transferred to the Red Sea. There he was wounded
in a scuffle on the Somali coast. It was impossible to print the
account of an action in which English had defeated Moslem. So
in the account published the captain's Moslem enemies appeared
as "large and ferocious monkeys."

The importation of books was severely supervised in the Customs. I protested against having a Koran confiscated ; and was
told it was "too good a book to be left to a Christian." Most
books were terribly mauled : the words "Christianity," "revolution," "Turkey," etc., were blacked over, or whole chapters
torn out. Schools not under foreign protection had to get their
textbooks through as best they could. I recollect that a col-
league's children lost their Christmas present because it contained
an illustration of Bluebeard—in a turban—and Fatimah. Our
Embassy, also, was asked as a favour, by Abdul-Hamid, to dis-
continue singing that "provocative anthem" "Onward, Christian Soldiers."

For such illiberalities Abdul-Hamid had the less excuse in that
as a young man he had been allowed more liberty than most
Ottoman princes. The Kafess had been abolished; but its
tradition still regulated princely education. In the school-books
of Abdul-Aziz, for example, which are preserved, every reference

to Christianity has been censored, the whole chapter of the French Revolution deleted, every Turkish defeat erased, and so on. Nevertheless, he allowed Abdul-Hamid to frequent foreign houses in Constantinople, and even to visit Paris with a single attendant. By a curious convention the Padishah was not supposed to know any Feringhee language. Abdul-Hamid, though a good French scholar, always carried on conversations through an interpreter. No doubt he found it convenient to have more time to prepare his reply. There can be little doubt, also, that he understood English ; for I remarked once, while listening to an interview, that although the question put in English had been incorrectly translated to him, the reply which he gave answered the English question correctly. The Emperor William, it is said, used to insist upon his dismissing his interpreter, and conversing with him alone. But the Germans had by that time established an ascendancy at Yildiz. The Sultan's favourite slave, a Christian girl, was generally reported to be in the pay of Von Bieberstein, the German Ambassador, and the head of the Palace secret service was a German, recommended by the Kaiser.

Some few concessions to publicity Abdul-Hamid made. One such was the Friday Selamlik, the weekly public appearance which, as we may remember, was maintained also by the Byzantine Emperors after they had sought safety in seclusion. The Sultan reduced it to the admission of a selected public, to see him drive to a mosque just outside the Yildiz gates. It was a quaint vestige of the old Byzantine ceremonial that took place. The background was provided by the Hamidieh Mosque : a building remarkable in that it combines in a common confusion the elements of the Persian, the Greek, and the Gothic styles. The foreground was filled by troops, mostly Albanian or Arab guards, but with a detachment representing also some favoured Anatolian regiment. Behind them stood a sparse gathering, women for the most part, such men as there were being spies. At one time foreign visitors were admitted to a pavilion overlooking the square. But this was eventually pulled down ; and then nobody could see anything, except such foreigners as obtained admission to the diplomatic pavilion. After a long wait a little cortège appeared : broughams containing princes in uniform and white-veiled ladies. The band played the Hamidieh March. You levelled your pocket camera and had it at once seized by " plain-clothes policemen." While you were still wrangling or wrestling with them, a small landau drawn by white arabs hurried across the square ; in which was seated a hunched, scraggy-bearded, and hook-nosed figure, in fez and frock-coat. The carriage was pursued on foot by fezzed eunuchs in black coats and a posse of fat Pashas in full uniform, panting and puffing, treading on one another's heels and tripping over their own swords. Arrived at the mosque-steps, the Sultan shuffled up, encircled by servile officials salaaming low. At the doors the Sultan turned for one hasty salute. Simultaneously the Palace dwarfs were supposed to cry the admonition: "O Padishah, be not proud—for there is One above!" But this Byzantine survival was not "featured," and the cracked voices of the dwarfs were drowned in the shout of the troops: "Padishahimiz chok yasha!" ("Long live our Sultan!"). When the service within was over, the Sultan reviewed the troops from a window on the north side of the mosque; and then emerged, entered a phaeton—this time—and drove himself off quickly into the safe seclusion of Yildiz.

A modern travesty of the past. They were all Byzantium in modern guise—the priests, the dwarfs, the eunuchs, the pages, the astrologers, the intriguing women, the Circassian odalisques, the imprisoned Prince, the shimmer of hidden treasure, the shadow of imminent death; and, most Byzantine of all, the "Great Assassin" himself, reading "djornals," signing death-warrants, and playing "La Fille de Madame Angot" on a cottage-piano to his little girls. His astrologers probably kept him moderately happy with reassuring prophecies; but Abdul-Hamid was shrewd, and must at times have heard the warning sounds which even the triple walls of Yildiz, the cloud of sycophants, and the swarm of crawling spies, could not keep out.

> For the kingdoms of Islam are crumbling
> And round me a voice ever rings
> That tells of the doom of my country—
> Shall I be the last of its Kings?

The short Indian summer of the age of borrowing was over, and the long winter of discontent was come. Disraeli and the British had put back the clock at Berlin in 1878, and the Sultan had restored Byzantinism at Constantinople. For a quarter of a century the Ottoman Empire is proclaimed by virtue of international law and Imperial irade to be standing still:—*e pur si muove!*

If we walk up to Yildiz through Beshiktash, we pass under the windows of the room where the Ambassadors' Conference met in 1882; when the Bulgarian province of Eastern Roumelia seceded from the Empire and joined the Bulgarian State. It had been Disraeli's great achievement to break up the Greater Bulgaria created by the Treaty of San Stephano, and leave Eastern Roumelia, with autonomy, and Macedonia, without autonomy, to Turkey. Now the rôles were reversed. It was Russia, afraid of Bulgaria, who opposed her aggrandisement, while we, through our Ambassador Sir W. White, supported it. Had Turkey fought to recover the province, there might have been another European war.

Sir William White was the antithesis of Stratford Canning. He was a diplomatist of the—then—new school, risen from the ranks of the Consular service; with a big brain, and a bluff manner that concealed a Bismarckian astuteness. The other Ambassadors were united in wanting to involve Turkey in war; and they exhausted every device of diplomacy to get rid of this parvenu. At last they did succeed in arranging a joint meeting without him. Hardly had they got to work, however, when the door opened, and he marched in; shouldered his way to the table, and deposited on it a large paper packet of sandwiches. Then for hour after hour the crowd outside heard the well-known voice booming through the open window—blurred occasionally by a sandwich—and drowning every proposal or whisper of intrigue, until the Conference, famished and enraged, broke up. In its way his influence with the Turk was as great as Canning's. The Sultan took his advice, accepted the *fait accompli*, and war was avoided. The first stage in correcting the mistakes of the Treaty of Berlin had been passed without bloodshed: not so the following stages.

In the valley just below the Pera Palace Hotel the house still stands where I remember watching the two-day siege of a Bulgar band who had been conspiring for the freeing of Macedonia. It could have been ended in two minutes by the guns from the artillery barracks. But in that case the sound of the detonations would have travelled to the ears of the gun-shy Sultan up at Yildiz—and the back-lash would have been dangerous to the gunners.

The Bulgars in Constantinople, however, were for the most part harmless market-gardeners; and they were not penalized for the desperate audacities of their compatriots in Macedonia. It is evidence of the purposefulness of Abdul-Hamid's policy that he took his measures at this time, not against the Bulgars and Greeks, in order to preserve his European provinces, but against the seemingly harmless Armenians. The Armenians were not in open revolt, and they were the money-merchants and market-porters of Constantinople ; as serviceable and sub-missive to the Hamidian regime as the Anatolian Turks them-selves. But they happened not only to share with the other Christians a claim to foreign protection, under the clause of the Berlin Treaty that pledged Cyprus to us, but also to be co-part-ners with the Turks in the only Asiatic territory possible as a national home for that race. Therefore, almost indispensable as they might be to the imperial rule at Constantinople, their pre-sence in Anatolia was incompatible with the idea of a Turkish national State in that region. Under the surface of the Empire of espionage and of its dissolving institutions this Turkish national impulse was steadily developing. Sooner or later the Armenians, who were also running a national movement of their own, were bound to collide with the Turkish movement. The Armenian Massacres of 1896 in Constantinople, which shocked all Europe, were not, therefore, as is generally supposed, a last desperate effort of Abdul-Hamid's to keep control of Constantinople ; they were the first combat in the struggle between the Turkish and Armenian races for a national home in Anatolia.

At the same time the massacres were as brutal and bloody a business as ever disgraced that City of Dreadful Night. The enterprise was carefully prepared. Russian consent was obtained by means of diplomatic intrigues which we cannot deal with here. European opinion was prepared by an attack on the Ottoman Bank, delivered by a gang of Russian Armenians, who shot the guard, menaced the European managers, held the premises for a day, and were then allowed to escape. Then, at preconcerted signals, organized bands of Moslem roughs, Laz boatmen, Softas from the Medressehs, Kurdish hamals and the dregs of the dock guilds, rushed through the streets of Galata, armed with bludgeons, and knocked on the head the panic-stricken Armenians. They broke down doors and broke through roofs, massacring all within. The Patriarchate and the churches, though crowded with refugees, were spared ; and hardly one Catholic Armenian perished. The organization in fact was so complete as to suggest to any observer the wide difference in thoroughness between the Turk acting as a nation, and adminis-tering an Empire. The Armenian porters let themselves be bludgeoned as helplessly as a drove of seals : a fact in itself expressive of the atmosphere of paralysis produced by Hamidian oppression. For, away from Constantinople, they often died fighting as fiercely as rats in a trap. In Constantinople alone nearly 3,000 perished; in Anatolia probably a quarter of a million. In the city the massacre had one definite economic object, in that it was directed chiefly against the Armenian hamals (porters). The Kurdish hamals replaced them, much to the detriment of trading interests. An incidental result was the disappearance of the Sedan chair, until then much used by Pera Society. When the reliable Armenian hamals were no more, the ladies soon found that the Kurdish porters were not to be trusted up and down the steep stony lanes in the dark.

Galata streets, that may seem so disappointingly dull to us to-day, were then, as often before and possibly so again, the scene of human agony too painful to describe. If I have given these dreadful massacres their place in the story of the city, it is because I want to transfer that butcher's bill and the others that followed from the account of the Turkish nation against which they have been entered to that of the imperial city. Had the Turk not become involved with the city, there would long before have been a national Turkish peasant State, not unlike Bulgaria, sharing Anatolia with an Armenian national State, not unlike Roumania. Nor must we forget, in reading accounts of such actions, that the minds of ninety-nine out of a hundred Turks of the present day are the minds of our own countrymen and neighbours during the Middle Ages; the minds of the men who burned Joan of Arc or beheaded Jane Grey, who planned the massacres of St. Bartholomew and of Drogheda.

With the Serbo-Bulgar War of 1885 and the Græco-Turkish War of 1898 we need not be concerned. They were more the results of the Disraelian reaction at Berlin in 1878 than of the subsequent Hamidian reaction in Constantinople.

But the long racial struggle in Macedonia has a closer bearing upon the story. It was the struggle which eventually effected the overthrow of Abdul-Hamid. For the Hamidian system had at last come to be recognized as ruinous to the Turkish race. The reform movement could be diverted no longer by the crafty Sultan. During the early years of this century the spirit of reform and revolt penetrated into the military college at Pankaldi, and thence spread among the Turkish troops.

The transfer of the headquarters of the Young Turks, and of the Committee of Union and Progress, to Salonika in 1906, marked the beginning of a new epoch. In Constantinople the movement could never have made good. It must have failed in a direct assault upon a corrupt despotism, just as the Russian revolution of 1904 failed. But away in Macedonia the movement was able to combine, as once before in 1876, the resentment of the reactionary Moslem against the Concert of the Powers and its Christian protégés, with the revolutionary demand for military and civil war. Bodies of Albanians began to appear in Old Serbia, and Turkish troops took to the mountains in Macedonia, both demanding the putting in force of the Constitution of 1876. So the great yellow barracks at Yildiz became a menace in place of a protection. The Constitution was proclaimed at Ferizovitch, on July 23, 1908 ; and the Sultan's private wire confirmed it the following day.

REVOLUTION AND REACTION

The swift success of the revolution let loose a long pent-up flood of Liberal sentiment. The Millennium had come, having chosen for its birthplace—of all places—Macedonia. In Constantinople the long reign of terror ended, like a bad dream. Abdul-Hamid proclaimed liberty for his subjects. The Moslem welcomed the Christian to equality. The rival races embraced in fraternity. " Henceforth," announced Enver Bey, a young relation of the Sultan and the popular hero of the revolution, " we are all brothers : there are no Bulgars, Greeks, Roumans, Jews, Mussulmans ; under the same blue sky we are all equal : we glory in being Ottoman." In the general effervescence of emotion there was no cynic to hint that there was one " glory " of the Greek, another of the Bulgar, and yet another of the Turk. The Palace of the Sleeping Beauty woke up; and went on with its work just where it had left off in 1876, when the evil magician, Abdul-Hamid, had laid his spell upon it.

The spectacle, in the great square outside St. Sophia, on December 17, 1908, seemed all but incredible to those who had lived through thirty years of Hamidianism. The inauguration of the Turkish Parliament took place in a building on the site of the Byzantine Senate House. There before you is the whole Hippodrome—a sea of red fezzes, green and white turbans, Albanian Guards in white uniforms, Syrian Zouaves in green turbans, students, clericals, and uniforms of every fashion. There are the red banners, the green banners, and the black banners with silver inscriptions. High above, under the silver crescent crowning St. Sophia, stands like a statue a green-turbanned mollah, his robe blowing out on the wind. A long procession of carriages, full of deputies, notables, ladies of the Hareem, ecclesiastics and Ambassadors, crawl up to the steps of the Parliament House. The procession is cut, and for ten minutes blocked, by a shepherd-boy and his flock, on their annual journey from Anatolian to Roumelian pastures—a journey which antedates Byzantium itself. The Turks are a pastoral people, so the Lancers hold up the Ambassadors and Pashas until the sheep are safely through. The carriages are at last emptied, the road cleared ; and all wait expectantly. A distant roar of " Padishahimiz chok yasha ! " comes rolling up the hill. A carriage, drawn by six white arabs, dashes up at a gallop. The horses blow and steam. The captain of the Lancer escort wipes from his forehead sweat sprung as much from fear as from heat. For he has brought the Padishah through from Yildiz at speed with no untoward incident, only—as they thundered across the bridge—an old Armenian woman has clamoured, " Give me back my sons ! "

The inside of the Parliament House is a blaze of colour. The Senators in gold lace and decorations ; the Sheikh-ul-Islam in white with a tall turban of yellow ; the Ulema in green robes, with red fezzes bound with white turbans and broad gold bands. The Persian Ambassador-poet glitters with jewels. The Patri-archs are gorgeous in their robes. In one box the Sultan's sons—jolly-looking boys; the white-bearded military chiefs in another. And then to the front of an empty box there shuffles a hunched, scraggy-bearded, hook-nosed Shylock, in a grey mili-tary overcoat with red facings and heavy epaulettes ; and stands there, propping himself upon a ponderous sabre, and shifting uneasily from one foot to the other. " He looked," writes one eye-witness, " like some obscene and treacherous beast of prey, that after hiding in a cave for years is finally trapped, caged, and brought forth, blinking and reluctant, into the blessed sunlight."

The imperial speech is read : " I have promoted progress in all parts of my Empire," etc., etc. Prayers follow. Outside, a dull booming from the cannon, and a dull roaring from the crowd. Inside, the deputies shout their allegiance in unison, " Wallahi ! Billahi ! " The Sultan, inaudible in the din, is understood by his gestures to be calling down the blessings of Allah upon the new regime.

Even Constantinople was carried out of itself ; when every day brought news of fresh marvels and miracles in Macedonia. Righteousness and Peace have kissed each other, the Greek archbishop and the president of the Bulgar Committee have embraced at Serres. The mighty are put down from their seat—a Moslem policeman has been imprisoned for insulting a

Christian at Drama. The lion has lain down with the lamb—
Sandanski the brigand has called on the Pasha at Monastir. But
above all Abdul-Hamid, the sower of tares, is bound, and Babylon
has fallen. " How has the oppressor ceased—the Golden City
ceased! The whole earth is at rest—they break forth into
singing ! " And among the choir was heard the voice of the
coolest of foreign secretaries of the coldest of Frankish peoples:
" The Macedonian question and others of a similar character
will entirely disappear."

But an " Ottoman Empire " was always " a lost cause and
an impossible ideal." It was fated from the first to collapse
as speedily in 1908 as it had in 1876. And yet who will say that
such fleeting moments of peace and goodwill have no value ?
The Macedonian revolution was a moral protest, one of the
great spiritual adventures of our time. The free wind of it
came driving through the Hamidian cobwebs and the carrion-
taint of Byzantinism like

> An air of the morning, a breath
> From the Springs of the East, from the gate
> Whence freedom issues and fate,
> Sorrow, and triumph, and death.

REACTION

These yellow barracks round Yildiz were the scene of the
next drama in the story of the city.

The policy of the Young Turks was not to take over the
government at Constantinople, but to remain at Salonika; and
there to hold a watching brief for reform, leaving it to the Sultan
and the Parliament to work out a compromise between the
reactionary and the revolutionary elements in the movement.
Their idea was that the Sultan as Caliph was to be a combination
of Pope and Permanent Secretary for Foreign Affairs ; while
the country was to be ruled by the Parliament and administered
by the Porte. The " C.U.P." (Committee of Union and Progress) was to supervise, and with its local committees " make
the elections." The aged Kiamil Pasha, a protégé of the British
Embassy, whose Hebrew origin had brought him into conflict
with the Hamidian regime, formed a government with the support of a Liberal party, which soon came to loggerheads with
the secret organization of the Radical C.U.P. The Liberal party
had an attractive programme on paper that seemed quite practicable : a reconstruction of the Empire on a federal basis, that would
give autonomy and representative institutions to all the dif-

ferent races. They had accordingly the support of the Greeks, Slavs, Arabs and Armenians, whose movements for national independence were anti-imperial, and of the British Government, and soon became suspect to the Turco-Jew Radicals, who desired a centralized Empire, in which they themselves would be supreme. Simultaneously the "Mohammedi" party, consisting of religious reactionaries, began to agitate against the whole reform movement, through the Hodjas and Softas.

This conflict between the Liberal Chamber and the Radical Committee soon developed into a duel between the British and German Embassies, those two portentous palaces on the Pera ridge. The German Embassy, in the Grand Champs des Morts, with its flapping eagles on the corners symbolically dominating the Bosphorus Palaces and looking out over Asia ; the British, in the Petit Champs des Morts, looking out towards Europe and a setting sun. The German Embassy had become the antechamber to the German Chancellorship ; and its occupier, the tall, thoughtful Baron von Marschall, was the coming man of the German Empire. Of him it was said that he never went for a walk without carrying two chess problems in his head, and that he never came back without two solutions for each of them. The British Embassy on the other hand was what it looked like—a mausoleum. Every few years a new Ambassador was interred there ; but the more he changed, the more he was the same thing—R.I.P. "Si monumentum requiris, circumspice."

The revolution, as it began, was a triumph for the British ; for the Germans had been deeply committed to Hamidianism. The Germans, originally encouraged by Sir W. White, our last dynamic Ambassador, and by the British government, to embark upon enterprises in Asia Minor in order to act as a bulwark against the Russian advance, had made themselves the paramount power at Constantinople. Turkey-in-Europe had become an Austrian sphere of influence ; Turkey-in-Asia a Prussian protectorate. The Turkish army was managed by German officers, the whole country was rapidly becoming mortgaged to German bankers. This whole structure of German control, this German strangle-hold upon Constantinople, was threatened by the revolution. But not for long. The indispensable German change of front and shift of grip gave the British a diplomatic opportunity. But the British policy, still imbued with the ideas of the age of Stratford Canning, remained unalterable.

To put it shortly—we again backed the wrong horse, this

time the Liberals. It was not a bad tip, but we plunged some-what heavily. A telegram from King Edward, advising Abdul-Hamid to pin his faith to Kiamil, offended the Young Turks, affronted the Osmanli, always resentful of foreign interference, and staked our influence upon the fate of a single faction. No doubt we thought that the " Liberals " represented in Turkey, as they would have in England, the " mass of moderate opinion." Whereas the Liberal party represented little but place-hunters and several ill-assorted " national " movements. The real reform movement was represented only by the Committee.

The British Embassy was for the Liberals, who were fighting against the Committee, and, in this way, for the Palace. There-fore the British Embassy was fighting against the revolution, and for reaction. It was a simple syllogism ; and one accepted throughout Constantinople during the winter of 1908–1909. That the inner truth of the situation was not realized at home was due to the dependence of the correspondents upon their official relations with the Embassy, and to the pro-Palace policy of the " Times " and " Morning Post."

There was much that was sympathetic, as we have said, in the policy of the " Liberal Union," the Ahrar. It was federalist, in contrast to the extreme centralism of the Committee. The Committee's idea of making the Empire one " grand sweet song," in which Greeks, Turks, Bulgars, Arnauts, Arabs, the old Sheikh-ul-Islam and all, would be changed in the twinkling of an eye into " Ottoman " citizens, co-operating loyally in a central government, was not practical politics. But the Liberal federalism, which was no more than the cloak for Greek and other separatism, would have led to precisely the same result. While our policy of supporting the Old Turks and Greeks against the Committee, led us into supporting Abdul-Hamid against the Reform in 1908 ; and our persistence in this policy in 1918 led us into supporting Constantine of Greece against the Turkish nation, fighting for its national home: in both cases with lamentable results.

The elections of November 1908 brought Turks and Greeks into open collision. The Greeks accused the Turks of " making the election " ; the Turks the Greeks of making the Constitution a cloak for their separatist intrigues. A compromise between federalism and centralism, such as was later contrived by the Moscow Communists, was beyond the C.U.P. Moreover this was not the main question for it. The real question, first to be settled, was whether reform or reaction was to prevail.

The Sultan had of course set to work at once to countermine the new Constitution. He had again taken to his "djornals" (like a drunkard going back to drink). Without a "djornal" (spy report) he found his daily breakfast of eggs and milk as tasteless and he himself felt as much out of touch with life as we should over our eggs and bacon without our "Daily Mail" or "Herald." He got his "djornals" smuggled in now, by his barber; and they were mostly written by the Anglophil editor of the "Ikdam," the only "daily" not enlisted by the Committee—and the German Embassy—in the cause of the reformers. For the Germans had by now established a close co-operation with the Committee, and the Committee organization itself had extended over the whole Empire. The German policy also was well served in its new orientation. German correspondents were not dependent as ours upon their Embassy for information; journalists like Weitz, bankers and business men acted as "intelligence service" of the German supremacy. As against this, we relied on "a secret treaty" between Liberal politicians, Porte officials, the sariklis (turbaned clericals), and "Abdul the Damned." The striking force was fifty thousand spies and spadassins of the old regime whose pay had been stopped.

In February 1909 came the first open breach between the Committee and the British Embassy. Kiamil, the British nominee, was replaced as Vizier by Hilmi, whose diplomatic abilities as Vali of Salonika had not recommended him either to the British or the Greeks. To set against this Committee success, the Sultan succeeded in buying over the Salonika chasseurs who had been sent to garrison Yildiz. He had also, by appeals to their religious feelings, managed to detach the bulk of the Constantinople Army Corps from their support of the Constitution. When, in addition to this, it came to be recognized that our Embassy, the Palladium of European Constitutionalism, was in opposition to the Constitutionalists of Turkey, Yildiz seemed to have won the game. It had nothing left against it but a sentiment. But that sentiment was strong. "In my experience of Turkey, dating from 1880," writes Sir William Ramsay, "there was never a time when such hostility to England was so openly expressed in Constantinople as in April 1909." It was less than a year since all Constantinople had been cheering outside the British Embassy.

But Macedonia had still to be reckoned with. And it was not long before Constantinople began to realize that the Macedonians meant business. At tea-tables our young diplomats talked mysteriously about an "arrangement." But people whose lives were at stake were more alive to the situation. What more likely than that the Sultan, if things went ill, might seek to compel foreign intervention by a massacre, like those at Adana ? At best there would be severe street fighting. For two thousand years the fever of fear has lurked in Constantinople. In times of crisis, such as this was, it stalks the streets.

Those who have known the city at such times have seen the paralysis of terror descend upon each family, and disfigure every passing face. The more fortunate fled to the steamers chartered by their wealthy co-religionists. The others moved aimlessly about and muttered in corners. A single word—" geliorlar " (they are coming)—a dog-fight or a door banging, was enough to set every one scuttling. There is a provision of Turkish martial law which prohibits running in the street ; so easily, there, is a stampede started. Anyone who could appeared in a tall hat, so as to take advantage of the immunity secured to Ambassadors.

The real diplomats were wrong; no arrangement was possible between Constantinople and Salonika. The quasi-diplomats in improvized tall hats were very nearly right. There was a counter-revolution that was little short of a massacre.

The Palace *coup d'état* started with a mutiny of the troops against their Young Turk officers. The slogan of the counter-revolution was " The Sultan and the Sheriat " (the Canon Law). But a very real motive for the mutiny was that the army had had to work under the Young Turks as it never had before, and that its pockets were now filled with Palace gold. The mysterious murder of Hassan Fehmi, editor of the reactionary and scurrilous " Serbesti," which was attributed by the Liberals to the Young Turk Committee, gave the signal for the outbreak. Hassan was given a public funeral in the Turbeh of Mahmoud the Reformer ; and although the Young Turk Committee, acting on the advice of Talaat, declared itself to have become a political party and to be no longer acting as a secret society, the mutiny or military counter-revolution thereupon broke out. The Hippodrome was filled with mutinous troops and reactionaries. The Parliament house was invaded by soldiers and fanatical Softas, half-daunted, half-defiant ; who engaged in absurd altercations with the deputies over such matters as the proposed Moslem Girls' School at Kandilli. But the character of their demands showed plainly enough that they were in revolt against the Committee, in particular, and against the Constitution in general.

Few lives were lost in the riot, and most of those by the

falling bullets of *feux de joie*. One deputy was murdered by mistake for a Committee man ; and this led to a revulsion of feeling which, later, stood the reformers in good stead. But, for the time, the Young Turks had to run for their lives. Many took refuge in foreign Embassies. The life of Moukhtar Pasha, who commanded in Constantinople, was saved by the courage of Lady Whittall, who faced the pursuers when they traced him to the Whittall house in Moda. Prince Aziz of Egypt disguised himself as a stoker in his own yacht ; Reschid Pasha as a European lady. Some fifty officers were less fortunate. The Ertogrul regiment held a sort of court martial on its officers, before a bench of Ulema and Khodjas, and executed them on the parade ground. The sole surviving young officer escaped, pale and breathless, into the Pera Palace Hotel.

The most dramatic of the murders was that of Kabuli Bey, captain of the cruiser *Assar-Tewfik*, who was accused of having ordered his crew to fire upon Yildiz. Nadir the Palace eunuch afterwards described it. He was brought in a carriage to Yildiz, bound hand and foot, and set on his feet on a gravel path outside the Mabein (Hareem). Abdul-Hamid leaned out of the window, and interrogated him ; then turned away, and left him to be assassinated. Two officers who took refuge in the Palace he ordered to be expelled ; but the implied sentence of death was not executed. Nadir also deposed that Abdul-Hamid tore up with his own hand the draft irade submitted to him by Tewfik the Grand Vizier, which ordered the assassinations to stop as contrary to the Sheriat.

The old diplomat of Yildiz, with the help of the old diplomacy in Pera, had turned the tables upon the Young Turks with remarkable promptitude and success. But the Sultan had shocked Moslem opinion by permitting the murder of Moslems, and he had scared supporters in Constantinople with the murders by his officerless mutineers—although these last had done little general damage. The murder of a Syrian deputy, the Emir Arslan, had shaken the allegiance of the Arabs. The Albanians, who might have supported reaction, were kept by Major Niazi, the hero of the July revolution, from attacking the Salonika army in the rear. And, of even greater importance, the Sultan's military commander, Edhem, the victor of 1898, was not allowed sufficient time by the Macedonian advance to get the mutineers in hand again, and organize them into a defensive force. Further, if the Sultan had ever calculated upon having bought Enver's support, by giving him a princess in marriage, the event proved him wrong. Incredible as it may appear, there was no traitor in the ranks of the Macedonians.

The General Commanding the advancing Salonika army was Mahmoud Shevket, an Arab, who owed his Liberal views to his experiences, on a mission to the Hedjaz, in a steamer which contained some 600 of Abdul-Hamid's political prisoners, and to his attempts to negotiate with the fanatics of Mecca. He was, moreover, what liberal leaders rarely are—a man of action. The Salonika forces moved on the capital.

When the news arrived that the Army of Liberty was actually on the move, at once the tables were turned again upon Yildiz, the reaction guttered out, and the general rally to the Palace died away. The " Times " scoffed at this army being able to reach Constantinople within three weeks : it arrived within three days, the remarkable rapidity of this operation being due to the assistance of the German military experts. For the Germans had not failed to profit by the British mistake, and had entered into close co-operation with the Committee. Co-operation worked the more smoothly in that Von der Goltz Pasha had been long associated with the army, and Enver Pasha had received his own military training in Germany.

THE CONSTITUTION AND THE COMMITTEE

The Army of Liberty consisted of the Third (Salonika) Corps, and of Christian volunteers, mostly Bulgars, and a few Greeks. The two reactionary Corps, the Fourth (Erzinghian) and the Fifth (Damascus), were out of reach. The Second Corps at Adrianople wavered, for it was devoted to Nazim, who was Kiamil's War Minister. But the Constantinople massacre of young officers decided it ; and it gave free passage to the Salonika Corps, remaining itself to guard the frontiers against any Bulgar coup. The attitude of the Fleet also was ambiguous. But the day before the final advance of the Macedonians it put to sea on manœuvres—Admiral Gamble, the Englishman in charge, thus securing its neutrality. Even so, the Army of Liberty was inferior in numbers and artillery to the troops collected in Constantinople. Had the Sultan decided to fight in Pera, or had he even fled across the Straits to Scutari, where there were large additional reactionary forces, the struggle would have been severe. It is reported that afterwards, in his exile, Abdul-Hamid lamented his error in mistaking what was a civil war for a " scuffle for power between different regiments "—one that did not, therefore, concern himself. " Nalet olsun ! " (" A

curse on it!") he would say, thumping the table, when he medi-
tated upon his missed opportunity. But he must have been
beaten, even had he fought. The catchword of the Macedonian
volunteers was "Baba Hamid bitdy!" ("Daddy Hamid is
done for!").

But the Sultan persisted in pacific persuasion even when
the Army of Liberty was before the gates of Constantinople. A steady stream of "sariklis" and spies with pocket-
fuls of gold trickled out to the camp. The Macedonians
proved incorruptible; but as a precaution their ranks were
stiffened by officers serving as privates. The rump Parliament
was as slow to recognize that reaction was at an end. The
Liberals, such as Ismail Pasha, the Albanian Chief, still hoped
to steer between the devil of Yildiz and the deep seas of Macedonia. The Chamber sat daily. But the few deputies who
risked attendance were principally occupied in searching for a
lost Byzantine subterranean passage, which was said to run
from the Old Palace to the Theatre—the site of the present
Akhmediyeh Mosque—and which might come in very conveniently in case of emergency.

The Sultan's first rebuff came over the body of the unfortunate
Emir Arslan. Syria threatened to come to Constantinople *on
masse* to retrieve it : and Yildiz gave it up. The Emir was given
a public funeral; to attend which the Committee deputies left
their hiding-places at the risk of their lives. In the course of it,
a Syrian Sheikh denounced the Sultan. The guard of honour—
composed, strangely enough, of the very Salonika chasseurs who
had sold their cause—was in the act of escorting the cortège down to
the Syrian steamer, when a young student stepped out in front
of the procession, stopped it, and resonantly proclaimed that
Niazi Bey had arrived at the Gates of Constantinople. Niazi's
was a name to conjure with ; for he had taken all the risks of the
July revolution, and refused all its rewards. For a moment the
student's life hung on a hair ; but conscience and the fear of
impending retaliation disarmed the chasseurs and they listened
in sullen silence.

Telegrams to the Chamber, denouncing the reaction, continued
to pour in from the provinces ; and from the outlying barracks the
troops began to desert to the enemy. On the 19th April, for
example, the Rancis barracks at the head of the Golden Horn,
where were quartered sixteen batteries of machine-guns, received
the Macedonians and opened the road over the downs to Yildiz.
In vain did Abdul-Hamid order new uniforms for all the cadets

in the military schools. The cadets marched out ; and did good service later, in guarding the Embassies.

On Friday, April 23, the Sultan mustered up enough courage to attend his last Selamlik. The signs were not encouraging. For the first time in his long reign there were no representatives of the Powers on the diplomatic terrace. The soldiers gave the usual greetings, and there were a sufficiency of Ulema and Softas. But the hunted look never left his foxy old face, and he seemed in a state of collapse, for the hounds were already running in view. The once dashing Ertogrul cavalry were dirty and dusty with continuous guard duty, and when that noon they returned to the Davoud Pasha barracks on the downs, it was to find the Macedonians in possession. Driven off by the machine-guns, they galloped into Stamboul, raised three battalions of regulars from the Fateh barracks, and returned with them to attack Davoud Pasha. They were repulsed, and retreated to rest in the barracks in Stamboul.

That night Constantinople lay shivering in darkness and silence. Only Yildiz flared with lights, until the Macedonian army, camped outside the city miles away, wondered what the illumination meant. From behind its high walls came the ceaseless tramp of regiments marching and counter-marching round and round the garden roads. As the Macedonian army came nearer the Sultan's terror of solitude and of darkness had grown ever greater. He moved restlessly all night from room to room, sending for Ministers and then forgetting what he wanted of them. At one moment, in a frenzy of fear, he was ready to fight like a cornered rat ; at another plotting some subterfuge which, by sacrificing all else, might still save his own life.

Constantinople was carried by assault before dawn. Flying columns were sent to march through Stamboul and seize the Seraskierate and the bridges. But the main attack had to be directed across the downs, against the barracks guarding Yildiz which were held by the renegade Salonika chasseurs. For these men could expect little mercy, and were certain to provide the backbone of the resistance.

The columns that entered Stamboul found the regulars and the cavalry in Fateh barracks asleep and resting after their day's exertions; and made them prisoners. The buildings of the Sublime Porte, the Law School, and the Officers' Club were, however, defended from daybreak to noon by chasseurs, who caught the Macedonians in a cross-fire and killed many. The Sublime Porte surrendered after it had been considerably ventilated by shell-fire, but the Law School held out until the evening. Another detachment reached the Stamboul terminus by train and seized the bridge. Meantime what was happening to Yildiz?

At the extremity of the Golden Horn on the eastern side, lies the old Jewish Cemetery—a bare hillside of enormous extent covered with ancient rough blocks of stone. At the southern edge of this desolation lived Salih Keramet, a Turkish shepherd. All Turkish peasants are superstitious, and after more than forty years spent in this lonely spot (the last ten years passed in solitude, for his childless wife died in the year 1899), Salih had become morbidly superstitious. On the night of Friday, April 23, he was suddenly awakened by the furious barking of his dogs. There was a feeble clouded moon, and by its light he could see his dogs barking at Something which to judge from their panic-stricken agitation was advancing on them from the Cemetery. Too horror-stricken to think of going out to see what that Something was, Keramet was on the point of banging and bolting the door, when there suddenly swept by a host of phantoms, rushing towards the city. Hundreds, thousands passed, paying no attention to him, all fearfully intent on their distant goal. He could hear no footsteps and their faces were cowled. The silent passing of this phantom army was terrible; but still more terrible was the distant thunder at dawn of day, from the city invaded by that silent army.

For it was the Macedonian Army of Liberty, hurrying from their barracks at Davoud Pasha over the downs to Taxim, and their phantom silence was due to their being shod with charik, the Macedonian pampooty, while their mouths, like all peoples of malarial regions, were muffled against the night air. Round Taxim they took up their positions, and so noiselessly that the reactionary troops were surrounded unawares in their barracks.

At 4.30 in the morning firing began at the Matchka barracks and the Pancaldi School. By 7 o'clock the Macedonian guns were in position, Armenian men and women having helped to drag them up from the valley of the Golden Horn to the heights of Tatavla. About 10 a.m. Major Moukhteir, in command of the Taxim attacking column, was killed. Enver Bey took command, and half an hour later the Taxim barracks were shelled out and captured. Tashkishla barracks, where the Salonika chasseurs held the north wing, were knocked to pieces by the guns. Some 150 chasseurs made a desperate sortie, but were shot down; others threw themselves from the windows. Another 200 or so of them barricaded themselves in a hayloft and opened a destructive fire on the Macedonians as they marched in to take possession. They were not subdued until 5 p.m. The Tophané barracks and depot surrendered after desultory firing. Round Yildiz itself the barracks were not attacked, but merely surrounded. By nightfall the fighting was to all intents over. Only the Marines, those spoilt children of the Padishah, continued to give trouble at Tershané until as late as May 1.

Abdul-Hamid either did not know what was happening or he thought it the wisest policy to pretend not to know. He gave no orders as to the defence or surrender, and remained shut up in his Little Mabein. Not even his intimate, the eunuch Nadir, knew what the Sultan was doing, or thinking. The guard at Yildiz and many of the Palace population flitted during the night of Friday. The Palace quarter was swept by spasms of terror, and during one of these the hundreds of women in the Hareem started screaming so alarmingly as to horrify the Macedonian cordon encircling the grounds. An aide-de-camp went out waving a tablecloth to signify formal surrender, and on Monday morning the Macedonians took possession of the Ogre's Castle.

The Young Turks lost no time in cleaning up Yildiz. Let us march in with them and see what they found there, for much of it, I believe, is still to be seen.

All the higher functionaries who had not fled with their ill-gotten gains were sent off to Prinkipo. Many, including all the eunuchs, had hidden in the Hareem. But a summons was sent in for their ejection, and the girls went over to the enemy, and threw their former tyrants out among the soldiers. Through Pera next day there passed a dismal procession, half a mile long, of servants, eunuchs, slaves, parasites, spies, astrologers, cooks, courtiers, and all the scum that for a quarter of a century had infested the Yildiz slum. They were kindly treated and soon absorbed into the more " Byzantine " districts of Stamboul. A few were executed as the result of the inquiry. One of these was Mehmed Pasha, known as Kabasakal or Twisted Beard—a formidable figure, prominent at Selamliks, and by profession the Palace executioner. His system was to take suspected persons out on the Marmara in a launch, and after examining them under menace of death, drown them by degrees. Yet another executed was Djevket Agha, head eunuch, a bloated brute of notorious cruelty. The hangings, which were performed on the bridge by gipsy executioners at 10s. a head, were very horrible; but the victims were carefully chosen, and they were regretted by none.

The two principal advisers of the Sultan towards the end of his reign had been Izzet Bey and Nadir Agha. Izzet, a Syrian of infamous character, fled at the revolution in a ship he had bought, took refuge in Switzerland, and for all we know " lived happily ever afterwards." Nadir, a young eunuch, saved himself with the help of the Germans by informing the Committee of the final intrigues of the Sultan, and of the hiding-places of his hoards. You may be fortunate enough to see him—a pleasant boyish-looking person, strolling in the Rue de Pera, dressed in the height of fashion. Nadir applied for the post of official guide to Yildiz. Had he been appointed, a tour of Yildiz with him would have been an illuminating experience.

The last imperial Hareem had a not unhappy ending. Most of the inmates were Georgians and Circassians, and telegrams were sent to such of their families as could be traced, inviting them to come and fetch them. So one day there was an interesting ceremony in the halls of the Old Serai. At one end of the hall sat a Young Turk Commissioner, down one side sat the ladies, and down the other a row of gaily dressed and heavily armed tribesmen. The ladies then unveiled, fell upon the necks of their particular mountaineers, and, after tearful partings amongst themselves, departed for the long-lost homes of their childhood. *Facilis descensus Averni*—it was no doubt an easier journey down from the mountain-huts to Yildiz than back again. As they milked the cows of a morning did they ever regret the pianolas, the petits fours and the Paris models of the Padishah ? But not all of them could be thus brought "back to the land." Some had disappeared—probably *spürlos versenkt*. Others of the more elderly could not face the change, and joined the remnants of past imperial Hareems in respectable retirement at Top Kapou Palace. Any young man thirsting for romantic adventure *à la* Pierre Loti, if he chance to stroll past its latticed windows, may yet find a scented handkerchief or a pink rose dropped upon his head, the gesture of some elderly ex-Sultana punctiliously keeping up the traditions of the service.

Abdul-Hamid himself was dealt with as promptly and sensibly. On the day of the surrender the Sheikh-ul-Islam authorized his deposition : " What shall be done with a Commander of the Faithful who has——" And here followed an indictment of the Sultan's crimes. " Can he be deposed ? " Which was answered with the single word, " Yes ! " A Commission of deputies was sent to Yildiz to announce this fetva to the Sultan. It was headed by Essad Pasha, an Albanian, and consisted of a Greek, a Jew, and an Armenian. In this matter, at least, the Young Turks would appear to have been thinking imperially. For Carasso, the Jew, the return must have been dramatic. Soon after the July revolution he had been arrested and taken to Yildiz, as he supposed to his death. After examination he was taken out in the fatal launch by Kabasakal, and gave himself up for lost indeed. But he survived—to return once more upon this Mission.

Upon their arrival they were warned by the secretary that Abdul was in a highly nervous condition—and a dead shot. Undismayed, the deputies proceeded to the Tchitli Kiosk, and they have left us a description of the scene. The door of the room opened upon a large Japanese screen. Behind it, sitting on a much-worn sofa, was the Sultan, in his grey military overcoat. Beside him sat his little boy Abdurrahman. On the other side was a small smoking-table, with a tin cigarette-box and a candle-stick with a guttered candle. In the middle of the room stood a round table, on which was a decanter full of a red medicine. In one corner a litter of cigarette ends, and crumpled " djornals " ; in another the Sultan's goloshes. All round the walls were mirrors —a precaution observed in every one of Abdul's rooms—and there were a great number of clocks. A piano, cheap ornaments and candelabra completed the setting.

Sensational accounts of the conversation are inventions. Abdul, who was in a condition of collapse, only replied to the announcement of his deposition, " I am not guilty : it is my Kismet. Will my life be saved ? " He was reassured, and the deputation left in a silence only broken by the sobbing of the little Abdurrahman. At midnight of the 27th there left Yildiz a cavalry escort and an armoured car, followed by a landau, containing Abdul, his three wives and two small sons, and other carriages with four concubines, five kalfas, four eunuchs and nine servants. The luggage had to be reduced to a minimum, and a number of large trunks were necessarily left behind, in which jewellery of great value was afterwards found concealed. At Sirkedji station the party were put on board the imperial train, which Abdul had had built, but had never even inspected, and at about three in the morning they left for Salonika. There, in the Villa Allatini, the deposed Sultan was installed in modest comfort. All that he asked for was at once sent from the capital. His first request was for his cat. His next list was for two white Indian cows, two black eunuchs, a lap-dog, his poultry yard, three hundred more electric lights and fifteen more ladies. And the load was at once dispatched.

The Young Turks could afford to be generous, for the clean-up of Yildiz proved to be very profitable. Since we have already seen something of the ceremonial buildings we can now enter with the search-party into the Hareem Dairessi, the inner recesses of the House of Fear.

Opposite the Great Mabein, containing the reception rooms, etc., is the Tchitli Kiosk, a long one-storied building. From it a secret door communicates with the Hareem, a large edifice at right angles in the rear. Opposite the Hareem is the Little Mabein, where Abdul lived. From the entrance, the way to the Little Mabein lay along a lane through soldiers' and servants' quarters. This Little Mabein is a two-storied, wooden bungalow, entirely commonplace, except that the lower windows are barred, and that the windows outside do not correspond with the rooms inside. This was the first of Abdul's dodges for baffling intending assassins. The sole interest of Yildiz, in fact, lies in the reflection which it preserves for us, in bricks and mortar, of Abdul's own mentality. In it we can see Abdul's mind to have been the mind of Byzantine Constantinople. Just as its purposes were continually shifting, so as to divide and distract the enemies which it had provoked and feared, so the arrangement of his apartments was continually altering, and altering again. As in a nightmare, rooms were perpetually dividing, passages and windows disappearing or altering their shape, new ones unexpectedly opening up. Every corridor was blocked with heavy furniture so that never more than one at a time might pass along it. The little court between his own rooms and the Hareem is only ten paces wide, and yet you will observe that it is crossed by several flying bridges—so that the Sultan never needed to use the same bridge twice running. For the same reason he slept in a different room, often in a different building, every night, and very rarely used the room which he had ordered to be prepared for him. Abdul's feeding was on the same devious system. The food was not prepared in the obvious, up-to-date kitchen, but in a heavily barred and bolted little room. Here it was wrapped in napkins and sealed, then carried to wherever the Sultan had appointed to dine. All who met it *en route* bowed, with their hands clasped over their stomachs. The Sultan broke the seal; the first helping was eaten by the cook, the next by some dog or cat, and then came the Sultan's turn. Thereafter the remainder of each course was distributed among the notables and courtiers, who were expected to provide evidence that they had eaten it. Often one met these little meal-time processions bearing dishes tied in cloths to dignitaries who might have some interest in a change of sovereign.

Another precautionary measure, common to all the Sultan's apartments, was the wall-covering of mirrors, already referred to. Not a gesture could be made that was not revealed and multiplied.

And yet another point we notice is the small size of the rooms, still further reduced by quantities of furniture, Abdul himself always sitting where no one could pass behind him. Beside any bed he used, beside his bath, everywhere, were little shelves, upon which lay revolvers ready loaded. In all over a thousand revolvers were found. His silk-quilted, bullet-proof cuirasses are, I believe, still on view.

Such was the manner of living of this descendant of the Osmanli warrior-Sultans. Such the effect upon them of three centuries in Constantinople. Something in the atmosphere of the city breeds cowardice as it breeds corruption, whether in the palace or the slums.

The Commissioners who first penetrated into the den moved from room to room and from rubbish-heap to rubbish-heap in fear of their lives, for Abdul had taken care to spread abroad the report of his numberless man-traps, pitfalls and spring-guns. But the probability is that he was too fearful himself of such apparatus to permit of its actual introduction, for nothing of the sort went off. On the other hand, the Commissioners found much to reward their intrepidity. Wrappings of rags concealed the seal in brilliants of Abdul-Aziz and jewels to the value, in all, of about three-quarters of a million sterling. Mouldering in damp cupboards were found bundles of notes and of securities. There were sacks of ancient gold bezants and of other coin, to the value of £60,000. One "mixed bag" disgorged a quantity of valuable rubies, 2,000 medals and orders, mostly in gold and jewels, 180 shares of the Bosphorus Steamboat Company, a pouch of jewels—the confiscated estate of a slave who had died at Medina—and a job-lot of neckties.

Objects of great historic or artistic interest there were none, for the Sultans have always neglected their opportunities for making collections of that kind. A few rare old volumes were the richest find. In 1924 this library, after many vicissitudes, passed into the possession of the British Museum. The 400 manuscripts, half of them in Persian, the other half in Arabic and Turkish, contained nothing individual to Abdul-Hamid. History, poetry, and religion were principally represented, with some unique works on archery and the management of the horse. There were also some invaluable early Arabic codices, a unique Persian MS. of the Maxims of Mohammed, Persian and Arabic legal treatises, a unique copy of a collection of Persian and Turkish "divans," or poems, of the fifteenth century, a unique Turkish history of the Ottoman Empire in the eighteenth century, by Adib Chelebi, and a great wealth of " divans," belonging to the middle and modern periods of Ottoman poetry, of which copies so far had not reached the West. In calligraphy, illumination, and binding, it is an exceptionally artistic collection.

There were no pictures of any interest, unless we may include among works of art a picture said to have been painted by the Padishah himself, which hung outside his bedroom. It portrays a company of black-gowned and bearded men, standing in a boat and playing upon musical instruments, while upon the shore naked girls are dancing, to whom the boatman is handing a purse of gold. What it means I have no notion. But Abdul was something of an artist, and a clever craftsman in wood inlay.

Round the inside of the high, inner wall of the precinct stood rows of cages, in which he kept his many thousands of pet birds. Gazelles, ostriches, rabbits and sheep, wandered at will about the grounds. In the gardens we can still see many traces of the childishness that distinguishes potentates. As one example there is the little canal, with its miniature landing-stages, named after the villages on the Bosphorus, and its little café, where the Sultan used to call for his coffee—always insisting upon the time-honoured formula of the waiter, and upon paying 10 paras for coffee and narghile.

That Abdul should not only have survived his deposition, but should have ended his life in tranquillity, is the best evidence that with the passing of his despotism Byzantinism itself, and all that it implied, was accepted as having come to an irrevocable end. On the outbreak of the Balkan wars he was brought back to Beylerbey, and lived there in dignified retirement, occasionally even advising his incompetent successor. We may indeed detect, in examining the whole conditions of his regime and his relations with the Army of Liberty at its close, a resemblance to—almost, we might say, a twentieth-century reproduction of—the conditions of the regime of Isaac Comnenus, and his relations with the Latin Crusaders.

This last capture of Constantinople by the Macedonian Army of Liberty terminates the story of the city as a centre of a peculiar imperial culture and of an international civilization. It was conquered, it is true, in the name of a new " Ottoman Empire," which was to be based upon constitutional liberty, on racial equality and religious fraternity. But this final " Imperial" experiment was fated to last no longer in 1908 than it had twenty years before.

CHAPTER V

THE TURKISH NATION

" Perturbabantur Constantinopolitani
Innumerabilibus sollicitudinibus "
("Eton and Westminster Verses.")

OLD AND YOUNG TURKEY

THOSE perturbed Constantinopolitans whose innumerable solicitudes we have followed through fifteen hundred years will be found in this last chapter causing the world more perturbance and solicitude than ever before.

The interval between the revolution of 1908 and the establishment of the Turkish Republic in 1923—the subject of this chapter—seems but a short distance to travel in time, as compared with the interval between the fall of the Byzantine Empire in 1453 and the final phase of the Ottoman Empire that began in 1908. But the second fall of Constantinople and its descent into a provincial port of a Turkish State, has been farther than its first fall, from the capital of a Greek Empire to the capital of an Osmanli Empire ; and these few years accordingly demand a fuller consideration.

Most of the sights of real significance in the city itself we have already seen ; and the best illustrations for our study of the last phase we shall obtain by making excursions into the environs—up the Bosphorus, to the Sweetwater Valley, and across to Scutari. Those who accompany us will see for themselves much that is still picturesque by the way. In the Turkish and Jewish quarters, especially, it is never wholly lacking.

The Turks and their loyal parasites the Jews are the two elements, the conservative and the progressive, the patrician and the proletarian, out of which a national republic is at present being built. They are now sole owners of Constantinople, and the heirs of its future—if it has any. Though the Turks only have any say in Constantinople, they are still a minority there, as they have always been also in most of the provinces of their

Empire. Only in Anatolia, the regions from Broussa to Aidin and Konia, do they form the bulk of the population.

The Osmanli have retained all the pride of a dominant race. The poorest Turkish peasant considers himself the superior of the Armenian banker or the Greek merchant. But the Turks have never evolved a ruling caste among themselves. The hereditary country gentry, the land-owning Beys, who were the descendants of the feudal fief-holders, the Sipahdars and Timariotes, never acquired any political power. The imperial government remained always Byzantine. The Palace government was a paradise for parvenus. Abdul-Hamid's principal advisers were in turn a slave bought at Tophané, a clown out of a circus, a son of a pastrycook, a performer in a Punch and Judy Show (Karagyöz), and a bootblack. Even the imperial family, for all its sacrosanct attributes, never formed a caste, and freely intermarried with subjects. Enver Bey, the son of a parvenu, became son-in-law to the Padishah. " Founding a family " was not in itself an idea that could be realized in Turkish society. The immense fortunes acquired by Palace favourites were dispersed at their death and as a rule not even the name was transmitted. Turkish surnames are still in the nickname stage, and generally have to do only with personal peculiarities. "Little Said," " Selim Humpback," " Hassan Pasha Broken-nose," were recent public characters. Titles were at the same democratic stage as in America, where " Colonel " or " Judge " is a distinction open to anyone with a certain local standing. The only official title of dignity, " Pasha," was conferred by the Sultan ; but it is also popularly attached to any powerful per-sonage. " Bey " implies a certain official significance ; " Effendi " a certain social status. " Agha " and " Tchelebi " are the " Colonel " and " Judge " of America.

But for all this absence of recognized class distinctions the Turk is, by temperament and tradition, aristocratic in his attitude. His personal dignity is as precious to the Anatolian peasant as to the Spanish grandee—although he can dissipate in season. He is easily offended by familiarity ; but he loves anyone who can joke with him as a friend. In short, nothing is less like the real Turk than our popular impression of him —formed as a general rule from contact with Levantine officials. At his best in the army or on the land, he is at his worst in Con-stantinople. Until recently the Turkish family life in a " Konak " in Stamboul was modelled upon the way of living of a small country town. It was passed in retirement in a secluded quarter in a rambling, ramshackle house surrounded by a garden. Whenever possible the ladies went out for a picnic to the shady banks of the " Sweet Waters " of Europe or of Asia. We no longer meet the closed carriages of veiled figures, with an ugly eunuch prancing alongside whip in hand, or see their graceful kaiks with gaily-dressed rowers sweeping past on the water. But the ladies among us may still find hareems to visit, and study a mode of life that has not changed since Byzantine days.

Those of us who were brought up on the tradition of the changeless East grew to look upon this way of life as peculiarly and permanently Turkish. We never dreamed it could all be swept away in a few years. But in the light of after-events we can now see that all the manners and customs which writers depicted for us as essentially Turkish were not Turkish but Byzantine. What the Turks slowly learned from Constantinople and its Byzantine Perso-Greeks, they have now swiftly abandoned again. The life of the hareem, its veils and eunuchs, sweetmeats and sacks, was borrowed from Byzantium, and was quite alien to the Turkish temperament. The haphazard way of living, the meals at any time or place, eaten from little tables brought in and set beside the divan or while squatting round upon carpets, the fashion of fishing out the food with the fingers, the very dishes themselves, were all of early Byzantine civilization, crystallized during the long Turkish occupation. The custom of sleeping upon pallets or rugs thrown down in any corner of a room, often interpreted as a vestige of the nomad past of the Turks, the washing arrangements—the hole in the floor of a marble-lined recess, the rosewater poured over the hands from a ewer—in like manner interpreted as a Turkish indifference to comfort, were again the borrowed manners of mediæval Constantinople. In shaking off Constantinople, the Turk has dropped his dusty peacock-feathers, and become again the plain jackdaw.

Ten years ago it was still possible to write :

Even now, interviews with officials, walks through the streets of Stamboul, the sights of each day remind one irresistibly of a chapter in Gibbon or some tale of wonder in the " Arabian Nights " (Hutton, "Constantinople," p. 229).

For the change then was proceeding only slowly ; and even though we might rarely find the colour that we sought, we could still assume or imagine it to be there. But to entertain you with descriptions of Turkish life in its borrowed plumage would at the present time be misleading. That Constantinople is already of the past; and we must not hope to find it else-where than in books or on the stage. But there is one thing that does not change with the passage of time; that has not changed with the passing of the Empires or the decline in the supremacy of the city, and that is the peculiar spell cast by Constantinople itself. It is a spell broken from time to time, and again broken to-day, but which is always renewing its irre-sistible appeal to the love of beauty and the lust for power latent in every human being. It is inexplicable in words: it is dis-coverable only in person, and in the atmosphere of the city itself. But no one who has not come under it, who has not visited the ruins of the succeeding centuries with an under-standing eye, and reconstructed the triumphs and the tragedies which they represent, can hope to hold the clue to that laby-rinth of shifting scenes, contradictory policies and changing racial characteristics, which makes up the story of Constantinople.

Friends in the Colony or at the Embassy may be able—with difficulty—to recover for us a glimpse of lost local colour, by arranging for us to visit some Turkish " interior," where a household may still be living *à la turca*. But otherwise we must be content to seek out what we can of " Old Turkey " among the back-streets of Stamboul. Perhaps we shall still find pil-grims from the Far East about the old khans in the Turkish quarter—Mongolians, Persians, men of Bokhara and Khiva, negroes from the heart of Africa, Circassians and Georgians in their native dresses, and armed many of them to the teeth. Round the fountains there will be groups of brightly dressed children. From the lattice windows of old Byzantine houses will come the tinkling sounds of Eastern music. Behind walls overtopped by trees we shall hear the voices of girls and laughter. Perhaps we may meet an old turbaned Turk riding in dignified ease upon his white donkey's tail, home to his Konak—a ram-bling wooden building with overhanging latticed windows; or we may come upon a row of bearded elders sitting on a stone bench in the shade.

But it is the Young Turk who matters now. He lives in a modern flat in the new residential quarters of Pera, very much *à la franca*. His pretty wife will be a rather silent but com-petent hostess. The family lunch, however, will be patriotically Turkish; and Turkish dishes are very full of local colour and historic flavour.

In greater matters than these the Young Turk may seem to us to have shed much that was attractive in the Old Turk, and kept much that is objectionable. Where the Old Turk had to work himself up to killing-point through a fever of fanaticism, the Young Turk can murder *en masse* for a cool economic object. He can be courteously cynical where an Old Turk would have been either foolishly generous or frankly greedy. Association with the Jewish attitude of mind has somewhat warped his native Turkish honesty. His idealist Liberalism, of British origin, has been hammered by rough contacts with imperialist foreigners, and with Greek and Armenian fellow-citizens, into something closely resembling a Prussian " Real-Politik." The merit of the change is that it has made him enthusiastic and efficient in a practicable cause, that of Turkish nationalism. Only a few years ago an Osmanli would have felt himself insulted if addressed as a Turk : he was an Ottoman of the ancient Moslem civilization of Constantinople, not a tribesman. To-day a Turk would take offence if addressed as an Ottoman—the offspring of a bastard Byzantinism. He is a free Turk. His is the pride of race, not of religion.

This contrast between Old Turk and Young Turk, between Imperialist and Nationalist attitudes of mind, invaded during the last century every region of national life. To a foreigner it is most apparent in the domains of literature and law. I wish I could allow myself an excursion into Turkish literature. It would be the best way of explaining how the great change that has come over Constantinople in our time was prepared. For, as usual, the national renascence was heralded by a literary revival. The literary language, which had become a clamjam-fry of Persian and Arabic and officialese, was purified and simplified back to its Turkish foundation. There is no language less capable of corruption than Turkish, whether by pedant or proletarian. It might have been invented by an Academy of philologists for use by professors. So perfect is it, as an instrument of exact expression, that it is almost unmanageable by everyday mortals. If you want to make an observation in Turkish, you have the following choice. You may think for several minutes, and then convey your meaning, to the last shade of accuracy, in one monumental verb built up of enclitics ; which the other man will in time take to pieces, and assimilate. Or you may use the Turkish roots, and Persian and Arabic constructions. Or you may pick out the most important idea, say the substantive, and throw it at the other man, adding, " Isn't it so ? " ; then the next most important, and drive that too home with a " deyil-my ? " ; and so continue down to the details.

And this also is a fine art. If, on the other hand, you try to construct a sentence, you will have to work just the other way about, beginning with the details, and reserving the main idea until the end. Your Turkish sentence, in this case, will run in the opposite sense to our Western thought. An example given by " Odysseus " will serve as well as another—

Der-saadet ile Varna beininde ishleyen Loid Kompaniassinin Vulcan vaporina rakiben Istambula gelioruz
(Capital and Varna between running Lloyd Company of Vulcan steamer upon Stamboul to coming are we.)

As for official documents, Byzantine clerical art writes them " all in a concatenation," without stops. Our own legal drafts-men still make paltry experiments in this style. But Turkish, with the help of gerunds, gerundives, and other strange forms of speech, can sustain the effort unfalteringly, page after page, for an indefinite length. Little wonder if, as " Odysseus " says:

The man who has decided on the grave step of writing a' letter com-municates the substance of what he has to say to the professional letter-writer, and the latter embodies it in suitable language, according to his powers of composition and the rank of the person addressed, for it would be a want of etiquette to address a high official in a style which every one can understand. If the recipient of the letter is himself not a literary character, he may require to have the document explained to him.

If we add to this that Turkish is as yet written in Arabic character, of course without vowel points, which is much as though you wrote Basque in British shorthand, reading it becomes a matter of guesswork.

Against all this Byzantinism the Young Turks declared war. Literary associations, notably the " Yeni Kalemler " (new pens), began a campaign under the Empire, which Angora has since prosecuted successfully. The vocabulary has been sifted, the style simplified. It is even possible that the Latin charac-ter may be introduced. For the present, however, Turkish literature remains a closed book for the majority ; and they must be content with translations, such as the Turkish poetry which the work of Mr. Gibbs has brought within our reach.

In Turkish Law a somewhat similar process has taken place. Under the Empire there were three bodies of law, and three benches of judges, functioning independently of one another. The Sheriat or Sacred (Canon) Law, based upon the Koran, regulated civil status, landed property, etc. ; each autonomous Church enforcing its own corresponding Canon Law. Secondly, a large body of Codes and Statutes regulated most modern commercial transactions. These Codes were borrowed largely from the French ; and they were applied in combination with a fluctuating mass of irades, or Imperial Orders in Council. Finally, there were the judicial Capitulations and the Orders in Council of foreign Powers, which regulated all the civil and commercial affairs of the foreign communities. Each of these bodies of law was administered by its own Courts ; and the tendency of recent years has been for the foreign Courts to encroach more and more upon the Ottoman, and the foreign-made law upon the Sheriat. No authoritative publication of the Law was ever made, even where it was not in dispute between the various authorities. To supply in some part the gap, I myself published early in the century a many-volumed "Corps de Droit Ottoman," which contained all that could be begged, borrowed, or burgled from the several Chanceries, Courts and Departments. And it has been interesting recently to find that although almost every practical provision therein contained has been in the interval repeatedly repealed ; yet, pending the time when Angora might take the whole matter in hand, it has been as often as not agreed to accept as the Law the codification so conveniently indexed and clearly printed by the Clarendon Press.

The problem for Angora, in this respect, is now much simplified. The Sheriat passed, with the failure of the Padishah to hold Constantinople in 1909. The Capitulations passed, with the failure of the Powers to hold it, in 1922. The ground is now clear for the legislation of the Assembly, and a Commission on the Codes has recently revised legislation and is now publishing it in convenient form.

It is curious how the struggle between Old and Young Turkey penetrates every expression of national life. If we look at the theatres we find it there too. I am not speaking of the obvious unlikeness between the theatres of Pera and the entertainments in Stamboul. The performances at Pera are much what we may expect to find in any East-European town. During the Allied occupation and the Russian emigration they sometimes reached a high level. But the Turkish restoration has had a depressing effect. The diversions of Stamboul, on the other hand, together with the less reputable Pera resorts, provide a type of entertainment of which the less said the better, except as a word of warning : if you go to such places don't go alone or with a hotel tout. Such an entertainment is that essentially Turkish puppet-show Karagyöz (Black Eye). This is a " shadow-show," on view at Ramazan and occasionally at other times. It is well worth seeing as a curiosity, but unless the performance is a private one, so that it can previously be censored, the local colour will be somewhat lurid. Karagyöz, the Punch, is a caricature of an Old Turk. He has a parrot nose and a beady eye which is represented full face on the profile ; the whole effect being strikingly like the lately discovered Sumerian reliefs, the oldest art we know. His huge turban covers a bare poll, and his dress is much that of our Punch. His companion harlequin, Hadji-Aivat, is as courageous as Karagyöz is cowardly ; and in essence, if not in intention, he is a contrasted Young Turk. For an account of the performance, I prefer to trust to a more competent Agag, Mr. Davey (" The Sultan and his Subjects," p. 241) :

Shall I ever forget that night ? When I shut my eyes the whole scene comes back to me : the long white-washed room with a curved roof which had probably been the apse of a church, the line of lighted horn-lanterns casting a dull glimmer on the faces of the crowd. In the front seats, in time-worn arm-chairs, were a few elderly Pashas, one or two in uniform, the rest in the hideous frock-coat of modern civilization, with fezzes on their heads. Their little bright-eyed children nestled close to them, watching proceedings in that earnest, half-listless way peculiar to Turkish urchins. A few old turbaned Turks sat gravely apart, smoking chibouks. The background was filled up with a nondescript crowd. In an obscure corner a group of Armenian and Greek women of the lowest class muffled in thick black shawls sat apart, whispering and occasionally bursting into ill-suppressed giggling as Karagyöz, growing bolder with approbation, became more rampant in his glaring impropriety. . . . Suddenly the lights were extinguished, and the sheet that was to serve for a stage showed opaquely transparent. The orchestra, two drums, a flute, a viola and a triangle struck up those quavering sounds which enchant the Eastern ear, but which nearly drive the European listener mad. Presently a little figure on a camel's back scurried across the transparency, followed by a cat running after a mouse. The cat played with the mouse an unconscionable time, and finally swallowed it whole. At this the orchestra emitted the most appalling noises, a sort of quivering shriek intermingled with a rumbling rattle, possibly to illustrate the luckless mouse in the cat's stomach. Then with a deafening tattoo on the drum it settled into silence : Pussy's repast was evidently over. The incident of the cat and the mouse had so delighted the audience that a little wave of admiring whispers rippled through the room, to settle into silence as the figures of two ladies were projected on the screen. One was dressed in Turkish, one in European fashion. They were joined by a Turkish masher in stambouline frock-coat with straight collar, lavender trousers, patent leather boots, etc. On his head was a fez. A prodigious moustache curled up under his nose. He slipped a piece of paper into Madame's hand, after which he made obvious efforts to elope with the Hanoum. But, alas, Karagyöz was at hand, making mischief, and bringing with him the outraged husband of the lady. Then there was much animation upon the sheet. The husband and the lover fought right valiantly, the husband, I am sorry to say, getting continually the worst of it; until he beat an ignominious retreat. . . . Nemesis was, however, at hand, in the shape of Karagyöz, who returned in company with Hadji-Aivat. Things now became very mixed indeed, for both these iniquitous little gentlemen, having cast a longing glance upon the ladies, determined to rid themselves of the masher. When least the luckless youth expected it they pounced on him, and literally pulled him in two. Then followed a scene with the ladies which I may not describe. . . . When the French Ambassador appeared on the sheet, Hadji Aivat conducted himself abominably. On beholding His Excellency, he fell prostrate at his feet, while Karagyöz limply rose and followed suit. The attitude of the Ambassador was exceedingly majestic, as addressing himself to one of his secretaries, who now slid on to the canvas, he raised his stick menacingly. At once the ladies rushed forward, apparently to beseech his protection. The Ambassador received them affably, and offered each an arm. On this Hadji-Aivat, who had got behind His Excellency, suddenly jumped on his back. In an instant his gold-laced coat was in tatters, his cocked hat cast to the winds, and the representative of la Grand République appeared a poor thin wretched individual, stricken with rheumatism and afflicted with gout. Howling with pain he rushed off, followed by his fair friends, while the orchestra struck a few chords vaguely recalling the Marseillaise. Karagyöz, evidently afraid of the consequences, promptly bolted, leaving Hadji-Aivat the hero of the field. . . .

All this time the Armenian behind the screen recited in a sing-song voice a dialogue in Turkish, full of preposterous double-entendres and questionable jokes. Occasionally he sang a few verses in those quavering nasal tones which Orientals admire. Alas, I must not translate for your benefit ! . . . nor may enter into further particulars of the exploits of Karagyöz; nor describe how he and Hadji-Aivat divested themselves of their last scrap of reticence and like a pair of little drunken satyrs, careered madly up and down the keyboard of equivocal conduct, provoking such roars of delight that the braided pigtails of the three little grand-daughters of a Pasha, who sat in the front row and nearly had a fit himself, vibrated with the intensity of their excitement, and their childish merriment rang through the building ! So on and on went Karagyöz, leaving no iniquity untried, until the old sinner tumbled, like Humpty Dumpty, off a high wall, and could not be picked up again. Then they buried him, Turkish fashion, hurrying him to his grave as fast as they could. But Karagyöz, who is immortal, pushed up the lid of his coffin, and sat upon it, roaring with laughter.

So much for a singular sidelight upon the primæval Turkish temperament, with its semi-prophetic caricature of the opposition between Old and Young Turks and its picture of their united hostility to all foreign intervention.

HASSKEUI AND THE JEWS

The Jews, as we have said, were the faithful assistants of the Young Turks in their new revolution of 1908 ; and we may well begin with an excursion to the Jewish quarter : through Hasskeui, over the Ok-meidan, and back by Taksim. Hasskeui is the principal Jewish quarter. Some of the families here are descendants of those who left Jerusalem after its fall, and settled in this suburb of Byzantium since they were not allowed within the city itself. The remainder, for the most part, are Spanish and Portuguese families, who fled from the Inquisition in the fifteenth and sixteenth centuries, and were welcomed by Bayazid II, who wished to repeople the city. Their language is still a bastard Spanish, as it is also in Salonika, their other large settlement ; and their Synagogues are still called after the Spanish cities of their origin—" Toledo," " Cadiz," " Grenada," etc. At first they were allotted the Balat quarter, round the Blachernæ, which had been wasted in the Siege. But they soon spread across the Horn. They were allowed autonomous privileges, like the Christian " millets " ; with whom, however, they were never on good terms. For they had fled from Christian persecution to Moslem protection ; and, so far as was permitted, they associated with the Osmanli, even copying them in costume. We cannot quarrel with their choice. For the greater number of these low-class Jews are Talmudists, and retain many of their peculiar rites. Wherever, therefore, as in Rhodes, they were under Christian domination, they were made the victims of charges of child-murder, etc., and subjected to " pogroms ": a form of sporadic persecution from which, under the Moslems in Constantinople, they remained immune.

Consequently, for a Jewish community, their history has been unusually uneventful ; and only two massacres are recorded. The first was when the Jewish doctor of Mourad II, the drunkard, forbade him wine. Mourad, in his annoyance, hanged all the Jews, to the number of several hundred, in whose houses wine was found. Again, in 1666, a Messianic excitement arose in the community, over the case of Sabatai Levi, a good-looking and eloquent young Jew, of whom Rycaut had a high opinion. He was denounced by a rival as a traitor to the Sultan, arrested, and, under threat of execution, professed Islam. The Jews rose to save him ; and several thousand were killed. In Salonika a large number of these families actually verted to Islam. They are the Donmés, or crypto-Jews, who supplied many leaders to the Young Turks.

But in Hasskeui the race seems as a rule to have known how to protect itself, and yet retain its religion. They made themselves in fact so useful to the Turks that they became more powerful than was supposed, owing to the appearance of poverty and humility which they affected. An episode of the eighteenth century gives striking proof of this. The Jews considered for some reason that they had been unjustly used. The whole community, therefore, lined both sides of the Golden Horn, waiting for the appearance of the Sultan's kaik on its way to the Sweet Waters. Simultaneously with its appearance, at a secret signal, the multitude broke into a Jewish hymn, producing so tremendous a volume of sound that the Sultan turned back in terror, and retreated to the Serai. Any other "millet" indulging in such a practical joke would have been made to sing small.

The steady impoverishment of the city has fallen hardest upon this parasitic people; now reduced, probably, to some 30,000. The squalor and poverty of their way of life is appalling, and the condition of the Kassim Pasha valley under the British Embassy has cost more than one young diplomatist his life. Leprosy is but one of the diseases, and it is no place to linger in. Not that things are always what they seem in Constantinople; and some of the picturesquely ruinous house-fronts conceal comfortable interiors. Conversely, the beauty of many of the young Jews and Jewesses who swarm about us may cover a multitude of sins. The individuals who infest the cheaper hotels, offering to act as guides to the less reputable sights, are mostly Jews of this quarter. On the other hand there have always been Jews in influential positions, and some of them have occupied the highest posts. Kiamil Pasha, of the Old Turks, was of Jewish extraction: so also was Djavid, Finance Minister of the Young Turks. When I knew the community, it was reflecting, characteristically, this political division in the ranks of its protectors. There were the Rabbis, representing the old religious tradition; and they were opposed by the young reforming Jews. In general, as their streets suggest, the Jews form the proletariat of the city. But it is possible that the recent expulsions of the Greeks and Armenians—that is to say, of the whole mercantile and money-dealing class, may, by transferring the whole business of the town into their hands, make them a ruling class.

When we leave the Jewish slums, we climb out on to the open down of the Okmeidan, or Bow Meadow. It was here that the Sultan and his Pashas used to practise archery; and the little stone columns mark their "record" shots. They did not shoot at a target, but aimed purely at length; and with the short Turkish bow and a long light arrow extraordinary distances were covered. The Meidan was also used for the ancient game of the Djerid, a dart-throwing tournament on horseback. Both these sports, which date back to the nomad days of the Osmanli, became extinct about a century ago. When I knew it the Okmeidan had been taken over by the British colony, for polo and golf. The usurpation had not the approval of the Turks, and the games were often conducted under difficulties. Once, while we were playing polo, a troop of Ertogrul cavalry rode up, deployed, charged, and swept us off the plateau. One of our players was unhorsed, and lay winded, upon the ground. A trooper rode back, inspected him, and I heard him report to the troop—" Mashallah !—the dog is dead ! " On another day our Military Attaché was attacked here by a fanatic with a yataghan ; but he succeeded in laying him out with a niblick.

Passing on over the down, we get a fine view over Stamboul, and an idea of the country round the capital.

Constantinople, even to-day, still ends abruptly in a desert. There are no long suburbs, no market-gardens, not even cultivated land : nothing but bare downs, with occasional barracks. The curfew regulations of the Hamidian regime may be held responsible for this desolation. After dark no one was allowed to traverse the roads outside the city. During my last two years at the Embassy I was engaged upon a compilation of Ottoman Law, which made it necessary to go to town every afternoon from the Embassy summer quarters, ten miles out at Therapia. The last steamboat back to Therapia had to reach there before dark, so usually I had to ride back, by night. This meant avoiding both the guard-houses and the cavalry patrols. The guard-houses could be passed by a detour over the down, or, if pressed for time, by a gallop past at the cost of a bullet whistling off somewhere. But the cavalry patrols gave me many a hunt. Even if you know every foot of the ground, and every leg of your pony, a hand-gallop over the down in the dark, with a troop of Turkish cavalry thundering behind, is very stimulating after a day spent among Armenian and Greek lawyers. After a time it became a game on both sides ; and if I was caught, I had only to pay by sitting up all night in the guard-house, swapping stories and cigarettes. Others were not always so fortunate. One day the Embassy out riding got into serious trouble which was hushed up with difficulty ; and one incident was so grave that foreigners riding far afield with ladies in company always went armed.

In the last chapter we saw the Army of Liberty hurrying by night across these downs to capture Yildiz and overthrow the reaction.

The Army of Liberty had captured Constantinople in the name of the Constitution. But the Committee, after their escape during the reaction, took no more chances with constitutional government. Mohammed Reshad, Abdul-Hamid's long-suffering brother, was proclaimed Sultan, as Mohammed V, at the age of 64. But there was never any question of his being allowed to rule. The first act required of him was to sign the death-warrant of his favourite son-in-law, who had been implicated in the reaction. The public humiliation took from this Sword of Islam any temper that may have been left to him after twenty-five years of solitary confinement. Abdul-Hamid was, at least, a personality. But according to a diplomatist who knew "Mohammed the Conquered " (" The Near East," p. 38):

His very appearance suggests nonentity : small and bent, with sunken eyes and lined face, an obesity savouring of disease and a yellow, oily complexion. There is little or no intelligence in his countenance. and he never lost a haunted, frightened look. . . . Abdul-Hamid hated and despised him, but feared to have him killed.

And little wonder !—" They will never kill me, Jamie, to make *you* king ! " was no doubt his calculation.

The Turkish Parliament had again to pitch its moving tent. The C.U.P., after their restoration, installed it in the Tcheragan Palace, which was almost immediately burnt down. It then travelled to a house near Yildiz ; and finally into the Palace of the Djemile Sultané, on the quays.

The Committee transferred their organization to Constantinople ; and made no further concealment of the fact that they were the real rulers. As such they came at once into violent collision with the other races : with results that proved fatal to the representative institutions of the Empire. From 1909 onward, in fact, the Turko-Jew government was practically at war with every other race in the Empire, and with one or two races outside it.

THE BOSPHORUS

Leaving Constantinople for the moment to the tender mercy of the Triumvirate and of the German Embassy, let us embark on an excursion up the Bosphorus, which will illustrate the chapter of small wars, 1910–14, that preceded and preluded the Great War.

We leave the Bridge by one of the Bosphorus steamers ; and pass the Galata quays and the Tophané arsenal. The Bosphorus palaces are on either side of us : Dolma Bagtché on the one, Beylerbey on the other. Above Dolma Bagtché towers the heavy four-square blockhouse of the German Embassy. Off Tophané, below, are the moorings, where once lay the little fleet of Embassy yachts. In pre-war days every Embassy, besides its palace in Pera and its summer-palace at Therapia, had a sea-going steam-yacht, in permanent commission, and one or more steam launches. The yachts were handy for picnics up the Marmara, or for shooting-parties up the Gulf of Ismid ; but as the Ambassador had to pay the coal-bill, the *Imogen*, for one, spent most of her time at her moorings. Besides the yachts, there were the stationnaires, nominally for the protection of the foreign colonies. An Embassy also had a State kaik, and two or three pair-oared kaiks : the rowers all in a uniform of Broussa silk shirts and baggy breeches. Until the War there was still an old kaik-builder at Ortakeui ; and his excellent examples of this admirable model have gone as far as the United States. But I doubt whether there is anyone now left who handles still less builds one of these cranky gondolas. To row a kaik was like paddling, with the canoe-paddle tied by a thong to a pin, and with its inboard end made bulbous, so as to balance it. The paddle was not levered against the water horizontally like an oar, but dug into the water vertically, with a screwing action, as in Canadian canoe-paddling or in sculling over the stern. In skilled hands the results in pace were as surprising as they were subversive to the unskilled. With a pair of expert kaikdjis, the long-nosed, fish-like craft seemed to wriggle its way through the swirling currents of the Bosphorus. Marine mechanics have achieved nothing more perfect or more peculiar. But I doubt whether of the sometime 30,000 kaiks on the Bosphorus there are now twenty still afloat. The British Embassy, when I was there, added to their fleet a " four-oar," from Salter's at Oxford. This strange craft was the cause of much tribulation to the police-boats. For the Bosphorus in summer was only calm enough for a four-oar after sundown, when the afternoon northerly breeze had dropped. On the other hand, under Abdul-Hamid no row-boat was allowed out after dark. Consequently, when the mysterious craft came sweeping up through the deep shadows under the quays, the six-oared police-boats would dash out of their lairs in pursuit. Confident that they could overtake any local row-boat, they would pound along, with many imprecations, to arrest the disturber of the absence of traffic, which, however, inexplicably kept ahead just out of revolver-shot. It was some time before the mystery of the " Sheitan-sandal " (the " devil-boat ") was cleared up ;

and the police-boats refused to be drawn any more into pace-making.

Above Dolma Bagtché we come to Beshiktash, a quarter formerly inhabited by Palace officials. From here the Sacred Camel used to embark annually for Scutari on its long journey to Mecca. The quaint ceremony lingered on into our time, when it had become about as impressive as a second-rate circus starting for a fair. A more enduring memorial is the turbeh of Khair-eddin Pasha, or Barbarossa, the great admiral who made the Crescent supreme in the Mediterranean, in the sixteenth century.

Over his bier hang the remnants of his green silk battle-flag, and the great poop-lantern of his galley. To this turbeh every admiral came to pray before setting out with an Ottoman fleet. Here too, as I remember, came the captain of the old Turkish cruiser, commissioned by Abdul-Hamid, during his pan-Islamic phase, to display the flag of the Caliph to the Moslems of Java and of the Far East. This was an adventure followed by Constantinople with the anxious pride that we take to-day in the progress of a round-the-world flight. Great was the pride of the Empire as, week after week, the old turtle of a boat ploughed along at a spirited five knots, keeping carefully in sight of any convenient coast. It reached Hong-Kong ; and was, I believe, eventually sold there, to pay expenses. These were the days when the Turkish Embassy at Madrid put the archives up to auction, in the hope of shaming the Palace into paying their salaries.

Ortakeui (Middle village) is recognizable by the white Mosque of Abdul-Medjid.

On the little promontory of Defterdar-Bournou stood once a temple of Proteus, the elusive Old Man of the Sea ; who might well have been the patron saint of all Ottoman Sultans. Here, also, was the magnificent palace, described by Lady Mary, which was built by Damad Ali Pasha, who died heroically at Peter-wardein. And here, too, was the Yali of the equally unfortunate Kara Moustapha Pasha, defeated at Vienna, whose skull is in the Vienna Museum.

Further round the point is Kuru-Tchesme (Dry Fountain). On the top of the rocky hill " Daniel of the Bosphorus " built, in 464, a lofty column, and lived on the summit of it for twenty-seven years. From the time of the Conquest this village was the centre of Greek culture at Constantinople, as distinct from the Phanar, the seat of Greek authority. A century ago its schools and churches were wiped out by Mahmoud II (v. p. 180).

ARNAUT KEUI AND FEMINISM

At Arnaut Keui we meet the current as it is thrown across to this side by the Kandilli point. Arnaut Keui was originally settled with the followers of Skanderbeg, by Mohammed the Conqueror. The Church of St. Michael is built on the site of a church built by Constantine, and pulled down again by Mohammed, who used its materials for the Castle of Roumeli Hissar. St. Michael is the Christian successor of Poseidon, to whom the Bosphorus was especially sacred. It was here, in consequence, that the ceremony of baptizing the water used to, and perhaps may still, take place. At the Orthodox Epiphany, the Patriarch in his robes, and attended by clergy, choirs and a great crowd, flung a gold cross into the water, which was dived for, and fished up by some fortunate swimmer. A mid-winter plunge into that current was certainly a robust act of faith. The Arnaut Keui of to-day has acquired more modern associations. High above on the hillside the white marble façade in Græco-American style is the American Women's College. It was transferred here just before the War. Its imposing appearance makes an appeal to Oriental imagination that can but assist the important work which it is doing for the education of the women of Constantinople. The success of these American educational enterprises, mission work in the best sense of the word, has been due to the almost unlimited financial support they have received. Similar efforts by the English and French have been entirely outdistanced. Although the Americans have not altogether escaped the Turkish suspicion of foreign influence—even stronger under the Republic than it was under the Sultanate—it is to be hoped that they will be allowed not only to carry on their work for Christian girls, but even to extend it to the Turkish and Moslem.

The future position of women is one of the most difficult points at issue between the Turkish race and the religion of Islam. The subjection of women is alien to the true Turkish temperament. The hareem was adopted from Byzantine civilization, and in deference to a religion adapted to the Arab mode of life. Mohammed, though he owed his career to the rich widow Kadijah, made the Koran a charter of men's rights over women. "The happiness of a woman is beneath the sole of her husband's feet," he picturesquely observes; and therefore the Islamic bride must crawl under the counterpane at the foot of the bed. "If your wives do not obey you, beat them," is another precept. And, although he originally favoured monogamy, his final decision was, "If one wife is not enough, it is lawful to take four."

Upon this basis a social system was built up by which woman was excluded from any independent existence. In return, she received the right of administering to and being maintained by some man. The Perso-Byzantine hareem system survived in Constantinople long after it had been abandoned elsewhere, not only on account of the licence it allowed to the ruling sex and the ruling race, but also because the female sex, subjected by Islam and the females of the races subjugated by conquest, obtained under it legal rights of value. Under the hareem system women could not recover their lost liberty, but neither could they lose their livelihood. The social status it gave to women was bad. But their economic status in a hareem was better than under the Western system of free contract.

There were hardships, no doubt. I recollect coming down to the Therapia Chancery early one morning, and as I passed along a passage a veiled Hanoum (hareem lady) dashed out of some hiding-place, embraced my knees and poured out her woes. It was a tangled tale, and even the plainest tale told in Turkish calls for quiet, calm deliberation. But it gradually emerged that she was a Circassian slave who had fled from her hareem because her Pasha wanted to marry her off to some friend of his. Rather than obey him she had taken sanctuary in the Embassy and embarrassed the relations between two Empires. Round the piers of the gateway peered the fezzes of her pursuers. They could not come inside; but a telegram from the Palace could, and so could telegrams from the Foreign Office. We had no right whatever to intervene. International law is sometimes quite like real law. Had she been black we might have protected her; since she was white, we might not. On the other hand the ladies of the Embassy declared that if she was surrendered they would know the reason why. The situation was extremely delicate. At anxious last a Secretary who had made a hobby of local law remembered that no Circassian can be a slave unless born in the slave caste, and that the Sheri Court could be counted upon to apply the Circassian law. Thereafter all was plain sailing. The Levantine dragoman produced the lady's " relations "—a poor-looking lot, but not expensive. They swore that she belonged to the military caste, and the Kadi accordingly emancipated her. And then, of course, no sooner was she free than she married the man she had risked death to escape.

In Constantinople this domestic slavery has practically come to an end. It was always limited to women and eunuchs, although some male servants were slaves in all but name. It was purely

Byzantine, the Koran positively prohibiting the enslaving of Mussulmans. In the provinces it may survive for a generation or two. But now that unveiled women can be employed in a Moslem household, and now that such households have got to be monogamous, the old wasteful patriarchal establishments will not survive long.

A few individual black woman-slaves are still to be found in Constantinople. But they are extinct as an institution. Formerly they had a regular organization of their own, with a Chief Priestess, the Kul Bashi (Head Slave), and a special pagan deity known as Yarrabox—a remarkable devil, worshipped with Voodoo rites. Their pagan temple was in great repute among the Turkish women. The hareems, indeed, lived in a twilight world, of white and black magic, of witch-doctors, wizards, wise women and mumbo-jumbo.

A picture of the life in a hareem before the War is given us by Mr. Davey (" The Sultan and His Subjects," p. 114). It is the description by a lady, one of those English governesses who were perhaps the most potent educational influence in Turkey at that time :

Fortunately the ladies in this particular Hareem were fond of the bath ; but all day long, especially in summer, they lolled about in their night-gowns, which were often not changed for a month. I have seen them when they had a reception wearing these dirty garments under an elaborate tea-gown worth £30 or £40. Some of the slave-girls wore very splendid costumes of velvet or brocade, and often more jewellery than their mistresses. These ladies did absolutely nothing from morning until night but eat, dine and sleep. Occasionally they went for a drive in a closed brougham, or sat by the hour under the trees of some cemetery, or lounged in a caïque on the Bosphorus. One or two of them spoke French fairly well and read French novels. There was one girl who played the piano. On the whole the monotony of their life was incredible.

Some time ago I was an inmate of the Hareem of one of the most powerful and wealthiest men of Turkey, a favourite minister of the Sultan. There were sixty-two women there, though he had only two wives. But besides these ladies were the seven wives of his three sons, the Pasha's mother and her two old sisters, and half a score of aged pauper female relations who, according to Turkish custom, must be clothed, fed, and housed gratuitously. The rest were slaves and servants.

One day a little grandchild of six fell ill. A wise women was summoned, who performed some incantation ; then incensed the bed : and finally, taking out of an embroidered handkerchief the jaw-bone of a man, scrubbed the child all over with it. After that she said a few prayers ; then, rising from her knees, took a spoonful of molten lead, and threw it into a vessel of water. It took a curious shape at the bottom, and from that she prophesied whether it was to recover. As a matter of fact it died in the night.

One day some very pretty slave-girls were brought to the Hareem to be purchased. It was a sickening sight to see the Pasha examining them, even their teeth, as if they were young animals. They did not seem to mind, and I am bound to admit that in all the ten years I have been governess in Turkish families I have come across fewer cases of ill-treatment of servants than I did in the same number of years in England.

It is not for me to reveal what I know of the moral atmosphere of the average Turkish household ; but, though I have come across a great many cases of women—and even very young girls—who had clandestine love affairs, and worse, yet, take her all in all, the average Turkish woman, were it not for her language, which to our minds is most indelicate, has a right to be considered " honest," as Shakespeare expresses it.

The all-too-Shakespearean "honesty" of language in the Turkish family circle was one of the early barriers to the education of Turkish women. Small Turkish girls were found, in this respect, to be altogether too advanced for foreign schools. When the Sultan withdrew permission for Turkish children to attend them, lest they should be corrupted by contact with foreign ideas, the lady-superintendents breathed again.

Angora, after various attempts, has succeeded in establishing monogamy. Polygamy, even before it was made illegal, had become economically impossible. So long as the Empire was wealthy and its revenues remained in the hands of its officials, the maintenance of a hareem was practicable. But for many years poverty had restricted the majority of Turks to one wife. Facility of divorce has, however, remained. And, not in this respect alone, the present transitional status of women in Turkey, both economically and socially, it not altogether enviable.

Women have played a conspicuous political part in the Turkish renascence. Halideh Edib Hanoum, a graduate of the American College, and married to Adnan Bey, one of the Nationalist leaders, has filled a place in the public eye during the dramatic national adventure second only to that of the " Ghazi " himself. This charming lady—a novelist, poet, and politician—was a host in herself whether raiding Constantinople in disguise, with a price on her head, or riding in uniform with the cavalry on the Anatolian campaigns. Turkish women, now that they are rid of Byzantinism, will not be long in recovering the social position that was theirs before the Osmanli conquered—and were conquered by—Constantinople.

There are wholesome signs that women are already regaining their freedom. Latterly, for instance, I read that the Vali of Constantinople has overruled a Kaimakam on the Bosphorus who had prohibited mixed bathing. This means more than it might seem to us in the West. The public bath was a historic survival of ancient Greek civilization, and it remained the healthiest element in Constantinople life. The sexes were, of course, separated, and costume was limited to a kindly covering of the old' and fat. A party of us were riding many years ago in the forest of Belgrade behind Therapia, and we came unexpectedly upon a picnic-party from some Pasha's hareem, bathing from one of the great marble dams that once supplied the capital with water. Some of the girls had swum across and stood in the nearer edge of the water, quietly watching us pass and merely screening their faces below their eyes with the broad green leaves of a water-plant. A prettier picture could not be imagined, and it held a promise, full of hope, of a Turkish womanhood enfranchised at last from Byzantine bondage and enjoying both the freedom of Turkish tribal society and the culture of classical Greece.

At Arnaut Keui we have arrived at the most striking reach of the Straits. Bebek (the baby), with its wooded ravine, is, as its name suggests, the pet of the Bosphorus villages. It possesses some delightful Yalis, including one belonging to the Khedivial family. It was the site also of a British colony.

On the Asiatic side, opposite, is beautiful Kandilli, a favourite resort for Europeans, where the wooden houses overhang the quay, and the slopes behind are covered with trees. From it a peaceful bay runs back to the valley of the Sweet Waters, and to the low-lying towers and walls of Anatoli Hissar, the Castle of Asia. But there is little to take a traveller over there to-day. The slow, muddy stream of the Sweet Waters has little beauty, and the picturesque picnic-parties in kaiks from the Constantinople Konaks and the Bosphorus Yalis are no more. Although the meadows in spring are beautiful and their flowers still attract the children of the neighbourhood, they can no longer be classed at other seasons with what the German guide-books call " seeworthinesses."

ROUMELI-HISSAR

Roumeli Hissar, the Castle of Europe, on its rocky bluff, is very different. There, side by side, stand a collection of buildings as interesting and incongruous as any to be found in Constantinople. On the top of the hill is the Tekke of the Bektash Dervishes, the free-thinkers of Islam. The modern buildings of Robert College look down towards Stamboul. And along the water-front, and climbing up the steep slope behind, are the massive towers and fortifications of the Castle of Mohammed the Conqueror. It is a good situation, and the Castle is worthy of it. It is in good preservation, though the conical roofs of the towers are gone, and some of the floorings. But the heavy oaken outer doors, sheathed in brass and iron, still hang as they were set up forty years before the discovery of America. The friendly Turkish families who live in the wooden houses clustering round the walls " keep themselves to themselves " as a community, and claim to be descended from Firuz Agha and the 400 Janissaries who were placed in charge here by Mohammed when he built the Castle before conquering Constantinople.

The plan of the fortress is visible at a glance from below, upended as it is upon the steep slope, and we can work out for ourselves how the contour is made to comprise the four Arabic characters, mim, heh, mim, dah, the letters of the Conqueror's name. Over every gate is a " mim," cut in the marble, and into the south-western tower, which faces Constantinople, is built a cannon-ball, as a symbolic warning of what the doomed city had to expect. Legends have gathered round the head and bust of porphyry, inserted in the western face of the north-western tower ; but they are all meaningless, and we may guess for ourselves what the builders may have had in mind. The great round towers were built exceptionally solid, in order to carry the monster guns of the day. The three largest towers are named after the rival Pashas who built them, Khalil, Saganes, and Saridja. That of Khalil was adjudged by the Sultan to be the best built, and upon it was mounted a cannon which threw a stone ball of 600 lb. across the Strait. It is recorded that the first Venetian galley that passed refused to heave-to and was sunk, and the crew as they swam ashore were killed. From that day onward the Turks have commanded the Straits, and the old Greek name, Laimo Kopion (the cut-throat) has become the Turkish " Bogaz-Kessen." But the strangle-hold of the Castle upon the throat of the Strait, through which has to pass the wheat of Odessa and the oil of Baku, has loosened with time. But for the War a great steel bridge would by now, in all likelihood, have bound Europe to Asia, and as we rolled across it, in the Boulogne-Bagdad mail, Constantinople would be no more than a wayside station, and Roumeli Hissar an incidental stone-heap.

After the Fall of Constantinople the castle became a prison. The Tower of Khalil, wh ch came to be known as the Tower of Blood or the Black Tower, soon acquired a very evil reputation. From the " Memoirs of Baron Wratislaw," written in 1599, from which I have already quoted, we gather that it was accounted worse than the galleys :

As soon as we heard the Black Tower mentioned and that we were to be put in so gloomy a prison we all with one voice began to lament. The other prisoners pitied us and wept with us and we would rather have undergone death than so unendurable a prison. . . . As soon as we ran ashore under the fortress a ladder was let down to us, up which, each carrying his wallet, we walked in after our reis. The great iron gates were opened to us and we saw a square with a gallery round it reaching to the Tower itself in which there was an iron door. The reis of our boat handed Mehemed the Agha of the Tower a letter from the Pasha, on reading which he said aloud : " What am I to do with these poor prisoners ? They have not deserved so cruel a prison. It is not just so to punish the guiltless." And looking at us who were all weeping, our eyes red with much weeping, he said, " Allah buickter, Kurtular Sise " (God is great, he can save you). He then ordered the iron door opened, and bade us enter. The Tower is high but not wide, so that the four already there and us twenty-two had scarcely room to lie down. Inside is an oaken grill like a lion's cage, that the guards can walk round while the prisoners sit inside. In the middle of the cage a glass lamp burns night and day and round are stocks on which we rested our feet. Our feet should have been fastened in but the Governor did not put us in the stocks except when Turks whom he did not know were coming to the Tower.

After the prisoners had escaped death by cold, by starvation, and by poisoning—the guard having given them by way of a joke an uneatable kind of ray—the Sultan who had imprisoned them died, and the prisoners managed to attract the attention of Mohammed III, by all shouting in chorus when they were told he was rowing past on the Bosphorus. Eventually they were released, after over two years in the Black Tower, owing to the intervention of the English Ambassador.

In the Black Tower, also, was confined the reforming Patriarch, Cyril Loukaris, the friend of Archbishop Laud, and the donor of our Codex Alexandrinus (v. p. 169). He was strangled here in 1638. He had, as we know, incurred the enmity of both Orthodox and Moslem by trying to give the Greek Church the vitality it had to have if it were to keep the Greek race alive. His body was dragged with a rope round its neck through the arched water-gate and thrown to the " devil's " current. Nor was there any miraculous recovery of it as in the case of more orthodox martyrs.

Robert College

Robert College, the adjacent modern building, was founded in 1863. In 1862 Tom Hughes, the author of " Tom Brown's Schooldays," published his opinion, after a visit to Constantinople, that the salvation of the Ottoman Empire would be the establishment of an English Public School. This struck our fathers and grandfathers as merely comical. But, as has often, fortunately, happened, America had either less sense of humour or more practical insight. A year later Mr. C. R. Robert, a New York merchant, stepped in and secured for America the responsibility of educating the Near East, which should have been our right. We have seen the great Embassies in Pera, whose contribution to the civilization of Constantinople was the Crimean War and the Great War. The contribution of Robert College also led, in the end, direct to war. But, whereas the cemeteries of Scutari and Gallipoli are the only memorials of the Embassy wars, the work of Robert College has its memorials in the liberty of at least one Christian nation, Bulgaria, and in the new life it has given to other races of the Near East.

The intention of the College was to offer an education to all Ottoman subjects, including Turks. But so long as the Hamidian regime lasted Moslem—except for one short period—were not allowed to attend. The scholars were mainly Greeks, Armenians, and last, but not least, Bulgars. For the foundation of the College preceded by a few years that of Bulgaria. Practically all the prominent men of Bulgaria not only received their education in it, but continued, after they had become Premiers and permanent officials, to look to Dr. Washburn, the Principal, for advice. In his study were debated in advance most of the dramatic developments in Eastern politics during the reign of Abdul-Hamid. It was not until Sofia had outgrown its mentor of the Bosphorus, and had substituted for the shrewd old New Englander that sinister scion of the Coburgs, Ferdinand, that Bulgaria began to blunder. In the early years of this century, when Bulgaria was still the model of a progressive and prudent State, and the laurels it had won by defeating the Serb invasion and the Russian intrigues were still green, I have often sat with Dr. Washburn on the terrace overlooking the Strait, and listened to prophecies that were a good antidote to the prognostications of the seers of Whitehall.

THE BALKAN WARS

The Bulgars and the Turks are racially akin, and by nature should be allies. It was Constantinople, and the empire which its possession gave the Turks, that made them political enemies. Until the Bulgar had freed his race from Turkish over-lordship there could be no real peace. The Treaty of Berlin, in order to strengthen Turkey's hand, had restored Turkish rule over the Bulgars and Greeks of Thrace and Macedonia. But, even so, had the policy of Stambouloff, of Dr. Washburn, and of Sir William White continued to prevail, Bulgaria, like Eastern Roumelia, might have come into its own without war. This possibility, however, finally vanished with the Ottoman Revolution, and with the ascendancy of the Young Turk Committee.

As we leave the College, where there is so much to recall to our minds our own missed opportunities and the mistakes of European policy, we may console ourselves with one anecdote of a different character. Dr. Washburn, in commenting on the complacency with which the boys, of several creeds, were all alike allowed to attend the short American school service, used to add, with a smile, " But they nearly all ask that their sons should be taught ' English morality.' "

We have brought the story of Constantinople down to the recovery of power by the Committee, in 1909. The break-up in the *status quo* in the Near East, produced by this revolution, was followed by a crop of small wars. The Austrians took the opportunity to annex Bosnia and Herzegovina. A war, however, in this case, between the two Empires was avoided; since the Treaty of Berlin had already surrendered to the Austrians the administration of these provinces. Italy seized Tripoli. And this led to a desultory war, which dragged along until the Young Turks found they had to defend themselves against the Bulgars ; and so, although still undefeated by the Italians, they preferred to put an end to it, in the first Treaty of Lausanne, 1912.

Negotiations for a Balkan coalition against Turkey had begun as early as 1910. Even so, the race hatred between the Slavs and Greeks would never have permitted them to co-operate effectively, but for the bellicose procedure of the Young Turks. Their hostile attitude towards the desire for autonomy on the part of the subject races in the Empire, forced on a war with Arabia and another with Albania. And in the spring of 1912, at a time when the Balkan States were concluding their coalition against the Imperialism of the Young Turks, the indomitable Turkish Triumvirate proceeded to " arrange " the elections so as to secure their authority. They had, however, antagonized some part of the Turkish army by their military failures. A Macedonian military organization, called the League of Military Unity, set itself against them ; and their regime collapsed, in June 1913, as abruptly as had Abdul-Hamid's. A ministry of Old Turks, with an average age of sixty-five, came into office, on a platform of making peace generally. The Young Turks at once set about preventing this, by a policy of provocations of every kind. One Young Turk minister to Montenegro even presented an unauthorized ultimatum, while " incidents " and intrigues of their manufacture put the peace parties in the Balkan capitals and in Constantinople in an impossible position. The inevitable war between the Balkan coalition and the Empire broke out that autumn. The war only concerns us indirectly ; because, although the possession of Constantinople was an unavowed article of the Greek policy, it was not the declared object—which was the partition of the European provinces of the Turkish Empire.

The Bulgars drove the Turks out of Thrace, and back behind the lines of Tchataldja, with an ease as flattering to themselves as it was humiliating to Young Turkey. But this success gave the war a direction very fatal to the Bulgars'; for their national objective should have been Macedonia, and their true national opponents were the Greeks.

The victory of the Bulgars over the Turks is often mistakenly described as that of a developing over a decaying race. This is only true in so far as the Turkish race was still tainted with the decay of its fatal Capital. In other respects Turkey, after the revolution of 1908, was more in the condition of a very crude European State than of a very corrupt Asiatic Empire. The campaign in Thrace revealed that the new vigour of the Young Turks had not yet had time to permeate the vast mass of militant Turkey. In certain directions it was already effective. The troops were better clothed, armed, and equipped, and, in a fashion, better commanded. But the commanding officers showed themselves incapable of manœuvring masses of men over the big distances of a modern battlefield. Modern appliances, field telephones and field railways were not available, or their uses were not understood. The commissariat failed even to supply bread and water on a short double railway line between two such centres of supply as Adrianople and Constantinople. The railways, indeed, only helped to disorganize the customary foot-crawl of a Turkish army. The lessons of transport learned from the Germans on the hurricane, but unopposed, advance from Salonika in 1909, were neglected. Lack of mobility had always been a defect of Turkish armies, but this campaign gave evidence of a new trouble, loss of *morale*. For this the Young Turk policy of recruiting Christians was largely responsible. The total proportion of Christians so admitted was very small, not more than some 5 or 6 per cent., of whom the Armenians, estimated at about 8,000, alone fought well. The additional men gained could not, therefore, have affected the result. On the other hand, the admixture was sufficient to affect prejudicially the racial and religious solidarity of the imperial army.

These defects were made good in the end, when the new national impetus had had time to penetrate further below the surface. The Turkish revolutionary government recovered its military efficiency as rapidly as did the French or the Russian revolutionary governments. Our own subsequent and bitter experiences in Mesopotamia and at the Dardanelles must bear witness to it. But, for the time being, these Balkan wars, provoked before the new leaven had had time to work, all but cost the Young Turks Constantinople.

On their side, the Bulgars were in a false position, politically and strategically. They were advancing successfully against Constantinople ; but Constantinople could be of no use to them. Their Thracian campaign, for this reason, was bringing them in no profits comparable to those rewarding the campaign of their allies in Macedonia. Macedonia, not Thrace, was the true Bulgarian political objective. Political prudence accordingly should have suggested to them the utmost economy of energy in Thrace. But war can never be kept in its place, as a means to an end. Invariably it becomes the end itself. It was not otherwise with the Bulgarians. Their Macedonian force, co-operating there with their Greek allies, became no more than a reserve, from which to draw reinforcements for their successful Thracian campaign. Their central reserve force was moved to the extreme left wing, at the end of the Thracian frontier farthest from Macedonia ; and it was there used for a vigorous offensive against the Turkish right. Thus the Bulgar armies were ultimately redisposed as though their political objective had become the capture of Constantinople and not, as it should have been, the capture of Salonika.

An immediate military success was thus made safe ; and an eventual political discomfiture made equally sure. The Turkish right was crushed at Kirk Kilisse, but clung, fighting fiercely, to the difficult country of the Istranja Balkan. The left held its own round Adrianople. But the centre was hammered in, and driven back, sagging southward over the open downs ; with the momentum of its amorphous masses of men and material travelling rearward instead of forward. Every mile increased its disorganization, hunger and hardship. There followed the five days of confused fighting known as the battle of Lule Burgas.

Hustled out of all formation the Turkish army staggered back, a starving and stricken multitude, behind the Tchataldja lines, with perhaps a quarter of its numbers still effective. The Bulgars, only less exhausted because stimulated by success, toiled after in slow pursuit; vainly hoping to reap the fruits of their victory in Thrace in time to hurry back and profit by a second harvest in Macedonia—where others were already reaping what they had sown. But want of cavalry, railway and road communications made their pursuit ineffective. Starving Turks without arms or formation could drag themselves quicker through the mud homeward than starving Bulgars invading a hostile country. For the Bulgars the railway through Thrace was blocked by Adrianople, the Black Sea route by Turkish cruisers. The barren downs and devastated Greek and Moslem villages of Thrace could not supply or shelter a regiment, much less an army. Every mile they advanced from their railway base at Yamboli added to the Bulgar weakness. Every loaf and cartridge had to be brought to the front, and every wounded man sent back to the rear, by buffalo transport, over unmade tracks. And buffalo transport could cover but five to ten miles a day, over lines of communication lengthening out for hundreds of miles.

It was done; but at an appalling cost to Bulgaria of its national capital—the peasant and the plough-ox. Doubtless it was this consideration which caused the Bulgars to hesitate before the further cost of storming Adrianople, and which decided them to try and force peace by threatening Constantinople. If so, it was a miscalculation. An Empire may be coerced by threatening its Capital: but a Nation cannot. What would have been effective against Abdul-Hamid was ineffective against Enver Bey. When, after a fortnight, the Bulgars had cleared Thrace and shut up the remnants of the Turkish forces in Adrianople and Constantinople, they found themselves no nearer a victorious peace. Winning a war can be only a little less disastrous than losing one.

It has been said that, on reaching Tchataldja, the Bulgars should have forced the lines at all costs, and dictated a peace at San Stephano. And again, that when the Turks first asked for an armistice, a peace should have been at once arranged. Both these courses were, in fact, tried. The attempt to force the lines was more serious than was realized abroad; it cost between ten and fifteen thousand men. Its failure forbad any further attempts. An armistice was then in the interests of both parties. Negotiations began outside Tchataldja on November 25, and were concluded in ten days. The Bulgars did their best to secure terms that would constitute a real treaty of peace. But all that they succeeded in getting was a truce which allowed their various enemies to prepare again for war. The Turks, on their side, had every inducement to evade a peace dictated to them under such unfavourable conditions; more especially because in holding themselves free to renew the war, they felt that they had the support of one of the great armed camps into which the Concert of Europe might at any moment resolve itself.

The procedure provided by London for the peace negotiations was one admirably adapted to the situation. It did away, as far as possible, with correspondence and circumlocution. One procedure provided for a reference to the representatives of the two groups forming the Concert, with a view to securing their joint recommendations on all questions especially concerning the Great Powers. The other procedure provided for a conference between the plenipotentiaries of the Balkan States, with a view to a final decision of all questions especially affecting the belligerents. Diplomacy is often abused for being stereotyped or stupid in its methods. But those who criticized British policy in the Balkans for its conventionality, as well as those who commended it for its correctitude, have alike overlooked the new procedure which it introduced at this time in the conduct of foreign affairs—a practical precedent, worth more than most proposals of unprofessional peacemakers.

The Turkish reverses had resulted in the fall of the Liberal ministry of Moukhtar. Since the outbreak of war, and the failure of its "Liberal" policy, this ministry had come under the influence of the Committee. It now gave place to one of distinctly anti-Committee tone, under the Anglophil Kiamil Pasha. The Committee and the Young Turks, therefore, constituted an opposition war-party; while the more prudent patriotism of the Elder Statesmen—as we may call the moderate Liberal government under Kiamil—was anxious for peace. The Concert jointly recommended that Adrianople should be ceded to the Allies, and that the Ægean Islands should be left to the disposition of the Concert. The Kiamil ministry received the recommendation on January 17, decided on its acceptance, and, in order to strengthen itself for its execution, summoned a "Grand Council" of the principal religious, military, and civil dignitaries; which gave its formal approval on January 22. Peace, on terms that formed a good basis for a permanent settlement, and at a time when a fresh outbreak of war might still have been prevented, seemed to have been achieved successfully, thanks to the mediation of London.

But, on the day following the decision of the Grand Council, the Committee effected another *coup d'état*, and assumed control of the government. The Porte was invaded by a small party, under the Committee Triumvirate, Enver, Talaat, and Djemal. All the leading Elder Statesmen were seized, and Mahmoud Shevket was made Grand Vizier. Nazim, the Minister of War, on hearing the uproar, came out, and faced the crowd, cigarette in mouth and hands in pockets. "Well, brothers," said he, "what's all this about ? " and fell, shot dead. It was an assassination which condemned the whole enterprise in the eyes of Europe ; and which later cost the Committee, in reprisal, the life of its most valuable member, Mahmoud Shevket himself. In the eyes of the Young Turks, however, the Elder Statesmen seemed doubtless to be guilty of a betrayal of their country, to say nothing of a breach of the Constitution. The Young Turk policy, in renewing the war, had also the excuse of being the policy of the Young Turkish people, as expressed through the only institution in working order at the moment, the Army. It was at all events immediately accepted as such abroad. The negotiations in London were broken off, and hostilities were resumed.

The Bulgars were given to understand by Petersburg that they might not occupy Constantinople or any point on the Sea of Marmara. For the same reasons Russian diplomacy deprecated the occupation by Greece of the islands commanding the Straits. Thus both Bulgarian and Greek ambitions were diverted from Constantinople to Salonika and Kavalla. But Bulgars and Greeks, who might have agreed as to the disposal of a conquered Constantinople, could not agree as to Salonika.

The reorganization of Turkish resistance by the Committee during the winter of 1912–13, after the break-up of the first Conference in London, was an astounding feat, comparable to that of the Committee of Public Safety in the French Revolution. But it failed. A naval offensive against the rear of the Bulgarian containing force, at Tchataldja, by way of the Black Sea, was repulsed with the loss of a Turkish ironclad. A flotilla of transports, under Enver Bey, which made a similar attempt on the rear of the Bulgar containing army by way of the Marmara, was also repulsed. On March 25 a Turkish force advanced direct from Tchataldja against the Bulgar front, and was driven off, with the loss of one-quarter of its strength. This last sortie from Constantinople having failed, Adrianople surrendered. The Turks immediately invited the mediation of the Powers ; and on March 31 they received the conditions of such mediation. These were the same terms as had been accepted by Kiamil in January. In the meantime, Janina had fallen on March 6, and Adrianople on March 26 ; Scutari did not fall until April 23.

When the Balkan plenipotentiaries again arrived in London, in May, they found that they had only been convoked in order to approve the terms of peace already drafted for them in the Ambassadors' Conference. This procedure was welcomed by the principal belligerents, Bulgaria and Turkey, whose delegates it was understood were ready to sign without delay. But the Greeks and Serbians were, for obvious reasons, not so well suited by this arrangement. Greece did not want the Second Conference to complete the peace until the Greeks were finally established in Macedonia and Albania ; even as they had not wanted peace at the First Conference until they were established in Epirus and the Ægean. The Greek delegates accordingly began a campaign of procrastination, which prolonged the proceedings until the end of the month. The treaty was eventually signed on May 30, under pressure from the British Government, the Secretary of State having curtly informed the delegates that they must sign the draft treaty, or leave London.

The terms of the Treaty of London afforded a sound basis for a permanent settlement. The Ottoman Empire was restricted to a strategic frontier, the Enos-Midia line, which secured the Turks their Capital and the command of the Straits. Of the remaining Ottoman territory, Albania, the Ægean Islands, and Mount Athos were taken *en dépôt* by the Powers ; and financial questions, such as the indemnity claimed by the Balkan Allies and the liability for the Ottoman Debt claimed by Turkey, were reserved for a special International Commission, to meet at Paris. The delay, however, in signing until the end of May, had unfortunately let matters drift too far towards the Second Balkan War—the War of Partition.

This was a war for Macedonia. Bulgaria was ranged against Greece and Serbia. Roumania joined in later in order to capture the Dobrudja from Bulgaria ; and Turkey likewise joined in, in order to recover Thrace and Adrianople from Bulgaria. Only in this last respect, therefore, does the war directly concern the story of Constantinople. But that the Turks should have been able to tear up the Treaty of London, which assigned

Thrace to Bulgaria, almost before the ink was dry, was ominous
for the peace of Europe.

On June 29 the war broke out ; and the Bulgars were driven
back behind their frontier by the Serbs supported by the Greeks.
On July 10, the Roumanians crossed the Danube ; and on
July 15 a Turkish army, under Enver, occupied Adrianople,
which had been practically evacuated by the Bulgars in order
to defend Sofia. The Turkish cavalry, under Rafet, then swept
the Bulgar population of Thrace over the frontier. The Treaty
of Bucharest, signed on August 10, left Bulgaria disarmed and
despoiled. Greece and Serbia divided Macedonia between themselves ; and Roumania took the Dobrudja. Bulgaria, after a
vain appeal to the Powers to maintain the Treaty of London,
made the best terms it could with Turkey, and signed the Treaty
of Constantinople on September 29, renouncing Thrace and
Adrianople, and retaining only Western Thrace and Dedé-agatch.

The effect of this swift spin in the wheel of fortune was to
put the war party of the Young Turks, and their patrons the
Prussians, in power at Constantinople, at an unfortunate moment
for our policy. Had we insisted upon the Treaty of London
being maintained, we might have brought our protégés, the Elder
Statesmen or Old Turks, back again. But such rebuffs must be
the fate of a democracy like ours, when it embarks on a diplomacy that only forcible intervention, at the right moment, can
put through : an intervention which, when the crucial moment
comes, public opinion will very rarely support. At Constantinople our democracy could only give " moral " support to
" moral " movements. But what we actually did was to collide
with such " moral " forces as there were—reform and nationalism. For this reason I know of no better introduction to a
study of the principles of foreign policy than the modern story
of Constantinople.

These Balkan wars have had to be treated somewhat fully,
not for their own sake, but because they were the preliminary
skirmishes in the great struggle for Constantinople between the
various nations composing the Ottoman Empire, and between
the European Powers. Behind and above the small, warring
Balkan States we seem to see throughout the Great Powers
looming, like the gods above the Homeric battles. When we
next resume the story of the city we shall find that the Olym-
pians have descended into the arena, and are themselves fighting
for Troy. Meantime let us return to the Bosphorus.

North of Roumeli Hissar there is a pleasant little inlet and valley, Balta Liman. It owes its name to the "Wood-cutter" admiral of the Conqueror, who built a Yali here, and used it as his naval base during the siege. We may recall that he was a Bulgar, and that the Turco-Bulgar combination has generally proved decisive in the story of the city. The notable villa was built by Reshid Pasha, the reforming Vizier of Abdul-Aziz, and it was given by that Sultan to his daughter Fatmeh. Here also were signed the treaties of 1838, 1841, and 1849—all as long-forgotten as these great people themselves.

Emirghian bears the name of a Persian Prince who sold Erivan to Mourad IV, in 1635; and thereafter for six years squandered here the proceeds of his treachery, until he was bowstrung by Ibrahim. Like all the Persian refugees he was an accomplished amateur, and he certainly chose a charming neighbourhood. On the cape to the north are the remains of the Yali of Khosrev Pasha, the Vizier of Mahmoud the Reformer, and his chief assistant in the destruction of the Janissaries. This fierce old man, who lived to nearly a hundred with scarcely diminished vigour, survived to become himself a monument of the Osmanli Empire. His palace was occupied, later, by the ex-Khedive, Ismail Pasha.

Yenikeui is picturesque, and as Western in character as Emirghian is Oriental. It is a gay little place; but its smart houses have also had their tragedies. One house was that of the Douzoghlou family, for two centuries jewellers and goldsmiths to the Sultans. In a single night they were wiped out, on an accusation afterwards proved to be false. The four brothers were hung from the windows, and the women died of grief and ill-usage. Another was the home of the Austrian Embassy. It was built by the Armenian banker Djezairli at a cost of £200,000. His wealth was confiscated before it was completed, and he died soon after of despair.

Between Yenikeui and Therapia is the Imperial Kiosk of "Kalender," the scene of an historic diplomatic encounter between Stratford Canning and the Porte, in 1812. He had been sent out to make peace between Turkey and Russia, so that Russia might concentrate against Napoleon's invasion. The last debate continued for sixteen hours; after which the Ottoman ministers collapsed, exhausted, and came to terms.

THERAPIA AND THE GREAT WAR

At Therapia diplomatic memories envelop us thickly. The pretty village was for a century the haunt of that octopus, the

Eastern Question, where it knotted and twisted its tentacles in floods of self-secreted ink. To-day it is deserted, and most of its summer Embassies destroyed. The French Embassy was a long, low, red wooden building, the picturesque home of the Phanar family of Ypsilanti. The British Embassy, a high, white, gabled structure, stood on the point, under a rocky cliff, in the delightful grounds of another Greek family, Dragoyannis. On the last occasion when I visited it nothing remained but fire-swept foundations; and under a wall, half-buried in creepers, were the remnants of an Embassy kaik. Verily, the glory was departed.

The German Embassy across the harbour still survives; as does the Russian Embassy at Buyukderé round the point. The Therapia Palace Hotel is gone. But Tokatlian's Hotel is open in summer, with motor services to Constantinople; as well as more modest hotels. Therapia has attractions for those who have leisure to explore something more of the country. To the valley of Buyukderé, where there is a reputed plane-tree of Godfrey de Bouillon's, is a pleasant walk. The Forest of Belgrade is a no less pleasant ride, with its marble dams built in the prosperous days of the Osmanli Empire. Across the Bosphorus we can make boat excursions: for one, to the charming Hunkiar-Skelessi (Monarch's Landing), with its magnificent sycamores, under the slopes of the Giant's Mountain. In 1832 the treaty between Turkey and Russia was signed here, which closed the Dardanelles to all the enemies of Russia, and nearly brought on the Crimean War twenty years earlier. Upon an obelisk is commemorated the fact that a Russian army, disembarked nominally for the protection of Constantinople, was encamped at that time upon this plain. Here, also, in 1869, Abdul-Aziz built a splendid pavilion for the Empress Eugénie; and at the house-warming 60,000 Ottoman troops were marched past in review.

Near by is Beikos (Walnut-tree), where there is a summer palace built by Ismail of Egypt. The whole region here is consecrated to memories of French, British, and Russian patronage of the Porte. In the Bay of Beikos, now solitary but for the " daglians "—the quaint, roofed perches, where the fishermen wait for the sword-fish—there assembled, in 1854, the Anglo-French fleet and transports, before they sailed for the Crimea.

It was just sixty years later, in 1914, at a time when the Summer Embassies were flirting, picnicking, and polo-playing as usual, that the crisis came which was to make Constantinople one of the battlefields and one of the prizes of the most terrible of wars.

In 1914 von Marschall had been succeeded in the German Embassy by von Wangenheim, a Prussian Junker, on his promotion to the Chancellorship. Of him Mr. Morgenthau, the American Ambassador, writes :

When I think of modern Germany, the massive figure of Wangenheim presents itself. He was six feet two ; his huge frame, Gibraltar-like shoulders, his bold defiant head, his piercing eyes, the whole physical structure pulsating with life—there stands the Germany whose limitless ambition transformed the world into a place of horror. Pan-Germany filled all his waking hours : the deification of his Emperor was his sole religious instinct. That aristocratic and autocratic organization of German society which represents the Prussian system was in his eyes to be worshipped. . . . Upon him depended the success of the German conspiracy for world domination. . . . Unless Germany could get the Ottoman Empire as its ally, there was little chance of success in a general war.

Turkey, as the ally of Germany, would not only redress the balance of man-power, which the adhesion of Russia had weighed down in favour of the Allies ; but also, by closing the Allied access to South Russia and opening the German land-bridge to Asia, would prevent the encirclement of the Germans in Europe. Wangenheim had one conspicuous and un-Prussian quality— and that was tact. But we well understood that behind all his gentleness there lay a remorseless ambition. I still recollect this huge man, as he would sit at a piano improvising upon some beautiful classic theme, and then suddenly start pounding uproarious German drinking songs. All life was a game to him. And in this greatest game of all—" World-empire or Downfall " (and he was himself to use the German phrase—" fire and flame " —for it)—he knew himself to be a strong player, set apart for a mighty task.

For such a personality the Entente Ambassadors were no match. Moreover, they were all obsessed with the delusion that the Young Turk Triumvirate, Enver, Talaat, and Djemal, could not retain power. They either ignored them, which was the British policy, or intrigued against them, which was the Russian policy. But they were not men who could be ignored. Enver, the debonair little Turk ; Talaat, the burly Bulgar gipsy ; Djemal, the white-faced, blue-bearded Asiatic, were all formidable factors. Mr. Morgenthau tells us of Talaat :

Physically he was a striking figure. His powerful frame . . . emphasized that natural forcefulness which made possible his career.

In discussing matters Talaat liked to sit at his desk, his shoulders drawn up, his head thrown back and his wrists, twice the size of an ordinary man's, planted firmly on the table. Whenever I think of him now, I do not recall so much his rollicking laugh, . . . the mighty stride with which he crossed the room, his fierceness, his determination, his remorselessness, so much as those gigantic wrists.

This was a new type of personality in Turkish politics. Enver was almost as much of a phenomenon. An adventurer of Napoleonic imagination, he was the "hero of the revolution," "Napoleonlik"—the little Napoleon. His clean-cut features, dapper figure and courteous manners concealed a cool head and a cold heart. These two were born leaders of men, and, until their deaths, they led. Enver staked his power on the German throw for world-empire; and when that was lost, he staked his life as boldly upon leading central Asiatic tribes on pan-Turanian crusades—and lost that. Djemal was a protagonist of a different mould. He was the Asiatic adventurer; and his ambition was a separate Sultanate in Asia Minor. By reason of this, the Entente Foreign Offices, early in the war, built much upon the chance of being able to bribe him. Djemal was the wire-puller and bow-stringer of the Young Turk government; Talaat was its organizer and administrator; Enver its man of action. Between them they converted Constantinople into a German camp; and thereby prolonged the war for a number of years. But even they could not have done this had not German diplomacy already defeated ours in direction and in detail. Well before the end of 1913 General Liman von Sanders had arrived in Constantinople with a large Military Mission, and had taken over executive control of the Turkish forces. Negotiations for a military alliance were completed by Enver before July 1914. If, upon the outbreak of the war, Turkey declared neutrality, this was no more than a blind. Nothing could have prevented the Triumvirate, under pressure from Enver, from joining Germany—except the presence at Constantinople of British warships, to counterbalance the presence of the German soldiery. Fortune even placed this weapon in our hands; and our ill-fated diplomacy threw this also away.

For our Naval Mission still had its hold upon the Turkish fleet; and, further, we had in our hands, in British dockyards, and ready to sail, two battleships ordered by the Turks. Had they been sent to Constantinople under the Turkish flag, with British crews, the game in that quarter must have been won or drawn. In place of this, we let the Admiralty put them into the Grand Fleet.   The ships had been paid for by popular subscription, with a view to a war against Greece.   Turkish women had even sold their hair to raise the money.   By their confiscation we forfeited the solid argument which their presence at Constantinople would have provided, and we outraged even friendly Turkish opinion.   With the trumps in our hands we let the Germans take the trick.

On August 9, passengers for Constantinople on the *Sicilia* were witnesses of a naval engagement—a light cruiser in pursuit of a large modern battleship and of a cruiser.   It was the *Gloucester* chasing the *Goeben* and the *Breslau* on their race for the Straits.   Two days later, the American Ambassador was sitting with Wangenheim in the German Embassy at Therapia.

Wangenheim's face was flushed, his eyes shining, he could not rest in his chair.   He was constantly jumping up and looking anxiously out over the Bosphorus, where lay his private wireless station, the *Corcovade*. "Something is distracting you," I said, rising.   "I will come some other time."   "No, no!" the Ambassador almost shouted, "I want you to stay where you are.   This is a great day for Germany.   Stay and you will hear a great piece of news!"   Then he rushed out on to the portico, and I saw a launch put out from the *Corcovado*.   Wangenheim hurried down, seized an envelope from a sailor, and a moment afterwards burst into the room again.   "We've got them!" he shouted.   "Got what?" I asked. "The *Goeben* and *Breslau* have passed the Dardanelles!"   He was waving the wireless message with the enthusiasm of a college boy whose team has won.   Then, checking his enthusiasm, he came up to me, solemnly shook his forefinger, lifted his eyebrows, and said: "Of course we have sold these ships to Turkey!" and he added with a wink, "Admiral Souchen will enter the Sultan's service."

So the *Goeben* and the *Breslau* became the *Sultan Selim* and the *Medilli*; and with their German crews in brand-new Turkish uniforms and fezzes they steamed up the Bosphorus, and anchored before the Russian Embassy at Buyukderé.   There the fezzes were replaced by German caps: "Deutschland über alles," and "Die Wacht am Rhein" were sung; the fezzes were resumed; and the ships returned to their station off Seraglio Point.

The story goes that many of the Turkish government were alarmed at this *coup de main*, and opposed the "sale"; but that Enver forced the transaction through, throwing his pistol on the Council table.   In Constantinople the majority would certainly have welcomed a naval counter-stroke by us.   But, when it came, it was too late.   Mr. Morgenthau tells us how Djavid, Minister of Finance, meeting a distinguished Belgian a few weeks later, said, "I have terrible news for you—the Germans have captured Brussels."   To which the Belgian replied,

" And I have even more terrible news for you, mon cher !—the Germans have captured Constantinople ! "

A few days later, Admiral Limpus and the British Naval Mission were unceremoniously dismissed ; and on September 27 the Dardanelles was closed to all shipping.

Never has any warship played a part of such immense import as that German warship the *Goeben*, which you can see to-day, under the name of the *Yavouz*, lying disabled in the Golden Horn. If the German navy had never done anything else, the services of the *Goeben* would have justified the sacrifices made to create it. That the *Goeben* and the *Breslau* escaped our Mediterranean fleet was the fortune of war. But it was not fortune that brought the *Goeben* and the *Breslau*, and not the two warships from British dockyards, to Seraglio Point on August 16. I do not hesitate to say that the arrival of two British-manned ships in July 1914 would have closed the blockade of the Central Powers on the eastern front, and would have ended the war in the course of 1915. Instead of which, the arrival of the two German ships kept open the line of German supplies from the East, crippled the supply of Russia, and made the winning of the war a matter of years and not of months. So exceptional is the position of Constantinople, and so vital was the control of its narrow Straits, that the timely presence of these ships enabled Germany completely to reverse the positions. In place of Russia closing the blockade of Germany upon the east, Germany had closed the blockade of Russia. Only Archangel and Vladivostock were left open for all the supply of the Russian armies.

If we, and not the Germans, had kept control of Constantinople, there would have been a short war and a long peace. Its occupation by Germany gave us a long war, and a peace that is barely even a peace in name. Nor was our failure due merely to the fortune of war, or simply to blundering. We failed to occupy Constantinople at the start for the same reason that we, later, failed in our efforts to capture it. Because we had already tied our hands, diplomatically ; and had surrendered Constantinople, in anticipation, to Russia. Russia, therefore, would not tolerate the idea of our naval occupation : just as Russia, afterwards, worked against our enterprise of military occupation.

Germany at once exploited her advantage ; and prepared to mobilize the Turkish man-power. Day by day motley crowds of half-clad, half-starved recruits straggled in through the streets from Asia Minor. Day after day parties of trim German engineers and experts arrived from the West. Day by day the requisitioning became more thorough. Everything was liable to be swept in, from the whole live-stock of a farm to the whole stock-in-trade of a shop. Enver boasted that he was recruiting and equipping an army for nothing. But the "nothing" cost the Turkish race nearly half of its population; and in the end practically annihilated the Greeks and Armenians.

In the meantime von der Goltz could be seen daily, dashing through the streets in his automobile, its panels painted with flaring German eagles, and a trumpeter blowing warning blasts. While, on the stone bench by the guardhouse, on the quay outside the Therapia Embassy, sat Wangenheim, the new conqueror of Constantinople. Except, we may add, when German reverses were reported, at which times he retired behind the Embassy walls.

Of the Triumvirate, Enver was all for war. Talaat explained his own policy to the American Ambassador very simply :

"Russia is our greatest enemy, and we are afraid of her ! . . . If, while Germany is attacking Russia, we can give her a good strong kick, and make her for a time powerless to hurt us, it is our duty to give that kick." And then, with a half-melancholy, half-defiant smile, he summed up, in his broken German—" Ich—mit die Deutschen ! " Djemal remained to the last an enigma. " If we accept your invitation to lunch for Talaat and myself," wrote Enver to Wangenheim, " that will mean Peace. If for Djemal also, then War." Djemal came. And a day or two later the *Goeben* and *Breslau* bombarded Odessa, and Russia declared war.

Mr. Morgenthau has left us a significant sketch of the fashion in which the curtain fell upon the passing of the once dominant Entente Embassies. The Turks had at the last moment upset the American arrangements for the departure of the Embassies and Colonies, and refused to pass anyone not personally vouched for as a diplomatist by Mr. Morgenthau.

People were running in all directions, checking baggage, purchasing tickets, arguing with officials, consoling distracted women and frightened children, while Badri (the Minister of Police) watched the whole pandemonium with an unsympathetic smile. Hats were knocked off, clothing torn, and, to add to the confusion, Mallet, the British Ambassador, became involved in a set-to with an officious Turk—the Englishman winning first honours easily ; and I caught a glimpse of Bompard, the French Ambassador, vigorously shaking a Turkish policeman.

Shades of the Great Elchi and of the Vicomte de Noailles !

In form, as in fact, the Turkish government had by now been reduced to the Triumvirate. The Minister of Finance, Djavid, a Judæo-Moslem; the Minister of Works, Mahmoud, a Circassian; the Minister of Commerce, Bustany Effendi, a Christian Arab; and the Minister of Posts, Oskan Effendi, an Armenian, had all resigned; and these were men of culture, who possessed public confidence. But the Triumvirate was by no means as strong as it seemed. Talaat was keeping the big motor of the Belgian Mission, and another car loaded with spares, tyres, and petrol, permanently ready, at Scutari, for a flight into Asia. The railway communication, also, between Berlin and Constantinople, ran still through neutral territory; so that there had been no means of fortifying the Dardanelles. In Constantinople it was generally assumed that the big guns of the British fleet would easily force the Straits. On January 28 orders were given to our fleet to do so; and it looked as if Wangenheim's bluff-blockade of Russia with two ships was about to be called. The Turkish government made all ready to withdraw to Eshki-Shehir, in Asia Minor.

GALLIPOLI AND THE ALLIED OCCUPATION

On February 19 the Allied fleets bombarded the outer forts, and put them out of action. Everyone, including the Turkish and German leaders, was looking daily for the appearance of the fleets off Stamboul. For the first time in his chequered career, Talaat became despondent; and busied himself with taking precautions against a rising. The Germans made ready to fight for their lives with a Turkish mob. The town was placarded with posters denouncing the Triumvirate. In a word, the distant thunder of the British guns was shaking the frail Turko-German alliance into ruins. Enver alone, just returned from a disastrous campaign in the Caucasus, kept a bold front, and prepared for a desperate defence. He was looked upon as a madman; and the evacuation was hurried on. The archives, the deposits in the banks, the Moslem women and children—all were sent into Asia Minor. It was arranged to leave the city in charge of the American Minister, of Badri, the Police Minister, and of a few Turkish officials of Anglophil Antecedents.

The attempt to force the Straits followed early in March. It resulted in the sinking of three old battleships, and the disabling of four other vessels, out of the sixteen capital ships engaged. This could not be regarded as a favourable beginning. But, on the other hand, the severity of the action had exhausted the Turkish ammunition. The Hamidieh fortress, the main defence, manned with Germans, and armed with Krupp guns that dated from 1885, had only seventeen armour-piercing shells left. Behind this, at Tchanak, was a battery that dated from 1878, and, at Nagara, two batteries dating from 1835, a minefield, and the *Goeben*. Had the Allies returned to the attack, the water-gate of Constantinople lay open to them. " I should advise you to get up at six to-morrow morning and take to the Anatolian hills—that's what we're going to do ! " said General Mertens, the German in charge of the defence, to an American correspondent. But the Allied fleets did not return. We could have taken Constantinople with two ships in 1914, and again in March 1915 with our sixteen ships, less casualties. We did not. As day after day passed, and nothing happened, the Turks plucked up heart ; and rallied again to the indomitable little Enver and the dominant Wangenheim.

During the last days of April the British force landed in Gallipoli, and began their desperate assault upon Sari Bair, the towering barbican which commands the water-gate to Constantinople. Thus it came about that whereas in the Crimean campaign we were defending the northern water-gate of Constantinople against attack from Russia, in the Gallipoli campaign we were attacking the southern water-gate of the Capital as the agents of Russia. In such a cause it was obvious that we could expect no support from the Greeks. Bulgar support we could have had ; but we were not prepared to pay the price they would exact, a repartition of Macedonia. Alternatively, a campaign of manoeuvre on the Asiatic side of the Straits might have met with success. But the course which we actually adopted, frontal assaults upon the entrenched positions of the Gallipoli heights, gave to the Turks every advantage, and, in addition, a form of fighting that best suited them.

Through May, June, and July, the fighting was as fierce as any in the war. On the Turkish side, the flower of the army perished. In August, reinforcements allowed of our making a flank attack on Sari Bair, from Suvla. For a few minutes the heights were actually won ; and our road to Constantinople lay open. But we could not make good the ground so hardly gained. At the same time our command of the sea-ways, which had been extended by our submarines into the Marmara, and even up to Constantinople, began to be threatened by German submarines. By October it was realized that retreat from the Gallipoli peninsula was inevitable ; and during the last week of December, this, the most delicate operation of the enterprise, was successfully completed.

Bulgaria, by this time, had been bribed over to the enemy by a judicious cession of territory in Thrace. Greece had withdrawn into neutrality. Serbia had been over-run. Constantinople itself had become no more than an *étappe* on the German line of communications to "fronts" in Persia, Afghanistan, Mesopotamia, Arabia, and Syria.

A Turco-German base the city remained until the end of the war : no more than a focus of the local friction between Turks and Germans, which steadily increased as fortune turned against them. Nevertheless, all attempts of the Allies to sow dissension between the Turkish leaders, or to detach them from their German confederates, failed. The heir apparent, Yousouf Izeddin, paid the penalty of his Allied sympathies, and of his opposition to the Triumvirate, by a "suicide" in 1916. Again, an intrigue to bribe Djemal with the promise of a throne in Armenia only contributed to the appalling "atrocities" which exterminated one-half of that unhappy people in 1915. It was a massacre disgraceful to the "reformers," for whom the Armenians had fought loyally during the revolution and in the field. The German patrons of Turkey must share the responsibility of what took place during the war.

The collapse of Bulgaria in 1918 was followed by that of Turkey. The Turks were left with no more than Constantinople and their home in Asia Minor. On October 29, 1918, Turkish envoys went on board the flagship, at Mudros, to ask for peace. The Triumvirate fled : Talaat to Berlin, to perish a year later at the hands of an Armenian ; Enver to Asia, to pursue his pan-Turanian adventure. Ten days later, the Allied fleet anchored off Constantinople. But there was no occupation ; and the armistice, while requiring demobilization, said nothing about disarmament. Like the Crusaders, the Allies had won Constantinople, and, like them also, they did not know what to do with it. Three Turkish Cabinets followed one another in quick succession, each of a more Anglophil and Old Turk complexion than the last. In March 1919 the Grand Vizier, Damad Ferid, journeyed to Paris to ascertain what the future of his country was to be. But the Allies, each and all, had conflicting policies ; and they were, in any case, too absorbed in dealing with problems nearer home. Damad Ferid was snubbed, and sent back again. So the moment passed in which Turkey would have accepted not only a disintegration of the Empire, but even a dismemberment of the nation.

For a generation the British Government had been supporting German enterprise at Constantinople and in Asia Minor, as a counterpoise to Russia. Not long before the outbreak of the war it was, however, decided that our weight must be transferred to the other scale, and the Russian claim to Constantinople was accepted. The reasons need not concern us here; but the results are material to the story. The principal result has already been explained. By our admission of the Russian claim to reconquer Constantinople from Islam, we lost the support which we might have had from all the young Christian nations of the Near East; and the lack of this support was the main cause of our failure at the Dardanelles. An even stranger result was that the Russian reconstruction of 1917 passed out of the hands of the " bourgeois " reformists into those of the Bolshevik revolutionaries. For the abandonment of the old Imperialist ideal of a Russian Constantinople was made in Russia the test as to whether or not Kerensky's government was genuinely inspired by a new spirit of reform, both at home and abroad. Milyukof's obstinate refusal to renounce the Russian claim to the city led, accordingly, to the overthrow of the reformists by the revolutionaries. No sooner were the Bolsheviks in power than they dropped the claim. But their renunciation profited them little. For Constantinople was made an advanced base in the south for the expeditions against the Soviet system, promoted by France and England. When the last of these, under Wrangel, had failed, it became a city of refuge for Russian émigrés. During the period of the Allied occupation no fewer than 200,000 Russians were crowded into its Levantine slums, in varying degrees of destitution. The Russian ruling class had at last attained its ancient ambition: it was occupying Constantinople.

I have seldom seen anything more harrowing than the fate of those Russian refugees. The Russian aristocratic class and army caste had sinned greatly against the people. But their punishment in being degraded into the parasites and pleasure-givers of a Levantine city was cruel. Those who had brought a few valuables with them took over every cabaret, cookshop, and café in Pera. The less fortunate ladies hired themselves out as waitresses or worse. The men hawked their clothes upon Galata bridge or sold their useless swords to any service. The gay courage shown by these mayflies was only equalled by their improvidence. The best of them, men and women, suffered the most. A Russian ambassador and his wife, whom I had last seen in semi-regal state, ruling Pera and the Porte, I found living by teaching. A commander-in-chief upon a war-front, who had made history, was growing cabbages, and not even his own cabbages. If we can trust Providence to apportion punishment to offence, then we may assume that the Russian aristocracy were mainly responsible for the war.

When the force of circumstances had brought nationalist Angora into close co-operation with socialist Moscow, and the Turks had returned to Constantinople, these *émigrés* fled farther westward : to become absorbed, we must hope, into less degrading surroundings. A vestige of their sojourn still survives, in the school for Russian orphans maintained by British benevolence at Moda. The circumstances of its origin and its object, compared with those of the American schools on the Bosphorus, will make us envy those who are laying the foundations of the future while we are still liquidating our liabilities to the past.

The collapse of Russian Imperialism had left us without a policy for the disposal of Constantinople. It was generally assumed at first that the city and the Straits would be internationalized; as also that the economic partition of Asia Minor provided for by the Secret Treaties and planned originally as a partition between Russia, France, and England, would be maintained. But Russia had dropped out. Italy, protesting strongly against her omission as injurious to her " moral prestige," had been admitted into partnership, and assigned the Adalia section. Greece, also, with the support of Great Britain, had obtained recognition of her economic and ethnic claims to Smyrna. Moreover, in the alarms of the domestic, economic and political disturbances which followed the war, the Imperialist ambitions of the Greater Powers had contracted ; and room was therefore left for the re-emergence of the old rivalry between Greek and Turk for the control of the Near East. The Greek homeland was the Ægean littoral and the Islands; the Turkish was the Anatolian highlands: and the two strategic points in dispute were Constantinople and Smyrna. In 1919 it appeared as if the rivalry might be settled without any actual contest. For the Turks were defeated and divided ; while the Greeks were not only armed, but in alliance with the Powers who were reconstructing the world at Versailles.

Asia Minor and Nationalism

But an unexpected factor appeared upon the scene. Under Moustapha Kemal, the Turkish nation revived, with an irresistible insurgence that overturned the whole structure of our Near-

Eastern diplomacy. It was unexpected ; but it might have been foreseen. Because it was not an isolated eruption ; it was the arrival, at its next geographic and historic stage, of the glacier-like advance of the Nationalist movements across Europe. Westward the Star of Empire takes its way—but eastward flows the tide of Nationalism

Moustapha Kemal was a typical " Macedonian " and Young Turk, in the widest sense of those terms. The son of a small wealthy Salonika official, he had made his mark as a man of character at the military school, passing out of it two years ahead of his future rival, Enver. His position in the school ensured his prompt exile by Abdul-Hamid, to Syria ; where he organized the Young Turk movement. He was restored to the army, returned to Salonika, and in the 1908 revolution became conspicuous as the reorganizer of the Army of Liberty, and as Mahmoud Shevket's chief-of-staff at the conquest of Constantinople. In 1910 he attended the French manœuvres ; and the relations he then established with the French brought upon him the enmity of Enver and of his German military associates. In 1912 he campaigned with Enver in Tripoli ; who then and thereafter kept him as much as possible in the background. Consequently he did not again become prominent until the days of crucial fighting at the Dardanelles, when his intelligence and his influence with the troops could no longer be ignored. Still retaining an inferior rank, and never referred to in the Press, he directed the defence of the Dardanelles. If it was Enver who carried the public with him, it was Moustapha Kemal who had the confidence of the troops and of the entire Command. Thence he went to the Asiatic front, still irreconcilable in his opposition to Enver and the Germans—at one time even to the point of resignation. This daring independence, which was manifested equally strongly in his hostility to the Russians and the English, had made him, long before the end of the war, and all unknown to the outside world, the Turkish Champion.

As Commander of the Yilderim (Lightning) Army Group, he was engaged upon preparing an offensive, when the Armistice intervened.

He returned to Constantinople, established friendly relations with the Allies, and showed himself ready to accept any reasonable terms for his country. This phase ended when Venizelos, the spoilt child of the Paris Conference, obtained, with British support, permission for Greece to " stake " her claims in Asia Minor. On May 15, 1919, the Greek troops disembarked at

Smyrna. On the 20th Moustapha Kemal, as Governor of Erzeroum, in company with a Turkish Military " Mission of demobilization," disembarked at Samsoun. The new national adventure had begun.

The situation may be shortly stated. The British covered Constantinople with their fleet, and controlled the Sultanate, the Caliphate, and the whole government machinery. The Greeks with a well-equipped force held Smyrna and the surrounding country. The Italians held Adalia: the French Cilicia; and the British again a circle of military posts through Persia and the Caucasus round to Samsoun itself. British agents, also, were engaged upon the creation of a Kurdish State, a Greater Armenia, and a Greek State on the Black Sea. On the other hand the Turkish army, although disbanded, had not been disarmed, and the German depots were still intact.

A bold bluff secured the Turks Samsoun. By July the leading spirits of the Young Turk movement had all fled from Constantinople to Erzeroum. The political machinery of the Committee of Union and Progress was converted into a Nationalist caucus; and an army was organized. A Nationalist Congress, held first at Erzeroum and then at Sivas, challenged the right of Constantinople to represent Turkey; and its proclamation of the " National Pact," containing a definite claim to Constantinople, Smyrna, and Adrianople, served at least as a rousing popular challenge. Even Constantinople felt the impetus. It responded by reopening a Parliament, and by replacing Damad Ferid with a government under Ali Riza and Young Turk supporters.

During the winter of 1919–20 a swift *rapprochement* was in progress between Constantinople and Angora, which had now become the Nationalist capital. The authority of Constantinople was confined to the Allied lines; while Angora assumed control of all Anatolia and most of Thrace.

On February 17, 1920, under pressure from Indian Moslem, Britain informed the Porte that Constantinople might remain the capital of the new Turkish State, provided that the Turks would leave the Greeks in possession of Smyrna and Adrianople, and would undertake not to attack either the Allies or the Christian minorities. This produced no effect. Constantinople became progressively more Nationalist, and we were forced to occupy the city formally on March 16. The leading Nationalists, including two deputies, were arrested, and deported to Malta. Damad Ferid was reappointed Vizier. We compelled the Caliph to outlaw the Nationalists as rebels, and the Sheikh-ul-Islam to denounce them as " traitors to Islam." These measures seemed likely to prove effective, more especially because the Nationalists, in order to inflame the East against our Empire, had been publishing their claim to be themselves the champions of Islam against the Infidel. Any advantage, however, that we might have gained by the enrolment of the religious authority of the Caliph and of the Sheikh, was neutralized by the racial antagonism aroused by our calling-in of the Greeks. For, in June, the Allies at last produced their proposals for the future of Turkey, in the Treaty of Sèvres ; and it was no longer left in doubt that we had decided to back the Greeks, as a solution of the whole Eastern Question.

This, the last-born of the Paris Settlements, was fated to be the first to die. And yet, severe as the conditions were upon Turkey, it cannot be considered the most impracticable of those treaties. It recognized nationality as a basis for racial and regional division. On the west, Greece received all Thrace, up to the Tchataldja line, and Smyrna with a hinterland of about 100 miles square. On the east, Arab and Syrian autonomies were recognized, and new Armenian and Kurdish autonomies were instituted. Constantinople with a broad zone along the Straits was internationalized, and the national State of Turkey was subjected to international control in respect of marine, armaments, etc. For all such provisions there were satisfactory precedents, or sound principles. In 1919 Turkey would have accepted them. But by 1920 the new Turkish nation looked upon the proposed racial and regional restriction as only provocative.

Moustapha Kemal at Angora and Jaffar Tayar at Adrianople nailed the national standard to the mast. Their political position had improved. Their military rear was already secure : the envelopment on the east had broken down and the British expeditions to the Caucasus had had to be withdrawn. At the meeting of the new National Assembly at Angora, on June 4, 1920, it was announced that Moscow would support Angora, and pinched between these forces the Armenian and Kurdish autonomies withered away. In the south, the Italians were—less openly—supporting the Turks against the Greeks and the French. The French, therefore, got into difficulties in Cilicia, and had to make terms in that quarter. The British, implicated with their Moslem sympathizers, and with their front on the Gulf of Ismid held by Indian Moslem troops, were even less able than the French to come to blows with the Turks. Moreover, British policy was confused by a domestic complication. In the Coalition Government the Conservative Imperialists, influential in the War Office, were for a policy of concessions to Turkish Nationalism. Whereas Mr. Lloyd George and the Liberals represented by the Foreign Office were for crushing Turkey once for all through the instrumentality of the Greeks. In the end this latter policy prevailed, but its prospects of success were prejudiced throughout by the pro-Turk faction.

At first things went well for the Græcophils. The Smyrna forces defeated the Nationalists near Ak-Hissar on June 23, and drove them into the interior. Another Greek army landed at Modania and, after a bombardment by the British fleet, took Broussa, and covered Constantinople. A third army cleared Thrace and Adrianople of the Nationalist levies under Jaffar Tayar. On August 10 the Constantinople government agreed to sign the Treaty of Sèvres, after obtaining some unimportant concessions.

But it was never ratified. The invasion of the Turkish homeland of Anatolia by the Greeks, with its inevitable accompaniment of exterminations and excesses, only served further to consolidate the Turkish people, and to drive them, heart and soul, into the Nationalist ranks.

The Treaty of Sèvres was torn up by the armed forces of the new Turkish nation. Yet they would never have been able to defeat the Western Powers and their agents the Greek armies in Anatolia but for the dissensions of those Powers themselves. The main trouble was that not only the Russian Republic but also the French Republic looked on the Greeks not as the mandatories of a Peace League, but as the mercenaries of the British Empire. Under the Treaty of Sèvres the whole Ægean had become a Greek lake, Greece holding both its European and Asiatic coasts. And though the Straits and Constantinople were in a way internationalized, yet it was pretty obvious that it would be only a very few years before a new Greek Empire was installed at its old capital. This was the apparent aim of the association between Mr. Lloyd George and M. Venizelos. But it suited neither the French nor the Italians. The French might have been satisfied with developing their historic claims in Syria, where they now proceeded to occupy Damascus and Aleppo. But there they came up against British support of Arab and Jewish autonomies and found themselves involved in fights and frictions that made the whole Syrian enterprise unattractive and unpopular. In these conditions it was inevitable that they should join the

Italians in supporting the Turks, while maintaining their contingents at Constantinople to prevent the British bringing the Greeks in there.

Thus in the autumn of 1920 the crazy structures that centred in our occupation of Constantinople began to crack and crash. The Caucasus had been evacuated and the Armenian, Georgian, and Tartar States there began to pass from British to Russian protection. The last and most formidable attack on the Russian Republic, that of the Poles and Wrangel, now also failed, and Constantinople was filled with the wreck of the " White " forces that had until then maintained a footing somewhere on the Black Sea littoral. Moreover, though the Greeks were by now in occupation of half Anatolia, the Anglo-Greek association was shaken. King Alexander had died, King Constantine had been reinstated, and M. Venizelos had resigned. The statesman was a possible partner for us in a policy aiming at an eventual and gradual restoration of the Greek Empire against the interests of all other European Powers—the King was not. For in the eyes of the British public he was a fellow-conspirator with the Kaiser; while in the eyes of the Greek public he was the long-predicted Emperor Constantine XIV, who had only to march his troops already in Thrace through the Golden Gate to join hands with their comrades from the Asiatic side and restore the Golden Age of Greece. So the Greeks with the spring of 1921 started pressing, in one campaign after another, for a military decision against an elusive enemy in the illimitable wilds of Anatolia. While the British in one conference after another pursued an equally elusive diplomatic decision through the no less interminable windings of " the official channels."

By the end of the summer of 1921 the Greek push at Angora had ended in a reverse on the Sakkaria and the Greek armies had retired again to positions covering Eski Shehir and Broussa. While the French, no longer afraid of backing a loser, in October concluded the notorious Franklin-Bouillon agreement with Angora. More fruitless conferences followed, but the fight for Constantinople was now fairly joined as one between Greeks backed by British against Turks backed by Latins and Russians.

What really happened in 1922 is still obscure. But it seems that the Greeks, rightly renouncing all hope of defeating the Turks decisively in Anatolia, withdrew the bulk of their troops to Thrace, leaving only a screen which should later become a garrison for no more than the Smyrna and Broussa regions. Then in the late summer the Greeks in Thrace launched a coup against Constantinople intended to convert the Allied occupation, in which their allies the British were neutralized by the French and Italians, into a Greek possession which would be a *fait accompli*. Undoubtedly a bold carrying-out of such a combination between the Greek armies outside Constantinople and the British forces and fleet inside would have secured the nine points so important in international law. But the plan, if such there was, was ruined by our army authorities, who were, as our ruling class always was, pro-Turk in sympathy. They therefore held up the Greek advance at Tchataldja.

Meantime, the Turks broke through the thin Greek screen in Anatolia and drove the demoralized and depleted Greek forces before them right back to Smyrna and Constantinople. Smyrna was hastily evacuated by the Greeks and burnt by the Turks, enraged at the part it had played in an invasion that had ruthlessly wasted the homelands of their race. " Ghiaour Ismirn " disappeared for ever, to be replaced perhaps some day by a Turkish seaport. A similar fate seemed in store for Constantinople, as the victorious Turkish armies swept up to the scattered outposts of British troops holding the " neutral zone." That keen-eyed war-hawk, Mr. Winston Churchill, with the same clear insight into the real issue that he had shown in attacking the Straits in 1915, sent his famous cable to the Dominions who might be supposed to be concerned in the fate of the City for which so many of their sons had died. His well-aimed blow had failed in 1915 because there was not enough force put into it and it was not swift enough. It failed again in 1922 because the peoples of the Empire had come to detest wars and to distrust Peaces. More than that. The blow, missing its mark, upset the tottering balance of the Coalition and threw Mr. Lloyd George and his pro-Greek policy headlong out of power. With him fell the whole framework of the future Greek Empire. King Constantine of Greece had soon achieved the unusual distinction of having been twice deposed.

The fall of Mr. Lloyd George and the pro-Greeks and the advent of Lord Curzon and the Conservative pro-Turks eased the rather risky situation as the Turkish advanced guards came up against the British lines covering Constantinople. Nevertheless, the " scrounging " of the Turks, who pushed their outposts in between and behind the British positions, created a most dangerous situation. A war between British and Turks had to be averted again and again by British withdrawals, before a meeting at Modania between the military authorities at last arranged an armistice, giving the Turks good guarantees for our evacuation. Even so the maintenance of peace was a matter almost of minutes. Before agreement could be reached the Turks required to see it all in Turkish. The translating into Turkish and typing in Arabic script of a lengthy document is a matter calling for prayer and fasting. All through that night the two armies stood to arms, finger on trigger, and the Chanceries of Europe sat up with eyes on the tape while the lady typist of the Turkish delegation tapped letter by letter with one finger. A momentous figure in history is that little lady, as obscure and ominous in her tapping as a death-watch beetle. In the morning the armistice was signed, the world gave a sigh of relief, and the Empire of the East that, as Roman, Byzantine, Latin, Greek, Ottoman, had existed for 1,500 years, drew its last breath.

But the City had still many alarums and excursions to experience before the Treaty of Lausanne finally surrendered it at discretion to the Turkish nation. For many months yet the Allied forces remained nominally in control while the Nationalist Turks gradually cut the ground from under their authority. One such crisis I well remember. All the wealthier Christians were using the respite given by the long negotiations at Lausanne to fly from the doomed city. Suddenly one day the Turks, who had already subterraneously ousted the Ottoman officials under British orders, established their own police and passport offices on the Galata quays and stopped further embarkations of Christians. To this open challenge there could be only one reply. A body of British Marines with machine-guns appeared on the quays and the Turks withdrew. But for weeks Constantinople lived under the shadow of death. The city could clearly not be held against the Nationalist rising that any unwelcome development at Lausanne might any moment excite. All preparations were made accordingly for immediately removing the Allied forces to Gallipoli. All night long on the foreign shipping men stood by the searchlights and steam hoses waiting for the warning signal on Galata Tower. All day long the wretched refugees lined up along the quays for the chance of a passage on an outgoing Greek steamer with a British name hastily painted on her bow and a makeshift " Jack " hoisted at her stern. It was the agony of 1453 over again, but long-drawn-out, and with the British in place of the Genoese.

Thus did Constantinople, after another occupation by Western Crusaders and another attempt to restore the Greek Empire, again fall to a Turkish Conqueror. I can still see, and probably always shall see, a scene silhouetted against the sinister shadows of Galata on a stormy night of November 1922. The dim light from a tavern window falls on a man coming into the roadway from one of the dark lanes leading down to the quays. He is walking backward, waving his hands with beckoning gestures, and making little whistling noises. It is the way Anatolian shepherds lure sheep through these streets to the shambles. Up from the dark of the water lane a moving mass comes slowly out into the light. Are they sheep or pack-animals? They are both. Old men and women, bent double under bundles of bedding and household gear, with a few children. No young men, and very few young women—for them there has been no escape. Asked in Turkish where they come from, each shies off into the flock just as a sheep would. Asked in Greek, one of the bolder says "From Trebizond." For these are the remnants of the Greeks of Pontus, a race that has held that region from time immemorial. A few hundreds of the thousands that had passed, or had still to pass, along the Via Dolorosa of deportation, the only way discoverable by European diplomacy out of the "minorities problem."

THE CALIPHATE AND EYOUB

Nor were Christians the only victims of the great spring-cleaning undertaken in Constantinople by the Young Turkish nation. The "Old Turks," the Ottoman officials who had taken service under the Allied authorities during the occupation, though they kept their homes, lost their jobs. First and foremost of these was the Caliph himself, who departed with more despatch than dignity in a British cruiser; and, by thus taking refuge with the infidel, automatically abdicated his authority and saved the Angora Turks the trouble of deposing him. Not without much opposition from the extreme Nationalists, it was decided to appoint a successor.

Let us pay a last visit to the Old Serai to attend the ceremony. As we cross the bridge there passes us at a trot an escort of Lancers, mounted lackeys in red, and a carriage and four with postilions. In it sits a portly person in a fez, frock-coat and green ribbon. It is Abdul-Medjid, son of that Abdul-Aziz who cut the tangled knot of his fortunes with a pair of scissors. Abdul-Medjid is on his way to be invested as Caliph. The carriage whirls into the inner court of the Old Serai. On the one side are the mediæval kitchens with their conical chimneys, on the other the cupolas of the hareem, at the end a Byzantine portico of marbles and coloured tiles, still delightful in its dilapidation. On the pavement in front of the portico stands the Golden Throne studded with jewels, looted from Egypt by Selim, the first Ottoman Caliph. In a circle round it stand a few reporters, some sight-seeing French and Italian officers, and some American ladies. No Britisher is there but myself. I venture to slip past the chamberlains through to the Bagdad Kiosk and so get a glimpse of that most sacred of ceremonies, the Investiture of a Caliph.

But what a travesty it is! Instead of the solemn ritual in the Mosque of Eyoub and a Sultan girded with the Sword of Osman receiving from the Sheikh of Islam the emblems of his spiritual power, here is a delegation of Angora deputies notifying an elderly dilettante that he has been elected by a majority vote like any Labour leader. There are the sacred relics, but the Sword of Othman remains at Eyoub to show that, though Abdul-Medjid is Caliph, he is not Sultan.

The new Caliph comes out to the portico for his Selamlik. A little ring of curious sightseers and correspondents crowds round, there is a short prayer, and a comic Palace dwarf, with some eunuchs, give a note of local colour. The chamberlains dislodge the American ladies from coigns of vantage where they would spoil the film ; some undistinguished frock-coats and fezzes, princes of the House of Othman, defile across with hurried salaams to a whir of cinemas. Dingy, pot-bellied officials trot across, muftis and dervishes follow, and the operators pack up. As soon as they do so, the ring is broken, the carriage drives up, and the eunuchs begin to take the throne to pieces. The Caliph climbs into his carriage, but this time not alone. Facing him sits a soldierly little figure, spare and spruce, with the profile of a sparrow-hawk—Rafet Pasha, the Nationalist Governor of Constantinople. The Caliph has been denied his Sword of Othman, but he has been given his Sword of Damocles.

From this Investiture of the last of the Caliphs let us go on our last excursion, possibly the most beautiful of all. The beauty of the village of Eyoub, and of the view that you get from it down the Golden Horn, will speak for itself. Whether, by the time you visit it, the Mosque of Eyoub, so jealously guarded for centuries against infidel eyes that no picture even of the interior was obtainable, will itself be open to you, I cannot say. Perhaps by then you will even be able to handle the sword of Othman itself, and see the magical inscription on the tomb of Abu Eyoub Ensari, the friend of the Prophet who died at the

Saracen siege of Constantinople. After the Ottoman Conquest
the existence of his tomb was revealed by a vision, and it has
ever since been a shrine of Islam second only in sanctity to those
of Mecca and Medina. There could be no better evidence that
the Ottoman Empire is to-day as dead as the Byzantine Empire
than the possibility that infidels like ourselves may be allowed in
the Mosque of Eyoub.

The Caliphate did not long survive the Sultanate. For the
stalwarts of Turkish Nationalism had determined to be rid of
every symbol of Ottoman internationalism, whether Islamic or
Christian, Asiatic or European. The Sultanate symbolized the
political system of an Empire, based upon the autonomies of
various races and religions. The Caliphate symbolized the internationalism of Islam. Not long after the last of the Caliphs
had followed the last of the Sultans into exile, there came the
turn of the Orthodox Patriarch. The Patriarchate had symbolized the internationalism of Eastern Christianity. Throughout the Ottoman Empire it had retained a large portion of the
political powers that had bridged the fighting front between the
Christian rayahs and their Moslem rulers. The Treaty of Lausanne now recognized the right of the Turkish nation to remove
this bridge, but tried somewhat feebly to secure the Patriarch
in his " Papal " position as religious head of the Orthodox Church
whether within or without Turkey. But the Turks were determined to make it clear that the Patriarch was, in future, to be
no more than the Christian Bishop to a religious sect of citizens
in a Turkish Republic. As Constantine V persisted in asserting
his ancient authority with a trust in Providence worthy of his
political namesakes and forerunners, at dawn one winter's morning representatives of the Angora government ordered him out
of his bed in the Phanar and put him on board ship. The effect
of this upon Eastern Christians was as decisive as the abolition
of the Caliphate on the Moslem world. Constantinople ceased
to be the capital of Eastern Christianity as it had ceased to be
the citadel of Islam.

At the same time Constantinople ceased also to be the commercial centre of the Near East. It had fulfilled its functions
in that capacity for a thousand years of Byzantine and Ottoman corruption and extortion, thanks to the international regime
of the capitulations. These rights of extra-territoriality were
originally granted, as we have seen, by Greek Emperors to
Italian commercial colonies, and continued by Ottoman Emperors to the colonies and commerce of the Great Powers of

Western Europe. As the Ottoman Empire declined, the rights of foreigners under this international regime had developed until, in the later years of the Empire, Constantinople in fact, if not in form, was internationalized. Abuses had no doubt grown up, but fundamentally the system was indispensable. It was very well adapted to the functions that the city had to perform as the commercial centre where crossed the land bridge between Europe and Asia and the waterway between Northern and Southern Europe ; and, without some such international regime, the complex web of international credit, commerce, and communications can at any moment be torn up by some explosive Nationalism or empiric Imperialism of the Near East. But the whole of this ancient international structure was sacrificed by the Treaty of Lausanne. The Turks recovered Constantinople when they defeated King Constantine in Anatolia. The question now is whether Constantinople will ever recover the no less decisive defeat they inflicted on Lord Curzon at Lausanne ?

In the helpless and hopeless position in which British diplomacy found itself at the opening of the Conference, it could only expect to get very little. It preferred that that little should be securing new rights for its warships in the Straits rather than saving ancient rights of British merchants or Christian minorities residing and trading in an international capital.

The Turkish National movement had learnt by bitter experience what would happen to it if it made its capital in Constantinople. Moustapha Kemal and the Nationalist leaders when they decided to stay at Angora showed that they were wiser in their generation than had been their predecessors the Young Turks. At Constantinople, exposed to the machinations of the foreign embassies and colonies, and to the menace of the foreign fleets, they would soon have been bullied and bribed into dependence on European finance and diplomacy. But merely staying at Angora and abolishing all the international symbols and systems of Constantinople did not solve the difficulty. It is not enough to deprive Constantinople of all means of existence and to deny that it exists. A white elephant is a white elephant, whether you trust yourself on its back or keep it tied up in a backyard. As yet, Angora does not seem to have any clear ideas as to what is to be done with Constantinople.

The Turks took back the City and Straits as a prize of war, as a protection against further wars and as providing them with a new province, Eastern Thrace. Their original idea was to clean up Constantinople and Turkify it—a labour of Hercules

made possible by the international sanction given at Lausanne
to the principle of " exchange of population." For though Constantinople was excepted, the exemption has been evaded. In
so far as government goes, they have been largely successful.
The trim villas of Angora, where the Turkish official now lives
strenuously, compare well with the Sublime Porte of the Empire.
The dingy passages and dirty rooms of the Porte were the run-
ways and rat-holes of predatory Levantines who kept alive the
worst legacies of the Byzantines. In the front rooms fezzed
and frock-coated Pashas, of dubious race and religion but of
indubitable rapacity, sat at the receipt of custom. And there
were no Capitulations to restrict those customs rates. In the
back rooms, crowds of seedy clerks scribbled on scraps of paper
held in the palms of their hands ; in the waiting-rooms foreign
officials and concession-hunters sat interminably on gilt sofas,
while their go-betweens slipped round by back passages on ear-
wigging and palm-oiling bent. And through all, like disease-
carrying bacilli, swarmed the spies. The atmosphere of Angora
is very different from this. Angora was absolutely, and still is
approximately, hardworking and honest.

But it is difficult to imagine a Turkish Constantinople as a
centre of world commerce. The whole business of the town was
in the hands of Greeks, Armenians, and Levantines. Many of
these have been deported or driven out of business ; yet there
are still enough left to demoralize and denationalize twenty
Turkish commercial centres. This is shown by the gravitational
pull of Constantinople on Angora, which is still that of a very
large and sophisticated city on a very small and simple country town. Turkish law says that a marriage with a fairy is
valid, but marriage with a Djinn is null and void. Angora has
married a Djinn, and the sooner it gets a divorce from Constantinople the better. It might do this perhaps by applying the
Fundamental Statute of the Turkish State which promised self-
government to Constantinople. As a free port with a full
autonomy Constantinople might be cut out of the Turkish body
politic in which it threatens to become a cancer.

ANGORA

There could be no greater contrast in cities than that between
Constantinople and Angora. Constantinople is, from outside, a
dream of beauty—Angora is not. Angora is, from inside,
virile and virtuous—Constantinople is not. Constantinople is
either a world capital or nothing. Angora may, in time and

with trouble, be made a respectable capital for a Peasant State.

Angora can now be reached with comparatively little delay and discomfort. But, for a tourist, the journey is not worth the trouble ; while the discomforts of a stay in Angora are still considerable. There is a large hotel building ; but meantime, a traveller has to take what is left in a town where members of the government are sleeping in their offices, and four or five in a room at that.

Angora, with its citadel on a bluff over a river, its main street with a few shabby shops, its villas doing duty as departments, its burnt-out Christian quarter and its scattering of new frame-houses, might be almost any Anatolian country town. But it has peculiarities of its own. It has the trying extremes of temperature due to its exposed position on a high barren plateau and the unhealthiness due to its surroundings of malarial, mosquito-haunted swamps.

Angora is no doubt a good place to work ; for there is nothing else to do. The Nationalist official has hitherto worked hard and honestly as no Turkish official has ever yet worked. But after some months of eating, sleeping, and working in an Angora office the less strenuous begin to look forward to a holiday in Constantinople with an almost passionate longing, while an appointment in Stamboul becomes their vision of bliss. But whereas life in Angora is possible on the modest pay which is all that the new State can afford, life in Constantinople means expensive motor-cars and mistresses and the money to pay for them. For the money is there for the asking. Those pleasant foreigners of gentlemanly manners who haunt the Constantinople clubs and hotels can always put an acquaintance from Angora on to a good thing. So it is coming about that though you cannot bribe an Angora Nationalist as you could a Pasha of the Porte, yet you will find he sometimes has a friend in Constantinople whom you will do well to make sleeping partner in your enterprise. It is all very well for strong spirits like Ghazi Moustapha Kemal to refuse to set foot in the accursed City. She has been stripped of her authority and wealth before now and yet as a captive slave has only made the quicker conquest of her new master. Age cannot wither her nor custom stale the infinite variety of her temptations.

So there let us leave the story of Constantinople, the City of Medea, of Theodora, of Roxalana, of Aimée de Rivery. The story is none the less real for being a romance. And if the heroine has no morals the story has many.

APPENDIX

RULERS IN CONSTANTINOPLE

Constantine the Great	330–337
Constantine II and } (his sons).	337–360
Constans	
Julian the Apostate	360–363
Jovian	363–364
Valens	364–378
Gratian (his nephew)	378–383

THEODOSIANS

Theodosius the Great	379–395
Arcadius (his son)	395–408
Theodosius II, the Younger (his son) . .	408–450
Pulcheria the Saint (his sister) . . .	450–453
Marcian (her husband)	450–457

THRACIANS

Leo the Great	457–474
Leo the Younger (his son)	474
Zeno the Isaurian (brother-in-law) . . .	474–491
Anastasius (his widow's husband) . . .	491–518

JUSTINIANS

Justin the Elder	518–527
Justinian the Great (his nephew) . . .	527–565
Justin II, the Younger (his nephew) . .	565–578
Tiberius (his son-in-law)	578–582
Maurice (his son-in-law)	582–602

Phokas	602–610

HERACLIANS

Heraclius	610–641
Constantine III (his son)	641
Constans II (his son)	641–668
Constantine IV, Pogonatus (his son) . .	668–685
Justinian II (his son)	685–694

Leontius	695–698
Tiberius III, Apsimaris	698–705

HERACLIANS RESTORED

Justinian II (restored)	705–711
Tiberius IV (his son)	711
Philippikos, Bardanes	711–713
Anastasius II, Artemius	713–716
Theodosius III	716–717

ISAURIANS

Leo the Isaurian	717–741
Constantine Copronymus (his son) . . .	741–775
Leo IV, Kazaros	775–780
Constantine VI, Porphyrogenitus (his son) . .	780–797
Irene (widow of Leo IV)	797–802

Nicephorus I, Logothetes	802–811
Michael I, Rhangabe (his son-in-law) . .	811–813
Leo the Armenian	813–820

ISAURIANS RESTORED

Michael II (son-in-law of Constantine VI) . .	820–829
Theophilus (his son)	829–842
Michael III (his son)	842–867

MACEDONIANS

Basil I . . . }	{ 867–886
Constantine VII (his son) }	{ 868–878
Leo VI the Philosopher (son of Basil) . .	886–911
Alexander (son of Basil)	911–912
Constantine VIII, Porphyrogenitus . . .	912–919
Romanus I (his father-in-law)	919–945
Constantine VIII (restored)	945–959
Romanus II (his son)	959–963
Nicephorus II, Phokas (his widow's husband) .	963–969
John I, Zimisces (son-in-law of Constantine VIII) .	969–975
Basil II, Bulgaroktonos } (sons of Romanus II) . .	{ 969–1025
Constantine IX }	{ 969–1028
Romanus III, Argyros (his son-in-law) . .	1028–1034
Michael IV, the Paphlagonian (his brother-in-law) .	1034–1041
Michael V, Kalaphates (his son-in-law) . .	1041–1042
Constantine X, Monomachos } (son-in-law and daughters of	
Zoe } Constantine IX) .	
Theodora }	1042–1056
Michael VI, Stratenikos	1056–1057

APPENDIX

KOMNENOI AND DUKAI

Isaac I, Komnenos	1057–1059
Constantine XI, Dukas (adopted)	1059–1067
Eudoxia (his widow)	1067–1071
Michael VII, Parapinakes ⎱(his sons)	1067–1068
Constantine XII ⎰	
Romanos IV, Diogenes (husband of Eudoxia)	1068–1071
Michael VII (restored)	1071–1078
Nicephorus III, Botoniates	1078–1081
Alexius I, Komnenos (nephew of Isaac)	1081–1118
John II (his son)	1118–1143
Manuel I (his son)	1143–1180
Alexius II (his son)	1180–1183
Andronikos I (nephew of John II)	1183–1185

ANGELOI

Isaac II, Angelus	1185–1195
Alexius III (his brother)	1195–1203
Isaac II (restored)	1203–1204
Alexius IV (his son)	1204
Alexius V, Mourtzouphlos	1204

THE LATIN EMPIRE

Baldwin, Count of Flanders	1204–1205
Henry I (his brother)	1206–1216
Peter (his brother-in-law)	1216–1219
Robert (his son)	1219–1228
Baldwin II (his brother)	1228–1261
John (his father-in-law)	1231–1237

LASKARIS (NICE)

Theodore Laskaris	1206–1222
John III (his son-in-law)	1222–1255
Theodore II (his son-in-law)	1255–1259
John IV (his son)	1259–1260

PALEOLOGOI (CONSTANTINOPLE)

Michael VIII, Paleologos	1261–1282
Andronikos II, the Elder (his son) ⎱	⎱ 1282–1328
Michael IX (his son) ⎰	⎰ 1295–1320
Andronikos III, the Younger (his son)	1328–1341
John V (his son)	1341–1391

CANTACUZENOI

John VI, Cantacuzene (his father-in-law)	1347–1355
Matthias (his son)	
Andronikos IV ⎱(sons of John VI)	⎱ 1355–1391
Manuel II ⎰	⎰ 1391–1425

John VII (son of Andronikos IV) 1399
John VIII (son of Manoel II) 1425–1448
Constantine XIII (his brother) 1448–1453

OSMANLI

Mohammed II, The Conqueror 1451–1481
Bayazet II. 1481–1512
Selim the Cruel 1512–1520
Suleiman the Magnificent 1520–1566
Selim II, the Sot 1566–1574
Mourad III 1574–1595

Rule of the Sultanahs

Mohammed III 1595–1603
Akhmet 1603–1617
Moustapha. 1617–1618
Othman II. 1618–1622
Mourad IV. 1623–1640
Ibrahim (deposed) 1640–1649
Mohammed IV (deposed) 1649–1687

Rule of the Veziers

Suleiman II 1687–1691
Akhmet II. 1691–1695
Moustapha II 1691–1695
Akhmet III 1703–1730
Mahmoud 1703–1730

Rule of the Chief Eunuchs and Janissaries

Othman III 1754–1757
Moustapha III 1757–1774
Abdul-Hamid 1774–1789
Selim III 1789–1807
Moustapha IV 1807–1808

OTTOMANS

Mahmoud II (the Reformer) 1808–1839

Rule of the Foreign Embassies

Abdul-Medjid 1839–1861
Abdul-Aziz (deposed) 1861–1876
Mourad V (deposed) 1876
Abdul-Hamid II (deposed) 1876–1908

Rule of the Young Turks

Mohammed V, Reshad 1909–1918
Mohammed VI (deposed), the last Sultan . . . 1918–1922
Abdul-Medjid (deposed), the last Caliph . . . 1922–1924

TURKISH REPUBLIC
(Deposition of Constantinople by Angora.)

INDEX

A

Abdul-Aziz, Sultan, 206–11
Abdul-Hamid the Damned, 207, 213, 215–22, 225–8, 231–43
Abdul-Medjid, last Caliph, 294
Abdul-Medjid, Sultan, 195, 201, 207
Aimée de Rivery, Slave and Sultanah, 131
Akhmediyeh Mosque and Fountain, 140
Akhmet, Sultan, 140, 150
Alai Kiosque, 143
Alexius Comnenus, 89–96
Alexius III, Emperor, 96
Alexius IV and V, Emperors, 99
Ambassadors, position of, 148, 186, 193
Anastasius, Emperor, 35, 41
— wall of, 68
Andronicus II, Emperor, 108
Anemas Tower and Prison, 84
Angelo Tower, 85
Angora, national capital, 286, 298
— Turks, 4, 20, 286–99. *Vide* Young Turks
Anna Comnena, historian Princess, 84, 91, 151
Anthemius, architect of St. Sophia, 42, 45
— wall builder, 33
Apollonius the Wizard, 57, 58
Argonauts, legends, 8
Armenians, 189, 214, 224, 284
Arms and Costumes collection, 24, 26, 144, 149, 151
Arnaut Keui Woman's College, 259
Athanasius Saint, creed of, 26
— Patriarch, curse of, 108
Attila, siege by, 34

B

Baldwins, Latin Emperors, 91, 102–5
Balkan Wars, 267–74
Balta Liman, Bosphorus village, 275
Balta-oglou, Turkish Admiral, 119
Barbarossa, Western Emperor, 96
Barbarossa, Turkish Admiral, 258
Basil Bulgaroktonos, Emperor, 83
Basil the Macedonian, Emperor, 81–3
Baths, 183
Bayazid, Sultan, character of, 132
Bayazidieh Mosque and Turbeh, 130, 131, 132
Bazaars, 171–5
Beikos, Bosphorus village, 276
Belgrade Forest, 23, 263, 276
Belisarius, triumph of, 55
Beshiktash, suburb, 258
Besma, the Washerwoman, Sultanah, 209–12
Beylerbey Palace, 209
Blachernae Palace, 74, 78–84, 99
Black Sea, route across, 7
Bosphorus excursion, 256–76
— origin of, 8
— scenery, 9
Bribes, 189, 217, 298
British Church, 201
— Embassy, 193, 207, 229, 254, 257, 260, 276, 281
— Naval Mission, 234, 278, 280
— policy, 150, 164, 176, 190, 195, 201, 206, 212, 222, 229, 231, 271, 278, 288, 294
Bucoleon Palace, ruins of, 34
Bulgarian Atrocities, 212

305